UNIVERSITY GOVERNANCE IN CANADA

# UNIVERSITY GOVERNANCE IN CANADA

Navigating Complexity

Julia Eastman, Glen A. Jones,
Claude Trottier, and Olivier Bégin-Caouette

McGill-Queen's University Press
Montreal & Kingston • London • Chicago

© McGill-Queen's University Press 2022

ISBN 978-0-2280-1144-6 (cloth)
ISBN 978-0-2280-1145-3 (paper)
ISBN 978-0-2280-1273-3 (ePDF)
ISBN 978-0-2280-1274-0 (ePUB)

Legal deposit third quarter 2022
Bibliothèque nationale du Québec

Printed in Canada on acid-free paper that is 100% ancient forest free (100% post-consumer recycled), processed chlorine free

Funded by the Government of Canada / Financé par le gouvernement du Canada   Canada Council for the Arts / Conseil des arts du Canada

We acknowledge the support of the Canada Council for the Arts.
Nous remercions le Conseil des arts du Canada de son soutien.

---

Library and Archives Canada Cataloguing in Publication

Title: University governance in Canada : navigating complexity / Julia Eastman, Glen A. Jones, Claude Trottier, and Olivier Bégin-Caouette.
Names: Eastman, Julia, author. | Jones, Glen A. (Glen Alan), 1961– author. | Trottier, Claude R. (Claude René), 1941– author. | Bégin-Caouette, Olivier, author.
Description: Includes bibliographical references and index.
Identifiers: Canadiana (print) 20220216878 | Canadiana (ebook) 20220217017 | ISBN 9780228011446 (cloth) | ISBN 9780228011453 (paper) | ISBN 9780228012733 (ePDF) | ISBN 9780228012740 (ePUB)
Subjects: LCSH: Universities and colleges—Canada—Administration—Case studies. | LCGFT: Case studies.
Classification: LCC LB2341.8.C3 E27 2022 | DDC 378.1/010971—dc23

---

This book was typeset in 10.5/13 Sabon.

# Contents

Tables and Figures   vii

Preface   ix

Introduction and Overview   3

**PART ONE | History and Current Context**

1   The History of Universities in Canada: A Synopsis   11
2   Canadian University Governance Today   55

**PART TWO | Findings from a Comparative Case Study of the Governance of Major Canadian Universities**

3   The Case Universities: Six Unique Histories   105
4   Trends and Themes in External Governance   136
5   Internal Governance   172
6   Updates and Observations   231

**PART THREE | Global Context and Reflections**

7   Governing Universities: The International Context   289
8   Concluding Reflections and Advice   330

Notes   369

References   373

Index   417

# Tables and Figures

## TABLES

2.1 National Survey of Student Engagement results for Canadian universities, 2017   95
3.1 Institutional-level interviewees by category   106
3.2 Institutional overview chart 2013–14   132
5.1 Composition of case universities' governing bodies   175
6.1 Updated institutional overview chart   247
6.2 Update on composition of case universities' governing bodies   282

## FIGURES

1.1 Number of Universities Canada/AUCC member institutions from 1790 to 2020   22
1.2 Number of *Maclean's* universities by category   23
1.3 Revenue structure of universities in Canada, 1921–2016   28
2.1 Major participants and forces in external governance of universities   66
2.2 Major participants in internal university governance   101
4.1 Major government influences on the governance of universities in Canada   165

# Preface

How well Canadian universities deliver on their educational and research missions is important – for their students, faculty and staff, alumni and partners, communities and country, and potentially even for humanity and life on the planet. Universities' performance is in part a function of governance – that is, how decisions are made within and about them. Literature on university governance in Canada remains sparse. This book examines how university governance in this country has evolved, how it varies by province, how it compares with other jurisdictions, and how it is changing. We hope the book will be a valuable resource for all who want to understand contemporary Canadian university governance in a global context.

The book draws upon higher education literature, data, commentary, and a comparative case study of the governance of six major Canadian universities that began in 2011. The study was jointly initiated by Julia Eastman and Glen Jones and conducted with funding from the Social Sciences and Humanities Research Council of Canada (SSHRC). Glen Jones, professor of higher education at the Ontario Institute for Studies in Education (OISE), University of Toronto, was the principal investigator. Claude Trottier, professor emeritus in the Faculty of Educational Sciences at Université Laval, was a co-investigator, as was Julia Eastman, then university secretary at the University of Victoria, now adjunct professor at its Peter B. Gustavson School of Business. The research team also included Olivier Bégin-Caouette, Sharon X. Li, and Christian Noumi, then doctoral students at OISE. Michael Skolnik, professor emeritus of leadership, higher, and adult education, and Grace Karram Stephenson, post-doctoral fellow, both of OISE, also contributed their knowledge and skill to the project. When Glen was appointed dean of OISE, Julia assumed the central leadership role for the project and was the first author of all English-language publications emerging from the study. She is the primary author of this book.

We are very grateful to the SSHRC for making the case study possible and to all who participated in the more than ninety interviews. Interviewees shared their knowledge, experience, and time very generously. The depth of their commitment to the work of the universities shone through their remarks.

The project's findings with respect to the external governance of the case universities were communicated in three articles. Two focused on provincial systems (Bégin-Caouette, Trottier, et al. 2018; Eastman, Jones, et al. 2018) and one article addressed the federal government's role (Eastman, Jones, et al. 2019).

Glen, Claude, and Olivier – now assistant professor in comparative higher education at the Université de Montréal – continued to work with Julia as she drafted this manuscript, providing invaluable feedback and suggestions. Makari Espe and Joshua Smith, former students at the University of Victoria's Gustavson School of Business, provided excellent research assistance to her in the final stages. Marie-Ève Lefebvre, doctoral candidate, and Noémie Deschênes, undergraduate student, at the Université de Montréal, assisted with translation. Alison Elizabeth Jefferson, PhD candidate at OISE, copy edited the manuscript and provided great advice on final revisions.

Herman Bakvis, Carmen Charette, Stéphane Dorge, Daniel Lang, Jeff Leclerc, Grace Skogstadt, Michael Skolnik, Richard Stubbs, Christine Tausig Ford, Reeta Tremblay, and David Turpin provided comments on sections of the manuscript, which were greatly appreciated. All errors and omissions are the responsibility of the authors.

The book draws on findings and insights from innumerable publications on university history and governance, higher education, research and innovation, and related public policy, in Canada and around the world. We are indebted to the authors of these publications for the benefit of their excellent work. Julia and Glen are also very grateful to the University of Victoria and OISE/University of Toronto for their support for this project.

We hope that the result will be helpful to all who have an interest or a stake in universities in Canada and want to understand better how they are governed, how their governance has evolved, and what the future may hold.

UNIVERSITY GOVERNANCE IN CANADA

# Introduction and Overview

People invest a great deal in universities in Canada, directly and through governments. First and foremost, they invest hope and expectations. Students hope that going to university will augment their knowledge, skills, social circles, and work and life prospects. Faculty members hope and expect to be supported in their research, scholarship, and teaching. Governments, business, other stakeholders, and the public expect that university activities will produce highly skilled personnel and valuable knowledge, while contributing to the quality of lives, communities, the economy, technology, society, and the environment. Immense amounts of time, effort, and talent are invested in university activities by more than 1.3 million students (Statistics Canada 2019) and by hundreds of thousands of faculty, staff, administrators, partners, and volunteers. Finally, large sums of money are provided to universities: in 2017–18, the combined income of universities in Canada was $39.2 billion (CAUBO 2019). At 1.7 percent of GDP in 2016 (OECD 2019, C2.1), Canada's total expenditures, public and private, on "long-cycle" tertiary institutions per full-time equivalent student were among the highest of all OECD countries (OECD 2019, C1.1).

Given all the aspirations, effort, and resources invested in Canadian universities, how they are governed is vitally important. In this book, governance refers to "how higher education systems and institutions are organized and managed [and] how authority is distributed and exercised" in relation to and within them (Harman 1991, 1280). External governance "refers to the system or macro level of authority and the role that the government (state, province or nation) and other external stakeholders play in governing higher education within their jurisdiction" (Austin and Jones 2016, 13). Internal governance concerns the distribution of authority and responsibility within the university. Governance is multi-layered, taking place at multiple levels within both institutions and national jurisdictions, shaped by international agreements and bodies and global forces.

Governance largely determines the extent to which universities meet the competing expectations of stakeholders, both external and internal. Resources are essential, but how those resources are obtained and deployed is a function of governance. External and internal governance arrangements can enable or constrain universities as they deliver on their missions, as well as the potential of their faculty, staff, and students and the resources invested in them.

The purpose of this book is to contribute to our understanding of how Canadian universities are governed – how their governance has evolved, how it varies across the country, and how it is changing – and to encourage consideration of what the future may hold. To that end, we will look briefly into the history of universities and university governance in Canada. We will reflect on their current state. We will learn about six major universities across the country, how they are governed, and how their governance has evolved and been tested. In the penultimate chapter, we will consider university governance in a number of other countries before contemplating possible directions for reform in Canada and their implications for actors in both external and internal governance. You may be among those actors. If so, we hope your reflections on aspects of this book will inform the roles you play in university governance and university life.

### OUTLINE OF CONTENTS

Following a description of the case study's theoretical foundations in the remainder of this chapter, the rest of the book consists of three parts into which you can dip depending on your interests:

Part 1, "History and Current Context" (chapters 1 and 2): Chapter 1 summarizes how universities and their governance evolved in Canada and around the globe. Chapter 2 looks at the state of contemporary Canadian university governance from the perspectives of scholars and commentators on higher education and public policy.

Part 2, "Findings from a Comparative Case Study of the Governance of Major Canadian Universities" (chapters 3 to 6): Chapter 3 introduces the histories and features of the six case universities. Chapter 4 presents findings concerning their external governance. Chapter 5 concerns their internal governance. Chapter 6 provides updates on developments at the six institutions and in their respective provinces in the years since the study.

Part 3, "Global Context and Reflections" (chapters 7 and 8): Chapter 7 describes international trends in governance and how universities are governed in three Anglo-American jurisdictions (the UK, Australia, and the United States), France, and China. Chapter 8 presents concluding observations about the state of university governance in Canada, advice to major players, and considerations for the future.

## THEORETICAL FOUNDATIONS

Pierre Bourdieu's writings have informed the case study and this book. So has Marginson's conception of the global higher education field, and so have Mintzberg's writings on the structure of organizations and, in particular, professional bureaucracies.

Bourdieu conceived of society as consisting of fields, that is, hierarchically structured networks of social relations in which individuals and organizations compete for capital and for position. Fields differ in the types of capital at play within them. The main types are economic, social, and cultural capital. The latter includes the knowledge, skills, and attainments of individuals, cultural goods, and educational qualifications (Bourdieu 1986).

Fields (e.g., the arts community, the technology sector, the university community) differ in their autonomy from economic and political power and in the extent to which they create their own values and principles (Maton 2005). Bourdieu distinguished between fields of "restricted production" – in which cultural capital has primacy and autonomous producers create cultural goods for other producers (e.g., academics write to be read by other scholars) – and fields of "large scale production" – such as the business sector, in which economic capital dominates, production meets pre-existing needs, and producers are subordinate to those who control the means of production (Bourdieu 1993).

Seen through Bourdieu's eyes, organizations compete for capital in order to move up or keep up in their fields. For research-intensive universities, acquiring and building cultural capital – in the form of highly qualified faculty members, students, staff, equipment, infrastructure, and so on – is key to maintaining or improving their positions. It is cultural capital that enables universities to generate knowledge, and that determines their faculties' and departments' prominence in disciplinary and professional fields. However, cultural capital is very costly. Given all the competing demands on the public purse, governments do not fund cultural capital – that is, the generation and dissemination of knowledge – for its own sake. Nor is the private sector a potential source of unrestricted funding on the scale required. In the context of a global knowledge economy and governments seeking tangible outcomes from mass higher education and research, universities in most parts of the world today must engage in other forms of knowledge production – in other words, they must harness their cultural capital to serve external needs, in order to generate economic capital. They do so in many ways, including by providing degree programs that students and/or governments value and are willing to pay for, by responding to funding conditions and incentives, by offering executive and continuing education, by conducting applied research, and by generating revenue through ancillaries.

Extrapolating from Bourdieu, a key challenge for universities in the Western tradition is to avoid becoming captive to either the state or the market in the quest to generate revenue. Either eventuality risks decreasing or destroying their capacity to generate knowledge. In a university subject to government control or akin to a for-profit corporation, political, bureaucratic, and/or commercial considerations would trump academic decision-making processes, undermining or suppressing the pursuit and dissemination of knowledge. Such a university would probably have adopted institutional planning, management, and control systems that tend to be inimical to the pursuit of knowledge, driving away sought-after scholars and their students. Finally, a university that acted like a corporation or a government department would soon be perceived externally as such – and therefore, as incapable of disinterested pursuit and dissemination of knowledge. The result would be to engender loss of public trust, cultural legitimacy, and public and private support.

Maintaining some distance from the state and the market is therefore necessary. The concept of "institutional autonomy" has been commonly used as a tool for understanding how the authority of institutional governance structures is limited by the external environment. Following Justin Thorens (2006) and others, we understand autonomy as the freedom that allows the institution to organize itself so as to carry out its mission effectively, and academic freedom as the right and the duty of professors to advance and disseminate knowledge without constraint. The extent of universities' autonomy varies greatly across time and within and between jurisdictions depending on national traditions, whether universities are public, private, or both, whether states are centralized or federations, and other factors (Thorens 2006). University autonomy is neither a necessary nor a sufficient condition for academic freedom.

Bourdieu perceived higher education as relatively autonomous from both the economy and the state. He identified higher education's roles in generating and legitimizing knowledge, and its control over the recruitment and appointment of its leadership and personnel, as explaining "its unusual historical continuity and stability, analogous more to the church than to business or the state" (Swartz 1997, 206).

In the years since Bourdieu's work, profound changes have taken place in the higher education systems of many countries. Some university presidents are no longer academics. Higher education is increasingly privately financed (Altbach, Reisberg, and Rumbley 2009). With the advent of university rankings, competition for position is more transparent, explicit, and extensive. The French universities that Bourdieu studied in the 1970s and 1980s were shaped principally by their national context; however, contemporary universities are better understood as both subject to and influencing global, national, and local forces (Marginson and Rhoades 2002).

Whereas Bourdieu stressed the competitive nature of individual and organizational behaviour and regarded the strategies of both types of actors as largely predetermined by their circumstances and dispositions, Marginson (2008) called attention to the extent of cooperation and creative imagination at work in global higher education. In this broader conception, universities are both competitive and cooperative; they are capable of both replicating and changing existing hierarchy and power relations. Bourdieu saw the education system as a whole as performing three main functions: conserving, consecrating, and disseminating cultural heritage; reproducing social-class relations; and legitimizing the cultural and social order (Swartz 1997, 190). But universities can also be forces for social, economic, and technological change. The extent to which universities replicate existing intellectual and socio-economic orders, or transform them, is in part a function of governance.

Especially for research-intensive universities, governance involves striking a fine balance between restricted cultural production and large-scale production – between fostering the exercise of academic judgment and academic freedom, and responding to the needs and demands of students, governments and other stakeholders, and society at large. The challenge in maintaining relative autonomy is to secure sufficient resources from the state and markets to sustain university activities while protecting and building cultural capital. This involves not only managing relationships with the state, other external stakeholders, and markets, but also putting in place internal mechanisms to foster institutional responsiveness to stakeholders' needs and demands. That said, as noted above, a university that goes too far in enlisting its members' activities in the service of external demands is likely to damage its capacity to generate knowledge, by driving away talent, depriving faculty members of the conditions they need to excel, and so on. So mechanisms to foster and protect cultural production are also required. Maintaining relative autonomy is thus both an external and an internal challenge for university governance, leadership, and management.[1]

It is also a challenge for governments. A government that harnesses universities too tightly to its own ends and processes risks decreasing their capacity to create knowledge and to innovate, hence the phenomenon (described in more detail in Chapter 8) of governments in some countries "stepping back." Mintzberg's writings on professional bureaucracy, summarized in Chapter 3, shed light on why governments' efforts to control universities tend to be counterproductive.

Many questions arise from the governance challenge of balancing academic autonomy and institutional responsiveness. What institutional mechanisms harness cultural capital to serve the needs of students, government, industry, and other stakeholders? What mechanisms constrain institutionalized responsiveness to external needs and protect space for restricted cultural production? What are the roles of boards, senates, faculties, university leaders, and other actors in facilitating or constraining responsiveness to external needs and in maintaining institutional autonomy, peer decision-making, and the conditions for the generation and dissemination of knowledge? What are the roles of governments? Can they encourage or require universities to evolve to better meet the needs of students, society, the economy, and/or the environment without undermining their capacity to produce knowledge? These are among the questions explored in this book.

PART ONE

# History and Current Context

# 1

# The History of Universities in Canada: A Synopsis

Universities are, of course, not native to Canada. They first emerged in Western Europe in the Middle Ages as academic guilds formed principally for defensive purposes (Kivinen and Poikus 2006, 189). After centuries in which Christian Europe had been an intellectual and cultural backwater (Lowe and Yasuhara 2017, 174), they represented a novel organizational form (Cobban 1975, 21), drawing upon scholarship generated in Arabic, Greek, Persian, Indian, and Chinese societies (Lowe and Yasuhara 2017).

The first universities emerged organically (Cobban 1992, 1247), but by the thirteenth century, only those with rights secured by the pope or emperor could call themselves a *studium generale* or university (Kivinen and Poikus 2006, 191). Early universities tended to follow one of two templates: the Parisian university of masters, to whom students were essentially apprenticed; or the Bolognese student-university, in which professors made their livings from student fees and were under bond to comply with regulations governing teaching (Ashby 1966, 3; Cobban 1992, 1247). When a new university was established, usually upon the initiative of a local prince or bishop, most often it was given a constitution modelled on Paris or Bologna; it then hired teachers from those or other established universities, established a given set of faculties, and adopted a standardized curriculum (Ashby 1966, 4). Latin was the common language. Since medieval universities fell under the jurisdiction of the Catholic Church, the authority of which spanned Europe, medieval universities were truly supranational (Ashby 1966, 3).

As early as the late medieval period, universities came under increasing state control (Cobban 1992, 1248). With the Reformation and the rise of nation-states, the uniform culture of medieval universities dissipated; universities became much more diverse as they adapted and responded to local circumstances (Ashby 1966, 4).

Despite the increasing differentiation and multiplication of institutional models (Frijhoff 1992), there was considerable continuity of institutional purpose. Kivinen and Poikus studied the charters of 225 universities around the world founded between 1224 and 1999 and found that, although the prominence of church and religion decreased over time, the *raison d'être* for universities remained similar. Throughout the centuries, the dissemination of knowledge and the development of human potential were viewed as reasons to establish universities, along with economic and social development, preparation of students for employment, and the promotion of local and national interests. In pursuit of these aims, prevailing authorities sponsored universities and gave them and their members privileges, ranging from exemptions from taxes and duties and special treatment in the courts in earlier times, to Humboldtian freedoms of teaching and learning in some parts of the world in recent centuries (Kivinen and Poikus 2006).

The universities' continuity of purpose was coupled with their perennial struggle to maintain autonomy. Cobban characterized this quest as "the persistent hallmark of the European university idea" (1975, 235). Likewise, Frijhoff (1992) observed that "the only recurrent element of continuity from 1500 to 1900 was the university's sense of autonomy as a prerequisite for true science, that is, independent learning, teaching and training" (1252).

Between fifteen and twenty universities were operating in 1300, and about seventy in 1500 (Cobban 1992, 1248). Universities spread throughout Europe and around the globe in what Ashby described as four major waves of intellectual colonization: the fifteenth-century spread in Europe; a wave in the sixteenth and seventeenth centuries that "carried higher education across the Atlantic to the New World"; another wave in the nineteenth century, "when for the first time universities were founded in non-Christian societies supplanting ancient indigenous centres of learning"; and finally, one in the twentieth century that spread them around the globe (Ashby 1966, 19).

By 1800, there were about 190 full universities in Europe and thirty in the Americas (Frijhoff 1992, 1252). According to Ashby, the impetus for establishing universities outside Europe had three sources. There were those set up by church and king (as in Latin America); those organized by settlers (as on the eastern seaboard of North America); and those initiated by governments – either by metropolitan governments (for example, in India and English-speaking Africa) or by national (as in Japan) or colonial governments wishing to import Western higher education

(Ashby 1966, 8). From our current vantage point, having witnessed the growth of the for-profit sector and marketing of higher education globally, a fourth source for the creation of universities can be discerned: organizations and individuals seeking profits from higher education.

Until the nineteenth century, universities were preoccupied with teaching in fields such as arts, law, medicine, and theology. The new model represented by Wilhelm von Humboldt's reformed University of Berlin – an autonomous state university that embraced research as a key part of its mission – greatly influenced the subsequent evolution of institutions in the US, England, Canada, and other parts of the world (Fallis 2007, 29–31). In other systems, including those of France and Russia, universities remained focused on teaching and research was concentrated in separate institutions for a much longer period (Altbach, Reisberg, and Rumbley 2009, 142). The Humboldtian model was based on principles of freedom in teaching and learning and encouraged the emergence of disciplinary structures (Altbach 2011, 14–15). The range and variety of subjects taught within universities multiplied, resulting in the creation of new chairs and/or departments (Shils 1992, 1261). Scholarly publication and the ethos of science blossomed (1262).

With the continuing reduction in churches' role in governance, universities generally increased their autonomy in the period leading up to the First World War. The distribution of authority within universities varied significantly by country. For example, in German universities full professors had extensive power, whereas in the US, presidents exercised great authority under that of boards (Shils 1992, 1261). Meanwhile, state universities and land-grant institutions in the US established in the nineteenth century embodied new conceptions of universities as servants of the public.

The First and Second World Wars disrupted the operations of universities at large and "the normal internationality of science and scholarship" (Shils 1992, 1264). The wartime roles of universities and their members in the UK, the US, and elsewhere paved the way for postwar changes in their roles in society. Expectations of universities became "much higher, more comprehensive, and more insistent … Esteem was replaced by expectations of practical benefits" (1267). Massive public investment followed in developed countries to enable universities to contribute to goals such as scientific and technological advancement, improved health outcomes, industrial and regional development, and social mobility (1267). The massification of higher education – that is, the increase in the number and size of universities to enable a much higher proportion of the population to attend them – began in many parts of the world. As Fallis observed, "the role of universities changes when a country commits itself to mass university education. The university system becomes the institutional embodiment of the commitment to equality of opportunity ... [It] becomes an institution for social justice, for changing the class structure of a nation, for including the previously excluded" (2007, 61).

In response to changing social expectations and campus unrest in the 1960s, university governance in many countries was democratized. Increased size, greater complexity, and broadened missions engendered more administration and gave rise to the Anglo-American "multiversity," that is, to large, complex, research-intensive universities offering undergraduate, graduate, and professional education and engaged in related functions, from running hospitals to managing endowments and intellectual property portfolios (Kerr 2001). As Fallis (2007) has pointed out, the advent of the multiversity was closely linked to the emergence of the welfare state with its expanded conception of the rights of citizenship, its confidence in the capacity of governments to solve problems, and its commitment to fund access to higher education.

As economic growth declined in the 1970s and government deficits and debt grew, universities were confronted by the partial roll-back of the welfare state and its ambitions (Fallis 2007). Public funding did not keep up with expanded missions, so universities sustained themselves by diversifying their revenues to the extent permitted by the state. Writing in the early 1990s, Shils observed:

> The power and multiplicity of the centrifugal forces working on the universities, from within and outside, have become very great since the 1950s ... Bureaucratization within the university has gone on apace. External bureaucratic and political influence ... has also increased. Universities out of financial necessity, out of the desire to be of service to their societies and out of the aspirations – intellectual, political and pecuniary – of their teachers, have been invited to accept many responsibilities outside the universities while performing their traditional functions.
>
> The modes of exercise of the external power of the state, in support of the universities, the exigencies and rewards of closer collaboration with business firms, the need for additional revenues to supplement what government and private patrons offer, and the greater opportunities for influence and rewards by public and political action outside the universities, have all had a disaggregative effect on the university as a community of learning ...

The tribulations of the university are the measure of its success. (1992, 1272–3)

Despite these tribulations, universities have continued to flourish as organizations. By 1985, 1,854 universities had been founded around the world, 202 of which had closed down (Riddle 1989, ctd by Kivinen and Poikus 2006). Since then, the growth in the number of universities has been explosive. In 2002, the World List of Universities catalogued 7,200 institutions (Kivinen and Poikus 2006). In 2015, the World Higher Education Database listed almost 10,400 institutions labelled as "university"; in 2019, it listed 11,078 (WHED 2019). Much of this growth has been in the private sector, particularly in Asia but also in Latin America, Africa, and Central and Eastern Europe (Altbach, Reisberg, and Rumbley 2009, xiv).

As Marginson observed, "higher education has become an essential passport to full-time work and effective social status" in many parts of the world (2015, 11). People and governments look to universities to advance goals such as human capital development, technological and social innovation, economic competitiveness, social mobility, and national reputation, in addition to their traditional roles of preserving, advancing, and disseminating knowledge. The attention given to university rankings by policy-makers, university stakeholders, and the public at large is an indication of universities' prominence. World rankings underscore the global dimension of higher education, reinforce the supremacy of elite Anglo-American universities, and promote isomorphism (Marginson 2008). Technology and converging approaches to quality assurance also foster conformity (Marginson 2008).

The world's universities nevertheless remain diverse. Diversity has arguably increased since the mid-1900s insofar as many new institutions called universities are not universities in the traditional sense. Some do not engage in research or entrust their faculty members with central roles in academic governance. Some lack physical premises. For-profit institutions typically operate on a business model in which students are regarded as consumers, boards and executives make decisions, and faculty "are viewed by the business side as being delivery people, as in delivery of the curriculum" (Ruch 2001, 115). There are numerous online mega-universities around the world, as well as innumerable smaller ones (Altbach, Reisberg, and Rumbley 2009, 130–1). Although their status as universities is sometimes contested, the rise of for-profit and online institutions can be regarded as expanding the already splendid diversity of the university field.

## ORIGINS OF HIGHER EDUCATION IN CANADA

The origins of higher education in this country have typically been traced to 1635. That year, the Jesuits established the Collège de Québec, which eventually offered the classical college course that would underpin the BA degree in francophone universities until the 1950s (Harris 1976, 14). Financed by donations from an aristocratic French family, the college combined the French classical program with practical subjects (Cameron 1991, 6). It served initially as an elementary school for children of settlers and Indigenous people (Harris 1976, 14), gradually introducing more advanced courses in mathematics and theology, which constituted the first higher education programs in Canada (Audet 1970, ctd by Jones 1996).

The establishment of universities and colleges was, of course, an aspect of European colonization, whereby European people gradually deprived Indigenous people of their lands, resources, and, eventually, languages, ceremonies, and indeed children. "Colonization advanced from the East to the West coast of Canada through active appropriation of lands justified through the denigration of Indigenous knowledges and Indigenous Peoples" (Cote-Meek 2020, xiv).

The Treaty of Utrecht (1713) awarded Acadia and Nova Scotia to the British. Fifty years later, under the Treaty of Paris (1763), Britain also obtained control of Quebec, giving it authority over almost all of France's North American colonies. Just over a century later, the British North America Act (1867) created the Dominion of Canada. The Royal Proclamation of 1763 had recognized the status of Indigenous nations, yet no Indigenous representatives were invited to the Charlottetown and Quebec conferences of 1864 that brought about Confederation (Papillon 2020).

Canada was initially a federation of four provinces (Ontario, Quebec, Nova Scotia, and New Brunswick). British Columbia (BC) joined the country in 1871 and Prince Edward Island in 1873. New provinces came into being in the west (Manitoba in 1870, Alberta and Saskatchewan in 1905), and Newfoundland became part of Canada in 1949. Canada also has three northern territories: Yukon, the Northwest Territories, and Nunavut.

The early universities and colleges in what is now Canada were essentially transplants, in that they were modelled on those in the UK and the US (Harris 1976, 37). According to Harris, "there was nothing notably Canadian about any of the institutions with degree-granting powers in 1849. What was being done at Acadia, Bishop's, McGill, Queen's, Victoria, and the three King's colleges was an imitation of what was being done at Oxford or Edinburgh or at [an American] college" (37).

Distinctively Canadian features began to emerge by 1860 with the founding of Université Laval, the creation of provincial universities in New Brunswick and Ontario, the incorporation of some applied programs into universities' offerings, and the emergence of a Canadian arts and science curriculum (37). In 1867, there were seventeen degree-granting institutions (Anisef, Axelrod, and Lennards 2012) and about 1,500 university students in the entire country (Jones 1996, 341). There were basically three models of university: the private, non-denominational institution (e.g., McGill[1]); the public university with a governing board composed of government officials (e.g., University of Toronto, University of New Brunswick); and sectarian colleges with external boards composed largely of church-appointed members, which comprised the majority and represented the dominant institutional form until well into the twentieth century (339–41).

The British North America Act (Constitution Act 1867) placed education, including higher education, squarely under provincial jurisdiction (Fisher and Rubenson 2014b, 14). Canada is typical of long-standing federations in that the lower level of government is responsible for higher education, and higher education has historically been an area of tension between the two levels of government (Watts 1992). Given the religious, linguistic, and cultural importance of higher education, the Quebec government has traditionally been a leader in protecting provincial jurisdiction from federal interference.

Section 91(24) of the Canadian Constitution gave the federal government responsibility for "Indians and the Lands reserved for the Indians." Federal authorities have discharged this responsibility largely through the 1876 Indian Act (Papillon 2020). The goal of that act was to assimilate Indigenous people (Dickason and Newbigging 2019). The 2015 report of the Truth and Reconciliation Commission concluded that education and, in particular, "the establishment and operation of residential schools were a central element of this policy, which can best be described as 'cultural genocide'" (TRC 2015a, v. 1, 3). The 1876 act provided that "[a]ny Indian who may be admitted to ... any [ ] degree by any University of Learning ... shall ipso facto become and be enfranchised under this Act," thereby losing Indian status (Stonechild 2006, 21).

In the late 1800s, universities and colleges in Canada were struggling financially, at a time when the rise of science was increasing the cost of education. These were very small institutions in which the president usually carried out the functions now associated with deans and a department often consisted of a single instructor (Boyko and Jones 2010, 4). Provincial governments provided annual grants to a small number of institutions, but overall, government funding was very limited (Harris 1976, 100). Much professional education took place outside universities at professional schools in fields such as medicine, engineering, dentistry, pharmacy, and agriculture. These professional schools were usually established by governments, but some were founded privately (116).

Prompted in part by its ties with Johns Hopkins University, the University of Toronto (U of T) established a research-based doctoral program in 1897. U of T and McGill University pioneered a Canadian version of the research university model (Lacroix and Maheu 2015, 121), but most Canadian universities remained teaching institutions for many decades.

By the beginning of the twentieth century, the governance of U of T was in disarray (Cameron 1991, 27). In 1905, the provincial government established a Royal Commission to investigate the situation and make recommendations. The Flavelle Commission concluded that

> one of the principal contributory causes of [the defects of the present system] is the exceptional and unsatisfactory method by which the powers of the Crown in relation to the University have been exercised. No parallel to this method exists either in Great Britain or in North America. The State-owned and State-supported universities of Michigan, Wisconsin and other States of the American Union offer the closest examples for comparison. In these cases the State invariably delegates its powers to trustees or regents ... To administer the affairs of a State university by a political government, occupied with different matters, constantly changing its party character, and gifted with no special talent for the management of universities, has not commended itself to a practical and progressive people. We see no ground for the belief that this plan of direct State control, rejected abroad and in ill-repute at home, can be made a success in this Province. (Royal Commission on the University of Toronto, Ontario 1906, xix)

The commission recommended a new governance model that would involve "dividing the administration of the University between the Governors, who will possess the general oversight and financial control now vested in the State, and the Senate, with the Faculty Councils, which will direct the academic work and policy" (xxi). The commission called upon the provincial government to delegate its power over the control and management of the university to a board of governors composed of government-appointed members. It also recommended that the president's role be strengthened, "making its occupant in fact as well as in name the chief executive officer (CEO) of the University" (xx). To avoid board overreach, faculty appointments, promotions, and dismissals were to be made by the board only upon the recommendation of the president (Cameron 1991, 28). Academic control of the university was to be vested in the senate, representative of faculties, graduates, the administration, and federated and affiliated institutions (Jones 1996, 346).

This bicameral model of university governance was eventually adopted by almost every Canadian university (Jones 1996, 346). Several others had long been bicameral (including Dalhousie, McGill, and Queen's), but it was the Flavelle Commission that articulated the underlying rationale and principles of bicameralism (Cameron 1991, 27). According to Harris, the 1906 charter for the University of Toronto provided a model for "almost every institution in English-speaking Canada which has been established since that time" (Harris 1984, 813, ctd by Jones 1996, 346). Some Catholic universities in Quebec and New Brunswick remained exceptions, continuing to be governed by a *conseil d'administration* (board of directors) that combined the functions of board and senate (Duff and Berdahl 1966, 15).

Over time, almost all the denominational institutions entered the public system either as autonomous institutions or as affiliates of larger secular universities (Skolnik 1997, 328). Provincial governments took different approaches to secularization. Nova Scotia was relatively tolerant of denominationalism (Christie 1997), but many other provinces actively promoted secular higher education, using tools such as legislation to create secular provincial universities, the withholding of degree-granting authority from denominational institutions, and the withholding of funds from denominational institutions. As of the mid-1990s, only a handful of independent denominational institutions in Canada continued to grant degrees – one in BC, one in Ontario, and a few private colleges in Alberta (Skolnik 1997, 328). By 2013, however, their numbers had increased; faith-based institutions could be found in five provinces (Li and Jones 2015), but they were small, and the university sector remained overwhelmingly secular.

For the first half of the twentieth century, universities served a small, relatively privileged fraction of the population and received little public and political attention (Jones 1996, 347). Most provincial governments paid scant attention to university matters, except when considering the annual grants provided to some institutions (Jones and Noumi 2018, 97). Overall, universities had meagre public funding but a high level of autonomy from governments (Jones 1996, 347).

In the 1940s, the federal government became a major force in the financing of higher education, with encouragement from the National Conference of Canadian Universities (NCCU). The NCCU was founded in 1911 and by 1920 was recognized both domestically and abroad as the voice of Canadian universities (Harris 1976, 210). After the Second World War, Ottawa provided financial support to veterans to enable them to attend university (Harris 1976, 457). Enrolments remained relatively high after the wave of veterans graduated, owing to an increase in both population and rates of participation. By 1951, 7.2 percent of 18-to-21-year-olds were attending university (Harris 1976, 457).

Federal funding for veterans' education "demonstrated both the value and the feasibility of federal money being used to support higher education" (458). In 1951, a federal royal commission recommended annual federal funding for universities proportionate to the population of each province (459). Parliament voted to implement the grants to universities, but the premier of Quebec objected, so grants to universities in the province were replaced with a fiscal transfer to the provincial government. In 1967, the federal government ceased providing direct grants to universities in favour of fiscal transfers to all the provinces. These later became unconditional (rather than earmarked for post-secondary education). According to Skolnik (1997), "with the apparent withering away of the major source of federal funds for postsecondary education, so, too, [did] the prospect for significant federal government influence over postsecondary education policy in Canada" (335).

In 1966, the federal government considered establishing an education office within the Department of the Secretary of State. This galvanized the provinces into creating the Council of Ministers of Education, Canada (CMEC), of which the federal government is not a member (Cameron 1991, 13). To this day, there is no minister, ministry, or department of higher education at the national level (Jones and Noumi 2018, 102). Ottawa's very limited role and capacity in this policy area places Canada firmly at the decentralized end of the world spectrum of federations (Watts 1992; Jones and Noumi 2018).

Though Ottawa withdrew from funding university education directly, it greatly increased its financial support for university research. Federal involvement in research dates back to the formation of the National Research Council (NRC) in the early 1900s. The NRC initially focused on industrial research and development, but it soon began to provide grants and scholarships for university research (Cameron 1991, 33). Federal support continued after the Second World War with the formation of the Canada Council in 1957, the Medical Research Council (MRC) in 1960, and the Natural Sciences and Engineering Research Council (NSERC) and the Social Sciences and Humanities Research Council (SSHRC), both in 1978.

Until the 1950s, most Canadian universities were principally teaching institutions. In his account of the development of universities in Canada, Howard Clark (2003) observed that during the 1950s and 1960s, "probably only McGill University and the University of Toronto were known outside Canada for research accomplishments and even they did not rank highly among the world's universities. Other universities were little more than undergraduate teaching institutions, and Canada's research effort, such as it was, was conducted at the National Research Council and in other government laboratories" (42).

The subsequent influx of funding for university research changed this situation so dramatically that a 1972 report commissioned by the Association of Universities and Colleges of Canada (AUCC, the successor to the NCCU) concluded that a "headlong rush of universities into graduate studies and research [had led to] neglect of undergraduate teaching [and] also uncoordinated research, much of which was of dubious quality" (Cameron 1991, 333). The Bonneau–Corry Report recommended that measures be taken at the institutional, provincial, and national levels to set research priorities, more rigorously assess quality, and support the development of centres of excellence, while rewarding faculty members for teaching and associated scholarship and removing requirements and incentives for research and publication (Cameron 1991, 334). The NRC began to promote the development of centres of excellence and links between university research and industry. Clark (2003) commented that "at the time, neither of these initiatives was welcomed in the universities; we much preferred to have increasing, unrestricted, individual research grants" (52).

In the meantime, on the educational front, the period from the late 1950s to the early 1970s saw the "identification and elaboration of provincial needs, innovation and expansion, and the establishment of what might be described as provincial systems of higher education" (Skolnik 1997, 329). Provinces took different approaches – some engaged in system visioning and planning, while others relied more on encouraging institutional initiatives (335). Nevertheless, there were common themes, including these:

- High public and governmental expectations of and faith in universities in the early 1960s, which would diminish in later decades (Fallis 2007).
- Expansion of the number of universities, particularly in the 1960s and 1970s. Figure 1.1 shows the number of Universities Canada/

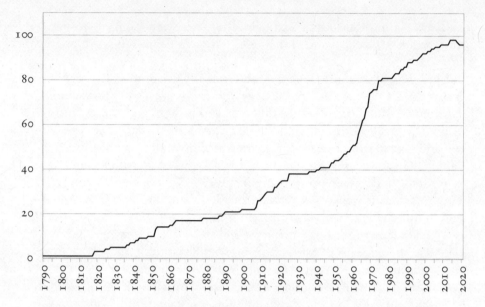

Figure 1.1 | Number of Universities Canada/AUCC member institutions from 1790 to 2020. *Source:* Turpin, De Decker, and Boyd (2014, 578). © The Institute of Public Administration of Canada/L'Institut d'administration publique du Canada, Toronto. Updated with data from Universities Canada.

AUCC member institutions from 1790 to 2020. As seen in figure 1.2, which shows the number of *Maclean's*[2] universities by category from 1950 to 2020, most of the growth was in the undergraduate and comprehensive categories.
- The creation of provincial higher education departments or ministries as well as policies, program approval and review processes, and funding mechanisms.
- Enrolment-based formula financing, practised by most provinces. Formulas are instruments of public policy for allocating funding to institutions. Their benefits include: a reduction in political influence and lobbying; provision of a basis for institutional and collective planning; assurance to donors that philanthropy will supplement rather than supplant public funding; and protection of institutional autonomy (Darling et al. 1989, 560).
- Ongoing prioritization by provincial governments of the goal of increasing access to higher education (Fisher and Rubenson 2014a; Jones and Noumi 2018).

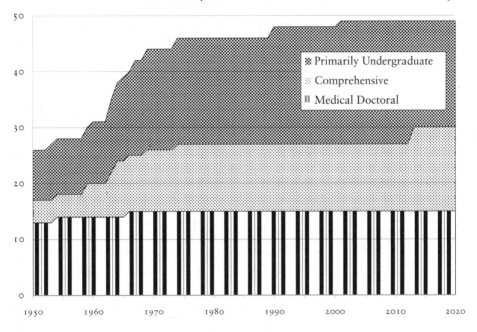

Figure 1.2 | Number of *Maclean's* universities by category. *Source:* Turpin, De Decker, and Boyd (2014, 578). © The Institute of Public Administration of Canada/L'Institut d'administration publique du Canada, Toronto. Updated with data from Universities Canada.

In the late 1950s, the federal Department of Indian Affairs began offering scholarships to enable "Indian" students to attend university or college. The formalization of the post-secondary assistance program in the 1970s led to a rapid increase in the number of students entering university, but completion rates were low (Stonechild 2006).

According to J.A. Corry (1970), the postwar period saw the transformation of universities "from private domain to public utility," from "nobody's business" to "everybody's business" (101–2, ctd by Jones 1996, 348). According to Jones, "the transition to mass higher education [ ] gradually led to the development of a relatively homogeneous university sector across provincial systems … and by the early 1970s [the] sector was composed of public, highly autonomous secular universities [with] similar governance arrangements" (206).

Changes in external governance were accompanied by reforms to internal governance. By the 1960s, prevailing models featuring powerful lay boards and presidents in English Canada and continuing Church control in francophone Quebec were being challenged by faculty members and students seeking greater say in governance. The Canadian Association of University Teachers (CAUT), a national association formed in 1951 to promote the interests of teachers and researchers, and the AUCC jointly sponsored a review of Canadian university governance. It was conducted by James Duff, former vice-chancellor of an English university, and Robert Berdahl, an American political scientist. Duff and Berdahl endorsed the bicameral model but concluded that it was not working well in Canada. Their 1966 report found Canadian boards to be too large, too homogeneous in composition (predominantly businessmen and lawyers), and out of touch with the academic community. They also found senates to be overly large, ineffective, diluted by non-academic members, and/or dominated by administration. They called for the reform of senates (including the reduction of their size, the removal of most external members, and a broadening of their mandates), adding faculty members to boards, and measures to democratize administration, such as the introduction of terms of office for deans and chairs.

Although the Duff–Berdahl Report did not recommend student membership on boards, students advocated strongly for membership on boards and other university bodies. In the ensuing decade, most Canadian universities reformed their senates, broadened representation on their boards, and provided for student participation in governance (Cameron 1991, 308). The proportion of boards that had faculty members increased from 9 percent in 1955, to 32 percent in 1965, to 92 percent in 1975; the corresponding numbers for students were 0 percent, 0 percent, and 78 percent respectively (314). In succeeding decades, other boards continued to add faculty and student representatives (Jones and Skolnik 1997).

Modernization also entailed movement toward open meetings. In 1967, no Canadian university had open senate or board meetings. By 1969, more than half allowed non-members to attend senate meetings, and ten boards had begun conducting open meetings (Cameron 1991, 311). Though the Flavelle Commission's recommendations were about establishing external accountability, "the governance reform movement of the 1960s can be viewed as an attempt to shift the balance of governance arrangements in order to increase accountability to internal constituencies" (Jones et al. 2001, 136). The reforms unleashed by the Duff–Berdahl Report also formalized granting of tenure and democratized decision-making (Cameron 1991). Universities began decentralizing decisions to "faculty members acting initially through departments" (316). They adopted the principle that academic administrators should make personnel decisions on the advice of faculty committees. They started appointing academic administrators for fixed terms after consultation with or election by faculty members. Democratization also featured in the extent of consultation of various forms, including in presidential searches. Thereafter, the selection of presidents and other senior university officials typically involved a search committee composed of representatives of major bodies and/or constituencies. In Quebec, some universities adopted an election process whereby rectors were elected by representatives of various constituencies (Jones 1996, 357). The upshot was a fundamental transformation of university governance – a significant shift in power from boards and presidents to senates and departments, as well as much greater faculty and student involvement (Cameron 1991; Jones 1997). Jones observed: "Within a few years faculty and student representatives could be found on almost every academic and administrative committee within the university, and few new initiatives were undertaken without first creating some form of broadly representative steering committee or task force. The governance process [had become] much more participatory, complex and decentralized" (1996, 357). According to Clark (2003), "boards and administrations lost much power and authority, although ironically they had to retain the ultimate responsibility for institutions they could no longer really manage" (182).

As economic conditions and public finances began to deteriorate in the mid-1970s, provincial governments – determined to maintain or increase access to university education, achieve economic and employment objectives, and constrain growth in expenditures – became increasingly concerned about institutional responsiveness, efficiency, and accountability. They sought to align universities' activities more closely with provincial priorities such as economic development, technological innovation, meeting labour market needs, and extending access to post-secondary education to historically underrepresented groups. Plentiful early funding for university expansion gave way to government efforts to rein in costs. As they tightened funding, provincial agencies tended to assume more control over program approval. Enrolment-based funding formulas coupled with regulation of fees encouraged universities to pursue enrolment growth and compete for students (Darling et al. 1989, 560).

The late twentieth century witnessed the following:

- A decrease in the proportion of university revenues coming from government funding and a corresponding increase in that coming from fees, to varying degrees by province (Usher 2018d, 27; Fisher and Rubenson 2014a, 346). Increased fee revenues resulted from

looser regulation of domestic student tuition fees, coupled with differential institutional latitude over international student fees (Lang 2019).
- Reinforcement by governments of market mechanisms in higher education and research by means such as competitive funding programs and matching-funding arrangements. The extent of such "marketization" varied by province (Fisher and Rubenson 2014a, 313).
- Disbanding of most provinces' intermediary bodies. The general purpose of these "buffer" bodies had been to provide governments with informed advice on university matters while avoiding government intrusion into university affairs. Their roles and powers varied across the country (Jones 1996, 355); some were advisory, whereas others had responsibility for allocating funding to institutions.
- Focus on preparation of students for employment and on meeting labour force requirements, which varied in extent and form from province to province and government to government (Fisher and Rubenson 2014a; Jones and Noumi 2018).
- Efforts by governments to align university research with scientific, technological, and economic policy and priorities. The federal government invested heavily in university research and sought to harness it to increase innovation, human capital development, and economic growth. Meanwhile, to various degrees, provinces developed their own research and development infrastructures. One of the more populous provinces, Quebec, developed a parallel system of agencies, and Ontario was an early and active participant in this arena. In contrast, BC introduced a few programs of its own but relied principally on federal ones (Fisher and Rubenson 2014a, 325).
- Broad governmental efforts to make universities accountable for outcomes and returns on public investment.

The 1996 Royal Commission on Aboriginal Peoples (RCAP) found that the proportion of Indigenous people attending university had increased to 8.6 percent by 1991 but that completion rates remained low (RCAP, vol. 3, 476). The percentage of Indigenous people over fifteen with a university degree was 2.6 percent in 1991, up from 2.0 percent in 1981; the equivalent figures for non-Indigenous people were 11.6 and 8.1 percent respectively (440). RCAP recommended that post-secondary institutions undertake new initiatives or extend current ones to improve Indigenous students' education and experience, including by appointing Indigenous people to boards of governors (478–9). In addition to calling for increased federal funding for students, RCAP also recommended that federal, provincial, and territorial governments establish and support post-secondary educational institutions controlled by Indigenous people (484). Stonechild wrote that "the role of Aboriginal post-secondary education has evolved from a tool of assimilation to an instrument of empowerment" (2006, 2), but there were many obstacles to this. Federal post-secondary funding was capped in 1996, and increases were limited to 2 percent per year, so many eligible students were unable to access funding for their education (Timmons and Stoicheff 2016). Many Indigenous people regard post-secondary education as an inherent or treaty right, yet the federal government viewed its involvement in funding higher education as a matter of social policy rather than a legal obligation (Shanahan 2015a). Universities continued to display limited capacity to meet Indigenous peoples' higher education needs, and Indigenous-controlled post-secondary institutions were poorly funded (Stonechild 2006). Indigenous governments increasingly asserted jurisdiction over higher education but faced challenging organizational, financial, and jurisdictional issues (124).

What did the above developments in the broader environment mean for universities? According to Capano (2015), by the 2000s, "federal and provincial strategies [had] led to the presence of increased ties, more targets to be met ... and a greater degree of 'targeted' accountability to be taken into consideration" (116). According to Cameron (1991), the cumulative result of resource scarcity, external and internal expectations and scrutiny, unionization, and institutional complexity was "a new form of centralization, as scarce resources must of necessity be carefully shepherded, as collective bargaining imposes uniform rules ... and as concerns for safety, equity and affirmative action cut across the university. This centralization has not yielded increased management discretion, however. Rather, discretion has been attenuated, as more and more decisions are either routinized or subjected to negotiation, or both" (448). Perhaps ironically, this perceived narrowing of management's role was accompanied by a growing sense among professors that they were losing their authority over their universities (MacKinnon 2018, 3). Bruneau (2012) observed:

> At a distance, the governance arrangements of the university look unchanged from a century ago. The academic senate looks after curriculum, the evaluation of teaching, and student discipline. The board of governors has fiduciary responsibility for the buildings, the funds, and the administrative and management systems of the university ... As before, the president or rector is at the administrative apex of the academic and the "business" side of the university.

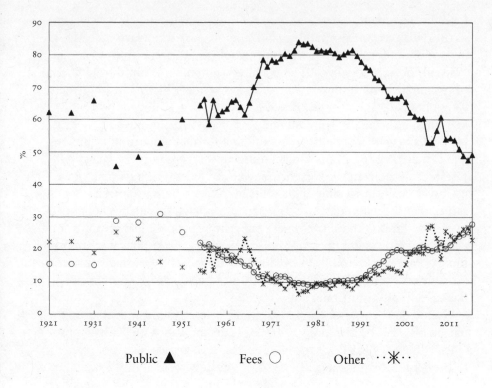

Figure 1.3 | Revenue structure of universities in Canada, 1921–2016
Source: Carpentier (2019, 25).

But ... appearances are deceiving. It looks as though the professoriate is still in the saddle. In the sight of the professors, it is not so. To them, the past 30 years have seen growing marginalization. (49)

Meanwhile, what happened to funding? Public funding for universities increased as a proportion of total university revenues from the 1940s through the 1970s before declining in relation to fees and other revenue sources (Carpentier 2019, 25).

For most of the 1990s, government funding fell in real terms. It then increased between 1998 and 2009 before beginning to decline again. Total university income has nevertheless continued to grow over the past decade owing to endowment income and international student fees (Usher 2019k, 32–3). Funding levels and trends vary substantially by province (40). By 2018, a number of major universities were receiving more money from international student tuition fees than from provincial operating grants (Usher 2018d, 1).

Canadian universities had traditionally been funded principally through block grants (Lang 2019, 2). However, by 2016, eight of ten provinces were employing some form of performance indicators, which were directly or indirectly attached to funding (Lang 2016a, 2). In 2019, the Ontario government announced that it would be moving to allocate 60 percent of grant funding to institutions by means of a new, performance-based funding formula (Usher 2019j). The Alberta government subsequently embraced performance-based funding as well (Usher 2020c), as did Manitoba (Foy 2021).

In the late twentieth century, many countries turned increasingly to private (including for-profit) provision of higher education – whether out of frustration with public institutions, a desire to increase diversity and competition, or simply an inability to pay for expansion – yet Canada moved only modestly in this direction. Ontario passed legislation in 2000 permitting private and out-of-province institutions to apply for university status (Anisef, Axelrod, and Lennards 2012). A number of other provinces also allow for-profit universities, but few have come into existence (Li and Jones 2015). As of 2020, the Canadian Information Centre for International Credentials (CICIC) listed five "recognized"[3] private universities in Canada, excluding theological schools. All were not-for-profit. The CICIC also identified twenty-eight university-type institutions authorized to grant specific credentials: nineteen not-for-profit and nine for-profit (CICIC n.d.). Some were foreign institutions permitted to offer specific credentials in one or more Canadian provinces.

In reducing the public share of higher education costs, opening the door to private institutions, and introducing more targeted, performance-based, and/or market-like mechanisms, governments in Canada were following a worldwide neoliberal trend in higher education policy (Schuetze 2012). That said, Fisher and Rubenson (2014a) concluded from a study of three major provincial post-secondary systems that Canada as a whole has retained its attachment to welfare liberalism and is among the countries "more affected … by the rhetoric, rather than the reality, of neoliberalism" (352).

Notwithstanding the common patterns and themes described above, the paths taken in the development of Canadian universities varied greatly from colony to colony and province to province. The next section of this chapter therefore offers brief sketches of the evolution of universities by major region, beginning with the origins of formal higher education in what is now Canada in seventeenth-century Quebec.

## EVOLUTION OF UNIVERSITIES IN QUEBEC

In 1663, around thirty years after the Jesuits founded the Collège de Québec, the first bishop of New France established le grand Séminaire de Québec for the training of members of the clergy. The college and the seminary were forced to close during the British siege of Quebec; the seminary resumed teaching in 1765, but the college never reopened (Cameron 1991, 6).

In the early years of the British regime, the Catholic Church was officially recognized but its activities were discouraged. Since the church was the primary sponsor of education in French Canada, access to higher education was meagre (Harris 1976, 17). In 1770, citizens of Quebec, Montreal, and Trois-Rivières presented a petition to the governor calling for the establishment of a university to

> élever la jeunesse dans les bonnes moeurs, dans la probité, dans la vertu, dans l'étude des langues, dans les sciences de la philosophie, des mathématiques, du génie, de la navigation, du droit civil, et généralement dans tous les arts et toutes les sciences humaines qui rendent l'homme utile à la société et qui font l'honneur d'une nation.
>
> [raise youth in good manners, in probity, in virtue, in study of languages, in philosophical sciences, mathematics, engineering, navigation, civil law, and generally in all the arts and humanities that make man useful to society and make the honour of a nation.]
>
> (Citizens' petition to Governor of Canada, 24 July 1770, qtd in Bizier 1993, 18)

The petition was not given serious consideration by the authorities in Britain (Harris 1976, 16).

Twenty years later, a special committee of the Legislative Council on Means for Promoting Education recommended the establishment of "a collegiate institution for cultivating the liberal arts and sciences usually taught in the European Universities – the Theology of Christians excepted" (17). The governor intended that this institution also govern the schools "so that the whole system may be animated by one common principle, under the eye and control of the crown" (17–18). The system was to be overseen by a body composed of the Catholic and Anglican bishops of Quebec and of an equal number of laypersons from the two denominations (Quebec 1963 [Rapport Parent], vol. 1, 23). Although the recommendation received enthusiastic initial support from the Legislative Council and many other quarters, it was temporarily set aside and never picked up again. The result was that, although the number of classical colleges increased in subsequent decades, there was little progress on the idea of a francophone university until the mid-1800s.

In the meantime, anglophone universities emerged in Lower Canada. McGill University was established in Montreal in 1821. Although chartered as a non-denominational institution, Anglican and Presbyterian influences dominated there until 1852, when its charter was amended, its board of governors reconstituted, and divinity removed from the subjects taught (Harris 1976, 6). The University of Bishop's College opened in Lennoxville in 1845 and was chartered in 1853. Its aim was to "promote sound learning and true religion amongst the inhabitants of this province, and to train up the rising generation in feelings of affection for the mother country and loyalty to their Sovereign" (*Journal of Education*, 1860, ctd in Harris 1976, 5).

The late 1840s saw the revival of the movement to establish a francophone university. With leadership from the Séminaire du Québec, a royal charter was obtained for Université Laval in 1852, creating the first francophone Catholic university in America (Bizier 1993, 42) and the British Empire (Cameron 1991, 14). In 1853, Rome granted Laval "les pouvoirs ordinaires d'une université catholique" (the ordinary powers of a Catholic university) (Harris 1976, 23). The process of affiliating existing colleges with the new university began. The latter was to consist of the traditional four faculties – arts, law, medicine, and theology – linked by "la grande Unité, qui est la Vérité incréée" (the great Unity, which is increate Truth) (23). Classical colleges comprised its faculty of arts (Quebec 1963 [Rapport Parent], vol. 34). Laval's 1852 charter provided for a unicameral governing structure, the basic elements of which remained in place until 1991, when it adopted a bicameral structure (Jones 1996, 355).

The establishment of a university in Quebec City under the authority of its archbishop did not, in the view of the bishop of Montreal, obviate the need for a university in his own city. He had supported the pursuit of a charter for Laval, because "il craignait que les laïques, au Québec comme en France, ne viennent à s'emparer de l'éducation" (he feared that the laity, in Quebec as in France, would take over education) (Lavallée 1974, 13). That objective having been accomplished, he now led a quest for a university in Montreal, and this led to an "academic civil war" between the two communities. Bishop Bourget petitioned Rome in 1862, 1864–65, and 1876, and the provincial legislature in 1872, for permission to establish an independent university in Montreal (Lavallée 1974, 15). His efforts were unsuccessful. A branch of Laval was established in

Montreal in 1876. Legislation to create the Université de Montréal was eventually passed in 1920 (Bizier 1993, 105).

In the latter part of the 1800s, McGill developed programs in the natural and applied sciences, including medicine and agriculture. The École Polytechnique de Montréal was established in 1873. Université Laval, having declined government funding for applied science education in the late 1800s out of concern about political interference, established schools of surveying, forestry, and chemistry beginning in the early 1900s and a faculty of science in 1937 (Quebec 1963 [Rapport Parent], vol. 1, 36).

Although other institutions were established in the Province of Quebec through private initiatives and under private charters (Donald 1997, 163), higher education remained relatively underdeveloped there until the 1960s, particularly for French-speaking people. Anglo-Canadian socio-economic dominance had led to a relative lack of economic and educational opportunities and role models for francophones. At the university level, Laval, Montreal, Sherbrooke, and several professional institutions served francophone students; McGill, Sir George Williams, Bishop's, and Loyola, anglophone ones. As the Parent Commission observed, except for a few schools established and maintained by the provincial government (e.g., l'École polytechnique, l'École des Hautes études commerciales) or the federal government (Royal Military College Saint-Jean), "tous les établissements universitaires qu'on trouve dans le Québec sont indépendants et doivent leur existence à des initiatives extérieures à l'État" (all the university establishments in Quebec are independent and owe their existence to initiatives outside the state) (Quebec 1963 [Rapport Parent], vol. 1, 75).

Since the BNA Act guaranteed the right to be educated in either the Catholic or the Protestant faith in Quebec, there were two separate school systems. Until 1960, education was church-controlled, poorly coordinated, and underfunded. Long-serving Quebec premier Maurice Duplessis opposed the creation of a Ministry of Education on the grounds that it would undermine religious schooling (Donald 1997, 162). Education was compulsory only until the age of fourteen (165) and only 63 percent of French-speaking students finished elementary school (Trottier et al. 2014, 215). In 1960, 2.9 percent of the French-speaking population twenty to twenty-four years old was enrolled full-time in a university, compared to 11 percent of the English-speaking population (Linteau et al. 1989, 344).

According to Lacroix and Maheu (2015), the leading francophone universities were handicapped by a number of factors relative to their counterparts in English Canada:

First, they were Catholic institutions in a highly conservative social milieu, led by clergy who often had no academic expertise. Rome exercised a great deal of control over these universities, and they essentially identified with the European network of Catholic institutions that was worlds away from the great German, UK, and US traditions that were blazing the trail for modern universities. In addition, little if any of the vast wealth in Montreal, which was such an asset to McGill, was available to these two francophone universities, which had to depend on the Catholic Church for their survival. Finally, they could not gain much from the French university model, as it generally had little to offer. Thus, Canada saw a two-tier development of universities and it was not until the early 1960s that francophone universities in Quebec began to catch up to their leading Anglophone counterparts. (121)

Trottier and colleagues (2014) studied the modern development of the Quebec higher education system up to 2011 and identified five stages: emergence (1960–70), consolidation (1970–85), evolution under the Parti Libéral (1985–94), evolution under the Parti Québécois (1994–2003), and changes under the Parti Libéral (2003–11).

The profound social transformation known as the Quiet Revolution started in 1960 with the election of a Liberal government. Modernization of the education system was a central component of that transformation. Reform involved "an affirmation of Quebec's own culture, which was in the process of breaking with Roman Catholic, French Canadian culture ... a commitment to social change associated with the transfer of responsibility for and control over education from Church to State ... [and] the promotion of French-speaking Québécois" (Ferretti 2000, ctd by Trottier et al. 2014, 215). The Quebec government established a Royal Commission of Inquiry on Education in the Province of Quebec (Parent Commission), which advocated state involvement in education, expanded access, secularization, and regional representation. The Parent Commission recommended that the public school system stop at grade 11 and that a new model replace the classical school structure (Jones 1996, 353). Its recommendations also included more democratic governance and management of universities (Donald 1997, 167).

The government responded to the Parent Commission's recommendations by creating a Ministry of Education, the Conseil Supérieur de l'Éducation (Superior Council of Education), the Université du Québec (UQ), and a new college network (Collèges d'enseignement général et professionnel: CEGEPs). The UQ was conceived as a system of public universities located across the province that would expand access to higher education and contribute to the socio-economic development of communities and regions. The rector of one of its constituent universities described it in 1969 as "une structure de concertation, une déconcentration géographique d'institutions autonomes et, finalement ... une idéologie universitaire nouvelle ... Le tout ... adapté et souple, à la mesure du Québec et de l'homme québécois d'aujourd'hui et de demain" (a structure of concertation, a geographic deconcentration of autonomous institutions and, finally, a new university ideology ... The whole, adapted and supple, worthy of Quebec and the québécois man of today and tomorrow) (Dorais 2002, 352).

The CEGEPs – public institutions offering both pre-university and advanced technical/vocational education – are another distinctive feature of the education system in Quebec. Colleges play a very important role in post-secondary education across Canada, including at the university level. Historically, people in many parts of the country first experienced university-level education at a college, because "one university" policies, fiscal constraints, and other factors limited the number of universities. Nevertheless, Quebec's CEGEPs are unique in that they serve all high school leavers.[4] Students go to a CEGEP after eleven years of school and take either a two-year general program leading to university or a three-year program leading to the workplace. These and other measures introduced in response to the Parent Commission report, at a time of rapid population growth, meant that, between 1962 and 1970, full-time enrolment in francophone universities tripled (Donald 1997). A Council of Universities was established in 1968 to strengthen coordination within the rapidly growing system.

Like other parts of the country and the world, Quebec in the 1960s and 1970s experienced social and campus unrest, democratization of universities' governance, reform of university management, expansion of the number and variety of programs, and growth of graduate studies and research.

The Université de Montréal was secularized in 1965 and Laval in 1970 (Donald 1997, 169). Professors at American universities began to unionize in the 1960s, and Quebec led the way in this in Canada: the Syndicat des professeurs de l'Université de Montréal, founded in 1966, was the first faculty union in the country, and an association of engineering professors at the University of Sherbrooke became the first certified faculty union in 1970. The Syndicat des professeurs de l'Université du Québec à Montréal came into being in January 1971, affiliated with the Confédération des syndicats nationaux; by October of that year, it was on strike (Cameron 1991, 346–8). In 1976, nine new university collective agreements were negotiated in the province, the Laval and UQAM campuses were beset by conflict, and the Council of Universities expressed concern about the impact of unionization (Donald 1997, 172). By 1979, 61 percent of professors in Quebec and all the francophone universities were unionized (174). Similar developments were taking place at a slower pace in other provinces: by 1980, there were twenty-two faculty unions across the country and a common pattern of collective bargaining had emerged (Cameron 1991, 359, 361).

In Quebec, the development of universities was intertwined with the development of scientific capacity. Francophone universities had been relatively slow to adopt research as part of their missions (Donald 1997, 163), but by the 1970s they were rapidly catching up.

The years 1985 to 1994 in Quebec were characterized by a focus on economic outcomes, accountability, and efficiency (Trottier et al. 2014). A recession in the early 1980s led to budget cuts, and universities had to accommodate increased enrolments with fewer resources. In its 1987–88 report, the Superior Council of Education noted that many universities were responding to increased student numbers and pressure to do research by relying increasingly on sessional lecturers for undergraduate teaching (Donald 1997, 181). Tuition fees were increased, after having been frozen since 1968. An Act Respecting Educational Institutions at the University Level was adopted, specifying which institutions could use the name "university." In 1993, the Council of Universities was abolished and the Conference of University Rectors (CRÉPUQ) assumed some of the council's responsibilities, which included developing a mechanism for university program evaluation.

Following the tradition of consultation established thirty years earlier with the Parent Commission, the Quebec government held Estates General on Education in 1994–95 to take stock of higher education. Recommendations included ensuring universities' accountability through stronger state involvement in planning and coordinating the higher education system. The government subsequently passed a Public Administration Act, a Policy on Universities, and a Policy on University Funding, which revised the funding formula, reinforced program evaluation, and introduced accountability agreements between universities and the Quebec Treasury Board (Trottier et al. 2014).

A Liberal government elected in 2003 initiated a "re-engineering of the State" based on new public management principles (Trottier et al. 2014). In 2007, mismanagement of a capital construction project by the Université du Québec à Montréal (UQAM) led government to amend the

Public Administration Act to strengthen ministry oversight over university capital projects. That episode also led the provincial government to turn its attention to university governance. It subsequently proposed two bills intended to alter the composition of university governing boards; neither, however, was ultimately approved by the legislature.

The Liberal government's plans to increase tuition fees by 175 percent over five years led in 2012 to the biggest student strike in Canadian history. By 22 March, 300,000 students (75 percent of the Quebec student population) were on strike and between 150,000 and 200,000 students and citizens were protesting in Montreal (Bégin-Caouette and Jones 2014, 417). A provincial election in the fall of 2012 resulted in the election of a Parti Québécois minority government. The new minister undertook broad consultations with stakeholders in higher education, leading to a Summit on Higher Education early in 2013, after which tuition fees were indexed according to per capita disposable income in Quebec. The Liberal government elected in April 2014 did not reverse this decision or follow through on several of the recommendations that emerged from the summit. It was succeeded by a Coalition Avenir Québec government in 2018.

The province's university sector is diverse. It includes six charter universities (Bishop's University, Concordia University, Université Laval, Université de Montréal, McGill University, and the University of Sherbrooke); two affiliated schools of the Université de Montréal (École des hautes études commerciales and École polytechnique); and the Université du Québec (UQ) Network, comprised of six universities, one engineering school, two graduate education institutions, and a distance education university.

The "charter" universities are those established prior to 1968 as private institutions (Trottier et al. 2014). Since each operates under its own charter or legislation, they are governed in different ways. For example, at Université Laval the rector is elected, whereas at the Université de Montréal he or she is appointed by the board. The members of the Université du Québec are public institutions, governed by the 1968 Act Respecting the Université du Québec.

Quebec's higher education sector has traditionally featured a large number of consultative bodies, commissions, and councils. Trottier and colleagues (2014), Donald (1997), and others have described this as characteristic of the province. Nevertheless, according to Trottier and colleagues (2014), recent decades have seen a concentration of power in the hands of the Government of Quebec, and especially the ministry responsible for higher education, as reflected in new funding mechanisms, new accountability requirements, and highly specific budgetary rules.

The Government of Quebec influences universities through funding, legislation, and regulations but delegates to other bodies the responsibility for quality assurance. Universities develop and manage their own programs, and the Bureau de coopération universitaire, which replaced the CRÉPUQ, administers the process for review of new programs. Programs are also shaped by professional bodies. In 2011, fifty-one occupations in Quebec were governed by forty-six professional associations, many of which had training committees concerned with preparation for professional practice (CRÉPUQ 2011). Many professional programs are also subject to quality assurance mechanisms at the national and/or international levels (CRÉPUQ 2011).

In sum, over 350 years of Quebec's history, the governance of universities and colleges changed dramatically. The Church, which exercised extensive control over education until the mid-twentieth century, receded abruptly into the background. The state assumed a "preponderant role in the management of the PSE system when compared to the role it plays in other systems" (Trottier et al. 2014, 286). Professional education, which initially took place largely outside universities, migrated into them. The Université du Québec was established alongside charter universities, as was the CEGEP network. Internal governance was also transformed. Governing bodies and administrations were laicized. Faculty members, many of whom were once members of the clergy, are now largely unionized professionals. Students became highly organized and politically effective. Quebec's system is distinctive, not only in Canada, but also on the international scene, in that it is a partial exception to trends toward neoliberalism and marketization in higher education (Trottier et al. 2014, 286; Metcalfe 2010).

## EVOLUTION OF UNIVERSITIES IN THE ATLANTIC PROVINCES AND ONTARIO

Although higher education in what is now Canada originated in New France, the first degree-granting institution was the University of King's College, established in 1789 in Windsor, Nova Scotia (Cameron 1991, 7). An example of a settler-instigated institution, it also had strong ties to the Church of England. It was established through the efforts of a group of United Empire Loyalists, one of whom had been among the founders of King's College in New York. The Loyalists, who migrated into the remaining British colonies in North America after the American Revolution, sought to strengthen British values and prevent the spread of republicanism. Having relocated to Nova Scotia, King's founders argued for the establishment of a college in the colony: otherwise "The youth of Nova Scotia will be sent for their education to the Revolted Colonies – the inevitable consequence [of which will] be a corruption of their religious and political principles" (7). The same argument would later be advanced for the establishment of colleges in other colonies.

King's College Windsor was the first institution outside the British Isles, in what later became the Commonwealth, to receive a university charter (Harris 1976, 4). Established in 1789 under provincial legislation, it received a Royal Charter in 1802 and annual grants from both the Nova Scotia and British governments. Its governors included the principal officers of the executive government of the colony and the Anglican bishop. Final authority to approve the college's regulations lay with the Archbishop of Canterbury. The combination of state and church control was not unusual for universities of the time. As Levy (1986) and Geiger (1991) have pointed out, historically, church and state control of higher education were intertwined.

> Until approximately the end of the eighteenth century, education was viewed as a combined responsibility of civil and ecclesiastical authorities. The universities of Oxford, Uppsala, Santo Tomas, and colonial Massachusetts – to take a sample – were all publicly supported (albeit irregularly) and privately governed in the presumably homogeneous interests of their respective societies. The rise of the secular state sundered this nexus and produced the distinction between public and private institutions. (Geiger 1991, 233)

King's required students to take an oath of allegiance to the Church of England in order to graduate, which was deeply problematic in a settler society, in which less than one quarter of the people belonged to the Anglican faith (Cameron 1991, 7). In Nova Scotia, and subsequently other colonies, the establishment of colleges identified with the Church of England prompted the establishment of colleges associated with other churches and of non-sectarian public universities, sometimes both.

In Nova Scotia, a multiplicity of colleges associated with different denominations emerged, competed, and struggled to survive, notwithstanding some concerted efforts in the 1800s to establish "One Good College" (Christie 1997, 227). By the mid-twentieth century, the province's higher education sector comprised one small, private university, numerous small, private colleges, and a few applied schools established by the provincial government. The private institutions resisted attempts to rationalize them in 1876 (through the creation of an examining University of Halifax, modelled on the University of London) and the 1920s (when a proposal for a University of the Maritime Provinces emerged from a study sponsored by the Carnegie Foundation, but failed to gain traction). The institutions subsisted principally on tuition fees, endowment income, donations, and, in some cases, funding from churches (Christie 1997).

New Brunswick and Upper Canada subsequently established their own King's Colleges. The former provided a charter in 1800 to a College of New Brunswick in Fredericton that became King's College in 1828 under Royal Charter. Like King's College in Windsor, the College of New Brunswick was modelled on King's College in New York (Jones 1996). In 1854, the recommendations of a Royal Commission led to its reorganization and rechartering as the non-denominational state-supported University of New Brunswick (UNB) (Harris 1976, 11). Other universities and colleges also emerged in New Brunswick, associated with the Methodist and Catholic churches, but the government provided operating funding only to UNB until 1951 (S. Brown 1997, 200).

The movement to establish an institution of higher education in Upper Canada was also led by United Empire Loyalists (Jones 1997, 137). King's College, York, was granted a Royal Charter in 1827. It was "in theory a provincial university, [but] was in fact controlled by the Church of England, and dissatisfaction with that arrangement ... led to its abolition by the legislature as of December 31 1849 and to the creation in its place on 1 January 1850 of a non-denominational University of Toronto" (Harris 1976, 8). Nevertheless, new denominational colleges continued to emerge in Upper Canada, and a number of technical, non-university institutions were founded (Jones 1997, 138). A reorganization of the University of Toronto (U of T) in 1887 enabled denominational colleges to enter into federation with the provincial university (Harris 1976, 99). This was spurred by the fact that Ontario had acted upon the jurisdiction granted to it under the BNA Act of 1867 by ending annual grants to denominational colleges (Harris 1976, 108).

As in French Canada, federation and affiliation played a huge role in the development of universities in English Canada (Harris 1976, 485). In some instances, federation was a means of bringing denominational colleges under one roof; in other instances, however, colleges started out as affiliates of established universities and became independent over time.

The late 1800s saw the opening of higher education in Canada to women. In 1874, Mount Allison Wesleyan College was the first university in what was then known as the British Empire to grant a bachelor's degree to a woman (11). By 1890, nine other Canadian institutions had done so as well (116).

As noted above, the 1906 report of the Flavelle Royal Commission led to bicameral governance at U of T and the emergence of a Canadian pattern of university governance. In 1920, Ontario appointed a royal commission on university finances that recommended capital and annual ongoing grants for U of T, Western, and Queen's universities (361). Even as late as 1940, these were the only three publicly supported universities; other institutions were ineligible for government funding because of their church affiliation (483).

As in Quebec, the 1960s witnessed the beginning of massification and steps to develop provincial or regional systems in Ontario and the Atlantic provinces. The provinces took different approaches. In Nova Scotia, general government funding of universities was restored in the 1960s after a hiatus of more than eighty years (Christie 1997, 231). As founding churches relinquished control to lay boards, many of the denominational colleges were rechartered as public institutions with degree-granting privileges (231–3). A University Grants Committee was established in 1963 – the first such buffer body in Canada. Along with its counterparts in New Brunswick and Prince Edward Island, it was succeeded in 1974 by the Maritime Provinces Higher Education Commission (MPHEC) (232).

Nova Scotia institutions successfully resisted another strong attempt to rationalize them in the early 1990s, but two specialized professional institutions subsequently merged with Dalhousie, the province's major university. Christie wrote in the 1990s that "sponsorship of university education in Nova Scotia has shifted from largely religious to primarily governmental and is now shifting again to a greater reliance on market support from fees, contract income and fundraising" (222). The province currently has one medical/doctoral university, five largely undergraduate universities, and four smaller, specialized institutions. In 2017–18, 48 percent of students in the province were from Nova Scotia, 32 percent were from out of province, and 20 percent were international (MPHEC 2018).

In New Brunswick, a Royal Commission established in 1961 recommended a new structure for higher education in the province, consisting of a two-campus University of New Brunswick, co-location and federation of one English university with UNB, continuation of the other, and the affiliation of the francophone institutions with a new Université de Moncton. The implementation of these recommendations in the mid-1960s led to the present structure. In 1968, formula financing of all the institutions was introduced and a Higher Education Commission was established, later superseded by the MPHEC.

In PEI, legislation turned the former St Dunstan's College and Prince of Wales College into the University of Prince Edward Island in 1969. After a decade of squabbling among the Maritime provinces over its location, the country's fourth veterinary college was established in 1986, at UPEI (Baker 1997).

Newfoundland, which joined Canada in 1949, had established the non-denominational Memorial University College in 1925. Although the University of London was the examining body, the college's two-year curriculum was modelled on that of universities in the Maritimes. In its early years, the college was dependent for funding on the Carnegie Corporation of New York (Bindon and Wilson 1997, 264). Public funding was later forthcoming. The college was subject to significant bureaucratic intrusion from government. In 1949, it became Memorial University of Newfoundland (MUN). MUN was regarded as a key player in the province's economic development from the outset and has always held a very important place in the province (Bindon and Wilson 1997, 266). However, university autonomy has continued to be an issue over the years (Bindon and Wilson 1997, 264, 267); in 2008, the provincial government denied the appointment of an internal candidate for the MUN presidency recommended by a university search committee (Simpson 2009). A 2017 review of MUN's governance noted that under the university's act, the province retained substantial authority over the institution (Lewis 2017, 5).

Whereas in the Atlantic provinces, most twentieth-century enrolment growth was absorbed by existing institutions (which, in NB and PEI, were reconfigured in the 1960s), Ontario created new universities and granted university status to former government institutions, in addition to expanding enrolments at existing universities. The new universities were secular, and their operating funds came largely from government grants. Denominational colleges continued to exist, but many of them federated or affiliated with public universities in order to secure government support (Jones 1997, 143). Until 2000, Ontario's policy was to prohibit private degree-granting institutions (Clark et al. 2009, 8).

Issues of language played a major role in the development of the higher education system in the bilingual province of New Brunswick. Addressing the needs of the francophone population was also a factor in the evolution of the higher education system in Ontario, as it would be in Manitoba.

As in Quebec, the latter half of the twentieth century saw changes in the internal governance and administration of universities in Ontario and the Atlantic provinces. Well into the 1950s and early 1960s, "benevolent dictatorship" characterized decision-making at most Canadian universities (Penner 1994, 49). Many institutions revised their governance structures in the late 1960s and 1970s to provide for increased faculty and student participation. Faculty members began unionizing in response to concerns about funding, job security, and changes in legislation favourable to the formation of professional unions (Cameron 1991, 350). The Canadian Association of University Teachers (CAUT), formed in 1951, was initially deeply ambivalent about the merits of faculty unionization (345). By the mid-1970s, however, it had become an advocate for formal collective bargaining, as well as a source of support to local associations in obtaining certification and in the negotiation and administration of collective agreements (364). "Unionisation [ ] shifted power and authority relationships within universities [insofar as m]any areas of university policy that had once been left in the hands of university administration or university governing bodies became subject to collective bargaining" (Jones, Shanahan, and Goyan 2001, 139).

Other internal governance changes in the late twentieth century included the following: reduction in the size of boards; growth in graduate programs, research centres, and institutes; and increases in administration in response to increased institutional size and complexity and external and internal demands (Jones, Shanahan, and Goyan 2001, 139). Universities sought to diversify their revenues through fundraising, the exploitation of intellectual property, increased fees, and other forms of revenue generation. Notwithstanding these efforts, cost pressures typically exceeded revenue increases, and many institutions responded by increasing student/faculty ratios and the proportion of undergraduate instruction conducted by part-time, sessional faculty (Clark et al. 2009, 80).

The Ontario university system, the design of which has changed little since the 1960s (Clark et al. 2009, 176), consists of around twenty relatively homogeneous publicly assisted universities and numerous federated institutions and theological schools (CICIC n.d.). The provincial systems in the Atlantic region are comprised of a provincial university (MUN, UNB, UPEI) or other major university (e.g., Dalhousie) and varying numbers of smaller and/or specialized institutions. The great majority of the universities, though regarded as public, are independent, not-for-profit corporations with bicameral governance structures operating under individual provincial acts.

## EVOLUTION OF UNIVERSITIES IN THE WEST

In the latter part of the nineteenth century, institutions of higher education emerged in western Canada. Manitoba became Canada's fifth province in 1870. St Boniface College – a small Roman Catholic institution founded in 1818 as a school where Latin was taught to boys from the French-speaking Red River Colony – offered a classical program in Winnipeg beginning in 1866. St John's College, an Anglican institution, began offering programs in arts and theology the same year, and a Presbyterian institution, Manitoba College, got under way shortly thereafter (Jones 1996, 344). Seeking to avoid repetition of the problems evident in the east, the province passed legislation in 1877 creating the University of Manitoba. The preamble stated that it was desirable "to establish one university for the whole of Manitoba" (Harris 1976, 114).

The university functioned at first as an examining body, with instruction being provided by affiliated denominational colleges. Over time, Manitoba – influenced by American models and in response to the need for science education – gave the university teaching responsibilities (Gregor 1997, 115). Largely because of resistance by the constituent colleges to the university becoming a full-fledged provincial teaching university, the process was fraught, and the University of Manitoba did not have a president until 1913. It did not come fully into being until 1920, after "at least eight legislative acts and a series of commissions of inquiry" (Harris 1976, 228). As a result of these tribulations, Manitoba became a pivot point in higher education in Canada. In bringing a set of denominational colleges together under one provincial university, it set the stage for other western provinces.

The desire to avoid the fragmentation and sectarian rivalry characteristic of higher education in eastern Canada informed the design of universities elsewhere in the west. The Anglican Church founded a college in the Northwest Territories in 1879 and obtained a charter from the Dominion government in 1883 for the establishment of a university; however, many residents objected to a denominational university (Muir 1997, 94). In 1890, a meeting of all university graduates held in Regina passed a resolution for the establishment of "one university for the whole of the North-West Territories" with which denominational colleges could affiliate (Harris 1976, 113). The spirit of this motion was acted upon fifteen years later, in 1905, when Saskatchewan and Alberta were carved out of the North-West Territories to become provinces. In the meantime, a number of small colleges were established in the territory, as well as in British Columbia.

The University of Saskatchewan, created by legislation in 1907, embodied a very different vision than those that had inspired universities in the east – that of a secular university dedicated to the service and advancement of the people of the province. In a 1908 speech, the first president of the University of Saskatchewan, declared:

> It is fitting for the university to place within reach of the solitary student, the distant townsman, the farmer in his hours of leisure, or the mothers and daughters in the home, the opportunities for adding to their stores of knowledge and enjoyment ... Whether the work be conducted within the boundaries of the campus or throughout the length and breadth of the province, there should be ever present the consciousness that this is the university of the people, established by the people, and devoted by the people to the advancement of learning and the promotion of happiness and virtue. (Thompson 1970, 44)

The University of Saskatchewan (U of S) was bicameral in that it had both a board responsible for financial affairs and a senate responsible for approving academic programs. However, it was unique in that the senate was elected by university graduates resident in the province; the senate, in turn, elected the majority of the members of the board of governors (Muir 1997, 100). Further bolstering the university's autonomy from government, the provincial government provided the bulk of its funding through a statutory grant (100). Whereas professional schools tended to arise outside universities in the east and Manitoba, the U of S's first president "strove from the first to involve the university in the process and criteria of accreditation and education of every profession practiced in the province" (95). Over time, the U of S's governance and funding became more conventional, and the board came to be comprised of a majority of government appointees (100). Nevertheless, according to Muir, writing in the mid-1990s, the province's universities "benefited from the traditional arm's length relationship with the civil power" (111).

Distance from government was less evident in Alberta. The new province passed a university act in 1906, before the impact of the Flavelle Commission's report. It provided for the university to be governed by a senate, the majority of whose members were to be appointed by the provincial government. In 1910, the act was amended and bicameralism was introduced; the board consisted of the chancellor, the president, and nine members appointed by the government. The president was also government-appointed (Cameron 1991, 29). Like Manitoba, Saskatchewan, and British Columbia, Alberta followed the "one university" principle.

The British Columbia legislature approved an act to "Establish One University for the Whole of British Columbia" in 1890. That did not come to fruition for twenty-five years, but in the interim, the legislature denied degree-granting powers to a number of denominational institutions (Harris 1976, 114). As in Saskatchewan and Alberta, there was intense rivalry between municipalities to be the site of the provincial university. This delayed its establishment, and in the early 1900s, it was McGill University College of British Columbia that offered undergraduate education in BC. The act to establish the University of British Columbia (UBC) was passed in 1908, and the university began operating in 1915 (Cameron 1991, 32). Its first president chose as its motto *Tuum est* (It is yours) (Jones 1996, 347). With an economy based on resource extraction and agriculture, the province's political leadership saw little need to invest significantly in higher education until the second half of the twentieth century (Dennison 1997, 32).

Given their "one university" policies, provincial governments in the west naturally took different approaches to postwar massification than their eastern counterparts. Manitoba passed legislation that allowed for the creation of additional universities by Order in Council (in essence, by the provincial cabinet). Under this legislation, pre-existing colleges became the University of Winnipeg and Brandon University in 1967, bringing the province's ninety-year-old "one university" policy to an end (Gregor 1997, 116; Jones 1996, 354). The U of S retained its monopoly on degree-granting for many years, but in 1959, Regina College became a second campus of the university, and in 1974 it became the University of Regina (Muir 1997, 101). Both institutions had networks of federated and/or affiliated institutions. Beginning in 1976 at the University of Regina, this included the Saskatchewan Indian Federated College sponsored by the Federation of Saskatchewan Indian Nations (Muir 1997, 101), which became First Nations University of Canada in 2003.

In Alberta, the Universities Act of 1966 made the University of Calgary an autonomous institution. That omnibus act provided for the establishment of other universities by regulation, and others were subsequently created. In the 1970s, Athabasca University was established with a mandate to specialize in distance education – the first institution of its kind in Canada (Andrews et al. 1997, 64).

In British Columbia, in 1963, Victoria College – an affiliate of UBC – became the University of Victoria and a new Simon Fraser University was created. At the end of the 1980s, a number of colleges were allowed to offer degrees through collaborative arrangements with universities, resulting in a distinctive set of "university colleges" (Dennison 1997, 45). A University of Northern British Columbia was established, along with an Open University as a distance-learning alternative to conventional universities. During the 1990s, the university colleges were given degree-granting status, as were a number of specialized institutions (48).

According to Dennison, British Columbia went furthest among Canadian provinces in the development of a provincial higher education system, with the exception of Quebec and possibly Alberta (51).

In many other respects, developments in the last half of the 1900s in the west were similar to those in other provinces. Like their eastern counterparts, the western provinces established bureaucracies, policies, and funding mechanisms and created, and subsequently disbanded, buffer bodies. They established research councils or foundations and began funding university research. An era of unprecedented institutional growth and expansion in the 1960s and early 1970s gave way to consolidation and constraint. As in other parts of the country, some western provincial governments became concerned about universities' effectiveness and efficiency. Illustrative of their sentiments was the 1993 report of the University Education Review (Roblin Commission) in Manitoba, subtitled *Doing Things Differently* (Gregor 1997, 129). Similarly, a 1994 policy document titled *New Directions for Adult Learning in Alberta* identified four major goals for the province's post-secondary institutions: increased accessibility, improved responsiveness, greater affordability, and more accountability (Andrews et al. 1997, 85).

Despite many commonalities with other provinces, universities in the west exhibited distinctive features. The missions of the provincial universities in Saskatchewan, Alberta, and British Columbia, informed by those of the American land grant universities, emphasized service to the people and communities of those provinces (Pocklington and Tupper 2002, 23). In Saskatchewan and Alberta, the provincial universities' governance structures reflected this conception as well. Like Manitoba, those provinces established convocations – bodies to be comprised of all graduates and faculty of the university, with functions including the right to elect some members of the governing body – at the outset, before the university had graduates, by including in the convocation graduates of any university in the British Empire resident in the province (Cameron 1991, 21). In addition to a board and a general faculties council (a body with academic responsibilities similar to those of an eastern Canadian senate), the University of Alberta (U of A) and the U of S both have a senate, composed in part of elected community representatives and designed to foster links with communities in their respective provinces. Those bodies perform functions such as approval of honorary degrees and act as "the university's window on the province and the province's window on the university," in the language of the University of Saskatchewan (University of Saskatchewan n.d.).

Alberta and British Columbia adopted collective or omnibus university acts. BC's 1963 Universities Act, which specified the powers, responsibilities, and internal governance arrangements of the province's three universities, was the first of its kind in the country (Cameron 1997, 113). Alberta passed an act in 1966 that applied to all universities. In 2004, the Alberta legislation was superseded by a Post-secondary Learning Act that encompassed universities, colleges, and other post-secondary institutions. The BC and Alberta acts distinguish between research universities and teaching or undergraduate universities, so there is more differentiation among universities there than in most other provinces (Howard and Edge 2014, 27).

At various times, the Alberta and BC acts provided for the existence of mandated post-secondary coordination structures. For example, a Universities Council was established in BC under the Universities Act of 1974 and abolished in the early 1980s (Dennison 1997, 44). As part of their efforts to develop university systems, BC and Alberta both established councils to promote transfer of credits between institutions (Skolnik 1997, 331).

Governments in western Canada tend to appoint a higher proportion of the members of university governing boards than their counterparts in the east, with the exception of Newfoundland and of Quebec (regarding government appointments to the boards of the UQ system). Based on a survey of Canadian university boards in 1994–95, Jones and Skolnik found that fewer than one quarter of Canadian university board members had been appointed by government (Jones and Skolnik 1997, 5). However, at the time, provincial governments appointed 53 percent of the members of the UBC board,[5] 47 percent of the University of Alberta board, 50 percent of the University of Saskatchewan board, and 52 percent of the University of Manitoba board.

Universities in BC, Alberta, and Manitoba have a different status relative to the government reporting entity (GRE) than most of their counterparts in the east. The GRE consists of those departments, agencies, boards, commissions, Crown corporations, and not-for-profit organizations whose finances are reported as part of a provincial government's financial statements. The fundamental principle is that "a government's] reporting entity comprises all organizations *controlled* by that government" (PSAB, n.d., 7). The Public Sector Accounting Board (PSAB) provides a definition of control and various indicators to assist governments in determining which organizations are within their control and are therefore to be included in their financial statements. Those indicators include factors such as whether government has the power to unilaterally appoint or remove a majority of the members of the organization's governing body and whether it has ongoing access to the assets of the organization, has the ability to direct the ongoing use of those assets, or has ongoing responsibility for losses (12–14). Historically, most Canadian universities have not been part of provincial governments' reporting entities, with a few exceptions (e.g., UQ institutions, two universities in Manitoba). BC universities were moved into the GRE in the wake of a recommendation from the province's Auditor General in 2003 that the "SUCH" (schools, universities, colleges, and health) sector be included, even though the universities opposed the change and the provincial government initially rejected the recommendation that universities be included. Alberta universities were included in the GRE in 2003 in response to changes in the *PSAB Handbook*.[6] Shortly afterwards, in order to maintain that province's universities' autonomy, the Saskatchewan government changed the acts of the University of Saskatchewan and the University of Regina so that the government would appoint a minority of board members (Saskatchewan 2005, 443–6) and so that universities would remain outside the government reporting entity.

The appointment by government of a majority of board members has implications for the continuity of institutional governance insofar as a change in government can bring about change within a board. For example, after the 2016 election in Manitoba, the new government revoked the appointments of seven members, including the chair, and made a total of eleven appointments to the twenty-three-member board of the University of Manitoba. This was reported in an article in the *Winnipeg Free Press* titled "PC replaces NDP [New Democratic Party] appointments on U of M board" (Martin 2017), as well as in the university's student newspaper ("Progressive Conservatives stock U of M board of governors" [Williams 2017]). According to a BC board chair interviewed for a 2009 thesis on university boards, the same practice had also been common in that province. The interviewee said that "the past practice – and all governments are bad for this, of firing boards wholesale when the government changes – it's never a good idea to run governance on that basis, but they all do it" (Trotter 2009, 84).

Provincial policies and priorities naturally vary to some extent with the political stripe of the government in power, but in provinces in which the government appoints a large proportion of board members, the effect can be magnified. The western provinces' university systems currently each comprise a provincial university, up to two other large, comprehensive universities, and a number of smaller primarily, undergraduate, specialized and/or denominational institutions.

## EVOLUTION OF HIGHER EDUCATION IN THE NORTH

Canada's North consists of Yukon, the Northwest Territories, and Nunavut, the latter having been carved out of the Northwest Territories in 1999 as the homeland of the Inuit people. They are vast territories with very sparse populations, high proportions of Indigenous and young people, and economies highly dependent on resource extraction and government activity. The peoples of the three territories have experienced massive changes in less than a century, and climate change, technology, and other forces are continuing to transform their societies and the environment in profound ways.

The history of non-Indigenous higher education is very recent. In the Northwest Territories (NWT), as of the mid-1990s, higher education consisted of two colleges, a federal delivery system moving toward more Indigenous control, and "a plethora of external university and college involvements, including distance delivery activities, articulation arrangements, and extensive national and international research" (Hilyer 1997, 301). In the mid-2010s, Aurora College provided university-level transfer, certificate, and diploma programs, as well as trades and adult education programs (Howard and Edge 2014, 34). Subsequently, the NWT government decided to transform Aurora College into a polytechnic university. A discussion paper released by the NWT Department of Education in 2020 called for it to have a bicameral structure and a twenty-member board, including at least five residents of the territory and three Indigenous members (Toth 2020).

By 2014, post-secondary education in Nunavut was being delivered primarily through Nunavut Artic College, which had transfer arrangements with numerous institutions across the west (Howard and Edge 2014, 34). Shortly afterwards, the Nunavut government hired KPMG to conduct a study of the feasibility of establishing a university. Phase One of the study identified five strategic options: the creation of an autonomous university eligible for Universities Canada membership, a joint venture, a satellite campus, an Arctic confederation, or a university college. The autonomous university option was found to entail challenges, including high costs (at a time of other pressing priorities), sustainability issues, and the possible duplication of the offerings of existing colleges and other institutions (KPMG 2016, 78). The Nunavut government identified two options for further investigation: the development of Nunavut Artic College into a university college, and a joint venture with a university (KPMG, 2016, 7).

In Yukon, a vocational training centre was first established in 1963. A group of people obtained letters patent for University Canada North in

1971, but the institution did not continue to operate (Senkpiel 1997, 288). Consultations during the late 1970s found little support for a university but great enthusiasm for a college (292). Yukon College was established under the College Act of 1988. In 2009, the Yukon government gave it degree-granting status (Howard and Edge 2014, 33). In 2019, Yukon's Legislative Assembly passed a bill to transform the college into Yukon University – the first university in the Canadian North. The new university's purposes as articulated in the legislation included these: to "honour and support ... reconciliation with Yukon First Nations [and] the jurisdiction of Yukon First Nations; ... [to] build[] capacity through education and research for and with Yukon First Nations; [and to] include, respect and honour Yukon First Nations' knowledge, worldviews, cultural and traditional practices and educational priorities in the university's educational programming, training, research, services, governance, administration, policies and facilities" (Yukon Legislative Council Office, 2019).

Canada lagged behind other circumpolar countries (Senkpiel 1997, 286), but it now has a truly northern university.

## UNIVERSITIES IN CANADA TODAY

The higher education systems of many countries, including Australia, China, France, Norway, the UK, and the US (Lang 2003; EUA 2019; Hanc 2019; Cai 2019), have witnessed waves of institutional amalgamation. Canada is not one of those countries; here, such mergers are rare (Eastman and Lang 2001). Over the past several centuries, Canadians have shown themselves to be enthusiastic about creating universities, prepared to sustain them, willing to see them federate or affiliate, and loath to see them subsumed or shut down.

The result is approximately one hundred universities in Canada today. The exact number is difficult to pin down, because the great majority exist by virtue of provincial legislation and there is no standard definition of what constitutes a university. The institutions are highly complex from a legal perspective, with most of them embodying not-for-profit corporate, collegial, charitable, and other dimensions (Shanahan 2019). In the absence of a national accrediting body, membership in Universities Canada tends to serve as a proxy for university status. In this regard, there were ninety-six institutional members of Universities Canada in 2020.[7] For its part, the CICIC identified 101 "recognized" universities in 2020, excluding theological schools (CICIC n.d.).

Though concentrated mainly in the southern part of the country, like Canada's population, universities are located across the continent, in small towns as well as the largest cities. Most of them are relatively small, serving fewer than 15,000 students. The smaller institutions include universities serving more remote regions, largely undergraduate colleges, specialized institutions (e.g., art schools), denominational institutions, and colleges associated with larger universities. In communities in remote or less prosperous regions, many small universities play an outsized economic role.

There are around fifteen "comprehensive" universities offering a wide range of undergraduate, graduate, and professional programs, typically with enrolments of between 10,000 and 40,000. There are an equivalent number of research-intensive universities with medical schools, the largest being the University of Toronto, which has more than 91,000 students (Universities Canada 2019a). Graduate education is concentrated at a couple of dozen universities, as reflected in the distribution of full-time graduate enrolment.

Above and beyond their other attributes, universities constitute an important economic sector. In 2018, universities, colleges, and other public post-secondary institutions generated around $46 billion, accounting for 2.5 percent of Canada's economy as measured by gross domestic product – more than the agriculture, fishing, forestry, and hunting industries combined (Usher 2018d, 26).

Though relatively homogeneous in institutional form – most institutions are engaged in both teaching and research and offer undergraduate, professional, and graduate programs (Jones and Noumi 2018) – Canada's universities vary greatly in program breadth and depth, as well as selectivity and prestige as measured by rankings. In 2019, ten Canadian universities were ranked among the top 250 in the world in the Times Higher Education World University Rankings, with five of those in the top 100. The 2018 Shanghai Academic Ranking of World Universities (ARWU) ranked nine Canadian universities in the top 200, and four of them (U of T, UBC, McGill, and McMaster) in the top 100. Unlike in many other countries, the highest-ranked Canadian universities are large ones.

There are indications of increasing hierarchy among Canadian universities, based largely on the intensity of research and graduate education. Fifteen major Canadian research universities, most of them with medical schools, formed an organization (the "U15") to represent themselves and their interests, separate from the national umbrella organization (Universities Canada). Partly in reaction to this, an Alliance of Canadian Comprehensive Universities emerged in 2011, attracting about forty members (Young and Kraglund-Gauthier 2015; ACCRU n.d.).

Research universities are expected to play crucial roles in national innovation systems. Largely because Canada's industrial sector is relatively weak, its universities account for a much higher proportion of national R&D activity than is the case in other OECD countries. In 2018, the higher education sector accounted for 42 percent of Canada's gross domestic expenditure on R&D; the equivalent figures were 25 percent in the UK, 12 percent in the US, and 17 percent for the OECD overall (OECD 2021). Universities potentially have an even more pivotal role in knowledge transfer and innovation in Canada than universities in other jurisdictions.

Bourdieu suggested that higher education tends to be characterized by tension between an élite subfield of restricted cultural production and a subfield of large-scale production for the mass market. This polarity is evident within numerous national systems, as well as at the global level, in the contrast between the "global super-league" of élite, largely Anglo-American universities at one pole, and institutions providing education on a commercial basis at the other (Marginson 2008). Evidence of such polarity in Canada is mixed. Universities in this country are relatively homogeneous, with a large "middle." Unlike in the United States, the quality of Canadian undergraduate programs has traditionally been perceived as quite comparable from institution to institution across the country, and students continue to enrol in universities close to where their parents live. Competition for undergraduate students thus takes a somewhat different form than in the United States, where students compete to enter high-status schools and there is a general belief that the quality of undergraduate education varies a great deal by institution (G.A. Jones 2018).

Some universities at the lower end of the hierarchy are heavily reliant on international students as a source of revenue; however, that is also true of many major research-intensive universities (Usher 2018a). There is also a large college sector, which varies in structure by province and competes with some universities for students and with the university sector as a whole for government support. The college sector is relatively well-funded: in 2016, Canada spent more per full-time equivalent (FTE) "short-cycle" (i.e., college) student than any other OECD country (Usher 2019f). In general, colleges are more heavily regulated than universities and are viewed more as instruments of public policy (Jones and Noumi 2018, 109).

Although universities are part of provincial "systems" and operate in a national context, they are also subject to global forces and mechanisms, which shape government policies and programs and thus the parameters within which universities function. International agreements – on trade, immigration, intellectual property, and other topics – affect matters ranging from who (i.e., which faculty and staff) the universities are able to recruit, to the competition they face, to the regulatory standards to which they are required to adhere. Global forces, of course, also shape the nature and extent of the opportunities available to the institutions and their members abroad.

The universities themselves, though subject to provincial legislation and oversight, are by no means "provincial." They are also players on the national and global stages: they recruit faculty and/or students nationally and internationally; they belong to national and international institutional networks; and they are attentive to their competition abroad and their places in rankings. Canadian universities, however, inhabit different global fields in the sense that some are anglophone, others part of la Francophonie.

Studies of governance tend to focus on institutions. Marginson and Rhoades's (2002) framework reminds us of the importance of the broader environment – of other agencies, associations, and networks at the global, national, and local levels. Government officials interviewed for the case study commented on the roles played by formal and informal international networks through which economic, science, and education policy ideas are disseminated. The networks of government officials to which they referred coexist with university networks, some of these general in membership (e.g., the Association of Commonwealth Universities, the Agence universitaire de la Francophonie), others more selective or special-purpose. There are also many international and national disciplinary and professional networks, which interact with university associations as well as directly with government bodies.

Bodies and mechanisms at the national level affecting universities include not only the federal government itself and its agencies, including research granting councils, but also bodies like the PSAB of the Canadian Institute for Chartered Accountants (which establishes generally accepted accounting principles for senior governments in Canada) and advocacy organizations representing universities, faculty and student associations, industry, labour, and other sectors. Many national advocacy bodies are replicated at the provincial level, where one finds not only governments but also research councils, advisory and other bodies with varying roles (e.g., Ontario's Higher Education Quality Council, Quebec's Conseil Supérieur de l'Éducation, the Maritime Provinces Higher Education Commission), professional bodies, and university, faculty, and student associations. As Harmsen and Tupper (2017) have pointed out, these provincial and national organizations constitute "an active policy community that lobbies governments, coordinates the sector and tries to educate public opinion" (23). Relatively little attention has been paid to these organizations.

In this context, the country's universities pursue their missions and compete for funding, students, professors, prestige, and rankings. At the same time, they and their members continue to collaborate through international, national, provincial, and other organizations, as well as on an *ad hoc* basis. Over the past century, they have taken on additional roles and responsibilities, including for the following:

- the advancement of knowledge;
- graduate education;
- education and research in new professional and applied fields;
- the education of women and, more recently, people of all genders;
- contributing to innovation and economic development;
- community service;
- equity and inclusion of members of groups that are underrepresented and have faced barriers to higher education;
- support of students' mental as well as physical health needs;
- Truth and Reconciliation with Indigenous Peoples; and
- sound environmental stewardship.

Each of these roles responds to deep expectations on the part of students, stakeholders, and society. How effectively are Canadian universities fulfilling these expectations? That is in part a function of their governance – the topic of the next chapter.

2

# Canadian University Governance Today

This chapter peels back the layers of governance of Canadian universities, starting with the overarching role of the state. It examines each of the major layers and invites you to reflect on its status and how well it is fulfilling its role in the larger governance system.

The chapter draws on literature, data, and commentary on both external and internal governance. It begins by inquiring into the nature of the state's role in a country like Canada, how that role is divided between the federal and provincial governments, and how those governments are perceived to be performing. Attention then turns to other external actors that control or influence aspects of university decision-making and activities. Related governance questions are briefly discussed. The second part of the chapter focuses on the university itself and on major bodies and actors involved in internal governance. By identifying and describing key participants in decision-making about and within universities in Canada, the chapter provides context for the case studies and comparative findings that follow.

## THE ROLE OF THE STATE AND ITS PERCEIVED PERFORMANCE

The state plays a primordial role in the governance of universities. Universities around the globe, both public and private, ultimately depend on the state for "their existence, their status and, directly or indirectly, for their funding" (Thorens 2006, 98). What is the role of the state in the governance of universities?

The nature of that role varies from one type of state to another. In a study of nine federal jurisdictions, Marginson and Carnoy (2018) identified three broad groupings: "comprehensive" states (e.g., Russia), postcolonial states (e.g., India), and "limited liberal" states. They characterized Canada as among the latter, along with Australia and the United States. In such states, "the sphere of government is separated from and variously opposed to the economic market, to civil society and to the sphere of the individual or family ... The state/university boundary is watched closely [and] university autonomy and academic freedom are core concerns" (7).

Although Canada falls within the Anglo-American mould, the state–university relationship in Quebec is distinctive. Notwithstanding the private origins of Quebec universities, by the 1980s they were subject to closer state supervision than those in other provinces, with the exception of Alberta (B. Clark 1983, 144). To this day, government plays a larger role in higher education in Quebec than in most other provinces or in Anglo-American states generally, as a result of Quebec's model of public management and of the central roles of the state and of higher education in nation-building (Toulouse 2007; Fisher and Rubenson 2014a, 337).

Does the state have a legitimate role to play in governing universities in countries like Canada? Many of those who work in universities are skeptical. We see the downside of government "intervention" and tend to think that the optimal role for the state is to provide funding. That perspective is myopic. As Duff and Berdahl pointed out more than fifty years ago – and as many people outside universities are acutely aware – a hypothetical, completely self-governing Canadian university would tend to act other than in the best interests of the public (1966, 14). Governments have a responsibility to ensure that the public interest is "heard and respected" by universities (14). It is appropriate for governments to exercise their authority "when universities are reluctant to undertake necessary reforms ... or are behaving in self-interested ways at the expense of students and public accountability" (Tupper 2013, 356).

Given the state's role in advancing the public interest, what are its responsibilities? Surprisingly little systematic attention has been given to this important question, but an answer can be gleaned from a variety of sources. The state's responsibilities include fostering aspirations, establishing high-level public policies, setting goals, and allocating resources, as well as holding accountable those who govern the university (Newman 1987, 2). In discharging these responsibilities, governments should avoid inappropriate intrusion of three kinds: bureaucratic (e.g., unnecessary or counterproductive regulations); political (i.e., the exercise of political power for self-interest); and ideological (i.e., efforts to impede university activities on ideological grounds) (Newman 1987).

The boundary between fulfillment of the state's role and intrusion is neither static nor clearly delineated. According to Fallis (2007), government could legitimately "determine whether to open a new medical school or engineering faculty; but most observers would argue that the social contract would be violated if government policy were to cut back, say, the English department and expand the biology department. Broad policy direction is fine, micromanagement is not" (117).

This notion of broad policy direction points to the state's role in coordinating a system of universities operating in pursuit of collective goals that a set of independent universities, acting on their own ambitions, would be unlikely to perceive, pursue, or achieve. To achieve a well-functioning system, government must pay attention to system structure. Having different types of institutions can result in more access, better quality, more responsiveness to students' needs, and lower costs (Clark et al. 2009). Unfortunately, institutions of higher education are prestige-seekers (Bowen 1980) and tend to emulate the research universities at the top of the hierarchy. "Left to their own devices, degree-granting institutions ... gravitate toward the same model of emphasizing research and having light teaching loads ... The only way to avoid ... [this] is through government action ... Institutions should be given autonomy with respect to how they carry out their missions ... but specifying the missions of the post-secondary institutions that it funds is a proper and responsible function of government" (Clark et al. 2009, 137).

Allowing universities a degree of autonomy within their mandates enhances their performance (Altbach and Salmi 2011; Newman 1987; Lacroix and Maheu 2015). Autonomy is part of the social contract between the university and liberal democratic society, as is academic freedom (Fallis 2007, 113). When it is absent or lacking, government intrusion can "trample upon academic values and micromanage institutions into mediocrity" (Duderstadt and Womack 2003, 151).

What is autonomy in practice? More than fifty years ago, Ashby identified these as its key ingredients: institutional freedom over the selection of students, recruitment of staff, setting of standards, awarding of degrees, design of curriculum, and allocation of funds, as well as freedom from non-academic interference in the academic governance of the institution (Ashby 1966, 296). In recent years, the European University Association has adopted indicators to measure and track university autonomy along four dimensions: organizational autonomy, financial autonomy, staffing autonomy, and academic autonomy (Estermann, Nokkala, and Steinel 2011).[1]

Autonomy is especially important for research-intensive universities (Altbach 2011). In order to perform at a high level, such universities need enough autonomy from the state to have strong institutional leadership, to generate funds from non-public sources, to provide salaries that attract and retain top academics, and to make decisions about academic programs, language of instruction, and foci of research (Salmi 2011, 331–2). Other factors in the success of research universities are a central role in the national research effort and exposure to markets (Lacroix and Maheu 2015).

In sum, the role of government vis-à-vis universities in a country like Canada includes the following:

- establishing goals, broad policy and system design;
- providing funding and/or opportunities to generate revenue;
- establishing mechanisms for monitoring performance relative to goals (i.e., accountability);
- according institutions sufficient autonomy to carry out their missions; and
- protecting and supporting academic freedom.

Note that in their interface with government, universities are more than just higher education and research institutions; they are also landlords, real estate developers, arts and cultural venues, health care and food service providers, day care operators, waste managers, animal care providers, operators of nuclear reactors, and so on. The complexity of universities' relationships with governments at all levels – and of their internal governance and administration – reflects the breadth and diversity of their activities. Major universities do almost everything and are regulated by the state in almost everything they do.[2]

Who fulfills the state's roles in Canada? Canada is a parliamentary democracy in which Liberal and Conservative governments have traditionally alternated at the federal level after one or more terms. At the provincial level, governments tend to alternate between centrist or centre-left parties and centre-right ones. Party identification has been relatively weak in Canada compared to the US and the UK, so large swings in votes and seats are not unusual.

Overall, how effectively is the state perceived to be fulfilling its role in Canada viv-à-vis higher education? The answer is complicated by federalism, varies by province, and appears to depend in part on one's political vantage point and one's perspective on how well the university sector itself is performing.

Much of the literature on the neoliberal drift in higher education policy is implicitly, if not explicitly, critical of governments in Canada and elsewhere for reducing funding for universities, fostering competition, and encouraging or requiring institutions to generate additional revenue from private sources. By 2016–17, the share of post-secondary institutions' income from non-government sources exceeded 50 percent in Canada (Usher 2019k, 9). As noted in the previous chapter, universities are increasingly dependent on revenue from fees – in particular, international student fees. The past decade has seen increases in enrolments in the great majority of provinces as well as in participation rates, including by racialized students and students with disabilities (16–17). In Ontario, university accessibility for students from below-average-income families increased between 1995 and 2015 (Ford, Hui, and Nguyen 2019, 77). Nevertheless, as governments' share of university income continues to fall in Canada, there are expressions of concern that reliance on fees and other non-governmental revenues may undermine the role of universities as public institutions, transforming them into institutions catering to the privileged – within Canada and from abroad – and causing Canadians at large to question the rationale for public support of universities.

Canadian universities' performance has received some attention from scholars, policy-makers, commentators, and others, but there is little consensus, in part because of a lack of commonly accepted definitions and measures of performance. Some argue that universities' outputs are too complex to be measured and that attempts to do so impose a corporate model on universities and distort their activities. Others counter that measurement is possible and legitimate but believe that existing performance measures are too simplistic to capture the diversity of universities' missions and contributions to society (Larouche and Savard 2019). Still others might be satisfied with fairly rudimentary indicators, but, this being Canada, nationally accepted definitions and measures of university performance are lacking, and there are major gaps in national data.

Against this background, what have observers concluded? Some identify serious failings. A 2014 report for the Canadian Council of Chief Executive Officers characterized the performance of Canada's post-secondary sector as poor, notwithstanding high total spending per tertiary student. It cited the fact that Canadian post-secondary graduates ranked low in numeracy, literacy, and problem-solving in the OECD's Program for the International Assessment of Adult Competencies. It pointed out that in scientific output and perceived university quality as measured by rankings, Canada lagged behind not only larger countries but also smaller ones like Switzerland. Paul Cappon, the report's author, attributed these deficiencies to the failure of federal and provincial governments to agree on a national strategy. He noted that Canada is characterized by an absence of national goals and "a hodgepodge of reporting – where it exists – using varied definitions, timetables and indicators across provinces ... [as a result of which] we know little about national performance or the comparative performance of individual provinces" (Cappon 2014, 30).

In the view of Coté and Allahar (2007), Canadian governments' emphasis on access has been misguided and resulted in large numbers of students who lack the interest, ability, and knowledge for university studies and who would be better served by other paths into the workforce. They suggest that lack of rigour in the school system and excessively broad access to university has resulted in serious grade inflation as well as faculty and student disengagement.

Other authors agree that the overall quality of undergraduate education in Canada is poor. Books including *No Place to Learn* (Pocklington and Tupper 2002) and *Academic Reform* (Clark, Trick and Van Loon 2011) argue that universities are neglecting undergraduate education in favour of research and other priorities. Universities are also criticized by some in business, government, and the media for preparing students inadequately for employment – a huge concern for students and parents in an era of diminishing "good" jobs.

Concerns about quality and employability are coupled with concerns about affordability. In the 1990s, tuition fees doubled or even tripled as government funding for universities was reduced (Lang 2019, 2). This led to student protests and widespread public concerns about affordability and student indebtedness. Although domestic tuition fees, adjusted for inflation, have been nearly flat for the past decade and the percentage of graduates carrying debt decreased from 45 to 40 percent between 2000 and 2018 (Lang 2019, 39), affordability remains a prominent issue.

Setting aside these concerns, other assessments of Canadian universities' performance have been more positive. Harmsen and Tupper (2017) disputed Cappon's characterization of the overall performance of the post-secondary education sector as mediocre, maintaining that "on the whole, Canadian PSE institutions perform well, both sustaining comparatively high rates of participation and ... attaining a satisfactory spectrum of results in international rankings" (26). They nevertheless agreed that the post-secondary sector is hampered by lack of coordination between the two levels of government (26).

Lacroix and Maheu (2015) concluded that "the Canadian university system has performed very well in terms of the number of world-class research universities it has spawned" (118). Lang (2020) concurs, pointing out that the performance of Canadian higher education is "well above average" compared to other jurisdictions and that "the quality of higher education is high" (1). In his view, the federal–provincial interface, while "appearing messy," divides mainly along lines between fiscal practice and program delivery. He suggests that "the system of higher education in Canada can be compared to a bumblebee: it shouldn't be able to fly, but it does, and well" (1). Higher education consultant and commentator Alex Usher (2019g) has argued that "depending on the measure of access one chooses, [Canada is] either above average or top of the pack ... On research, we punch at or above our weight ... [On the educational front, we] don't have an Ivy League, which means money is spread around widely [and] lots of students attend good schools." Usher attributed these successes to "happy accident [and the fact] we spend boatloads more money on higher education than do most countries," rather than to effective government or institutional performance. In his view, lack of coordination of federal and provincial policies, atrocious data, and "a fundamental national fear of accountability" mean that the performance of the university system is far from what it could and should be, given the amounts invested in it (2019g).

In sum, assessments of the performance of both Canadian universities and the Canadian state differ widely, but there is general agreement about this country's lack of a national strategy, lack of coordination between the two levels of government, lack of adequate data, and, hence, lack of transparency and accountability. Is federalism itself at the root of these problems? According to Cappon, no. He argues that other federal countries and the European Union (EU) itself have been far more effective than Canada in developing strategies, pursuing common goals, and measuring performance (Cappon 2014). In other words, these are problems of *Canadian* federalism, rather than of federalism itself.

Others view Canadian federalism in a more positive light. Paul (2014) noted that lack of coordination, while detrimental in some respects, "protects universities from the sort of national intervention in their mandate, organization and governance" seen in other countries, because such reforms would "require ... the collaboration of thirteen ministers of education and their respective provincial cabinets!" (Paul 2015, 4). While acknowledging problems associated with lack of coordination, Jones and Noumi (2018) suggested that a decentralized approach to higher education policy is fitting, given interprovincial differences in culture, language, and economic make-up: "The end result, after all, is a collection of different but high access provincial systems of higher education that provide a quality of education that is well-respected by other jurisdictions, and includes a number of internationally recognized research universities" (123).

What about autonomy? In recent decades, governments in this country have sought to align university activities and outputs more closely with public policy priorities; even so, Canadian universities continue to be regarded as highly autonomous by international standards (Capano 2015, 117; G. Jones 2018, 201; Jones and Noumi 2018, 109; Pennock et al. 2015; Jamet 2014; Lacroix and Maheu 2015; Anderson and Johnson 1998; Richardson and Fielden 1997). According to Jones and Noumi, "Canadian universities continue to have a relatively high level of autonomy, especially over decisions about academic programs, program standards, the admission of students, faculty and staff employment, internal financial decisions and institutional direction. Even quality assurance, now a major mechanism for steering universities in many jurisdictions, has been largely left in the hands of institutions or in the hands of leadership of the university sector" (121).

While generally high, university autonomy varies from province to province. Lacroix and Maheu (2015) observed that "systematic assaults on the autonomy of universities [are] regularly observe[d] in Quebec" (238). According to Clark and colleagues, the situation in Ontario is very different. In their view, successive Ontario governments have been overly deferential to universities, which have resisted system planning and policy (2009, 46). In Usher's estimation, provincial "governments' inclination to engage in detail grows as one goes further west across the country" (2018d, 4).

In sum, the role of the state in a country like Canada appears to be to nurture aspiration on the part of universities; to establish goals, policies, and system design; to provide funding and/or access to resources; and to monitor universities' performance and hold them accountable, while respecting their autonomy and their faculty members' academic freedom. Opinion is divided on how well governments in Canada are performing and on the performance of universities themselves. Many authors and commentators are implicitly or explicitly critical of the performance of governments and universities. Others rate the outcomes of Canadian federalism and of government and university activities highly. Some in both camps argue that the outcomes of universities' activities should be even better, given the resources invested in them.

## THE ROLES AND IMPACT OF OTHER EXTERNAL ACTORS IN GOVERNANCE

Other than federal and provincial governments, what external actors are involved in the governance of universities?

Municipal governments, which are creatures of the provinces, have authority over matters such as land use, roadways, parking, local transportation, water systems and, in some cases, policing. Several First Nations governments play roles in board appointments. For example, under the Yukon University Act, Yukon First Nations nominate some members of the university's board of governors. They are also consulted by the minister on the development of institutional performance and accountability measures (Yukon Legislative Council Office 2019). A commission of the Federation of Saskatchewan Indian Nations ratifies the appointment of members to the board of First Nations University of Canada (First Nations University of Canada Act, 10 June 2010, s. 30). The boards of Algoma University and Lakehead University include members elected or recommended by Indigenous student or other bodies (Foy 2021, 75; Algoma University 2020; Lakehead University 2019). Universities may engage in consultation with nearby First Nations on matters involving land. The Crown has the duty to consult First Nations on matters affecting their rights (Imai and Stacey 2014), but provincial governments may expect public sector and other entities to consult local First Nations on proposed dispositions of land. More broadly, universities across the country also engage with Indigenous communities in pursuit of reconciliation – the "ongoing process of establishing and maintaining respectful relationships" between Indigenous and non-Indigenous peoples in Canada (TRC 2015b, 6, 16). A 2017 Universities Canada survey found that 70 percent of universities had a partnership with Indigenous communities or organizations to foster dialogue and reconciliation (Universities Canada 2017).

Non-government actors also play roles in university governance. Churches, though much less powerful than in previous centuries, continue to participate in the governance of some institutions. For example, the board of St Francis Xavier University in Nova Scotia includes the bishop of the local diocese, two members appointed by the bishop, and six members elected by priests of the diocese (Nova Scotia 2014).

Standard-setting and regulatory bodies with responsibility for matters such as accounting, safety, and animal care govern activities in those areas. The impact of their decisions can be significant. For example, changes in the PSAB *Handbook* informed the transfer of universities in Alberta and BC into those province's government reporting entities, which reduced their financial autonomy.

Professional and accrediting bodies have a strong impact on universities and faculties offering programs in their fields by virtue of their authority to accredit programs and/or to determine the competencies required to practise. Accreditation is the process whereby an external body determines whether a university program is capable of producing graduates with professional competence to practise. In some cases, the external body's authority is based in legislation or regulation; in other cases, it is not (Harvey 2004). In Canada, universities are not subject to formal institutional accreditation, as is the case in many other countries. The Canadian tradition has been "accreditation by legislation" – that is, institutions authorized by government to grant degrees have been deemed legitimate (Marshall, ctd by Shanahan 2015b). Accreditation of professional programs is, however, widespread. The Association of Accrediting Agencies of Canada was founded in 1994 and had twenty-four full members as of 2021 (AAAC n.d.).

More than fifty years ago, the Parent Commission expressed concern that professional bodies in Quebec were too heavily involved in program development and even student selection (1964, vol. 2, 273). What is the state of the relationship between professional bodies and universities today? What is the balance between university autonomy and professional control? There is little Canadian literature on this. Harvey's (2004) study, which included some input from this country, reported that participating academics identified benefits associated with accreditation (the capacity to attract well-qualified students, benefits to graduates in obtaining employment, internal and external recognition) but also had concerns about the extent to which accrediting bodies prescribed program content and delivery and stifled innovation.

The courts also shape university decisions and activities (Edmondson 2020). Canadian courts were long loath to intervene in university matters, but over time "universities have become captured by developing case law and statutory frameworks" Shanahan 2019, 5). A recurring issue in court cases is whether Canada's Charter of Rights and Freedoms applies to universities. The Charter applies to "government." In 1986, the Supreme Court of Ontario ruled that the Charter did not apply to universities, primarily because they are autonomous (Darling et al. 1989, 565). In 1990 the Supreme Court of Canada determined that the fact that universities are created by legislation and receive public funds does not mean they are part of government or under government control. In 1997, however, the Court also held that the Charter applies to an entity that is "putting into place a government program or acting in a governmental capacity" (Rogers and Taylor 2018), which opened the door for arguments that the Charter applies because universities are implementing government programs (MacKinnon 2018). In recent years, courts in different provinces have reached different conclusions about whether, and in what ways, the Charter applies to public universities in Canada. According to Marin (2015), "the continued uncertainty over the constitutional status of universities [ ] reflects notions of academic freedom and institutional autonomy, which are not easily reconciled with governmental control" (30). If universities were deemed to be subject to the Charter, it would change how they operate, potentially compromise their autonomy, and expose them to costly litigation (Dea 2020a).

In short, the state has ultimate authority over universities, but other external actors also exercise authority over aspects of university decision-making. Their decisions constrain or shape university activities in potentially significant ways, but their roles have to date received little attention.

## OTHER EXTERNAL STAKEHOLDERS AND MARKETS

Governments and other actors exercise various kinds of authority over universities. There are also stakeholders who lack authority but engage with universities and may exercise influence. They include business, labour, foundations, donors, lenders, bond-rating agencies, community organizations, and policy, advocacy, and interest organizations. Some are based in Canada, others abroad (e.g., foreign research funding agencies, ranking businesses, and bond-rating agencies). Furthermore, to degrees that vary by province, universities have been exposed to the market – or, more accurately, to markets. Markets are of course not actors, but engagement with them also shapes university decision-making and activities. Figure 2.1 depicts participants and forces in the external governance of universities in Canada today.

Universities and their members look to a wide variety of non-state actors for favour, funds, opportunities, and partnerships. Engagement produces many benefits, but it may be deleterious for universities to adapt or conform to such actors' wishes or interests, be they lenders, donors, community, or advocacy organizations. Many stakeholders do not appreciate the balance that needs to be struck between partnership and service to others and institutional autonomy and academic freedom (Fallis 2007, 177). The governance question that arises in this context is: How well does the university's internal governance equip it for engagement with external stakeholders and markets? Does it enable and support positive engagement while minimizing risks? How well do universities' governance, leadership, and policies enable them to partner with others and to attract opportunities, support, and resources while avoiding or rebuffing consequences inconsistent with their missions? The answer no doubt varies from university to university, but it is an important issue for all – especially as universities look increasingly

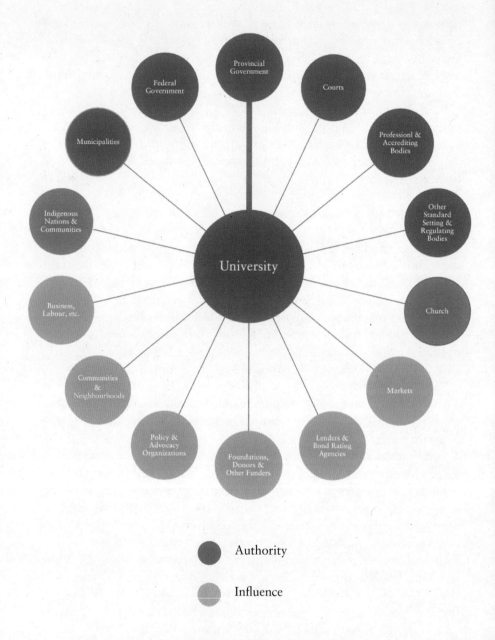

Figure 2.1 | Major participants and forces in external governance of universities

to private sources for revenue. The question is not what control these external entities possess, but what control or influence the university should or should not be prepared to cede to them in return for access to opportunities or resources. Autonomy is an increasingly important consideration, not only in relation to the state but also with respect to private interests and community stakeholders.

## THE STATE OF THE UNIVERSITY

What about the university as an actor? What are its organizational traits, and how has it evolved? Many different portraits of the university have been advanced over the years: a loosely coupled agglomeration of disciplines, a collegium, a political organization, a bureaucracy, an organized anarchy, a corporation, and a multitude of others. Which description is most apt varies by time and place and from university to university.

One compelling conception dates back to the 1970s and Mintzberg's early work on the structure of organizations. He described universities as embodying professional bureaucracy, an organizational configuration typically found in environments that are complex but stable (1979, 366). In such a setting, power rests largely with professionals who work relatively independently of one another but closely with clients (349). Outputs cannot be measured readily (349), and goals are not easily agreed upon, so institutional strategy tends to be an agglomeration of individual strategies and initiatives (364–5).

Since the work of a professional bureaucracy is too complex to be standardized or supervised by managers (357), middle management is minimal. Mintzberg cited the example of his own university, McGill University, and provided an organizational chart to illustrate the dearth of technostructure. Professionals obtain collective control of administrative decisions that affect them "by ensuring that [the middle line of the organization] is staffed with 'their own'" (358).

Professional bureaucracies have many virtues, but also problems (Mintzberg 1979), notably:

- problems of coordination: "they are collections of individuals who join together to draw upon the common resources ... but otherwise want to be left alone" (373).
- problems of discretion: they "cannot easily deal with professionals who are either incompetent or unconscientious" (374).
- problems of innovation: they tend to be inflexible (375). "Power

for strategic change is diffuse. Everybody must agree on the change ... So change comes slowly and painfully" (376).

As seen in the previous chapter, the environments in which Canadian universities operate have changed greatly since the 1970s. Governments have sought greater control over universities' outputs, even as the public share of total university revenue has declined. Mintzberg posited that the greater the external control of an organization, the more formalized and centralized its structure would be, the more power would be concentrated at the top, and the more rules and regulations would be used for internal control (289). He cited Holdaway's 1975 findings with respect to higher education institutions in the US – that formalization and centralization were highest in agricultural colleges and technological institutes, which were controlled directly by governments, next highest in public colleges, which were controlled by public boards, and lowest in private colleges, which were controlled by independent boards (289).

Given the increase in external control over Canadian universities over the past half-century, one would predict a corresponding increase in hierarchy and formalization. That is indeed what happened. Heightened government expectations, strengthening ties, and new targets and accountability mechanisms "in practice forced universities to adopt more managerial, verticalized internal governance modes" (Capano 2015, 117). An immense amount of literature and commentary on universities and university governance in Canada concerns what is often referred to as corporatization, that is, the adoption by universities of features of corporations. Based on a review of thirty years of scholarly literature on university governance in Canada, Hurtubise (2019) declared corporatization the second most dominant theme. Corporatization is what Demers, Bernatchez, and Umbriaco (2019) – espousing a definition of governance quite different from ours – characterized as "gouvernance," that is, "l'ensemble des pratiques de régulation, de gouverne et de gestion qui ont pour effet, sinon pour but, de transformer les universités en entreprises" (all the regulatory, direction-setting, and management practices that have the effect, if not the goal, of transforming universities into enterprises) (7). Corporatization has many dimensions, including the following:

- Managerialism. Increased emphasis on professional management, formal planning, systematic performance evaluation, centralized resource allocation, and directive leadership. (Hardy 1996, 3).
- Commercialization and "academic capitalism" (Slaughter and

Leslie 1997). These phenomena encompass branding, marketing, net-revenue-producing academic programs, research contracts and consultancy, patenting and licensing, exclusive vendor contracts, and other forms of revenue generation, at the institutional, unit, and individual levels.
- Growth of administration. This can be measured in terms of the rate of increase in administrative and staff positions and non-academic expenditures relative to academic ones. In the decade before 2016, expenditures on administration increased only slightly as a percentage of total university spending (Usher 2018d, 29); however, levels of administration have increased over a longer time period.
- Private fundraising. Unlike for-profit corporations, universities are typically charities (Davis 2015). Relative to American universities, Canadian universities receive only a small proportion of their income from donations and gifts (Fallis 2007, 175). In 2016, charitable gifts made up about 4 percent of revenue, and endowment income comprised just over 1 percent (CAUBO 2017, ctd by Lang 2019, 26). Nevertheless, with cost increases outstripping public funding, private fundraising is a significant source of funds for a few universities and a key strategy for most.

These and other aspects of corporatization have generated widespread comment and concern. Critics of corporatization have suggested that: institutions seeking revenue and professors capitalizing on intellectual property are inconsistent with the "disinterest" expected of universities and erode public trust (Fallis 2007); managerialism is a misguided and ineffective approach to bringing about change in a university (Hardy 1996); and universities are compromising their autonomy and academic freedom in the quest for support from donors, corporations, and other sponsors (CAUT 2013). The university has been described as having become "une organisation, formellement autonome, mais assujettie à des exigences de rendement et d'utilité économique qui lui sont imposes de l'exterieur" (an organization, formally autonomous, but subject to performance and economic utility requirements imposed on it from outside) (Demers, Bernatchez, and Umbriaco 2019, 7). Many fear that corporatization is impoverishing universities and that in the process, their activities are being debased – "education becomes [ ] increase in human capital; research becomes [] the creation of intellectual property[]; the university becomes a provider of educational services, and students become clients or customers" (Fallis 2007, 292).

An additional concern about corporatization is its impact on internal dynamics. Mintzberg observed that governments, clients, and other stakeholders often grow frustrated with professional bureaucracies and try to exert greater control. These efforts tend to be dysfunctional, because the resulting internal changes reduce professionals' discretion, which demotivates them and spurs them to resist. This observation was prescient. As described in the previous chapter, another major late-twentieth-century trend in Canadian higher education was near universal faculty unionization. Higher education has become one of the most unionized sectors in Canada (Butovsky, Savage, and Webber 2015, ctd by Bégin-Caouette et al. 2021). As Webber and Butovsky have observed, "a high rate of unionization among full-time, permanent Canadian faculty members offers a legal structure of support for resistance against intrusions on academic autonomy" (2018, 166). While resulting in greater procedural fairness and equity, unionization also engendered more formalization and bureaucracy.

Universities, like many other organizations, are hybrids and draw upon multiple organizational models. Machine bureaucracy characterizes the administrative side of the university. Research-intensive universities exhibit features of "adhocracy" – that is, the configuration associated with creativity and innovation, in which experts work together in organic multidisciplinary teams, mutual adjustment is the principal form of coordination, ambiguity is high, efficiency is low, and politics and conflict are inevitable (Mintzberg 1979, 463). Many multiversities take on a divisionalized form, that is, a form in which a set of semi-autonomous divisions is linked by a central headquarters.

Handy (1989) predicted that corporations would become more like universities, while acknowledging that universities could benefit from becoming more like corporations (142). It appears that both developments have occurred. In the decades since Mintzberg's classic work, new forms of organization have emerged – including network organizations, heterarchies, and post-bureaucratic organizations – many of which exhibit some traditional features of universities, including loosely coupled structures, staff consisting of professionals and experts, and overlapping managerial and technical functions (Heydebrand 2002, 188; Schoellhammer 2020).

Some authors depict the corporatization of universities as essentially evil; some, as inimical to the academic mission or simply misguided. Others see the capacity to generate revenue from non-government sources as both a sign of and a contributor to institutional dynamism, quality and autonomy, and have a more positive perspective on the costs and benefits of corporatization.

What are the costs and benefits of corporatization? How and to what extent does it contribute to or undermine stability of mission and responsiveness to society? To the extent that corporatization is necessary or inevitable – or, indeed, beneficial – are there ways of containing or minimizing the associated risks or damage? Concerns about corporatization are real. Whether driven by state regulation or by the need to generate revenue or by the desire to be of service to society, corporatization could, taken to extremes, transform universities into something else. The question is: what is the alternative? Given all that society invests in and expects of universities, lack of coordinated action is not an option. Norms and shared professional values and modes of conduct are insufficient. Alternatives to corporate management practices have been suggested (e.g., Hardy 1996) but have to date not supplanted such practices broadly. To what extent are universities capable of other modes of achieving collective goals?

That extent appears to vary between institutions. Corporatization is often portrayed as a phenomenon affecting all universities, but the typology developed by Larouche and her colleagues reminds us that every university has its own distinctive mission and characteristics. Their typology encompasses seven different conceptions of the university – academic; public service; entrepreneurial; market-driven; politically engaged; quality of life (*milieu de vie*); and learning organization – reflected across seven dimensions – values and principles; governance system; strategies; research; teaching; modes of evaluation; performance criteria. Based on an analysis of the mission statements and strategic plans of seventeen Quebec universities as of 2014, Larouche and Savard (2019) found that the predominant conceptions were academic, quality of life, and public service. The entrepreneurial conception was dominant at two of the institutions, the market-driven at none (96–7). Although the higher education landscape in Quebec is unique, these findings call into question depictions of the university sector in Canada as uniformly corporatized. They suggest that, in fact, some universities are more corporatized than others and that other models of the university continue to hold ground.

## THE STATE OF UNIVERSITY BOARDS

Overseeing the archetypical Canadian university – and in the eyes of some, abetting its corporatization – is the board of governors. At the interface between the university and society, boards are part of the internal governance structure, but they can also be seen as external (Austin and Jones 2016, 4). They have "ultimate responsibility for the university and [are] therefore the most important body in the legal sense" (Davis 2015, 68). Boards feature prominently in university governance in the Anglo-American world. The power of lay trustees has been especially notable in American universities. The founders of the first two colleges to be established in North America[3] apparently intended that they be governed by their members, like Oxford and Cambridge; however, early American colleges rapidly came under trustee control (Ashby 1966, 12). Boards of trustees gradually ceded more authority to presidents and teaching staff, nevertheless, in the early 1960s, "the power of lay trustees in American and Canadian universities [was] still strong" (13).

The board's role is to govern the university for the long term. In the case of public institutions, the public interest in the governance of the university is delegated to the board (Duff and Berdahl 1966, 12–14). It thus protects the university from direction or micromanagement by the state. The board is expected to interpret the needs of society to the university and to ensure that the university is accountable to society, while advocating for it and protecting its autonomy and academic freedom (Fallis 2007, 129). Boards have broad authority and responsibility for the following: universities' missions, strategies, and objectives; leadership; institutional and fiscal integrity; accountability; stakeholder engagement; and asset and risk management (AGB 2007, ctd by Lang 2016b). Specific board responsibilities typically include these: appointing, supervising, supporting, and evaluating the president; approving the university's strategic plan and overseeing its implementation; approving budgets, including fees; financial oversight; approving senior administrative and professorial appointments and employment arrangements; approving property transactions and overseeing property matters; overseeing risk management; and ensuring legal and regulatory compliance. Many boards also have disciplinary power over students and staff and responsibility for overseeing matters such as equity and safety. Board approval of senate recommendations for the creation of new faculties, schools, or programs is a common mechanism for confirming the availability of the required financial resources. The role of the board is to govern. Cameron (1991) underscored that "the board cannot manage the university. To do so would destroy academic self-government ... The true function of the board is not to manage the university, but to ensure that it is well-managed" (449).

How do university boards compare with boards in other sectors? Hatton (1990) conducted interviews with individuals who had served on both for-profit and not-for-profit boards, including those of publicly supported Ontario universities. Interviewees described the autonomy and authority of university boards as much more limited than that of boards in other sectors, because of the role of government, the role of the senate, and the presence of "stakeholder" board members (i.e., members appointed by government or elected by internal stakeholders), and because universities tend to be large, bureaucratized, and heavily unionized (113–15).

In Jones and Skolnik's 1995 survey of Canadian board members at forty-five institutions (to which 49 percent of members surveyed responded), internal and external board members had similar perceptions of the role that governing boards should play. Both groups agreed that a board member's role is to make decisions that are in the best interest of the university as a whole. However, internal members tended to see part of their role as representing the interests of a specific constituency. Respondents agreed that boards should regularly review the university's performance in academic areas, act as a "watchdog" on behalf of the public interest, ask "tough questions" of senior university administrators, periodically review the performance of the president, periodically review its own performance, and lobby for change in government policy (Jones and Skolnik 1997).

How are Canadian university boards composed? Jones and Skolnik's 1995 survey found considerable variation in board size and composition by institution, but the average size was twenty-seven members. Lay members accounted for 50 percent of the board; faculty, 17 percent; students, 9 percent; and alumni, also 9 percent. Overall, fewer than one quarter of board members were appointed by government. Presidents were members of all the boards surveyed. In other words, around one third of the members were internal (faculty, students, president) and two thirds were external (board- or government-appointed) (Jones and Skolnik 1997). With respect to occupation, about 37 percent were from the education sector (including the internal members), 26 percent were from the business sector, 13 percent self-reported as "professionals" (e.g., lawyers, accountants), 11 percent were from "other sectors," including the not-for-profit and government sectors, and about 11 percent were retired (Jones and Skolnik 1997). A 2020 report on board diversity across five sectors in eight Canadian cities found that women held 43.1 percent, and racialized people 14.6 percent, of board positions at universities and colleges in those cities[4] (Diversity Institute 2020).

The great majority of board members serve without remuneration: only two institutions surveyed by Jones and Skolnik reported that they provided honoraria to board members. One paid only students. Board members were asked how much time they spent preparing for and attending board and committee meetings: the mean number of hours was 10.3 per month (Jones and Skolnik 1997). Hatton's interviewees said that they volunteered because they perceived universities as uniquely important for the country's future and enjoyed the opportunity to interact with diverse, intelligent people. In interviews with BC university board chairs and members, Trotter (2009) found that they were motivated by public service and the desire to "give back."

Although the great majority of boards in Canada are composed largely of external members, a number of Quebec universities have boards with internal majorities. Governance reform bills introduced by the Quebec government in 2008 and 2009 in the wake of the Îlot Voyageur project at UQAM would have ended that practice. The fate of that capital project led the provincial government to question the effectiveness with which university boards were fulfilling their duties. In 2008, the government proposed a bill according to which two thirds of university board members would be independent and the chair would be accountable to the minister. In response to widespread opposition, the government replaced the proposed legislation with Bill 38, which required 60 percent of board members (instead of 66 percent) to be independent. However, it died on the order paper, so neither bill became law.

The 2013 working group on a legal framework for Quebec universities received forceful and conflicting arguments about how boards should be composed. Co-chairs Bissonnette and Porter wrote:

> Le débat s'était souvent cristallisé autour de stéréotypes. Pour les uns, les "externes" garantissaient un regard indépendant sur la conduite des affaires de l'université, tandis que les "internes" frôlaient constamment le conflit d'intérêts. Pour les autres, à l'inverse, les "externes" étaient au mieux ignorants des particularités de l'université et au pire affiliés aux intérêts des milieux d'affaires, tandis que les "internes" avaient mieux à coeur, par définition, les intérêts et l'avenir d'une institution qu'ils habitent. (Bissonnette and Porter 2013, 29).
>
> [The debate had often crystallized around stereotypes. In the view of some, the "externals" ensured an independent perspective on the conduct of the university's affairs, whereas the "internals" were constantly enmeshed in conflicts of interest. In the view of others, conversely, "externals" were at best ignorant of university's particularities and, at worst, affiliated with the interests of the business community, whereas "internals," by definition, took to heart the interests and future of their institution.]

The working group concluded that neither model should be imposed. Diversity of composition – and disagreement – continue to exist today in Quebec.

North American university boards felt the repercussions of the corporate governance scandals of the early 2000s and the 2009 financial crisis. These events gave rise to new expectations and standards for the operations of corporate boards, including greater independence from management. This led to more focus on governance in many other sectors, including universities (Bradshaw and Fredette 2009, 123). University board members with corporate board experience – along with governments, other external stakeholders, and the public at large – expected university boards to follow "best practices." Public outrage at the damage caused by corporate failures forcefully reminded boards and board members of their oversight responsibilities, of potential liabilities, and of the rigour called for in decision-making. The workload of board members increased, along with the attention and resources devoted to governance. Whereas board members surveyed in 1995 reported devoting a mean of 10.3 hours per month to their work (Jones and Skolnik 1997), several BC board chairs and members interviewed by Trotter in 2009 indicated that board members typically devoted six to ten hours per week[5] to their responsibilities, and board chairs, fifteen to twenty hours per week (2009, 75–6). Boards placed additional emphasis on member orientation and training. Governance support functions were professionalized, and university secretaries were hired to lead and manage board (and, in many cases, senate) support functions. In the past, Canadian university boards may have been "appurtenances of the university president's office" (Bruneau 2012, 53), but recent years have seen indications of greater board independence or activism.

How well are Canadian university boards perceived to be performing? Many people are critical or concerned. MacKinnon (2018) concluded that boards are struggling with the weight of their responsibilities – challenged by increased size, complexity, and regulation, and "tested by fractiousness, and by uncertainty among their members about whose interests they serve" (119). Some individual boards have faced extensive scrutiny and criticism for decisions about matters such as presidential appointments, executive compensation, property transactions, tuition fees, and board practices. Among the headlines: "Scandale financier de l'îlot Voyageur – L'UQAM s'endette" (*Le Devoir*, 7 June 2008); "Concordia University orders audit amid spending scandal" (*Toronto Sun*, 13 March 2012); "How UBC lost a president a year after they hired him" (*Globe and Mail*, 26 August 2015); "Western University looks into president's pay" (Canadian Press, 28 September 2015); and "Indigenous board member accuses Dalhousie University of 'entrenched' racism" (18 October 2017). Calls for more openness and transparency have been widespread (MacDonald 2018). That said, high-profile real or alleged governance failures at a few institutions do not necessarily mean that board governance at large is deficient. In a decentralized system, the quality of governance can be expected to vary from institution to institution. As Paul (2015) observed, "one must be careful in generalizing about university boards in Canada" (185).

One perspective on board performance is provided by board members themselves. Respondents to Jones and Skolnik's 1995 survey wanted to improve several aspects of their roles. Internal members tended to be somewhat more critical of board performance than external ones. That said, overall, board members "generally thought that the boards had relatively clear roles, they were fulfilling those roles, and they were reasonably pleased with the way the board was functioning" (Jones 2013b, 8).

A more recent study also found that board members perceived university boards to be functioning effectively. Chan and Richardson (2012) reported on a survey to which 133 board members at twenty-eight Canadian universities responded (representing 8 percent of board members at the sixty-three English-language universities surveyed). While identifying some areas for improvement, the authors reported that board members "seem to have a good understanding of their roles and responsibilities" and that "boards are involved in setting strategic directions, goals, and objectives ... making operating and capital resource allocation decisions ... monitoring the performance of the university and the president, and are involved in recruiting, succession planning, and determining the president's compensation package" (32). Respondents to their survey reported that the board committee structure and the support provided to board members allowed them to discharge their responsibilities properly.

Notwithstanding their members' perceptions of their effectiveness, boards have come under criticism from internal constituencies, as well as from others with a different conception of how boards should be composed and/or operate. In the preface to a recent book, the president of the Fédération québécoise des professeures et professeurs d'université (FQPPU) argued that, coupled with increased accountability requirements, "des conseils d'administration composés majoritairement de membres "indépendants"... dénaturent l'institution universitaire" (university boards composed mainly of "independent" members ...

distort the academic institution) (Lafortune 2019, vii). In this view, such boards import corporate practices into universities that should be governed and operate in a collegial manner. According to the CAUT, contemporary board structures and codes of conduct limit effective faculty, staff, and student representation (CAUT 2018, 1). Its position is that

> for decades, shared governance has been at the heart of how universities run ... But shared governance is under attack. University and college boards are increasingly controlled by corporate appointees with little understanding of important academic matters. Decision-making powers are concentrated in the hands of a few – who act behind closed doors – while the voices of academic staff and other key stakeholders are being weakened or silenced. (CAUT n.d.)

Of particular concern for CAUT are board policies that require board members to maintain confidentiality and to "speak with one voice" once a decision has been made. The organization thus calls for "reclaiming collegial governance" (CAUT 2018, 1).

The CAUT, the FQPPU, and some student groups regard boards as ill-equipped to govern because they are dominated by corporate and other external perspectives, but others see boards as excessively aligned with internal stakeholders and/or as having conceded too much authority to be able to govern universities effectively in the public interest (Cameron 2002; H. Clark 2003). Various government reports over the years have questioned "whether the movement toward decentralized, participatory governance structures went too far" (Jones 1996, 367), particularly when coupled with high levels of unionization. The increase in government regulation of universities in recent decades may be a sign that governments are losing confidence in boards' capacity to represent the public interest. Those who share that concern contend that more board authority and autonomy from internal stakeholders would strengthen governance.

## THE STATE OF ACADEMIC GOVERNANCE

Academic governance refers to "the internal governing mechanisms and bodies that shape the borders of authority and responsibility for academic activities within a university" (Austin and Jones 2016, 124). Traditionally, "the professoriate is granted authority and responsibility [for these matters] as individual professionals and through internal academic bodies" (124). The presumption that expertise is the basis for academic decision-making means that faculty "sovereignty" and professional authority are paramount (138). Collegial decision-making thus involves "conferring, collaborating and gaining consensus" (125).

Growth in centres and institutes, and inter-institutional partnerships and linkages, notwithstanding, departments and faculties remain the building blocks of academic organization in Canada (Boyko and Jones 2010). "Within their own departments, professors [ ] control the requirements for the degree, what is taught in the courses, the assessment of students, who is hired, and who is given tenure. They prepare academic plans and determine the evolution of their discipline. Collegial self-governance is realized through department meetings and a committee structure – hiring committees, tenure committees, curriculum committees, and so on" (Fallis 2007, 130).

Departments are organized principally along disciplinary or sub-professional lines. They are local outposts of international academic and professional fields, which – though global in scope and often massive in membership – tend to function as relatively self-contained communities in which an individual's position depends largely on the esteem in which they are held by peers (Bourdieu 1993). "In the omnipresent academic evaluation system known as peer review, peers pass judgment ... on the quality of work of other community members. Thus they determine the allocation of scarce resources, whether these be prestige and honors, fellowships and grants to support research, tenured positions that provide identifiable status and job security, or access to high-status publications" (Lamont 2009, 2).

Disciplines and professions differ enormously in their objects and concerns; their intellectual traditions and cultures; their epistemologies, theories, and practices; and their approaches to producing and evaluating knowledge (Lamont 2009). Pocklington and Tupper (2002) wrote that "in this environment, university departments have little contact with each other. The Department of Economics, for example, has few links with the Departments of Political Science and Sociology, let alone the Departments of Accounting, Physics or Corporate Law ... Each discipline is in charge of its own affairs. In Canadian universities, botanists hire other botanists, English professors evaluate English professors, and biochemists assess the research of other biochemists" (33). For approval, departmental recommendations typically go to the faculty level, where committees often consider matters before faculty-level approval. The composition and role of faculty councils are usually – but not always – set out in legislation or university by-laws (Pennock et al. 2015, 508).

Academic decision-making thus tends to be bottom-up, even though, as MacKinnon (2014) points out, it is subject to university policy and to the statutory and other authority given to presidents, deans, and others. Collegiality, coupled with the need for scrutiny at multiple levels, means that decision-making takes time. According to Clark and colleagues (2009), "university governance is marked by a level of decentralization that is matched in few other organizations. At every level, consensus is the holy grail of decision-making and its pursuit can easily lead to the delay or derailing of substantial proposals for change" (73).

At the pinnacle of the academic governance structure at most universities is the senate or an equivalent body (e.g., general faculties council, *commission des études*). Senates are responsible for matters such as admissions policy, academic programs and curriculum, academic quality, scholarships and awards, student appeals, and granting of degrees. Most senates also play roles in strategic planning, research policy, and the budget process (Pennock et al. 2015). Senate decisions with financial implications are typically subject to board approval. A 2011 survey of Canadian senates, which reaped data from about thirty-eight senates, found that their average size was seventy-seven – with large, older research universities tending to have larger senates than newer institutions. Overall, faculty made up 48 percent of senate membership; senior academic administrators (who typically also hold faculty appointments), 23 percent; and students, 16 percent. Eighty-four percent of the senates were chaired by presidents (Pennock et al. 2015, 507); others had elected chairs.

As described in the previous chapter, many Canadian university senates were reformed in the late 1960s and 1970s to reduce their size, reinforce their academic focus, and increase their effectiveness. University governance in this country as well as abroad underwent significant democratization so that students and junior professors obtained voices in matters previously decided by senior academics (Demers 2019, 41) and/or by the administration. A relatively benign external environment and funding for growth made possible substantial autonomy for universities and centrality for senates in their governance. Over time, however, power shifted to boards and administration (Hurtubise 2019). Faculty unionization also weakened senates insofar as matters formerly within senates' purview were moved to the collective bargaining arena (Penner 1994; Jones, Shanahan, and Goyan 2001; Pennock et al. 2015). In Cameron's (2002) view, faculty unionization upset the "harmony in the design of bicameral government:

> At the heart of [the Canadian model of bicameral university government] was the juxtaposition of a faculty senate, to represent faculty interests in shaping academic policy, a lay board of governors, to safeguard the public interest especially but not only in financial matters, and a strong president to provide leadership and direction to the institution. There was a harmony in the design of bicameral government...Faculty unionization destroys this harmony. It substitutes an adversarial relationship between faculty, on the one hand, and board and president (or "the administration") on the other. (151)

What do we know about the state of the senate in Canada today? In response to Pennock and colleagues' 2012 survey of Canadian senators (to which 23 percent responded), 51 percent of respondents agreed with the statement "our senate is an effective decision-making body" – up 7 percent from a similar 2000 survey (Pennock et al. 2016, 79). Administrators, graduate students, and external members were more likely to agree with that statement than faculty, undergraduate students, and support staff (12).

Pennock and colleagues found significant gaps between what respondents said a senate should do and what they said the senate of their institution was doing. For example, whereas 93 percent of respondents agreed that a senate should regularly review the performance of the university in academic areas, only 48 percent agreed it did. Whereas 91 percent agreed a senate should play a role in determining the future direction of the university, only 49 percent agreed it did. The survey revealed ambivalence on the part of senate members about the role of faculty unions. Forty-one percent of respondents disagreed with the statement that "the role of our senate has been strengthened by the work of the faculty association/union"; 30 percent were neutral; 28 percent agreed (83).

The authors identified a number of other themes in the responses, including concerns about the size of senates; lack of faculty engagement; ambiguous relationships between senates and faculties; and role confusion, power imbalance, or other tensions between the senate and the board or between the senate and the administration. They concluded that senates continue to have an important role but that there is room and need for improvement (86).

Based on eight interviews with current or recent former senators at a BC university in May 2012, Lougheed and Pidgeon (2016) concluded that the senate in question was fulfilling its obligations under the University Act, but that whether it was fulfilling its larger role as institutional steward of academic governance was "at best[,] up for debate" (101). Numerous other authors have expressed similar concern about senates' power and effectiveness and the level of faculty engagement (Hurtubise 2019), as well as about the deleterious impact on academic governance at some institutions of involvement by faculty unions (Foy 2021, MacKinnon 2014). Ambivalence about the roles of senates was also expressed by the eleven current or former university presidents interviewed by Paul for his book *Leadership under Fire*, first published in 2011. According to Paul, the presidents agreed on many issues, but "the role and effectiveness of the senate was not one of them. Some see the senate as an important instrument of governance and academic leadership in the university, while others are more skeptical of its power and impact" (2015, 195).

A 2009 CAUT task force concluded that "university senates have not proven to be reliable and consistent vehicles through which academic staff can ensure their proper role in the academic governance of their institutions" (CAUT 2009, 1). It encouraged faculty unions and associations to turn to collective bargaining to secure participation in academic decision-making as part of their terms of employment (1). Although the Supreme Court ruled in a case related to teaching evaluations at UBC that a board cannot intrude into the jurisdiction of a senate, the CAUT's position is that both "the Board and Senate should operate within the context of procedures and rules set out in legislation constituting the institution and in collective agreements negotiated between the institution and its academic staff association" (CAUT 2019).

Some object to blanket characterization of senates as ineffective. In a 2014 book on universities and public policy, MacKinnon (2014) observed that their effectiveness varies from university to university – some senates are better, others worse (107). Bradshaw, a former senate chair at York University, acknowledged the shortcomings of senates but expressed concern about typical criticisms of them because "we may lose a forum in which we can exercise governance and a challenge of the leadership function of the university's administration." She wrote that "despite its inefficiencies and problems, [the senate provides] an important check and balance within the institution over time ... one that, with all the emerging changes in both the internal and external contexts of universities, is perhaps at risk of being lost or trivialized" (Bradshaw and Fredette 2009, 132).

## THE STATE OF THE PRESIDENCY

Mintzberg observed in the late 1970s that, compared to their counterparts in other organizations, managers in professional bureaucracies "certainly lack a good deal of power" (Mintzberg 1979, 361). They might be powerful relative to others within their organizations, but they "keep [their] power only as long as the professionals perceive [them] to be serving their interests effectively" (363). Senior administrators were expected "to protect the professionals' autonomy [and] to 'buffer' them from external pressures ... [while] woo[ing] ... outsiders to support the organization both morally and financially" (361–2).

To what extent has the role of a university president changed since the 1970s?

> The role of the university president has shifted from that of primarily an academic leader to a position combining academic leadership and the responsibilities of leading a large, complex, multi-stakeholder business enterprise ... Presidents now require professional management skills and experience in addition to those developed in their academic career. The president's job description now involves leading off-campus ventures, major business enterprises, responding to media requests and dealing with a wide variety of external partners and stakeholders. (Turpin, De Decker, and Boyd 2014, 585)

Presidents' roles have common elements but also vary to some extent by province and region, as well as with institutional scale and mission (Paul 2015, 16–21). Their authority and responsibilities are typically set out in legislation, institutional policy, and/or position descriptions. Nevertheless, the president's role tends to be ambiguous:

> The modern university president has spheres of activity, numbers of constituencies, and diffusion of authority that make for ambiguity in defining the role, determining its responsibilities, and measuring success ... [The role] is complicated by internal structures that at their best constitute a system of checks and balances, and at their worst can be obstructive to change, even paralytic. And yet a president today is expected, externally at least, to "get the university's act together" – to manage, not merely to broker different interests, contain others, check intrusions, and produce calm. (Mackinnon 2014, 132–3)

How are presidents appointed, compensated, supervised, and evaluated? In English Canada, presidents are typically appointed by boards. The search process is usually conducted by a committee, chaired by the board chair, and composed of representatives of institutional constituencies (e.g., board, senate, faculty, students, alumni, staff) (Turpin, De

Decker, and Boyd 2014). The committees typically advertise the position widely and seek and consider nominations and applications. Assessment of candidates generally occurs in stages: identification of a "long list" of candidates who meet the desired criteria, winnowing down to a "short list" of candidates who are interviewed; and, ultimately, formulation of a recommendation to the board of governors. The size of candidate pools appears to be shrinking (Paul 2015, 29; Usher, McLeod, and Green 2010), so search committees can't assume an abundance of well-qualified candidates or that their preferred candidate will accept an offer. Executive search firms are typically engaged to identify and screen candidates.

Searches can be "open" or "closed." In an open search, the names of short-listed candidates are made public and members of the university community can learn about them, sometimes meet them, and provide feedback to the search committee. In a closed search, only the search committee and those they invite to meet with short-listed candidates know the candidates' identities. The rationale for open processes is to obtain community input, feedback and buy-in. The primary rationale for closed searches is to broaden candidate pools: potential candidates serving in senior positions tend to be reluctant to participate in open searches at other institutions because their capacity to do their current jobs would be compromised if it were known they were interested in leaving (Usher, McLeod, and Green 2010, 23). Senior administrative interviewees for a 2010 report on senior hiring at Canadian universities suggested that searches for president and provost tend to be closed, whereas searches at other levels were becoming more open (23). The authors observed: "the trade-offs that universities must make to attract candidates and build candidate pools while still satisfying the demands of democratic university culture result in contradictions that possibly, or even probably, cannot be completely overcome" (40).

The practices of many francophone universities in Quebec are different. At some charter institutions, including Université Laval, the rector is elected by an electoral college or assembly (Paul 2015, 17). In the UQ system, rectors are appointed by the provincial government on the basis of board recommendations and election results (17). The open nature of the processes tends to mean that rectors' positions are filled by internal candidates (26).

Overall, however, most Canadian university presidents are appointed from outside their institutions. Paul's analysis of the most recent presidential searches prior to November 2010 at forty-seven "established" universities found that 90 percent of the appointees were external (Paul 2015, 30). Few came from outside the country, and according to

Paul, "few of those who have assumed a presidency without significant prior experience as academic administrators in Canada have fared very well" here, owing to differences in university leadership style between countries (10).

Changes in the nature of the president's role notwithstanding, Paul concluded that the backgrounds of Canadian university presidents are "not much different from what they were in 1960 ... Almost all come to the position with previous experience as a vice-president, dean or president in a Canadian university" (13). There have been recent exceptions involving the appointment of former politicians, public servants, and businesspeople, but according to Paul, "it [is] not clear [ ] that such appointments are a trend or even a new phenomenon" (34), given the incidence of the appointment of presidents from outside academia in the past.

A Universities Canada survey of its members conducted in 2019, to which eighty-eight responded, painted a slightly different picture. It found that more than three quarters of presidents had been recruited from outside their institutions.[6] Forty-three percent had been vice-presidents prior to becoming executive heads, 23 percent deans, and 17 percent presidents; another 10 percent had worked in government, non-governmental organizations, or the private sector (Universities Canada 2019c, 14).

In terms of disciplinary background, Paul found that the presidents of the forty-seven universities he surveyed were quite evenly distributed across the sciences (16), the humanities and social sciences (15), and professional schools (16) (2015, 35). In contrast, the Universities Canada survey found a higher relative proportion from the arts, and social sciences and humanities, relative to STEM and health fields (Universities Canada 2019c, 14).

With respect to gender, the number of women presidents of the forty-nine "*Maclean's* group" of universities remained one or two from 1950 until the late 1980s, rising to approximately 20 percent by the late 1990s (Turpin, De Decker, and Boyd 2014, 579). Paul (2015) found that "only nine of the more than 50 long-established Canadian universities were led by women" (28) and that "the number of women who lead top universities in Canada is lower than it was just a few years ago" (29). Thirty-two percent of the eighty-eight institutions that responded to the Universities Canada survey were led by women presidents (Universities Canada 2019c, 14).

The report on the Universities Canada survey did not include data on the proportions of presidents who were racialized or Indigenous persons, or persons with a disability, because the size of the data in the relevant cells was too small to display; however, they did find that 8.3 percent of presidents were LGBTQ2S+ (2019c, 15). With respect to senior leadership as a whole – defined as "deans to board members" – the report stated that:

- Racialized people are significantly underrepresented in senior leadership positions at Canadian universities and are not advancing through the leadership pipeline. While racialized people account for 22% of the general population, 40% of the student body, ... 31% of doctoral holders and 21% of full-time faculty, they comprised only 8% of senior leaders at Canadian universities in the sample.
- Similarly, people with disabilities account for 22% of the general population and 22% of faculty but only accounted for about 5% of senior leaders at Canadian universities ...
- Indigenous people constituted 3% of senior university leaders, which is lower than their representation in the general population (5%), but higher than the proportion of full-time faculty and doctorate holders, and similar to the proportion of the student body population. (Universities Canada 2019c, 10)

Presidents serve for fixed terms – typically five years (Turpin et al. 2014) – which may be renewable. Compensation has traditionally been determined by boards. In general, presidents are paid more than other public sector leaders, with the exception of some Crown corporation and hospital CEOs (Paul 2015, 43). More and more provincial governments are now regulating presidential compensation, effectively taking this authority away from boards.

One of a board's primary roles is to oversee, guide, and support the president in their work. In practice, the bulk of this responsibility falls to the board chair, with whom the president typically communicates on a regular basis between board meetings. Many boards have an annual process for evaluating the performance of the president. Should a president wish to be considered for reappointment for a second term, a review committee is typically struck to take stock of the university's leadership needs, assess the incumbent's performance in that light, and make a recommendation to the board. At francophone universities, an incumbent rector interested in reappointment is more likely to have to participate in a full competition (Paul 2015, 26). At some universities, it is possible for a president to serve a third term (after a second review), but this is quite rare.

How effective are current appointment, compensation, supervision, and evaluation practices in securing, supporting, and sustaining good leadership? This is difficult to assess, but one measure is whether those appointed as presidents complete their terms and are reappointed. Turpin, De Decker, and Boyd (2014) examined total length of service and average years of experience of presidents of Canadian universities from 1840 until 2011. Between 1840 and 1875, length of service averaged approximately twenty years; by the early 1880s it had stabilized at about fifteen years. During the 1960s, length of service declined further; during that time, the number of institutions increased, term limits were introduced, and the challenges of the job escalated. Between the 1970s and the mid-1990s, length of service levelled off at approximately ten years (579). The average number of years of presidential experience of incumbents declined in the 2000s, from 4.9 years in 2004 to 3.6 years by 2010.

Recent years have witnessed a striking increase in the number of "early departures" (i.e., presidents who resigned having served less than three years in office). There were three such departures from the forty-nine universities included in the *Maclean's* rankings between 1996 to 2000 (2 men; 1 woman); four departures between 2001 and 2005 (3 men, 1 woman); and twelve between 2006 and 2010 (9 men, 3 women). Turpin, De Decker, and Boyd (2014) noted that early departures occur for many reasons, but "anecdotal information suggests that the majority of the 2004–2010 departures were board terminations" (585). Paul's examination of data for forty-seven universities confirmed the increase in the number of failed presidencies (up to 27 percent in years prior to 2015) and the trend toward shorter presidencies (2015, vii–viii). With respect to what he described as the "precarious presidency," MacKinnon (2014) calculated that approximately twenty presidencies at ninety-seven Canadian universities had ended prematurely in the previous decade (132).

Why is this happening? Turpin and colleagues cited a number of possible reasons for the increase in premature departures, including the rapidly changing external environment, increased complexity of the role, difficulty attracting qualified candidates, features of the search process, board activism, and board turnover. Cafley (2015) interviewed six former presidents who had not completed their first term. They expressed significant concerns about the following: board governance (including board members' understanding of the board's role and of university governance); the adequacy of communication between the board, the board chair, and the president; the hiring process (e.g., lack of board engagement, lack of disclosure of key information); lack of trust within the executive team; lack of transitional support and mentorship; and a strongly dominant male culture (Cafley 2015, 160–1). According to MacKinnon (2014), "one of the principal reasons why the modern university presidency is precarious [is that] presidents increasingly are held to account for results over which they have little control" (135). As leaders of organizations rooted in professional bureaucracy, they have little actual hierarchical power – and encounter resistance to the degree they use it – yet they are expected to achieve results akin to those of a corporate CEO.

In March 2019, Daniel Woolf – then principal of Queen's University – commented on his Principal's Blog that

> there have been many examples of prematurely terminated presidencies, usually involving either failures in governance or breakdowns between Boards and the leaders they hire ... The bicameral nature of universities (which often have, in addition, certified faculty trade unions), place senior leadership at the nexus of often irreconcilable views of the university and its purpose and functions, and in the position of having to satisfy multiple stakeholders with often incompatible goals (and who sometimes do not even speak the same "language" in discussing the future of the institutions).

## THE STATE OF "ADMINISTRATION"

What do we know about other levels of administration? The next level of administration usually consists primarily of vice-presidents, the number of whom depends partly on the size and complexity of the institution. Vice-presidencies with responsibilities for academic matters are typically filled by academics with ongoing faculty appointments serving for fixed administrative terms (e.g., five years), which may be renewable. In contrast, vice-presidencies with responsibility for finance, administration, external relations, student services, and other non-academic matters are typically filled by non-academics serving "at the pleasure of the board," subject to periodic reviews. Foremost among the vice-presidents with academic responsibilities is the academic vice-president or provost, a position that typically involves leading and overseeing academic planning and program delivery, academic personnel processes, faculty collective bargaining, and financial management of the academic sector, and to whom deans of faculties usually report.

Deans' appointments are typically approved by the board of governors for terms of three to five years (Boyko and Jones 2010, 16), which may be renewable. In Quebec, decanal appointments may flow from election by an electoral college or be at the recommendation of a search committee. Whether the selection of a dean is considered an institutional prerogative or a faculty prerogative varies from university to university (Mackinnon 2014, 147). Deans are to their faculties what the president is to the university as a whole – they are leaders, responsible for academic, administrative, and financial matters (147). They are "important opinion leaders who can foster either institutional collegiality or parochial interests among faculty members" (Hardy 1996, 193). The leadership capacity and competence of deans are critical to the success of faculties and of the institution as a whole (MacKinnon 2014, 147). Deans are typically viewed as part of management (Jones 2019, 250). Like other academic administrators, they serve for fixed terms in their administrative roles (250).

Large faculties are usually composed of departments, which are headed by department chairs. A study of anglophone universities found that chairs are usually, but not always, faculty members who are members of the faculty union or association; they are regarded as "team leaders allied closely to faculty" (Boyko and Jones 2010, 8). A 2006–7 study of the policies of thirty Canadian universities found that chairs were typically tenured professors who served three- to five-year terms and were eligible for reappointment (11). The chair's role was that of "a senior officer, responsible for leading and administering the human resource and financial aspects of a department within a faculty, facilitating research and teaching, and representing the department and its interests within the institution" (14). Chairs were appointed either by direct faculty election (at seven of the thirty institutions), upon decision by a departmental committee elected by the faculty (at sixteen institutions), or upon the decision of a dean after consultation with the faculty (at three institutions) (11).

Chairs have a difficult job. They have important leadership and administrative responsibilities but are usually union members. They take up the chair's role for a few years – often reluctantly and with little advance training – and then "return to the ranks." They receive communications from both the administration and their union. Many are naturally reluctant to take decisions or steps that will alienate their colleagues.

The people who work within faculties, which typically report to an academic vice-president or provost, include not only academic administrators and faculty members but also professional and administrative staff. Other such staff work within units reporting to other types of vice-president. Some staff work in research centres and institutes or as grant-paid employees in professors' labs. Many research staff are very highly qualified, full-time employees who play vital roles in the preparation of grant applications, the conduct of research, the management of data, and other aspects of research. Other staff work in central administrative services, student services, information technology, physical plant, residence services, external relations, regulatory functions, and so on. Although everything outside the academic and research vice-presidents' portfolios (and some things within it) tends to be regarded by faculty as "administration," the functions involved are diverse and increasingly professionalized.

How much "administration" is needed? Is its size and nature sufficient to meet external demands and internal needs while supporting and giving primacy to the academic mission? In the view of many faculty and student groups, and of some governments, growth of administration is something between a cause for concern and completely out of control.

"The Financial Information of Universities and Colleges," prepared annually by Statistics Canada and the Canadian Association of University Business Officers, makes it possible to track expenditures for central administration. It divides university operating expenditures into six functional categories: instructional (i.e., spending by a unit reporting to an academic dean or faculty), administration, libraries, student services, ICT, and physical plant. As of 2017–18, administration (including external relations) made up around 13 percent of total university operating expenditures, while instruction accounted for 59 percent, student services and physical plant each for approximately 10 percent, ICT for 4 percent, and libraries for 4 percent (Usher 2019e). Over the previous five years, spending on student services had increased by 21 percent. ICT expenditures increased at the next highest rate. Those on administration and physical plant maintenance had increased by 10 to 11 percent – roughly the rate of overall spending growth – while instructional spending had increased by approximately 9 percent (Usher 2019e). Over the decade prior to 2016–17, administrative spending had increased very gradually as a percentage of total spending (35). Although administrative costs have not ballooned in recent years, growth of administration remains a subject of comment and concern.

## THE STATE OF THE PROFESSORIATE

In 2017–18, there were more than 46,000 full-time tenured and tenure-track professors at Canadian universities – a number that, while stable more recently, represented an increase of approximately 37 percent from a modern low point in 1997–98 (Usher 2019k, 26). Twenty-one percent of professors worked in social and behavioural sciences and approximately 14 percent in humanities. Business, architecture/engineering, and physical/life sciences each accounted for slightly more than 11 percent. Also, 74 percent of professors were between forty and sixty-five, and 10 percent were over sixty-five (Bégin-Caouette et al. 2021). A 2019 Statistics Canada survey of university professors, instructors, teachers, and researchers found that 51 percent were male, 48 percent were female, and 0.2 per cent were gender-diverse. Approximately 19.4 percent identified as a "visible minority," 2.0 percent were Indigenous, 6.7 percent had a self-reported disability, 90.6 percent were heterosexual, and 7.6 per cent were gay, lesbian, bisexual, or pansexual (Statistics Canada 2020b). The composition of tenured faculty was less diverse and more predominantly male (Statistics Canada 2020c). Although the number of women in academic positions has increased over time, the proportion of full professors who are women remains relatively low, and the proportion of faculty members who are women varies greatly by discipline (Bégin-Caouette et al. 2021).

Canadian universities have a more or less common system of tenure-stream academic ranks – typically assistant, associate, and full professor. Academic positions are widely advertised, often both nationally and internationally. Promotion and tenure are based on an assessment of whether the candidate has met the criteria established by the collective agreement or institutional policy (Jones 2019, 249). Practices vary from institution to institution, including with regard to the respective roles of faculty committees and academic administrators in these processes (248). Tenure is a permanent appointment without term, and provision for tenure is the norm at universities across Canada for regular faculty (Bégin-Caouette et al. 2021).

Salary levels vary across institutions, by region, and by institutional type (Jones 2019, 249). Using Statistics Canada data, Bégin-Caouette and colleagues (2021) found that full-time professors' salaries tend to be commensurate with those of other professional sectors in their respective provinces. Associate professors in Ontario received a median salary of $169,245 in 2017, relative to median household income of $74,287 in that province. Their counterparts in Nova Scotia earned around $116,633 per year in 2017, relative to median provincial household income of $53,900. Whereas in both Ontario and Nova Scotia, associate professors earned approximately 2.2 times the median household income, those in Quebec received a median salary of $117,321 – 1.96 times the median household income (Bégin-Caouette et al. 2021).

Canadian professors are typically responsible for both teaching and research, as well as service. In a 2017–18 survey of full-time professors, 73 percent of respondents indicated that they preferred to engage in both teaching and research, whereas 10 percent preferred to engage primarily in teaching and 17 percent preferred research (Karram Stephenson et al. 2020, 32).

How do professors feel about their jobs? In the 2017–18 survey, the statement "I am satisfied with my job" earned a score of 3.88 on a scale of one (strongly disagree) to five (strongly agree) (Banks 2019). Around 72 percent of faculty rated their satisfaction with the status and salary of their position as high or very high. Less than half of faculty (45%) rated their satisfaction with their workload and working conditions as high or very high. Around 45 percent agreed or strongly agreed with the statement that their job "was a source of personal strain." Fifty-four percent said that "this is a poor time for any young person to begin an academic career in my field," but only 13 percent agreed or strongly agreed that they would not become an academic if they were making the decision again (APIKS 2018).

More than 80 percent of Canadian academics belong to a union (Butovsky, Savage, and Webber 2015, ctd by Bégin-Caouette et al. 2021). Faculty unions' early focus on salaries, gender parity, and benefits has expanded to include advocating for academic freedom, deciding what constitutes academic work at a given institution, and outlining the process of faculty appointments, tenure, and promotion (Bégin-Caouette et al. 2021). Concern has been expressed by MacKinnon (2018), Foy (2021), and others about faculty unions' efforts to advance their members' interests through their members' participation in governing bodies. That said, Webber and Butovsky (2018) suggested – based on semi-structured interviews with ten individuals involved in executive or other roles with five Ontario faculty associations – that faculty unions tend to operate as "business unions – ones that are concerned with workplace issues" (174). Although the authors themselves advocated a broader role for faculty unions, they concluded that "faculty associations, for the most part, have shied away from that direction (as evidenced by associations' unwillingness to mount partisan campaigns for political candidates, reluctance to run slates or organize attempts to take over academic senates, and so forth)" (176). They attributed this reluctance to "professional discourse that casts political action as 'unprofessional'" (176). However, they found that administrative initiatives that threaten to reduce faculty autonomy lead faculty members to call on their unions to take broader action (176). Notwithstanding reluctance on the part of faculty members to depart from traditional professional roles, Canadian campuses have witnessed numerous faculty strikes over the years.

Although the number of tenured and tenure-stream professors in Canada has been stable in recent years, increases in enrolments, faculty salaries, and other costs, and professors' research commitments, have left a gap in teaching capacity that has led many universities to engage new categories of academic staff (Jones 2019, 257). Arrangements vary from institution to institution. One new category consists of teaching-stream faculty positions, frequently full-time, that offer substantial job security after a probationary period. Teaching expectations are higher and salaries lower than for regular faculty positions. A second category of appointments consists of part-time contract "sessional" appointments, usually on a per-course basis. Recent studies in Ontario found that sessional instructors in that province were almost all unionized but that there was considerable variation from institution to institution in both salaries and working conditions, as well as in the number of sessional instructors relative to other academic appointments. On some campuses, teaching assistants and post-doctoral fellows have unionized as well (258–9). A survey of sessional lecturers at twelve Ontario universities found they have serious concerns about their compensation and working conditions and "frequently feel marginalized and unsupported by administrators and academic colleagues" (258).

Reliable national data on the numbers of sessional instructors are not available. One analysis of publicly available data at a small number of Ontario universities suggested that growth in sessional lecturer appointments varied greatly by institution. It had far outpaced the growth in tenure-stream faculty at some institutions, but the opposite was true at others (258). With respect to trends in spending, the amount spent by Canadian universities on sessionals was relatively flat between 2012–13 and to 2016–17 (Usher 2018b). The proportion of total academic wage spending going to sessionals had fallen gradually since the mid-2000s to just under 25 percent (Usher 2018b).

Many professors who carry out grant- and contract-funded research hire contract-based research personnel to assist them. Based on an exploratory study, Université Laval's Union of Research Professionals estimated that there were around 20,000 non-student research associates at Canadian universities in 2016 (SPPRUL 2016, ctd by Karram Stephenson et al. 2020, 29).

Regular faculty members are generally entitled to participate in decision-making in their departments and to serve or elect colleagues to serve on faculty councils, senates and boards; other categories of instructional and research staff typically have much less opportunity to do so.

## NON-ACADEMIC STAFF

National data on the number of non-academic staff at Canadian universities are not available. Their roles, employment conditions, and experiences have received virtually no attention in the literature. Based on the "Financial Information of Universities and Colleges," Usher (2019k) compared aggregate salary expenditures on full-time academics to aggregate salary expenditures on non-academics and found that in the 1980s and 1990s, spending shifted toward non-academic staff; however, since the early 2000s, the balance of spending on academic and non-academic salaries has been stable (2019k, 28). As noted earlier, the work of university staff is very diverse and increasingly specialized and professionalized. Non-management staff are typically unionized.

Relative to professors and students, staff play a very limited role in university governance. Boards often include a non-academic staff member (Jones and Skolnik 1997), and a significant number of senates have a non-academic staff member as well (Pennock et al. 2015, 507). Overall, however, non-academic staff play a much smaller role in institutional governance than faculty members and students.

## THE STUDENT BODY

Who is coming to study at Canadian universities? Of the more than 18,000 respondents to a Canadian University Survey Consortium (CUSC) survey of students starting their first year in September 2018, 85 percent were Canadian citizens, 9 percent were international students, and 5 percent were permanent residents. Sixty-five percent identified themselves as women, 35 percent as men, and less than 1 percent as "other." Forty-four percent described themselves as a "visible minority"; 4 percent were Indigenous. Around 24 percent self-identified as having a disability – most often, a mental health issue (14 percent) (CUSC 2019).

Students are represented on boards, senates, faculty councils, advisory committees, and other bodies. They also form student unions, which by the 1960s were receiving mandatory student fees to fund member services and facilities, as well as advocacy within and outside universities (Bégin-Caouette and Jones 2014, 413). Umbrella student organizations exist at the provincial and national levels and have played important roles in discussions of tuition fees, student financial assistance, and other issues (414). In some institutions and provinces, graduate students have their own organizations. Currently, there are two major national organizations: the Canadian Federation of Students, representing members of eighty university and college unions, and the more recently established Canadian Alliance of Student Associations (CASA), representing around thirty student organizations across the country (414). Neither national organization has strong links with Quebec student organizations, which are unique in Canada in terms of their organization, activism, and history of obtaining gains through strikes related to fees and financial assistance (416).

Many graduate students (and some undergraduate students) who are employed as teaching or research assistants are unionized. Other categories of student employees (e.g., residence assistants) also belong to unions at some institutions. The relations between universities and many of their students are thus complex, in that the latter are both students and unionized employees.

In response to student pressure, the majority of Canadian universities adopted policies providing for faculty-wide teaching evaluations beginning in the late 1980s (Bruneau 2012). Many universities also conduct surveys of their students – including the National Survey of Student Engagement, an instrument developed in the United States – and/or participate in the CUSC (Paul 2015, 178).

In spite of these mechanisms for advocacy, representation, participation, and feedback, Pocklington and Tupper (2002) argued in *No Place to Learn* that "students are not a major force in Canadian universities, although they have some influence" (50). According to these authors, students' greatest power is "vot[ing] with their feet." "Departments of Classics ... were once big items; now they are tiny or merged with larger units. In contrast, Faculties of Business, which used to have weak standards, now have high entrance standards and attract far more students than they can admit" (50). Students' power to reshape academic units through their program choices notwithstanding, Pocklington and Tupper noted that students still "have to put up with huge, impersonal lectures, multiple-choice and fill-in-the-blanks examinations, and advanced undergraduate courses that have much more to do with the professors' research interests than the students' need or wants" (50).

Overall, how do students feel about their experience at Canadian universities? In 2017, 130,291 first- and senior-year undergraduate students at seventy-two Canadian universities participated in the National Survey of Student Engagement (NSSE), representing a response rate of 37 percent (Dwyer 2018). One of the questions was, "How would you evaluate your entire educational experience at this institution?" The percentage of senior-year students who described their experience as excellent ranged from 78

Table 2.1 | National Survey of Student Engagement results for Canadian universities 2017

| Institution | Excellent (%) | Good (%) | Institution | Excellent (%) | Good (%) |
| --- | --- | --- | --- | --- | --- |
| Quest | 78 | 20 | Brock | 29 | 54 |
| Trinity Western | 69 | 25 | Carleton | 29 | 51 |
| Ambrose | 62 | 35 | UNB (Fredericton) | 29 | 52 |
| Tyndale | 58 | 30 | Victoria | 29 | 52 |
| King's (Edmonton) | 54 | 39 | Winnipeg | 29 | 53 |
| Briercrest | 53 | 36 | UBC (Vancouver) | 28 | 54 |
| Saint Paul (Ottawa) | 53 | 42 | McGill | 28 | 52 |
| Mount Royal | 51 | 40 | Memorial | 28 | 54 |
| St Francis Xavier | 51 | 40 | ACAD | 27 | 57 |
| St Thomas | 51 | 41 | Concordia | 27 | 53 |
| Mount Allison | 48 | 43 | Dalhousie | 27 | 49 |
| Acadia | 47 | 41 | Laval | 27 | 57 |
| Guelph | 46 | 42 | Brandon | 26 | 47 |
| Sherbrooke | 46 | 46 | Sheridan | 26 | 57 |
| Queen's | 44 | 41 | Montréal | 25 | 56 |
| Trent | 44 | 46 | UPEI | 25 | 58 |
| Wilfrid Laurier | 44 | 43 | Saskatchewan | 25 | 58 |
| MacEwan | 43 | 46 | UOIT | 24 | 51 |
| NSSE 2016 & 2017 average* | 41 | 44 | Toronto | 24 | 49 |
| Brescia (Western) | 40 | 51 | Calgary | 21 | 54 |
| Cape Breton | 36 | 49 | Moncton | 21 | 51 |

Table 2.1 | National Survey of Student Engagement results for Canadian universities 2017 (continued)

| Institution | Excellent (%) | Good (%) | Institution | Excellent (%) | Good (%) |
| --- | --- | --- | --- | --- | --- |
| McMaster | 36 | 47 | Ryerson | 21 | 51 |
| Mount Saint Vincent | 35 | 44 | Laurentian | 20 | 52 |
| Thompson Rivers | 35 | 50 | Simon Fraser | 20 | 56 |
| Western | 34 | 48 | UQAM | 19 | 62 |
| Saint Mary's | 33 | 48 | York | 19 | 54 |
| UBC (Okanagan) | 32 | 51 | Windsor | 18 | 53 |
| Nipissing | 32 | 52 | Lakehead | 17 | 50 |
| Alberta | 31 | 51 | Ottawa | 17 | 57 |
| Lethbridge | 31 | 54 | Manitoba | 16 | 56 |
| Waterloo | 31 | 52 | OCAD U | 15 | 53 |

Senior-year students' responses to "How would you evaluate your entire educational experience at this institution?" In 2017, 130,291 students at 72 Canadian institutions took part in this American survey, for an average response rate of 37 percent.

Source: Dwyer, M. 2018. "National Survey of Student Engagement: Results for Canadian Universities." *Maclean's*, 21 December.

* The NSSE average is the average score for all Canadian and US universities and colleges that participated in the 2016 and 2017 surveys.

percent at Quest University to 15 percent at OCAD University (see table 2.1). Overall, 41 percent of senior-year students at Canadian and American universities who participated in the 2016 and 2017 surveys described their experience as "excellent" and 44 percent described it as "good" (Dwyer 2018). As is typical of NSSE results, students at smaller universities tended to describe their experience more positively than their counterparts at large, research-intensive universities (Clark et al. 2009, 125).

How are university students feeling generally? Some insight is provided by the National College Health Assessment, a survey conducted by the American College Health Association (ACHA) in 2016 in which 43,780 students at forty-one Canadian universities participated (representing a response rate of 19.2%) (ACHA 2016). Almost 60 percent of the respondents reported they had "felt things were hopeless" at some point within the previous twelve months. Forty-four percent reported they had "felt so depressed that it was difficult to function," and 64.5 percent had "felt overwhelming anxiety" at some point during the year. Thirteen percent had "seriously considered suicide" (ACHA 2016).

In response to the rising incidence of mental illness and to deficiencies in provincial health care systems, universities have injected more resources into mental health services. A 2017 *Toronto Star*/Ryerson survey of fifteen universities and colleges across Canada found that all but one had devoted additional funding to mental health over the previous five years and that the average increase was 35 percent (Cribb et al., 2017). Catherine Munn, lead psychiatrist at the Student Wellness Centre at McMaster University, identified reasons for which students seek help, from developmental challenges, to identity issues, to recent or prior trauma, to psychosis or other serious psychiatric illness:

> All of them, and others, line up for care on campus at health and counselling services, if it's available ... Often the students who need the services most are the least likely to seek and find the care they need. Bottlenecks are common, given decades of under-funding of mental health and addiction services for children, youth and emerging adults at the federal and provincial level. Thus, students keep flowing in the doors to campus services, but only rarely and slowly flow out to other services, even if they have severe and persistent mental illness. (Munn 2019)

Why are university students reporting such high levels of distress? Does their experience reflect that of young people at large? One explanation for the data is that stigma is lessening, so students are more willing to acknowledge their struggles. Young people with mental illness are being accommodated in the school system; they now have the opportunity to attend university and need and expect continuing support. Other potential factors cited range from massification to financial stress, to the impact of social media, to parenting and school practices that result in lack of youth resilience. Another possible factor is uncertainty. Today's university students are a hugely varied group – in age, level and field of study, academic preparation, socio-economic status, culture and race, and other attributes – but in an era of rapid technological change and associated labour market changes, heightened income inequality, climate change, species extinction, a global pandemic, and shifts in the world political order, one thing they share is an uncertain future. A survey of leading-edge Generation Z (18- to 24-year-old) and Millennial (25- to 40-year-old) Canadians conducted by Environics in 2020 concluded that "Canadian youth are cognizant of the serious challenges facing society, and likely less optimistic about the future than were youth in previous generations" (Environics 2021, 3).

## THE STATE OF THE UNIVERSITY COMMUNITY

Universities have never been easy to govern or lead. Increases in size and complexity, centripetal forces, and the pace of change have compounded the challenges. The multiversity is, in Kerr's words, "so many things to so many people that it must, of necessity, be partially at war with itself" (2001, 7). Small universities may be less fragmented than large ones, but several developments in recent decades have affected the fabric of universities of all sizes.

Advances in information and communication technology have altered university activities, from teaching and learning to administration, library services, research production and dissemination, and student life (Altbach, Reisberg, and Rumbley 2009, 124). Convenient as it is, the electronic availability of classes and course materials, library resources, and a host of administrative and other services has diminished the importance of universities as physical places where people meet (Fallis 2007). Technology has enabled universities to function remotely. Even before the current pandemic, people had much less need to come to campus. At many academic departments, few faculty members were typically "in," and this lessened the sense of community within departments, faculties, and universities as a whole. As Fallis observed, "in a sad irony, the atomization of faculty because of IT is greatest in the humanities ... [because s]cientists still come to campus for their labs" (220).

Online social media platforms have affected the nature of discourse and frayed the boundary between "inside" and "outside" the university. Such platforms can empower Indigenous, racialized, and other marginalized members of the academy (Moeke-Pickering 2020) but can also expose them to cyberbullying and harassment. In their current form, these platforms do not lend themselves to thoughtful listening and discussion; indeed, they tend to fuel reaction and division. News about conflicts or controversies or allegations moves rapidly onto the internet and into the mainstream media, potentially making the matters at stake more difficult for universities to resolve and generating controversy on and off campus.

Diversity of students, faculty, and staff contributes to diversity of views. According to Clark, Moran and colleagues, "as a consequence of ... increasing diversity [of academic staff], one can no longer assume widespread agreement with [previously prevalent] institutional norms, values and assumptions ... including ideas about what constitutes quality in academic work ... It may be increasingly difficult to gain consensus on institutional priorities and important academic decisions, and traditional governance processes may come under considerable strain" (2009, 18).

Finally, there is a "fierce clash between the modern and the postmodern within the multiversity" (Fallis 2007, 222). Whereas modern thought believes in reason and truth and progress, postmodern thought rejects the possibility of objective understanding of reality and sees not progress but power. Although, according to Fallis, some academics regard postmodernism as a fad or simply hope it will go away, "postmodernism is not a fad and it will not go away. Its controversies rage in many disciplines, in literature, political science, sociology, law, social work, and education, in some cases so intensely as to debilitate whole departments" (228). Above and beyond its impact on academic debate and community, postmodern thought challenges universities and their governance in a number of ways. It disputes the advancement of knowledge – the basis for the university's claim for society's support and resources. It sees the university as an institution – and those in positions of authority within the institution as forces of oppression (Fallis 2007). Perhaps most fundamentally, it is at odds with the presumption that valid knowledge exists and that expertise is the basis for academic decision-making.

Universities have long been loosely coupled constellations of disciplinary and professional departments. As a result of the forces just described, the ties that bind their members have diminished further, even as universities have become more regulated, corporatized, and unionized. Boards have now come under greater external and internal scrutiny. There are widespread doubts about the effectiveness of senates. The president's role has become more complex and precarious. Tenured and tenure-stream teacher-scholars have been supplemented by other types of instructional staff and are surrounded by more non-academic staff than in earlier times. Although professors appear to be satisfied with their jobs and are well-represented both in institutional governance and by their unions, many feel marginalized within their universities (Bruneau 2012; Mackinnon 2018, 3). Instructors, lacking professors' governance prerogatives and employment arrangements, feel even more so. Staff are increasingly professionalized and are critical to universities' operations, yet they are relatively unheard. Most students describe their educational experience as "good" or "excellent," yet more than four in ten young Canadians (44%) are pessimistic about the world's direction (Environics 2021, 16), and many report personal distress and need support.

Despite all the changes that have taken place since the 1970s, formal governing structures have changed very little. There are more universities, and most provinces have eliminated intermediary bodies. Alberta and British Columbia have made some changes in the design of their systems, but by and large, provincial structures remain much as they were in the late 1970s. Internal governance structures have also been very stable. Figure 2.2 depicts major participants in the internal governance of universities in Canada today. The model of bicameralism proposed by the Flavelle Commission, modified in the wake of Duff–Berdahl and Parent, continues to prevail. New constituencies and interests are not formally represented on internal governing bodies. Faculty and student members are typically elected or appointed from constituencies defined by traditional disciplinary and professional boundaries, without regard to factors like gender, race, and sexual orientation (Jones 2002). Part-time faculty, interdisciplinary educational and research initiatives, and non-academic staff are often not represented.

Participation in governance continues to be, by and large, voluntary. Service on boards by external members is still regarded as a form of unpaid public service and even a privilege. Yet demands on board members have escalated, particularly for those who serve as chairs of boards or board committees. Faculty and student engagement in academic governance is perceived to be suboptimal or, at best, uneven. The senate survey conducted by Pennock and colleagues found that the difficulty of getting faculty members and students to participate in collegial governance was a major issue (2016, 85). Student groups at some institutions have called for their members to be compensated for serving on university bodies and committees. Pennock and her co-authors recommended that deans, department heads, and other senior academics encourage junior faculty members to participate in academic governance and that universities recognize such service in tangible ways, like making it count for promotion, tenure, and merit pay. Their call for participation in governance to be regarded and recognized as part of a professor's duties was echoed at a conference on governance held by the Confederation of University Faculty

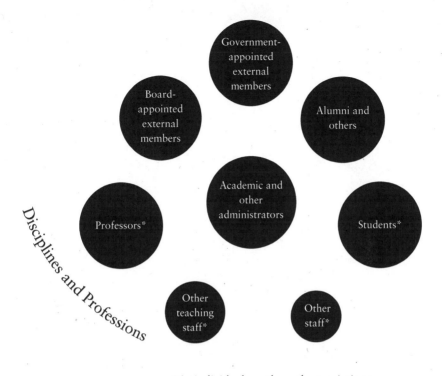

*As individuals or through associations

Figure 2.2 | Major participants in internal university governance

Associations of BC in 2012. In a paper introducing the proceedings, Kool wrote: "Our membership in the academy ... comes, as with citizenship, with rights and responsibilities. If academic freedom is our right, then academic governance is our responsibility" (Kool 2013, 86).

Whether professors are falling down in their governance-related responsibilities or whether it's natural – and perhaps desirable – for them to prioritize teaching and research over service, these phenomena likewise raise question of motivation, incentives, recognition, and, possibly, remuneration for participating in governance.

Is it time for a change? Are Canadian universities' governance structures fit for purpose in the twenty-first century? The changes this century will witness are unimaginable. Will the way Canadian universities are governed stand them, their students, and society in good stead? We will return to these questions at the end of the book.

PART TWO

# Findings from a Comparative Case Study of the Governance of Major Canadian Universities

# 3

## The Case Universities: Six Unique Histories

The study that led to this book encompassed six remarkable Canadian universities – one each in the Atlantic region, Ontario, the Prairies, and British Columbia and two in Quebec. Five of them – the University of British Columbia, the University of Alberta, the University of Toronto, the Université de Montréal, and Dalhousie University – are the largest institutions (in terms of student enrolment) in their respective provinces (Universities Canada 2019b) and have a broad range of doctoral and professional programs. These five institutions fall within *Maclean's* category of "medical/doctoral" universities and are part of the "U15" group. The Université du Québec à Montréal – the largest institution within the Université du Québec (UQ) network – falls within *Maclean's* "comprehensive" category and was also included, so as to capture both a charter university and a UQ member in Quebec.

This chapter introduces you to these six universities, their histories, and their status at the time of the interviews for this study, which were conducted between 2012 and 2014. First, a few words about methodology.

### CASE STUDY METHODOLOGY

The six case universities comprise a small, distinctive subset of Canadian universities. Given the multitude of variables that characterize universities across the country, focusing principally on provincial "medical/doctoral" universities was an efficient way to capture differences across provinces and regions – a major goal of the study. Such universities are also of particular interest because of the importance of autonomy for research universities (Altbach 2011; Altbach and Salmi 2011). In Canada, research universities account for a large proportion of total enrolment: around 50 percent of all full-time students and 45 percent of all students were enrolled at U15 member institutions in 2018–19 (Universities Canada 2019b).

Table 3.1 | Institutional-level interviewees by category

| | |
|---|---|
| Board (or equivalent) chair or member | 11 |
| Senate (or equivalent) chair or member | 5 |
| Governance or related professional | 6 |
| President or vice-president* | 18 |
| Dean* | 10 |
| Department chair* | 7 |
| Student or faculty association leader* | 11 |
| Total | 68 |

*An interviewee in this category may also be a voting member of the senate and/or board or equivalent body. For example, a student association leader who is also a board member is counted as a student association leader in this table and is not included in the board tally.

We conducted a qualitative multicase study (Stake 2006). Given the multilevel nature of university governance, our interest was in understanding the provincial context, university structures and arrangements, and the perceptions of those who were directly engaged in governance. Data for five provincial case studies (one comprising both Quebec universities) were obtained through a systematic analysis of government, institutional, and other documents, in addition to detailed, semi-structured interviews (Galletta 2013) with government officials, university officials and members (including board members, presidents and/or vice-presidents, deans, chairs, and student and faculty association leaders), and others within the sector in each province. In total, eighty-six interviews were conducted at the provincial and institutional levels (sixty-eight at the institutional and eighteen at the provincial level). Table 3.1 provides a breakdown of the institutional-level interviewees. Most interviews were conducted between 2012 and 2014. In 2015, a final set of six interviews was conducted with seven current and former federal government and other Ottawa officials in order to shed light on the impact of federal policy and programs on universities and university governance.

We then conducted a multiple case study analysis (Stake 2006) of the five provincial cases (and the institutional governance of the six universities) along numerous dimensions in order to identify the following:

commonalities and differences among case provinces and the selected case universities; changes over time as described by interviewees; implications for the governance of the universities and their relative autonomy; and insights into how the external and internal governance of the universities fostered the exercise of academic judgment and responsiveness to the needs and demands of external stakeholders. Given that the case institutions are not representative of Canadian universities at large, the findings cannot be generalized to all.

You will now be introduced to the six universities, beginning, as did the founding of universities in Canada, in the east.

## DALHOUSIE UNIVERSITY

Dalhousie is in Halifax, the capital of Nova Scotia, a small province on the Atlantic coast, accounting for less than 3 percent of Canada's population (Statistics Canada 2020a). Founded in the early 1800s, Dalhousie was initially a reaction to the denominational forces that had shaped higher education in the colony (Cameron 1991, 12). At the time, there were two institutions of higher learning in Nova Scotia – the Anglican King's College in Windsor, and Pictou Academy, effectively a Presbyterian institution. The lieutenant-governor of the colony, Lord Dalhousie, saw the need for a different type of educational institution in the province, modelled on the University of Edinburgh. He obtained Royal approval in 1818 for the founding of what he envisioned as "an institution at Halifax in which the advantages of a collegiate education will be found within the reach of all classes of society, and which will be open to all sects of religious persuasion" (Waite 1994, 21). The idea of a "godless" college was quite radical at the time. Lord Dalhousie was able to secure a small endowment for the college and a building, but, lacking a natural constituency in a deeply sectarian society, the college foundered after he left Nova Scotia and did not function as a college until the 1860s, when it was revived under Presbyterian auspices (Waite 1994, 37).

The Dalhousie Act of 1863 gave the board of governors, the members of which were appointed by the governor-in-council (effectively, the provincial cabinet), power to appoint the president, professors, and other college officers and to approve policies established by the senate – the latter body being composed of the professors and responsible for the university's internal government. This approach embodied a Scottish model of bicameral university governance (Cameron 1991, 17). No religious test was required of professors or students.

By 1910, the college had more than 400 students in faculties of arts and science, law, medicine, and dentistry (Waite 1994, 291). In the mid-1930s, the Dalhousie Act was amended for the first time since 1863, giving the institution a board of governors composed of thirty-five members (twenty-two appointed by the governor-in-council, nine alumni representatives, two representatives from King's College, the United Church governor, and the mayor of Halifax). The senate's membership continued to include all professors (Cameron 1991). At the time, the university sought to end the practice of cabinet appointments to its board, but the legislative committee reviewing the Dalhousie bill decided to continue the practice (Waite 1998, 75, 431). In 1949, a faculty of graduate studies was established.

By the mid-1950s, Dalhousie was a small university by Canadian standards, with around 1,500 students and fifty full-time faculty in arts and sciences, eighteen in medicine, seven in law, and one in dentistry. Faculty salaries were low (179, 408). Federal funding for universities had begun in 1951, but since it was calculated on a per capita basis and Nova Scotia had more university students per capita than any other province, the province received the lowest level of funding per student in the country (188). Lacking ongoing provincial funding (for fields other than health), Dalhousie continued to be much more dependent on endowments and fees than most Canadian universities.

Like other universities across the country, Dalhousie grew rapidly in the 1960s and early 1970s. Resumption of provincial operating funding in 1963, coupled with provincial capital funding provided through a University Grants Committee established in 1963, enabled the university to expand and to develop new doctoral programs and expand its research capacity; however, faculty and staff salaries remained low relative to other Canadian universities.

The 1960s and 1970s saw considerable democratization of the university. In most faculties, department "heads" were replaced by "chairmen," who served fixed terms of office. The appointment of deans, previously a presidential prerogative, began to take place upon the recommendation of committees representative of the faculties. Students obtained more representation on the university's governing bodies (Waite 1998, 299–319). Clerical staff unionized in 1974 and faculty members and librarians in 1978. The "benign dictatorship" (402) of the then president, which had been characterized by informality, ad hocery, and lack of accountability, was replaced by codified rights and responsibilities, explicit criteria and procedures, and a more legalistic and adversarial climate (389).

Some members of the senate, wishing to enhance its role relative to that of both the administration and the faculty association, took steps to give that body "a decisive place in policy making, including all aspects of physical, academic and financial planning" (392), on the premise that the senate should plan and legislate and the administration carry out its policies. Two referendums on changing the composition of senate (which still included all full professors) were held in 1979 and failed. However, the senate's committee structure was reformed, and the president was replaced as chair of the senate by an elected chair (392–3).

In the 1980s, Dalhousie struggled to cope with reduced government funding, a large accumulated operating deficit, and unfunded capital debt. The university's faculty struck for the first time in 1988. By 2002, Dalhousie had had four faculty strikes – more than had taken place at any other university in Canada (Cameron 2002, 153).

The 1990s brought changes to Dalhousie's board and senate. Each of the constituencies represented on the board of governors agreed to reduce its membership, thus reducing the board to thirty-three members without a change in legislation (H. Clark 2003, 140). The members of the senate voted to turn it into a representative body of around seventy.

After province-wide reviews of academic programs in a number of fields, initiated by the Nova Scotia Council on Higher Education in the early 1990s, the provincial government passed legislation to close the teacher education programs at several universities, including Dalhousie. In 1997, the Technical University of Nova Scotia (TUNS) amalgamated with Dalhousie, thus adding TUNS's faculties of architecture and engineering to the array of existing faculties at Dalhousie; it also led to the creation of a new faculty of computer science from the merger of two pre-existing units (Eastman and Lang 2001). In 2012, an additional faculty was added when the Government of Nova Scotia and Dalhousie confirmed an agreement to merge the Nova Scotia Agricultural College in Truro (founded in 1905), with Dalhousie, creating a Faculty of Agriculture.

As indicated in the institutional overview chart (table 3.2) at the end of this chapter, as of 2013,[1] Dalhousie had around 18,560 students (AUCC 2013) studying in twelve faculties. More than 52 percent of its students came from outside the province (Dalhousie 2013, 6). Several of its professional faculties offered programs serving the Maritimes or the Atlantic region as a whole (e.g., medicine and dentistry respectively). In 2013, Dalhousie ranked fifteenth among Canadian universities in sponsored research income received (RE$EARCH Infosource 2014). It was, and still is, the only Atlantic member of the U15 group of Canadian research universities. In 2013, it was ranked sixth among medical/doctoral institutions in Canada by *Maclean's* and among the top 300 universities in the world in the Academic Ranking of World Universities (ARWU) Shanghai Jiaotong ranking.[2] In 2013–14, provincial funding accounted for 46.5 percent of operating revenue, and tuition fees for 37.5 percent (CAUBO 2015).

### THE UNIVERSITÉ DE MONTRÉAL

Montreal is the largest city in Quebec, which accounts for around 23 percent of Canada's population (Statistics Canada 2020a). At the time of the last census, 77 percent of Quebeckers spoke French as their mother tongue, compared to 3.6 percent in the rest of Canada (Statistics Canada 2016). Clearly, Quebec is a distinct society in a country and on a continent where most people speak English.

The Université de Montréal began as a branch of Université Laval in Quebec City, the provincial capital. In 1878, Catholic clergy in Quebec City obtained approval from Rome to establish a branch of Laval in Montreal, over opposition from clergy and others in Montreal, who wanted an autonomous institution. At the outset, the new campus had eighty-six students in three faculties (theology, law, and medicine) spread over three different locations. The archbishop of Montreal was its highest officer, and its president and secretary-general were also members of the clergy (Université de Montréal 2015).

In 1889, the institution was granted a measure of administrative autonomy from Laval, including the right to hire its own staff. In 1895, its operations were consolidated in a single building in downtown Montreal, with room for approximately 1,000 students (Hébert 2008). Affiliation agreements were developed with École Polytechnique in 1887 and with the École des hautes études commerciales in 1915. In the early 1900s, the institution began to de-emphasize religion and to move away from the French model that had shaped its origins, toward the North American model of universities (Bizier 1993, 79).

The university was finally granted full autonomy through a pontifical charter in 1919; the following year, it acquired a provincial charter. The Université de Montréal's motto was *Fide splendet et scientia* ("Elle rayonne par la foi et la science"; Shines through faith and knowledge) (Université de Montréal 2015). Although its leaders had hoped that an autonomous university would attract philanthropic support from Montrealers, the university struggled financially. Faculties and schools that had affiliated with the university objected to its budget decisions and the degree of central control, and pushed for decentralization and continued autonomy (Bizier 1993, 107).

After a series of fires in university facilities between 1919 and 1922, it was decided to move the university away from its confined location downtown. This proved to be financially disastrous, because the institution lacked the means to build a campus at its new location on Mount Royal. Construction had to be halted, and the Great Depression worsened the situation. In 1939, the provincial government passed a Loi pour venir en aide à l'Université de Montréal. This effectively placed the university under receivership and imposed civil authority over its administration. It was not until 1946 that the university moved to its new campus (Université de Montréal 2015). Throughout these years, the university maintained its ties with the Catholic Church. In 1965, Roger Gaudry became its first lay rector (Université de Montréal 2015). The 1967 charter officially secularized the institution and brought an end to a yearly tradition of professors taking an oath to uphold moral Catholic values in their teaching (Hébert 2008, 18).

Under Gaudry's administration, the university developed in the realms of graduate education and research, and its administrative and faculty structures were reorganized. The size of the student body and of the faculty and staff doubled between 1963 and 1970 (Université de Montréal 2015). In 1975, thirteen years after the creation of the first staff union, the university's faculty unionized. The following year, the Fédération des associations étudiantes du campus de l'UdeM (FAECUM) was established as a federation of associations representing students across the university[3] (Université de Montréal 2015). In 2005, the faculty went on strike (Sauvé 2006).

Except for the UQ as a whole, the Université de Montréal is the largest university in Quebec in terms of student enrolment and by many other indicators. As of 2013, it had 46,980 students (AUCC 2013). It had thirteen faculties and three other major academic units covering a wide spectrum of disciplines and professions; it also continued to be affiliated with the École des hautes études commerciales (HEC) and École Polytechnique. Including the latter two institutions, enrolment totalled 67,240 (see table 3.2). In 2013, the Université de Montréal ranked third among Canadian universities in the amount of sponsored research income received (RE$EARCH Infosource 2014). The same year, it was ranked twelfth among medical/doctoral institutions in Canada by *Maclean's* magazine, and among the top 150 universities in the world in the ARWU Shanghai Jiaotong ranking. Provincial funding accounted for 71 percent of its operating revenue, and tuition fees for 19 percent (excluding affiliates) (CAUBO 2015).

With more than a dozen faculties, multiple campuses, and affiliated schools and health institutions, the Université de Montréal has a large physical and economic presence in and around the Montreal metropolitan region. A number of interviewees described it as the flagship of the Quebec university system and as one of the most important universities in the French-speaking world. In the rector's annual speech to the university assembly in November 2014, Guy Breton said that "l'Université de Montréal est un trésor national. C'est l'une des grandes réussites des Québéçois. Qu'un peuple sous-scolarisé ait pu bâtir une université qui est devenue, en l'espace d'un siècle, l'une des 100 meilleures du monde, c'est un véritable exploit" (The Université de Montréal is a national treasure. It is a tremendous achievement that a people who lacked education built a university that became, over the course of a century, one of the hundred best in the world) (Université de Montréal 2014).

### L'UNIVERSITÉ DU QUÉBEC À MONTRÉAL

The Université du Québec à Montréal (UQAM) was born of a very different era. The Université de Montréal grew up as a Catholic institution in a traditional society; UQAM was an exuberant child of the 1960s. The recommendations of the Royal Commission of Inquiry on Education in the Province of Quebec (Parent Commission) included that an additional French-language university be founded in Montreal (Corbo 2012, 11). Quebec's premier, inspired by the example of the University of California, envisioned a network of universities (Guillemet 2012, 260). After a number of additional studies, the Université du Québec (UQ) was established in 1968. Central to its mission was the expansion of access to post-secondary education and of universities' contributions to communities across the province (Donald 1997, 170).

Established in 1969, UQAM was located in the Quartier Latin, where the Université de Montréal had been situated before moving to Mount Royal. It brought together five pre-existing educational institutions (Corbo 2012, 12). UQAM was part of a wave of new universities created in the 1960s to educate rapidly expanding youth populations in North America, Europe, and other parts of the world. In Canada alone, thirty-eight new universities were founded between 1960 and 1970 (Roy and Gingras 2012, 3). These new universities were emphatically secular, public universities. They tended to define themselves as innovative, open, and egalitarian, and many of them, like UQAM, adopted innovative technology and/or organizational structures (Roy and Gringras 2012).

The mandate of UQAM, the largest member of the UQ, included the provision of education from the undergraduate to the doctoral levels, teacher training, research, and service to the community. Its mission included expanding access to education and knowledge for people who had not traditionally benefited from universities. This informed its location (close to the Métro) and its approaches to admissions (which took into account age and prior experience), scheduling (e.g., offering classes in the evening as well as during the day), and ancillary fees (which it sought to keep below those of other universities), as well as its decisions about program design (such as that all programs be offered both full-time and part-time) (Corbo 2012; UQAM 2014). Most of UQAM's initial offerings were in education, the fine arts, the humanities, and the social sciences, but it soon expanded into legal studies, health and other sciences, management, and other fields. Like many new universities, it was a leader in interdisciplinary education and research. By 1979, it offered twenty-three master's programs and five doctoral programs (UQAM n.d.).

According to former rector Claude Corbo, its development was informed by three grand and divergent visions of the university:

- The vision held by senior provincial officials of UQAM and other UQ institutions as modern, public universities, akin to state universities in the United States, responsive to the needs of the province's regions, the labour market, and development priorities identified by government.
- A Marxist conception of the university as an instrument of economic and social revolution. In this view, UQAM was a forum for critical analysis of society and capitalism, for advancement toward an alternative social and economic order, and for the education of citizens committed to social transformation.
- A conception, informed by elements of May 1968 in France and the counterculture of the 1960s, of UQAM as an anti-authoritarian, anti-utilitarian university in which faculty and students would come together to create new forms of knowledge and culture. (Corbo 2012, 13–14)

Faculty members at UQAM unionized in the summer of 1969, and staff followed suit the following year (Bertrand 2012, 214). In the winter of 1970, the non-renewal of the contracts of approximately forty professors led the Canadian Association of University Teachers (CAUT) to censure the UQ and UQAM. Besides demanding their reinstatement, CAUT strongly criticized UQAM's governance structure on the grounds that it did not respect the rights of professors (Bertrand 2012, 230). In the spring of 1971, staff went on strike across the UQ, eventually securing significant improvements in their compensation, job security, and benefits. The faculty went on strike in the fall of 1971. One of their union's demands was that it be recognized as the sole representative of the faculty, not only in matters of labour relations but also in university decision-making. Although the union did not succeed in gaining such recognition, it did secure some acknowledgment of departmental autonomy in matters of faculty hiring, evaluation, and professional development, as well as recognition of the powers and composition of the *commission des études* (Bertrand 2012, 233–4). In 1976–77, there was a four-month faculty strike, which led to the resignation of both the rector and the president of the UQ (Fournier and Antonat 2012, 39).

UQAM's first decade witnessed recurring conflicts among the administration, faculty, students, and staff (UQAM 2014). In Bertrand's view, these crises had various sources. Some were caused by external events such as the language crisis of 1969 and the October Crisis of 1970. Some resulted from unfortunate senior administrative decisions. A third category arose from the new organizational structures put in place within the UQ and UQAM, which tended to foster conflict. According to Bertrand:

[L]'Université du Québec et l'Université du Québec à Montréal apparaissent très tôt comme des lieux de luttes multiples pour le pouvoir, comme il n'en a jamais existé dans l'université québécoise francophone d'avant 1960, qui était fondamentalement cléricale et hiérarchisée ... Les tensions et conflits se retrouvent à tous les niveaux: luttes entres l'Université du Québec et les autres structures organisationnelles provinciales ... conflits entre de siège social de l'Université du Québec et l'Université du Québec à Montréal; confrontations entre les différentes constituantes du réseau ... oppositions des dirigeants de l'Université et des représentants des étudiants; difficiles relations des départements et des modules; affrontement du pourvoir patronal et des forces syndicales de regroupement des professeurs et des employés de soutien. (Bertrand 2012, 222)

[The Université du Québec and the Université du Québec à Montréal (UQAM) emerged very early on as sites of multiple struggles for power, such as had never existed in the pre-1960 French-speaking Quebec university, which was fundamentally clerical and hierarchical ... Tensions and conflicts were evident at all levels: struggles between the Université du Québec and other provincial organizational structures ... conflicts between the headquarters of the Université du Québec and UQAM; confrontations between different components of the network ... opposition between university leaders and student representatives; difficult relations between departments and modules; confrontation of the power of employers with that of faculty and staff unions.]

A legacy of its early years was that UQAM received "le mépris affiché à l'endroit d'un établissement turbulent dans sa vie interne et contestant volontiers l'ordre universitaire établi – et où elle se sent peu aimée des gouvernements québécois, malgré son statut d'université publique" (the contempt displayed for a turbulent institution that willingly contested the established university order – one that felt unbeloved by Quebec governments, despite its status as a public university) (Corbo 2012, 15).

During the 1980s, UQAM developed additional graduate programs, research, and creative activity. This caused it to become more like traditional universities, because getting program approvals and funding required adherence to external disciplinary and professional standards (18). Intensifying financial constraints may also have caused UQAM to become gradually less distinctive, insofar as they compelled new universities to enter into competition with others for students, donors, contracts, and government funds (Roy and Gringras 2012).

Almost from the outset, the leaders and members of UQAM – which was much larger in size and more comprehensive than the other UQ member universities – had chafed at the constraints resulting from membership in the UQ (Bertrand 2012). In 1989, the legislation governing the UQ was amended by the National Assembly to give UQAM the status of a "université associée." This status, unique within the UQ system, enabled UQAM to recommend the appointment of its rector directly to the Quebec government, to grant degrees, and to enter into agreements with other educational and research institutions.

In 2005, UQAM embarked on a major capital initiative – the Îlot Voyageur project – which involved partnering with a real estate firm to develop academic and office buildings, residences, and commercial space. The project was poorly planned, managed, and overseen and exceeded UQAM's financial capacity. When the extent of the losses came to light in the fall of 2006, the rector resigned. In 2007, the Quebec government indemnified UQAM for the financial consequences of the project, asked the Auditor General of Quebec to conduct a special audit of the project, and reached an agreement with UQAM and the UQ on steps for restoring the financial equilibrium of the university (Vérificateur Général du Québec 2008). UQAM had financed the project in part by issuing bonds. Concerned about the potential impact of UQAM's borrowing on the reputation of the Quebec public sector in financial markets and on future public sector borrowing costs, the Quebec Ministry of Finance bought up most of the bonds issued and associated long-term debt (Vérificateur Général du Québec 2008, 101). The Auditor General's report, issued in June 2008, found that the losses incurred by UQAM had been caused by the following: poor management of the project by the rector and others; lack of respect and transparency on their part toward the governing bodies of UQAM, the UQ, and the Ministry of Education; and deficiencies in governance on the part of the Board of Directors of UQAM and its audit committee, the UQ Board of Governors, and the ministry. The report included recommendations to UQAM, the UQ, and the Ministry of Education. The spectacular public failure of the project had profound consequences not only for UQAM and the UQ but also for government legislation concerning universities, public and governmental perceptions of the competence of university governance and administration, and the extent of the regulation to which all Quebec universities are subject. In 2009, there was a prolonged faculty strike (Meunier 2009). According to union representatives, the resulting collective agreement was ultimately negotiated directly with the provincial government. In 2010, the university administration removed deans from the faculty union; this was appealed by the union but eventually upheld by the courts.

One of the five working groups established by the Quebec government in the wake of the summit on higher education in early 2013 focused on a legal framework for Quebec universities. That group's report concluded that the UQ network, having enabled its member institutions to develop and flourish, had become superfluous; it recommended that the UQ be dismantled and that all universities in the province be part of a single public network. This recommendation was opposed by the president of the UQ, some other UQ member-institutions, and Quebec student and faculty associations. Shortly after the report's release, the minister of higher education told the Canadian Press that "the network will not be dismantled; it's here to stay" (Lambert-Chan 2013).

UQAM thus remains the largest constituent university within the UQ, as well as one of four major universities in Montreal. As of 2013, it had 42,040 students, around 60 percent of them full-time, the rest part-time (see table 3.2). It comprised a school of management and six faculties. In 2013, UQAM ranked twenty-second among Canadian universities in the amount of sponsored research income received (RE$EARCH Infosource 2014). It was ranked thirteenth among comprehensive universities by *Maclean's*. The Université du Québec as a whole was among the top 500 universities in the world in 2013, according to the ARWU Shanghai Jiaotong rankings. In 2013–14, provincial funding accounted for 73 percent of its operating revenue, and tuition fees for 23 percent (CAUBO 2015).

## THE UNIVERSITY OF TORONTO

The University of Toronto (U of T) is located in the capital city of the Province of Ontario. That province accounts for 39 percent of Canada's population (Statistics Canada 2020a). The university's origins date back to the early 1800s.

In 1798, the Executive Council of what was then the colony of Upper Canada set aside half of a 550,000 acre land reserve to endow a university, but progress on the initiative stalled until the 1820s (Cameron 1991, 10). Those who advocated for the founding of a university in what was then the town of York were motivated partly by a desire to reduce the number of young Upper Canadians going to the United States for higher education. Anglican bishop John Strachan wrote that a university was needed because, in the United States, "politics pervade the whole system of instruction. The school books ... are stuffed with praises of their own institutions, and breathe hatred to everything English ... Some [Upper Canadian students] may become fascinated with that liberty which has degenerated into licentiousness, and imbibe, perhaps unconsciously, sentiments unfriendly to things of which Englishmen are proud" (Friedland 2002, 6). Strachan went to England in 1826 to argue the case for the establishment of a university. A royal charter for King's College, which subsequently became the University of Toronto, was issued the following year. That charter prescribed that its president be the Anglican archdeacon of York and that the members of its governing council (composed of the president, the chancellor, and seven professors) subscribe to the Thirty-Nine Articles of Religion of the Church of England. The college was endowed with 225,944 acres of land and given a grant for building purposes (Friedland 2002). Although it was more denominational in character than the university Lord Dalhousie envisioned for Nova Scotia, the religious character of King's was by no means unusual. Indeed, the absence of a religious test for students made it more liberal than Oxford or Cambridge – or its counterparts in Nova Scotia and New Brunswick – were at the time (8).

Although the Anglican elite of Upper Canada saw its church's interests in the realm of higher education as synonymous with those of the state, members of other faiths took a different view. When the elected legislature of Upper Canada met in January 1828, it sought an inquiry into whether "the principles upon which [the university] has been founded shall, upon enquiry, prove to be conducive to the advancement of true learning and piety, and friendly to the civil and religious liberty of the people" (Friedland 2002, 10). In March, it sent an address to the king and the colonial secretary requesting that King's charter be cancelled. It argued that by making the college subservient to one church, the charter excluded "from [the college's] offices and honours" "the great body of Your Majesty's subjects in this Province" (10). The petition was referred to a select committee of the House of Commons in London, which concluded that no religious test should be required of officials or professors of the college. Its report stated that "in a country where only a small proportion of the inhabitants adhere to [the Church of England], a suspicion and jealousy of religious interference would necessarily be created" by the existing charter (10). Strachan refused to surrender the charter, but the opening of the college was delayed until 1843 by opposition to it, the rebellions of 1837, and the subsequent reunification of Upper and Lower Canada. In 1849, the parliament of the province of Canada underscored the distinction between public and private higher education, passing legislation to transform King's College into a secular institution, the University of Toronto. The legislation completely secularized the university, eliminating any publicly funded chairs of divinity and all religious tests for any member of the university (24).

The U of T came into existence on 1 January 1850. Three years later, the legislation concerning it was again changed. U of T became an examining body, modelled upon the University of London, with University College as its teaching arm. It was thought that this would pave the way for denominational colleges established in the 1830s and 1840s to affiliate with the larger institution, but that did not occur. The 1853 Act also gave the government control over appointments and major decisions at the university (Friedland 2002).

Confederation and the assignment of responsibility for higher education to the provinces was realized under the British North America Act in 1867. The government of Ontario moved swiftly to discontinue all grants to denominational colleges and universities (Cameron 1991).

In 1887, Ontario passed legislation to create a federated University of Toronto, whereby the university would assume responsibility for the sciences, and the professions and the colleges would suspend their degree-granting authority and teach specified subjects, principally in the humanities.

The "new University of Toronto was very much a state university" (Cameron 1991, 26). It was governed by a senate that included ten government appointees, among them the minister of education. Decisions of the senate required approval by government. The president and all the professors were appointed, their salaries determined by the government. However, problems in the governance and management of the U of T led the Ontario government to establish the Flavelle Royal Commission in 1905, which, as described in chapter 2, led to the delegation of state powers "in respect to the control and management of the University" to a board of governors, the introduction of bicameral governance at U of T, and its extension to other universities across the country (28).

The U of T influenced other Canadian universities, not only by demonstrating the possibilities of bicameral governance and federation but also by simple virtue of its size. In 1867, U of T was one of only five Canadian universities that had as many as one hundred students (19). In 1954–55, only twenty of Canada's approximately 180 degree-granting institutions had more than five hundred students. Of these, only four had more than 5,000 students and only U of T had more than 10,000 (59–60). By virtue of its size and the breadth of its programs, U of T over time became an important source of faculty members, university administrators, and advice for other institutions.

Before becoming president of U of T in 1958, Claude Bissell served as president of the new Carleton University in Ottawa. In a memoir, he contrasted Carleton, with its youthful energy and strong community ties, with "the University of Toronto, [which], for all its size and international prominence, was self-contained and introverted" (Bissell 1974, 32). With respect to his installation speeches at the two universities, he wrote: "My Carleton installation speech had tried to sketch out a role for the new university – a middle power with its special concern for national Canadian problems. In the Toronto speech I was saying, not directly, but not too obliquely either, that the University of Toronto was the great Canadian university" (51). The years of Bissell's presidency saw immense changes:

> The first ten years of my term of office were the final period of the old feudalistic university ... a final triumphant flowering of the old regime. The university ... was sustained by nineteenth century liberalism: the belief in progress through knowledge, and the striving for

objectivity through balanced support from private business and the state ... The faculty seemed for the most part happy with the compact whereby they handed over power to a lay board in return for safety, security, and the illusion of freedom in a separate, protected kingdom; the students accepted distinctions on the basis of measured intellectual achievement ... There was ... a mood of optimism, and the sense of a great intellectual ferment ...

After 1968, the basis of the old structure began to crumble: the hierarchical separation was challenged, first by the staff and then by the students; the alliance of the university with business and government was attacked, on the left from staff and students, who saw it as corrupting, and on the right by government, who rejected an alliance of partners and called for a masterservant relationship. (191)

In 1971, the university abandoned bicameralism in favour of a unicameral structure, consisting of a fifty-member governing council with responsibility for both academic and business matters, composed of sixteen government appointees, eight alumni, twelve faculty members, eight students, two senior administrators, two non-academic staff members, the president, and the chancellor (Cameron 1991).

The changes in the governance and culture of the university from the 1950s to the 1970s were accompanied by immense changes in university finance. Until the late 1950s, university life in Canada had been characterized by "genteel poverty" and professors were poorly paid. U of T initiated a series of annual faculty salary increases that "by 1958 had given the university primacy in Canada" (Bissell 1974, 44). The 1960s saw massive publicly financed growth in higher education to accommodate Ontario's baby boom, but, by the early 1970s, an "atmosphere of dour economy" had set in. "Politicians and newspapers [proclaimed] that the university had been profligate and should address itself to stern economies, to greater productivity or, as the minister for university affairs briskly put it, to turning out 'more scholars for the dollar'" (186–7).

The years that followed were difficult ones. By 1980, funding per student in Ontario was 25 percent below the provincial average. In 1979, U of T's president told the governing council that "the University is at the edge of decline" (Friedland 2002, 581). Cutbacks continued throughout the 1980s and 1990s. In her study of selected Canadian universities' retrenchment strategies in the 1980s, Hardy depicted U of T as having an administration that was large, remote, and bureaucratic, and a governing council that was "managed" by the administration most of the time but never entirely predictable. There was frustration and ambivalence within the university community – some of its members called for decisive leadership, while others gave every indication that any attempt at providing such leadership would be resisted (Hardy 1996). In 1987, the president reported "widely shared concerns in the University, a sense of frustration, of undesirable limitations, and of hopes not realized or deferred" (Connell 1987, 107).

During the 1990s, cutbacks in provincial operating funding continued. The total number of full-time faculty members at the university fell from 2,919 in 1990–91 to 2,628 in 2001 (Statistics Canada 2003). By the turn of the century, however, new federal and provincial programs, philanthropy, and other sources of revenue were "putting wind in [the university's] sails." Robert Prichard, U of T's president from 1990 to 2000, wrote: "At present, we have a quite remarkable alignment of federal and provincial forces all blowing basically in the same direction. As a result, for institutions like the University of Toronto which has, in effect, a very large spinnaker, we are going to pick up a lot of speed and leave a lot of distance between us and other institutions" (Friedland 2002, 652).

In 2013, U of T was still the largest Canadian university in terms of student enrolment, with 84,400 students. It accounted for almost 18 percent of the university student population in Ontario, and almost 80 percent of its first-year students came from within the province. The university had eighteen faculties or equivalents, and three Toronto area campuses. In 2013, U of T ranked first among Canadian universities in the amount of sponsored research income received per full-time faculty member (RE$EARCH Infosource 2014). It was ranked third among medical/doctoral institutions in Canada by *Maclean's* and twenty-eighth in the world in the Shanghai Jiaotong rankings. It is a member of the U15 group and one of only two universities in Canada that belong to the Association of American Universities. In 2013–14, provincial funding accounted for 35 percent of its operating revenue, tuition fees for 59 percent (CAUBO 2015).

## THE UNIVERSITY OF ALBERTA

Alberta, one of Canada's prairie provinces, is home to 12 percent of the Canadian population (Statistics Canada 2020a). Alberta became a province in 1905 and passed a University Act the following year. The act reflected westerners' determination to "avoid a repetition of evils" associated with many competing higher education institutions in eastern provinces (Harris 1976, 224). It would do that by creating a single, modern, secular university for the province. The legislation was also progressive in that it specified that the university's governing body must "make all provision for the education of women within the university in such manner as it shall deem most fitting, provided [ ] that no woman shall by reason of her sex be deprived of any advantage or privilege accorded to male students of the university" (Macleod 2008, 7).

Many Calgarians assumed that their city would be the site of the new university, given that Edmonton had been designated the province's capital (Macleod 2008, 4). But in the event, Edmonton was selected for the site, and the University of Alberta (U of A) began offering classes there in a temporary facility in 1908. The university had one governing body, the senate, made up of five members elected by the convocation (defined as all residents of Alberta holding a degree from a Canadian or British university who chose to register), and ten government appointees. The university was modelled on American institutions, not British ones: "There were faculties, departments and courses, not colleges, tutors, and gentlemen's pass degrees" (15). The university's first president said in a speech at its first convocation ceremony that "the modern state university is a people's institution. The people demand that knowledge shall not be the concern of scholars alone. The uplifting of the whole people shall be its final goal" (15).

In 1910, a new University Act gave U of A a bicameral structure. A board of governors was created, made up of eleven members: the president, the chancellor, and nine government appointees. It was responsible for all matters related to the business administration of the university. The senate's powers were restricted to academic matters, and it was enlarged to about thirty members.[4] The president was to be appointed by the provincial Cabinet (20). The act also gave legal status to the student union (26).

The university grew substantially before the First World War, enrolling students from across the province, some of whom were taught by faculty who travelled to distant communities to give classes. For two decades after the war, the university laboured under severe financial constraints due to Alberta's struggling economy, which was heavily dependent on agriculture. Nonetheless, it continued to grow in number of faculties, students (more than 2,000 of them by the end of 1930s), and other respects.

In 1940, the province's Social Credit government was re-elected under Premier William Aberhart. The senate of the university had previously granted honorary degrees to provincial premiers embarking on second terms. A senate committee unanimously recommended Premier

Aberhart for an honorary degree; he was invited and agreed to give the next convocation address. The senate itself, however, narrowly rejected the recommendation. The perceived affront to the premier triggered the resignations of the university president and the chairman of the board and eventually led to a re-examination of the university's governance arrangements (Macleod 2008, 124–7). The recommendations of a University Survey Committee, struck by the provincial government in 1941, brought significant changes to the university act: the board of governors was given more powers, most academic matters were delegated to a general faculties council (GFC) with greater faculty and student representation, and the senate was reduced in both power and size (138). The university president was still to be appointed by the provincial cabinet.

Although resources became somewhat more plentiful in the early 1940s, the province did not show much enthusiasm for the provincial university after the war and into the 1950s. According to Macleod, it treated the university "as if it were a minor government agency" and its president "as if he were a junior and rather badly paid civil servant" (2008, 162). The university was under chronic financial constraints even while taking in more students. The quality of education was not keeping up with that of other major Canadian universities. In 1956, the university and the province experienced a wake-up call when the Faculty of Medicine was put on probation by an external accreditation body. Provincial and federal funding subsequently increased, and the university expanded rapidly in student numbers and physical space. This led to a review of the legislation that governed it.

The new act of 1966 accorded the board of governors the power to appoint the president, removed the *ex officio* positions of the deputy ministers of education and treasury board from the board, and gave two seats on the board to nominees from the general faculties council, two seats to the alumni association, and one seat to the senate (Macleod 2008, 193). The GFC became a much more democratic body. The revised act did not provide for student representation on the board; however, students finally won two seats in 1969, a time of student activism in Alberta and beyond. Students later achieved parity of representation with faculty members on the GFC (223).

During the 1980s, the university again faced financial constraints, but the provincial government was unsympathetic. According to Macleod, "if anything, the government's attitude was hardening. There was no political opposition in Alberta ... and low student enrolments meant no pressure from the public to increase university funding" (MacLeod

2008, 249). Public board members at U of A found themselves in a quandary about whether to support government policy or advocate for an increase in provincial support (257).

In the early 1990s, a new government-appointed board chair, concerned that the university and its administration were resistant to the radical changes he believed necessary, began to take steps to bring about change. Some of those steps were perceived by members of the administration as interfering with their responsibility for day-to-day leadership and operation of the university. By the beginning of 1993, the relationship between the board and the president had become dysfunctional (Macleod 2008, 284). In June 1993, the board of governors voted to establish a presidential selection committee rather than reappoint the incumbent. The latter said he would not be a candidate and was quickly snapped up by another university (287). The government appointed a new board chair shortly thereafter. According to Macleod, "after the failure of its attempt to control the university directly through the board of governors, the government fell back on a more arm's length approach" (306).

Faced with continued provincial funding restrictions, the university had to eliminate or restructure some departments, including merging the Faculty of Dentistry with the Faculty of Medicine. The university conducted several ambitious fundraising campaigns in the 1990s, increased tuition fees substantially, succeeded in attracting external research funding, and was able to make many new faculty appointments. Nevertheless, in terms of revenue per full-time student, it was unable to catch up with U of T or UBC until the new millennium (308).

In the early 2000s, as Alberta's economy boomed, the university's financial situation improved, and it entered a period of major expansion (Macleod 2008, 310). Indira Samarasekara, appointed president in 2005, espoused the goal of making U of A one of the top twenty public universities in the world by 2020 (311). In 2006, the university adopted a vision statement, *Dare to Discover*, aiming "to inspire the human spirit through outstanding achievements in learning, discovery, and citizenship ... building one of the world's great universities for the public good" (University of Alberta 2007).

By April 2014, U of A had sixteen faculties, two colleges, and two branch campuses. Its enrolment totalled 37,730 (see table 3.2). Provincial funding accounted for 57 percent of operating funding for the fiscal year ending in 2014; tuition and other fees accounted for 29 percent (CAUBO 2015). In 2013, the U of A was ranked fifth among medical/doctoral universities in Canada in the *Maclean's* rankings. It was fifth among

Canadian universities in the amount of sponsored research income earned (RE$EARCH Infosource 2014) and ranked among the top 150 universities worldwide in the Shanghai Jiaotong Academic Ranking of World Universities.

## THE UNIVERSITY OF BRITISH COLUMBIA

The main campus of the University of British Columbia (UBC) is in Vancouver, the largest city in the province, which is home to 14 percent of the Canadian population (Statistics Canada 2020a). The populous parts of BC are to the west of the Rocky Mountains. Owing to its geographic remoteness, the Pacific Northwest was difficult for settlers to reach and colonization took place relatively late. For millennia, the bountiful coastal environment had supported large First Nations with complex societies and elaborate cultures, whereas Indigenous people in the interior tended to be nomadic (Canadian Encyclopedia 2019).

The first permanent European settlement in the area followed the rise of the fur trade in the early nineteenth century. In 1849, the British government granted Vancouver Island to the Hudson's Bay Company for colonization, and in 1858 it created the mainland colony of British Columbia. After long debate, the 12,000 non-Indigenous residents of the colonies agreed in 1871 to join the new Dominion of Canada on the condition that the federal government build a transcontinental railway. By 1881, the white population had grown to 24,000, while the Indigenous population was estimated at 25,000 (Canadian Encyclopedia 2019), having been decimated by colonization and disease. Well into the twentieth century, the settler economy was based largely on resource extraction – forestry, fishing, mining, and hydroelectric power – and agriculture. The ability of settler British Columbians to earn a good living by these means meant there was little perceived need to invest in post-secondary education (Dennison 1997, 31–2).

An act to establish a university in BC was passed in 1890 but lapsed before the university was legally constituted, because of rivalry between Vancouver and Victoria over the proposed site of the institution (Harris 1976, 226). McGill University College of British Columbia provided undergraduate education in Vancouver and Victoria in the early 1900s. In 1907, the BC legislature passed Bill 25, An Act to Aid the University of British Columbia by a Reservation of Provincial Lands. That act called for up to 2 million acres of Crown land to be set aside and administered under the Land Act; all revenues from the sale or disposition of the lands were to be devoted to the maintenance of the university. The minister of education of the time hoped that UBC would be financed by this means and, thus, independent of the annual legislative appropriations process (Logan 1958, 34).

The 1908 Act established a non-sectarian university with a bicameral structure modelled on that of U of T (Cameron 1991, 31). UBC's board of governors would be appointed by the provincial government; the senate, chaired by the university's president, would consist of the deans, two elected members of each faculty, the province's minister of education and Superintendent of Education, three government appointees, individuals elected by the convocation, and others (Logan 1958).

The opening of the university was delayed by continued rivalry between municipalities to be the university's site and by the province's fiscal problems. The issue of location was addressed by the establishment of a university site commission, composed of "disinterested educationalists residing outside the Province"; it recommended a site on Point Grey near Vancouver (Logan 1958, 41). The government duly set aside 175 acres on that site, and the search for a president began. The province's minister of education and superintendent of education conducted a wide search, interviewing potential candidates across Canada and the United States (21). The successful candidate, then dean of medicine at the University of Minnesota, saw UBC and other public universities as vital elements of socio-economic as well as individual development – places where, in his words, "we may design and fashion the tools needed in the building of a nation and from which we can survey and lay out paths of enlightenment, tunnel the mountains of ignorance and bridge the chasms of incompetence" (46).

The University of British Columbia opened in 1915 in the former McGill University College facilities in Vancouver, with thirty-four faculty members and 379 students studying in three faculties (Logan 1958). Unfortunately, UBC's original endowment lands produced no cash income. They were exchanged by the provincial government in the early 1920s for lands adjacent to the Point Grey campus, in the expectation that the latter would appreciate in value because of their proximity to the city (87). Even then, the university did not derive revenue from its lands until late in the century. Meanwhile, the university depended on provincial grants. UBC was founded on the idea that higher education should be free for all qualified students, and in this respect, it was initially unique among provincial universities in Canada (88). Within a few years, however, the government indicated that it could not meet UBC's budget requests and that it would have to begin charging fees.

After the end of the First World War, enrolments increased and classrooms became crowded. In 1922, students started a campaign to induce the provincial government to continue investing in construction of the Point Grey campus. In 1925, UBC finally moved to that site. Student self-government gained official recognition through an amendment to the University Act in 1927. Amid the financial difficulties of the Great Depression, provincial funding dropped sharply, as did salaries (Logan 1958).

At the end of the 1920s, a minister of education critical of the university began attending board meetings and accusing the university of mismanagement. He announced that funding would be reduced and that enrolment would have to be limited. According to Logan, the board "acknowledged that the question of [whether or not to limit enrolment] was a matter for the Government to decide since it paid for the support of the institution" (Logan 1958, 113). Shortly thereafter, the minister advised the university to deal with another reduction in the funding it expected to receive by cutting the Faculty of Agriculture. The president and the board defended that faculty, but several other faculties – naturally, preferring that it absorb the cut – opposed them (113). The upshot was a senate vote of no confidence in the president and the eventual appointment by the province of a one-person commission to inquire into the university's problems. It recommended replacement of the existing board and the appointment to its successor of three additional members appointed by the senate (Cameron 1991, 39). A further consequence, according to Logan, was that "from about this time each of the Faculties began to regard University financial problems almost entirely from the Faculty point of view – began to demand what they regarded as their fair share of student fees and of the Government grant" (115).

In 1943, the university advertised for a president who would, in the words of the search committee,

> be a man of sufficient imagination to envisage the enormous future potentialities of our Institution as a main source in the Province of humanitarian culture and scientific research ... With this quality should be coupled enthusiasm, firmness of character and strength of will as will cause the new President to pursue unflaggingly the task of transmuting these potentialities into realities as far as possible despite the discouragement almost necessarily incidental to the leadership of an institution practically unendowed and dependent for its support mainly on Government grants. (ctd in Waite 1987, 111)

By the late 1950s, UBC was English Canada's second-largest university (Logan 1958, 210), with around 9,000 students. The size of the cohorts working their way through the province's public schools led UBC's fourth president to believe that for UBC to attempt to meet the demand would be fundamentally incompatible with quality. He undertook a study of how BC's needs for higher education could best be met and proposed "expansion and diversification through the creation of new autonomous institutions" – specifically, a new four-year degree-granting college in the lower Fraser Valley; independence for Victoria College (then a four-year institution affiliated with UBC); and the creation of three two-year colleges that offered academic and vocational programs. He intended that the two four-year colleges be undergraduate institutions and that graduate and professional education be concentrated at UBC; however, the premier wanted two full-fledged new universities instead. In 1963, the government passed the University Act – the first of its kind in Canada – governing UBC and three other universities (Hardy 1996, 18).

During the 1970s, BC's universities were relatively well-treated by their provincial government, receiving the second-largest increase in government operating grants per full-time equivalent student in Canada (Hardy 1996, 31). In the midst of that decade, UBC's faculty considered unionization, as did faculty members at many Canadian universities. By September 1974, a majority of the university's faculty members had expressed support for unionization, and their association applied for certification as the faculty's bargaining agent. However, the board of governors agreed the following month to voluntary collective bargaining with the association as the sole bargaining agent. This enabled opponents of unionization within the faculty to muster sufficient support among their colleagues that the application for certification was withdrawn (Cameron 1991, 373).

In 1977, the BC government followed that of Alberta in banning certified trade unions, by adding a provision to the University Act (since repealed) stating that the provincial Labour Code did not apply to the relationship between a university and its faculty members (374). The minister of education, a medical professor on leave from UBC, said at the time that the model embodied in the University Act was "based upon the traditional university model" comprising four principles: academic freedom, collegiality and shared management responsibility, tenure, and the pursuit of individual excellence (374). He said that if a majority of faculty at any university were to vote in favour of a trade union model, he would introduce amendments to permit that, but "at the same time the Ministry of Education [would] adjust its policies to suit the trade union model" (374). In 1983, the province's Social Credit government passed legislation that would have enabled tenure to be abandoned if it impeded a university in effecting budget reductions. In the wake of protests, the government agreed to exempt universities that negotiated mechanisms (e.g., clauses permitting layoffs as a result of financial exigency) such that tenure would not be an obstacle to addressing financial problems. UBC and its faculty association agreed to such a clause in 1985 (Hardy 1996).

The finances of BC's universities deteriorated abruptly in the early 1980s: grants were frozen in 1983–84, reduced by 5 percent in 1984–85, and cut by another 5 percent in 1985–86. Dramatic tuition fee increases failed to compensate for a real decrease in operating grant per full-time-equivalent student of 18 percent between 1976–77 and 1986–87 – the largest such decline in the country (Hardy 1996, 31). Facing an estimated $6 million deficit (in a province in which universities were prohibited from running deficits), UBC made major budget reductions, closing several programs and ending the employment of twelve professors, nine of whom had tenure. As of the early 1990s, it was the only Canadian university that had laid off tenured faculty members in recent decades (80–1).

In her study of selected universities' retrenchment strategies in the 1980s, Hardy characterized UBC as a political organization (in contrast to U of T's federal bureaucracy) – that is, a university in which deans were powerful, behaved as CEOs of their faculty fiefdoms, and fought with one another and with the central administration (86). The university's board, most of whose members were government-appointed, was perceived to be supportive of the government and, if pushed, willing to overrule the university's administration. In Hardy's view, the university took the exceptional step of closing programs and terminating tenured professors partly to demonstrate to its board and to the outside world that it was capable of "tough decisions."

The president who took office after the program closures forswore further such dramatic measures and negotiated generous severance arrangements with those affected. He also took steps to centralize policy development, budgeting, accounting, and information management to a greater degree, thereby reining in the faculties and deans (Hardy 1996). That was, however, by no means the end of retrenchment. In the late 1990s, the BC government imposed a six-year freeze on tuition fee increases, which ended in 2002. During the tuition freeze, the province required the university to take in additional students without commensurate (indeed, in the first two years of the freeze, without *any*) increases in operating funding. Total enrolment at UBC rose from 29,358 in 1990-91 to 35,968 in 2000–01 (Statistics Canada 2003) – an increase of 23 percent over ten years – while the number of full-time faculty members fell from 1,888 in 1990–91 to 1,772 in 2000–01 (Statistics Canada 2003). In 2002, UBC's operating expenditures per weighted full-time-equivalent student amounted to $6,981 – less than any of the country's other fourteen "medical/doctoral" universities (*Maclean's* 2002, 56).

While noting UBC's research and other strengths, the university's academic plan, issued in 2000, observed that "offering quality education and sustaining superior research and scholarship is increasingly difficult in a context of declining revenues per student. Staff and faculty continue a long tradition of outstanding, productive work, but increasing demands on time and reduced revenue strain the capacity for quality learning and research" (University of British Columbia n.d.).

UBC was among the first Canadian universities, if not *the* first, to systematically pursue the education of international students as a means of generating revenue and achieving other goals (Eastman 2005, 181). In the late 1980s, the university's president had become aware of the potential during visits to Australia, and he encouraged deans to identify opportunities for their faculties in the international higher education market. In 1996, UBC's board of governors launched an initiative to attract undergraduate and professional graduate students to the university from abroad at fees that would, at a minimum, recover full costs. Another element of UBC's revenue generation strategy was the development of its lands as a source of revenue, as envisioned many decades earlier.

Emphasis on internationalization continued under the presidency of Martha Piper (1997 to 2006), and UBC was an active member of the Association of Pacific Rim Universities (Paul 2015). In 2004, UBC acquired Okanagan University College in the province's interior, which became UBC's Okanagan campus. The merger eventually gave rise to the new governance and administrative structure described in Chapter 6.

As of 2013, UBC had seventeen faculties on its two campuses (see table 3.2). Its student population was 58,030 (AUCC 2013), and around 19 percent of the students at its Vancouver campus were international (UBC 2013). In 2013–14, provincial funding made up 50 percent of its operating funds, and tuition and other fees accounted for 40 percent (CAUBO 2015), with the remaining 10 percent from endowment income, ancillary revenue, and so on. In 2013, UBC was second among Canadian universities in the amount of sponsored research income earned (RE$EARCH Infosource 2014). Nationally, it was ranked second in the medical-doctoral category by *Maclean's*. It placed fortieth in the Shanghai Jiaotong Academic Ranking of World Universities in 2013, second among Canadian universities after the University of Toronto.

Our case study examined six major urban universities – five older medical/doctoral universities and one "new" comprehensive one. Three of these, established in the 1800s, were initially associated with churches. The two western institutions were founded as secular, public, provincial universities. One was created as part of Quebec's public university system. They varied greatly in size, from the University of Toronto with almost 85,000 students, to Dalhousie with just over 18,500, as well as in the breadth of their faculties and their sources of funding. Two are francophone; four, anglophone.

Established at different times, their origins reflected evolving conceptions and expectations of universities as what is now Canada was colonized from east to west. Each had its own particular roots, character, and path. Spanning a large country of diverse regions, the six universities were very much creatures of their provinces. At the same time, their activities extended far beyond provincial boundaries – all six were active in different ways, to various extents, and in different realms on the national and international stages. Their unique trajectories were shaped by many factors, including their external and internal governance – the subjects of the next chapters.

Table 3.2 | Institutional overview chart

| University | UBC | U of A | U of T | U de M[1] | U de M[2] | UQAM | Dal |
|---|---|---|---|---|---|---|---|
| Total 2013/14 enrolment[3] | 58,030 | 37,730 | 84,400 | 46,980 | 67,240 | 42,040 | 18,560 |
| % full time | 74 | 94 | 90 | 73 | 70 | 60 | 88 |
| % graduate | 18 | 20 | 19 | 25 | 25 | 17 | 21 |
| % international | 19[4] | 17[5] | 15[6] | 10[7] | 12[7] | 8[7] | 14.5[8] |
| faculties & equivalents # | 17[9] | 18 | 18[10] | 16[11] | 18 | 7 | 12 |
| FT teaching staff 2013-14[12] | 2,769 | 1,662 | 2,712 | – | – | 1,098 | 942 |
| FT teaching staff 2013–14 excluding med & dent[13] | 2,067 | 1,452 | 2,244 | – | – | – | 633 |
| research $ per faculty member 2013[14] | $235.9 | $248.2 | $467.3 | – | $281.0 | $65.6 | $139.1 |

| University | UBC | U of A | U of T | U de M[1] | U de M[2] | UQAM | Dal |
|---|---|---|---|---|---|---|---|
| total income 2013-14[15] | 2,296,421 | 1,903,619 | 3,594,322 | 1,276,336 | 1,641,911 | 511,431 | 663,075 |
| general operating income 2013-14[15] | 1,205,036 | 1,061,748 | 1,924,073 | 718,995 | 965,797 | 398,088 | 447,895 |
| % from govt[16] | 49.7 | 56.6 | 34.6 | 71.2 | 70.1% | 72.6% | 46.5% |
| % from tuition & fees[17] | 39.5 | 28.5 | 58.5 | 19.1 | 20.8% | 23.2% | 37.5% |
| endowment net asset balances 2014[18] | 826,127 | 993,688 | 1,880,821 | 276,490 | 310,140 | 0 | 376,424 |
| Macleans[19] ranking 2013 | 2 | 5 | 3 | 12 | -- | 13[17] | 6 |
| ARWU[20] ranking 2013 national | 2 | 5-6 | 1 | 5-6 | -- | 19-23[19] | 8-16 |
| ARWU[21] ranking 2013 international | 40 | 101-150 | 28 | 101-150 | -- | 401-500[19] | 201-300 |

NOTES TO TABLE 3.2

1 Without affiliated institutions.
2 With affiliated institutions: École des hautes études commerciales (HEC) and École Polytechnique.
3 AUCC (2013). 2013 preliminary full-time and part-time enrolment at AUCC member institutions. http://www.aucc.ca/canadian-universities/facts-and-stats enrolment-by-university/headcount, rounded to nearest ten.
4 UBC. 2013 Annual Report on Enrolment. https://senate.ubc.ca/files/downloads\va_2013w_enrolment_report.pdf. Data are for UBC-Vancouver.
5 Government of Alberta. International Headcount Enrolment within the Alberta Post-Secondary Education System Website: https://open.alberta.ca/opendata/system-wide-headcount-enrolment-within-the-alberta-post-secondary-education-system. Document: https://open.alberta.ca/dataset/9d5b3f25-3fa5-4600-a48c-ba200ca6c4a8/resource/5776c043-d497-45bb-acb4-f63293443043/download/international-headcount-enrolment-within-the-alberta-post-secondary-education-system.xlsx
6 University of Toronto. Enrolment Report 2013-2014. http://www.planningandbudget.utoronto.ca/Assets/Academic+Operations+Digital+Assets/Planning+$!26+Budget/Enrolment+Report$!2c+2013-14.pdf
7 Québec. Ministère de l'Education supérieur, Recherche et Science, 5 May 2014 http://www.education.gouv.qc.ca/fileadmin/administration/libraries/documents Ministere/acces_info/Statistiques/Etudiants_internationaux_universitaire Etudiants_intenationaux_Universitaire_2013.pdf.
Autumn trimester international enrolments for 2013: U de M: 4,491; HEC: 1,833; EP: 1,691; UQAM: 3,153. Denominator: AUCC 2013 data.
8 MPHEC. Enrolment Statistics. Table 5: Enrolment of International Students by Province, Institution, Registration Status, and as Percentage of Total Enrolments, 2012–2013 to 2016–2017 http://www.mphec.ca/media/158817/enr_table5_2016_2017_e.pdf.
9 UBC. Office of the Senate. There were 12 faculties at UBC Vancouver and 6 at UBC Okanagan in 2013, including one dual faculty.
10 https://data.utoronto.ca/wp-content/uploads/2018/05/2013-Facts-Figures.pdf – accessed 18 November 2020.
11 U de M. Rapport du recteur 2013. https://secretariatgeneral.umontreal.ca/public/secretariatgeneral/documents/doc_officiels/documents-institutionnels/rapport-annuel/Rapport-du-Recteur-2013-Fr.pdf.
12 Including medical and dental teaching staff. Statistics Canada: Number of full-time teaching staff at Canadian universities, by rank, sex.https://www150.statcan gc.ca/t1/tbl1/en/cv.action?pid=3710007601.
13 Excluding medical and dental teaching staff. Statistics Canada: Number of full-time teaching staff at Canadian universities, by rank, sex.https://www150.statcan gc.ca/t1/tbl1/en/cv.action?pid=3710007601.
14 Sponsored research income per faculty member in $000s. Research Infosource Inc. Canada's Top 50 Research Universities 2014. https://researchinfosource.com pdf/Canada_s%20Top%2050%20research%20universities%202014.pdf.

15  In thousands of dollars. Canadian Association of University Business Officers (CAUBO) Financial Information of Universities and Colleges 2013–14.
16  Percentage of general operating income from government. CAUBO. FIUC 2013–14.
17  Percentage of general operating income from tuition and other fees. CAUBO. FIUC 2013–14.
18  Net asset balances in the endowment fund, end of fiscal year 2013–14. Canadian Association of University Business Officers (CAUBO) Financial Information of Universities and Colleges 2013–14.
19  2013 *Maclean's* university rankings, http://www.macleans.ca/education uniandcollege/2013-university-rankings.
20  UQAM was ranked 13th by *Maclean's* in the comprehensive institution category. All other institutions in this table were ranked in the medical/doctoral category by the *Maclean's*.
21  Academic Ranking of World Universities 2013, http://www.shanghairanking.com ARWU2013.html
22  This ranking was for the Université du Québec, rather than for UQAM.

# 4

# Trends and Themes in External Governance

External governance encompasses the complex relationships that universities have with external stakeholders that control or mould the university's mission, structure, direction, finances, policies, and activities. For publicly funded universities, relationships with government, often framed by legislation, regulation, and funding mechanisms, are key elements of external governance. However, as seen in chapter 3, many other bodies and agencies are also involved.

This chapter summarizes our findings about the universities' external governance in the mid-2010s, based on documentary sources and interviews with university members, government officials, and others. We begin by describing key aspects of provincial government oversight and similarities and differences across the five jurisdictions. We then review the role and impact of the federal government before turning our attention to professional bodies and other stakeholders and, finally, to the behaviour of the universities themselves.

## PROVINCIAL OVERSIGHT

The provincial governance of the case universities appeared to be broadly similar insofar as the universities all operated under provincial legislation, received provincial operating funding, and were subject to similar policy and regulatory regimes. Also, provincial governments appointed some of the members of their boards. That said, there were also differences regarding several of the following dimensions of the universities' external governance.

## INSTITUTIONAL ARRANGEMENTS

Each provincial government had a department or ministry responsible for policy and programs related to universities, as well as to colleges and other post-secondary institutions. In some cases, the department also had responsibility for science and innovation policy; in others, for labour market initiatives and training. Universities interacted at the provincial government level not only with the department responsible for higher education but also with other departments of government (e.g., science and technology, labour, health, forestry, or agriculture), and the objectives, policies, and programs of these latter departments did not always align with those of the former. In some provinces, other bodies played roles in the external governance of universities, either by virtue of their own authority or through the provision of advice. These bodies ranged from the Maritime Provinces Higher Education Commission, to the Superior Council of Education in Quebec, to the more recently established Higher Education Quality Council of Ontario.

At the time of the study, in all the provinces except Quebec, universities advocated collectively with their respective provincial governments through organizations such as the Research Universities Council of BC and the Council of Ontario Universities. This was in addition to their individual advocacy.

### LEGISLATIVE FRAMEWORKS

There were differences among provinces regarding whether universities operated under a post-secondary sector act (Alberta), a university system act (BC), individual acts (Ontario, Nova Scotia), or both university system and individual acts (Quebec). The existence of an individual act appeared to create a different dynamic between the university and the government than existed where there were collective acts. Universities operating under collective acts tended to get swept up in legislative changes aimed at the sector at large – or intended to address situations at other institutions – whereas those with their own acts appeared to have somewhat more control over their governance.

The legislation under which the case universities operated as of 2013 varied greatly in longevity – Dalhousie (Dal, 1863), l'Université de Montréal (UdeM, 1967), l'Université du Québec (UQ, 1968), the University of Toronto (U of T, 1971), the University of British Columbia (UBC, 1996), and the University of Alberta (U of A, 2004). The acts also varied in levels of specificity and prescriptiveness. The "act" seemed to figure much more prominently in the thinking of university and government officials in some provinces than in others. An interviewee at U of A said:

> I don't know, for example, in Ontario, how regularly people refer to the legislation, but here everything is referred to the legislation.

So shall we do this, how are we empowered by the legislation, what does the legislation say, what kind of language is in the legislation? So it certainly has an impact on how we think about ourselves ... If you say PSLA, people know what you are talking about.

At the time of the interviews, some officials at both Dal and UdeM regarded aspects of their acts as less than optimal, but they appeared reluctant to seek revisions for fear of opening themselves up for unwanted changes. The comments of a government official in Alberta suggested that governments also pick their moments carefully in opening up legislation: "Obviously, you do that in political cycles, right? ... So if there's going to be any legislative changes, those would likely follow [an election], probably in the first year of the government mandate."

The governing structures provided for under the acts differed significantly: four of the institutions were described as bicameral (Dal, UQAM, U of A, and UBC); one was tricameral (UdeM); and one was unicameral (U of T). For those universities with boards or equivalents, external members were in the majority (counting alumni as "external"), except in the case of UQAM, where the board had an internal majority. As noted in Chapter 3, the existence of a majority of external members on university boards appears to be taken for granted in most of the country; that said, the appropriate balance between internal and external board members has long been a major issue in Quebec.

Legislative diversity notwithstanding, all of the acts assigned responsibility for initiating important academic matters to the university – more specifically, to the senate or equivalent body within the internal governance structure. The legislation was thus foundational in protecting academic autonomy. An interviewee who had served in senior positions in the Ontario public service commented: "The governance structure is one statute away. Honestly, anyone who has done their thinking about the whereabouts of the governance structure, it's one piece of legislation away, and one party away, and you get in a party, a neo-con party, that wipes this out, it will wipe it out." As deeply engrained as bicameral governance is in Canada, universities' legislation may be a fragile foundation for their autonomy and capacity for academic governance.

### ACCOUNTING STATUS

Provinces differed as to whether they were deemed for accounting purposes to "control" their universities and in whether universities were within the government reporting entity (GRE). Because universities in BC and Alberta were within those provinces' GREs, they had less authority over their finances than universities in Nova Scotia and Ontario, and their capacity to respond to other needs (e.g., to borrow money to build infrastructure or residences) tended to be correspondingly less. Although charter universities in Quebec were outside the GRE, all Quebec universities were required by law to obtain provincial approval for major infrastructure projects.

### PROVINCIAL POLICY AND REGULATORY DIRECTIONS

All five provincial governments appeared to be seeking to align universities' activities or outcomes more closely with desired public policy goals. Provincial governments were described as increasingly concerned about ensuring that universities' activities address labour market needs and contribute to economic growth and innovation. The instruments the provincial governments employed or contemplated varied, from mandate letters or MOUs, to funding mechanisms, to legislation, official policy statements (*énoncés de politique*), and regulations. Quebec universities were required to report annually to the Commission de la culture et de l'éducation de l'Assemblée nationale and to appear before the commission every three years. In some cases, a province appeared to have adopted an idea from another one. For example, the practice of providing government letters of expectation to universities appeared to have migrated from BC to Alberta. In all provinces, regulation and accountability requirements were said to have increased substantially in recent years.

### PROVINCIAL ROLES REGARDING INSTITUTIONAL GOVERNANCE AND LEADERSHIP

In Alberta, the province appointed the university's board chair and all non–*ex officio* board members, some as public board members and the rest upon nomination by constituency groups. According to an interviewee, the provincial government ran "the process [for appointing the chair and public members] very much like filling a human resource vacancy ... in government." In BC, the government appointed more than half the members of a university board (including alumni association nominees). In contrast, Order in Council appointees made up less than one third of the members of U of T's governing council and around one third of UdeM's board, and the Nova Scotia government made appointments to the Dalhousie board only upon nomination by that board. Except for the rector, the members of the board of UQAM were all appointed by government, most of them upon designation by university bodies or groups, and some as representatives of the college sector and of the social, cultural, business, and labour communities.

Most of the case universities recommended to government external candidates for appointment to their boards, using some form of skills matrix to identify and assess candidates for particular vacancies. In the case of Alberta, the process was unique in that the provincial government sought and screened applications and then invited the board chair to review the results and make a recommendation. At five of the six universities, the president or rector was appointed by the board. At UQAM, the rector was formally appointed by the government upon the recommendation of the UQAM board of directors, but this took place after a consultation by means of a ballot and the process was described by interviewees as an election. Except at UQAM, provincial governments did not play a role in the appointment of the president at the time of the interviews. In BC, the president's compensation required approval by the province's Public Sector Employers Council.

There were differences between provinces in the ways that governments related to universities. In Nova Scotia, Quebec, and Ontario, presidents were the principal interlocutors with governments on behalf of their institutions. A board chair might accompany a president who was meeting with a minister or other government official on a particularly important occasion, and/or board chairs might receive periodic communications from government to make sure they were aware of developments or obligations; normally, however, it was the president with whom the government communicated. Depending on their particular backgrounds and connections, board leaders or members might communicate with government officials on particular issues, but this was typically at the request of the president or rector rather than at the behest of government. In Alberta, by contrast, there were direct and formal relations between government officials and board chairs (Alberta 2013). In BC, the government required board chairs to sign government letters of expectation (since replaced by government mandate letters) on behalf of the universities.

In most provinces involved in this study, presidents (rather than board chairs) were described as the principal interlocutors with governments. But it seemed that roles might be evolving. For example, board chairs in Ontario had begun meeting together and had recently undertaken to organize an annual governance conference, with the assistance of the Council of Ontario Universities. At the same time, the Ontario government was beginning to view chairs as important and to communicate with them.

## IMPACT OF PROVINCIAL HISTORY, POLITICS, AND POLICY

Despite the many similarities in provincial governments' goals vis-à-vis universities at the time of the interviews, their goals varied in specifics and in flavour, and there were differences in how governments pursued them.

*Nova Scotia*

Historically, Nova Scotia universities had been relatively autonomous. As seen in chapter 2, for most of their history they had been essentially private in funding and control. A Report on the University System prepared for the premier in 2010 (the O'Neill Report) described them as follows:

> Universities are independent entities, not government departments. They have their own assets, both tangible (e.g., buildings and equipment) and intangible (most notably reputation). The faculty, staff, and administrators are not public servants ... Although the government may appoint some of the members, the boards of governors are autonomous agents responsible for the oversight of the individual institutions. This implies that the institutions can and should be responsible for their own operation and for the strategic directions they choose to take. It is true that they rely to a considerable extent on government funding and are affected by tuition fee policy choices. Ultimately, however, their financial fortunes are determined by decisions they make about such things as cost levels and structures, program design and delivery, and student and faculty recruitment ... While government policy can set the broad framework within which they operate, the universities have and should continue to have considerable authority over and responsibility for their own success or failure. (Nova Scotia 2010, 16)

Nova Scotia's fiscal capacity was, and still is, very constrained. The province faces serious challenges, including an aging population, low rates of economic growth, and relatively poor population health status. Owing to the large proportion of university students from outside the province, provincial operating funding per student was among the lowest in the country at the time of our study, even though operating funding per capita was third-highest (Dalhousie 2013, 13). Although the number of university-level institutions in Nova Scotia had decreased as a result of the merger of two smaller ones into Dalhousie, with ten such institutions as of 2013, Nova Scotia continued to have a large university sector for a province of its size. To varying degrees, the universities faced the prospect of declining enrolments (due to demographics and increased competition for international students) and deepening financial challenges. According to the O'Neill Report and officials interviewed for this study, the province was not in a position to solve the problem through increased funding. The sustainability of the university system was in doubt. At least two of the province's university-level institutions were in very serious financial straits. Government officials were concerned about whether the university boards as presently composed had the capacity and expertise necessary for sound decision-making.

Provincial officials echoed the O'Neill Report in stating that the government did not want to control the universities. With respect to one institution in financial distress, a senior official said: "We don't want to own them, we don't want to have to consolidate their financial debt situation into the province's financial books." Concerning the universities generally, he noted that "they're relatively large organizations, so they need long-term scope in order to be well managed, and to undertake the things that they do – for example, fundraising and capital campaigns are very important – they need to have autonomy, and scope, and time to work."

According to provincial interviewees, the universities were not operating as a system. One said that in meetings with university presidents, "we say to them: 'You are a system; you need to work together … [Does it make sense to have] eight business schools for a province with 950,000 people? Maybe we need one business school, but delivering programs on eight campuses' … And [the presidents are] just saying: 'No, no; not going to talk about that; that's not our business; I'm here to run and represent my university.'" This official went on to say: "We in the government are trying to deal with the universities as a system. The current governance structure – there is no system – there's just ten separate institutions each with its unique context, environment, needs and challenges … We need a system solution and, on the governance level, there is no system."

In light of the challenges facing Nova Scotia, the provincial government wanted universities to contribute more to the economic and social development of the province. For their part, university officials perceived government as having become increasingly engaged with their sector, tending to intervene in university matters in an inchoate manner. Government officials acknowledged that they were expecting more from universities, even while reducing funding. Their apparent strategy was to secure changes in the structure and behaviour of the universities through memorandums of understanding (MOU) between the province and the institutions. Whereas the first two MOUs had been negotiated, key elements of the third had been imposed by government. A provincial official described the purpose of the third MOU as

> to bring about restructuring of the university system in the province [and] to achieve [ ] apparently contradictory objectives ... First, ... to reduce the cost structure of the system to something that the province can support, which may or may not be in contradiction with the second objective, which is better outcomes from university education in terms of our skilled labour force needs and also in terms of research and development and alignment with economic development and social development priorities. We're asking for more, better, at the same time we're reducing the funding level.

It was envisioned that the next step might be an arrangement "where we basically fund the universities through a five-year contract – and in this contract [with individual institutions] you have to deliver this, this, and this – and if you don't do that, we can step in and we can require you legally to fulfill the requirements of the contract."

### Quebec

As described in chapter 2, the higher education system in Quebec is distinctive in Canada. Its development has been influenced by nationalist ideology, a provincial tradition of consultation, and an incremental approach to policy-making. It features a unique, two-level (CEGEP and university) structure and the coexistence of charter universities with a provincial network. Other distinguishing features relate to the extent of student activism, the policy of low tuition fees, the strength of unions, and the early creation of provincial research-funding agencies. Despite periodic turbulence, there has been considerable continuity in Quebec higher education since the great changes of the 1960s (Trottier et al. 2014).

At the time of the interviews for this study, a Parti Québécois (PQ) government – elected in the wake of the Maple Spring – was in power. The new minister had undertaken broad consultations with stakeholders leading to a Summit on Higher Education early in 2013, followed by the establishment of four working groups on key dimensions of higher education (e.g., framework law, finance). Interviewed in June 2013 for the purpose of this study, a senior government official described the Quebec higher education scene as "en pleine ébullition" (in a state of ferment).

It was a time of great uncertainty for stakeholders in higher education, because the extent and nature of the changes that would emerge from the working group process were unknown. The process appeared to have succeeded in calming tensions within the sector, but strongly divergent views remained. Major changes in the structure of the system were expected or feared, depending on one's vantage point. Provincial student union and faculty union leaders looked forward to a new framework law and council of universities, believing that these would constrain institutional, board, and executive autonomy and power. Some faculty union and student leaders interviewed said that the state should oversee universities, rather than boards with a majority of appointed members. On the subject of university autonomy, a faculty union official had this to say:

> Il faut faire attention avec ce concept puisque nos gestionnaires aiment à se servir de ce concept pour se retirer de la surveillance gouvernementale. On fait une distinction entre l'autonomie de la mission intellectuelle et scientifique de l'université qui est fondamentale et protégée. Tous les professeurs doivent se battre pour la protéger. Derrière ce combat se cache quelque chose de vicieux, c'est que les administrateurs veulent la récupérer et l'appeler "autonomie universitaire" qu'ils assimilent à une autonomie de gestion et là on n'est pas d'accord parce que c'est le rôle de l'État de garantir l'autonomie intellectuelle des scientifiques.
>
> [One must be careful with this concept because it can be used by university administrators to justify withdrawal from government oversight. We make a distinction between [their misguided conception of autonomy and] the autonomy of the intellectual and scientific mission of the university, which is fundamental and protected. All professors must fight to protect the latter. Behind this fight hides something vicious – namely, administrators appropriating the concept of "university autonomy" and subsuming it into management autonomy. That, we disagree with, because it is the role of the state to guarantee the intellectual autonomy of academics.]

In contrast, some university officials were concerned about the prospect of *more* government and/or union and/or student association influence or control over universities. Fundamental questions about university education in Quebec raised in recent years – about the level at which universities would be funded and the sources of that funding, the relationship of government to universities, and the structure of the university sector – remained unresolved. Furthermore, the PQ government had introduced into the National Assembly in the fall of 2013 a charter of secular values that would have prohibited public sector employees – including university employees – from wearing religious symbols (e.g., turban, hijab, kippah). This would have applied not only to faculty and staff but also to students employed as teaching or research assistants. The rectors of a number of charter universities and the rector of UQAM publicly opposed the proposed legislation on various grounds, including that it infringed on university autonomy (Charbonneau 2014).

After the turbulence of 2012, Quebec universities did not speak with a common voice. Differences among them resulted in the dissolution of the Conference of Rectors and Principals of Quebec Universities (CREPUQ) in 2013. Following its demise, each university spoke on its own behalf to government, the media, and the public, while an Office for Interuniversity Cooperation (BCI) administered previous agreements on program evaluation, registrarial matters, libraries, and the like. In the words of one ministry official interviewed, universities were expected to "use public funds wisely. Avoid waste and implement tight cost control. Contribute to the development of the Quebec population through high-quality education. Be sensitive to the job market in training highly qualified personnel. Contribute to the economic growth of Quebec with high-quality and specialized research."

The university officials we interviewed complained about the increasing regulation and new accountability requirements since the 1990s, as well as the associated paper burden. The UQ had prepared a heuristic chart indicating Quebec universities' accountability requirements to the provincial government in 1990, 2000, and 2012. It showed that in 1990, four laws governed the sector (some applicable only to the UQ, others to all universities) and regulation and reporting requirements were relatively minimal. By 2000, reporting requirements had expanded significantly, principally under an Act Respecting Educational Institutions at the University Level. By 2012, many new acts governed the sector, including laws on financial administration, the governance and management of information resources, and anti-corruption measures, resulting in a host of new approval, policy, procedural, and reporting requirements. There were, for example, new approval requirements for borrowing, capital projects, financial contracts, and agreements with the federal government. Requirements to provide projections and reports ranged from employment-related matters (salaries and benefits, staff composition and advancement, etc.), and budgetary and financial matters, to matters of library resources, community service, support for Indigenous students, health and well-being initiatives, and inter-institutional collaboration.

Institutions were required to have ethics policies and to report violations of them. New regulations on funding, contracting, tuition and other fees, balanced budgets, reduction of administrative expenses and staff, and other matters had also been introduced during the intervening decade. External governance was also exercised through funding, in that highly specific budgetary measures gave the government influence over universities' governance and strategic choices (Trottier et al. 2014). According to one government official interviewed, the government recognized that accountability requirements had burgeoned and was seeking to develop a streamlined and more effective approach to regulation of the sector.

Although Quebec universities are subject to a common policy framework, the status of charter universities differed from that of members of the UQ system in several respects. Charter universities are outside the government reporting entity; by contrast, the UQ falls within that entity, which means that its financial statements roll up into those of the province. This meant that the UQ was subject to public sector accounting standards, which was described as somewhat of an administrative burden. A ministry official interviewed cited two larger implications of the UQ's status with respect to the reporting entity: first, as illustrated by the Îlot Voyageur incident at UQAM, the effects of financial mismanagement within the UQ showed up on the province's books; and second, salaries for senior administrators within the UQ were subject to government caps. According to a number of system-level interviewees, the salaries of the rectors of major charter universities were perceived by many in government and the media as excessive, while at the same time those of rectors, deans, and others within the UQ were not competitive. This compensation gap between the two segments of the university sector was said to negatively affect UQ institutions' capacity to recruit senior administrators.

Provincial-level interviewees tended to characterize UQ institutions as close to the state. One said:

> Le modèle de l'Université du Québec est plus près du Gouvernement, ce qui fait que les dirigeants des universités du réseau sont un peu comme des fonctionnaires de l'État avec des conditions d›emploi décidées par le [Secrétariat de]s Emplois Supérieurs du Québec. Le recteur a un salaire déterminé par la Loi et donc, même s'il ne remplit pas de commandes, la gouvernance est beaucoup plus encadrée.
>
> [The Université du Québec model is closer to Government, which means that leaders of universities in the network are a bit like government officials, with terms of employment determined by

the Secretariat for the Employment of Senior Officials of Quebec. The rector has a salary determined by law and, even though they don't actually follow orders, institutional governance is much more constrained.]

## Ontario

With respect to external governance, one government official interviewed said that, although there are other models, "in Ontario we tend to focus on setting policy and using funding levers and instruments to try to achieve our desired outcomes, rather than explicitly articulating a prescriptive kind of policy framework or entertaining governance reform or restructuring. That has tended to be the way in which we've operated in the past, tying some level of funding to key performance indicators and multi-year accountability agreements."

This interviewee explained that the government recognized and supported institutional autonomy, provided that it was "exercise[d] within a context of the need for productivity, fiscal sustainability, value for money, and the exercise of responsibility for the significant investment the government is making with taxpayers' dollars." This official went on to say:

> While we may expect different things from different institutions in the system, depending on their mandate and areas of strength and excellence, our overall approach (from the government point of view) will be one of setting government policy within which the universities operate and using funding levers to achieve the policy objectives. We transfer $3.5 billion in operating transfers to the twenty universities. So, in exchange for our writing those cheques, there are some expectations, I guess, with respect to accountability and alignment with government policy objectives, and achieving some value for money.

The Ontario government viewed itself as having made major investments in universities and as providing fiscal stability and predictability by signing Multi-Year Accountability Agreements with them, in the expectation that government goals with respect to access, quality, and accountability would be met. At the same time, the government was seeking to increase differentiation and innovation within the system by striking three-year Strategic Mandate Agreements with universities. It was anticipated that the latter – described by one university official as akin to "job descriptions for universities" – would increase differentiation, innovation, and accountability, as well as strengthen the link between funding and outcomes. There was also expected to be continued focus on fiscal sustainability and productivity increases.

At the time of the interviews, provincial funding had dropped to 42 percent of universities' operating income (CAUBO 2014), and operating funding per full-time-equivalent student was the lowest in the country (COU 2012). The great bulk of provincial funding came through the basic operating grant and other enrolment-based mechanisms (e.g., graduate expansion, funding for medical and nursing programs), supplemented by smaller performance and special-purpose grants. The funding formula was said by university officials to have provided a level of predictability and consistency that was very helpful in long-term planning.

Although the proportion of university operating income from the province had fallen, provincial expectations and regulation had not. A government official said:

> In the four years that I have been in this position, I have seen an increase in the desire to align university outcomes with government priorities ... with respect to access and quality, as well as accountability ... A more significant focus on that, as well increased accountability and transparency for the use of funds not just [for] universities, but any publicly funded body or institution that receives significant public funds, to make sure that there is good value for money and that there are demonstrable outcomes and results.

The combination of reduced government funding per student, increased expectations and regulation, and limits on tuition fee increases was challenging for the institutions. One university official observed that "as the public support goes down, the degree of regulation and regulatory intervention goes steeply in the opposite direction, which is on one level deeply ironic, on another level incredibly frustrating. So it's as if the edicts multiply daily from Queen's Park, and yet there is no corresponding increase in the resources that they either give us directly or enable us to raise for ourselves."

*Alberta*

The Alberta government began implementing Campus Alberta – described as a learner-centred, collaborative, accessible, innovative system of post-secondary institutions – in 2002 (Alberta Learning 2002, 1). As of

May 2014, the province had twenty-six publicly funded higher education institutions, categorized according to a six-sector model. All were governed by one piece of legislation: the Post-Secondary Learning Act (PSLA).

The Alberta government sought to coordinate activities within the post-secondary sector. To that end, a Campus Alberta Strategic Directions Committee, chaired by the minister, was established in 2008 under the PSLA, composed of board chairs of publicly funded post-secondary institutions. Its purpose, according to the ministry's website, was to "communicate provincial-level directions" and "enhance collaboration among institutions in order to further the vision of Campus Alberta." Government officials also met with vice-presidents academic, vice-presidents finance, and student representatives on a quarterly basis.

Beginning in 2003, publicly funded universities and colleges were included in the government reporting entity. Legislation introduced in the spring of 2015 stipulated that institutions in the "SUCH" sector (school boards, universities, colleges, and health entities) "be included directly in budget revenue, expense, assets and liabilities" (Government of Alberta, Treasury Board and Finance 2015). The province's Auditor General audited most post-secondary institutions, including the universities. A university official said that in Alberta, "[universities] have no degree of separation from the Crown. We are viewed by the Auditor General as part of the government and the only difference between the department and the university is that we are part of the broader public sector."

So strong was the assumption in government that it could direct post-secondary institutions that the involvement of the Auditor General on university audit committees was said to help protect institutional autonomy. The above interviewee added:

> Overall, I'd say, given Alberta, it's a positive thing to have the Auditor General in the audit committee, because in ten or eleven years, more often than not, the Auditor General has acted to keep the government out of our business by invoking the standards of independent board-governed institutions. So the Auditor General holds us to account on our macro financials, which is not bad in an era of accountability. On the matter of autonomy under the rules, the Auditor General keeps telling the minister, "If you want to do that, you've got to change the rules, you've got to change the legislation."

Board chairs, who were appointed by the province, were in many ways the conduit between their institutions and the government. Unlike in the eastern provinces, there were direct and formal relations between board chairs and government officials. Whereas presidents tended to play the lead role in communication with governments in other provinces (supplemented on occasion by board chairs), according to interviewees, "in Alberta amongst the senior public service, its board chair speaks to minister, president speaks to deputy minister." Letters of Expectation, introduced by the government in 2013 and signed by the board chair (representing the institution) and the minister (representing the government), set out the parties' respective responsibilities and expected outcomes. The province also required the board of each public institution to submit accountability reports annually, including a comprehensive institutional plan, an annual report, and a business plan – all approved by the board and signed by the board chair. In addition, the chair was responsible for signing a mandate and roles document that set out the respective roles of the board of governors and the ministry.

As well as appointing university board chairs, the province appointed all non-*ex officio* board members – some as public board members and the rest upon nomination by constituency groups. In the case of public members, the provincial government sought applications, assessed them, and typically gave the board chair of the university in question an opportunity to provide nominations or a recommendation before making an appointment. The government sought to ensure that all public board members knew they were there to act in the best interests of the province and taxpayers.

Given that one political party (the Progressive Conservative Party of Alberta) had held power in Alberta for more than four decades at the time of the interviews for this study, and that the government appointed board chairs and public members, there tended to be ties between the party and members of boards. One interviewee commented that "when [a recent major budget] cut happened to universities and post-secondary institutions, that create[d] an odd internal tension within the PC party, because you have these PC lifers [on boards] who are very influential who are now angry. So it's a bizarre and very personal relationship here in Alberta ... There is [a] tremendous amount of awkwardness, to say the least, between the institutions and the government."

Notwithstanding the longevity of the party in power, there had been rapid turnover of ministers responsible for post-secondary education – six different ministers in the previous six or seven years, according to one university official. The latter described relationships between university and government officials as having two aspects – the formal relationship governed by the PSLA, and the personal relationships between university leaders and members of government – with the latter relationships more important than the former. Each time the minister changed, the university needed to restrike that relationship, which could be stronger or weaker as a function of the minister's personality, knowledge, interests, and other factors. Turnover of deputy ministers was also perceived to be increasing.

While appreciating the great work universities were doing and describing government's relationship with them as "pretty healthy, solid, [and] functional," provincial officials appeared to be concerned about universities' efficiency and responsiveness to evolving external needs. A government official said:

> We have been closely working with institutions and with learners to make sure that our advanced learning system is going to meet the needs of learners today and tomorrow. And quite frankly, I worry about universities in particular and their ability to adapt, to be agile to change in the face of very restrictive faculty agreements, onerous decision-making processes that take years, and the ability of institutions to adapt and change in a timely fashion to meet learner demands.

In the previous budget, the government had significantly reduced operating funding to institutions even while expecting further progress on strategic directions and outcomes established for the system. Asked what was next, a government official said:

> The main piece over the next twelve months is we are going to have to redefine accountability and what accountability means. Again, just from [the ministry responsible for post-secondary education] alone, [there is] 2.2 billion dollars' worth of investment this year and there is probably another ... five or six hundred million dollars of investments that flow into the institutions across the province, whether it's on the research side of the equation, or health, or education, or whatever. So with 10 percent of the operating budget of the Government of Alberta going to post-secondary institutions, I think the accountability equation is changing a little bit and will continue to evolve as it relates to what Albertans and learners expect from a quality perspective coming out of their institutions.

### *British Columbia*

As of 2013, British Columbia had twenty-five public post-secondary institutions, including eleven universities, five of which were special-purpose teaching universities in operation since 2008. Most universities were governed by the BC University Act. A notable feature of that act was that it spelled out not only the minister's powers but also things the minister was *not* entitled to do: "The minister must not interfere in the exercise of powers conferred on a university, its board, senate and other constituent bodies by this Act respecting any of the following: (a) the formulation and adoption of academic policies and standards; (b) the establishment of standards for admission and graduation; (c) the selection and appointment of staff."

The Liberal government in power at the time of the interviews was strongly focused on ensuring that the province's post-secondary sector equipped students with the job skills demanded by the labour market. It placed great emphasis on trades training and encouraged all post-secondary institutions to focus on preparing students for jobs. The ministry also wanted to see an increase in the number of international students and had launched an initiative to reduce administrative costs through joint service delivery.

The government had implemented a results-based accountability framework for the public post-secondary system beginning in 2003–04. Under that framework, universities prepared an annual accountability document, including a three-year plan and report. These institutional accountability plans and reports included goals, objectives, and performance measure results for each institution along with contextual information to describe the institution's role in providing services to their students and communities. Every year, the ministry provided the universities with budget letters that outlined the student enrolment targets and operating budget allocations to support targeted programs and priority issues for the coming fiscal year. Tuition and mandatory fee increases for domestic students were limited to the rate of inflation.

Beginning in 2008, the government required each university to sign a government letter of expectations, reflecting agreement on respective roles and responsibilities, including high level strategic priorities and public policy issues. The letter was to be signed by the minister and the university board chair. The universities objected to numerous items in the initial letters. According to one interviewee, the letters were based on models used by government in sectors over which it had more direct control and did not take account of distinctive features of universities, such as bicameral governance. Some aspects of the initial letters were described as highly intrusive and inappropriate; for example, they sought to regulate what could be sold in vending machines on campus. The more recent versions were regarded by university officials as "better in the sense that [they don't] try to reach [in] too directly to determine what decisions we might make within the university." The letters of expectation were replaced by annual mandate letters after the government issued new Taxpayer Accountability Principles in June 2014.

In BC, as in Alberta, universities were included in the government reporting entity (GRE). BC universities had been moved into the GRE in 2003 at the insistence of the province's Auditor General, even though the universities opposed his recommendation and the provincial government initially rejected it. As the consequences of inclusion within the GRE became apparent, the universities had had discussions with the provincial government about getting out, but those talks had not come to fruition because of the extent of the debt that the universities would have had to assume. The general trend over successive governments had been toward gradual tightening of government oversight and institutional accountability through reporting. Universities and colleges were required to report financial results and budget projections on a quarterly basis to the Ministry of Advanced Education and follow the government's accounting standards. All debt financing had to be approved by the provincial government. University collective bargaining took place within mandates set by the Public Sector Employers Council, and boards were not allowed to borrow, sell assets, sign collective agreements, set executive compensation, or establish new academic programs without government approval.

Although there were many similarities in provincial governments' goals vis-à-vis universities, there were variations in the substance and flavour of those goals and the ways governments pursued them. Interviews at the provincial and federal levels suggested that governments' goals and approaches also varied within jurisdictions with changes in the party in power. For example, both the Parti Québécois (PQ) government in power at the time of the interviews (in 2013–14) and the Liberal government that preceded it prioritized access to higher education and economic contributions, but it appeared that the PQ assigned relatively more importance to the former and the Liberals to the latter. In addition to variations in policy emphasis between governments of different political stripes, there were variations in the nature and strength of governments' relationships with stakeholders. For example, interviewees indicated that the PQ government was in communication with student and faculty union leaders to a much greater extent than the previous Liberal government, and assigned their views more salience.

The nature of the relationships between governments and universities varied between provinces. Some very positive things were said by interviewees representing both "parties." At the same time, there appeared to be elements of mutual frustration and incomprehension between university and government officials. To the latter, universities could appear unresponsive, intransigent, and ungrateful for the massive public funding they received. For their part, many university officials interviewed said that members of the provincial ministry or department responsible for higher education had little understanding of universities. Even in some large provinces, it was observed that ministries lacked strong policy capacity (and here, one university official observed that lack of policy capacity could be a blessing: "In a way, it's lucky because if they really had the capacity to drive what they say they want to do, I'd be worried"). The result, however, was that government policies were often out of touch with institutional realities and did not achieve their intended objectives.

Oddly, even though it was provincial legislation that provided for universities to govern themselves in accordance with bicameral principles and to protect and foster the exercise of academic judgment, examples of government/university interactions were cited in which government officials appeared not to understand how universities are governed. For instance, the first version of the BC government's letter of expectations "didn't understand the distinction between what the Board of Governors had authority over and what the Senate had" and was thus inconsistent with the University Act. Similarly, an official at U of A said that when the provincial government

> started talking about Campus Alberta and thinking about the system as a whole and how the pieces fit into the system, I don't think they had a plan ... [or] a lot of policy depth ... The government ... wanted to get their hands on things and shape things, but because institutions run independently, over the years they had actually lost some of their understanding of how things worked. So when they started talking about taking a stronger leadership role, sometimes they didn't seem to know what they were talking about.

University and other interviewees indicated that ministries or departments tended to be restructured every few years and that not only ministers but also deputy ministers and assistant deputy ministers turned over frequently, causing discontinuity in relationships and the need to orient people anew. A number of government officials acknowledged this phenomenon and suggested it was not likely to diminish.

According to one Quebec official, that province had long followed the practice of appointing to a senior position in the Ministry of Higher Education an individual who had been a senior academic administrator at one of the province's universities. That practice meant that at least one senior official had personal experience in the university world, "got" how they functioned, and could serve as a point of contact and even an interlocutor for universities with the ministry.

One long-serving public official, who had had the opportunity to observe interactions between provincial officials and university officials for many years, identified several factors that may help explain the nature of the government/university relationship. First, deputy and assistant deputy ministers have complex and demanding jobs and tend to serve for relatively short periods in any given department. Second, those serving in the higher education department or ministry may have little understanding of how universities are governed and how that constrains the authority of presidents and boards; as a consequence, these people may apply to universities approaches originating in other sectors. Finally, governments and universities operate on different time scales. "Governments change visions every time a new government is elected," and senior officials naturally pursue what ministers want, whereas universities tend to have longer-term agendas.

A number of university board members and senior administrators also commented on the discrepancy in time horizons. A board chair described the mission of the university as "creating a great future for society" whereas "governments need to produce satisfaction in the very short term in order to get re-elected." A university official reflected:

> If you think about it, [for] an undergraduate, typically it takes four years and some would argue for four and half years [to graduate]. That's longer than a government's mandate, so our ability to turn on a dime when we have commitments that we must make to the students is not as easy as government might think it is ... And then if you have a different government or change in cabinet, you might totally get a different turn, therefore different expectations, therefore different targets. So that's kind of our reality.

An additional factor, identified by a provincial official in Alberta, was that in a province, the "revenue reality [of which] change[s] very dramatically on an annual basis ... the expectations of resource availability from institutions doesn't necessarily match up with government's ability to provide that level of stability on an annual basis."

Whether universities in a given jurisdiction are public or private depends on a number of factors, including legal status, control, finance, and common usage (Levy 1986). Public or private status is thus more ambiguous than status relative to the GRE. Although, with a very small number of exceptions, Canadian universities are regarded as public, we found that the status of universities in relation to the public sector differed significantly among the five provinces. The Report on the University System for Nova Scotia stated in September 2010 that "universities are independent entities, not government departments" (Nova Scotia 2010, 16); yet in BC and Alberta, universities were deemed to be part of the public sector (and thus within the GRE). In Quebec, universities' statuses differed for accounting purposes (charter universities being outside the GRE and UQ institutions within it), but all universities were deemed to be public for other specific purposes (e.g., under the Loi sur l'accès aux documents des organismes publics [LRQ, C A-2.1]). There were instances in BC and Alberta, but also in other provinces, of policies, procedures, and mechanisms developed for other parts of the public sector being applied to universities.

Seen from a distance, it appeared that the case universities were all experiencing increased state supervision, but that they were all at different points on the state supervision/autonomy continuum. At the time of the study, universities in Nova Scotia and Ontario appeared to be more independent of government than those in the West, insofar as they came under individual acts rather than a common act, had proportionately fewer government appointees on their boards, were outside the GRE, and received a relatively low proportion of their total revenue from the province. Alberta's university sector appeared to be the most public insofar as board chairs were appointed by the provincial government (which advertised and conducted a search and selection process) and were deemed to be accountable to the minister. Quebec was unique in that, although all universities in the province were subject to common policy and funding regimes, the province had both charter universities (which had individual acts, proportionately fewer board members appointed by government, and rectors who were not appointed by government, and were outside the GRE) and the UQ, which was within the GRE and subject to more state control.

The case universities were members of provincial university systems. However, they stood out from their provincial counterparts because of their histories, size, program breadth and depth, and research and related capacity. Their status and needs could pose a dilemma for provincial governments. For example, a Nova Scotia official said:

We in Nova Scotia and in the Atlantic region need a strong Dalhousie. We need that research capacity here. How does that play out in a system where everything is supposed to be equal, where, when you establish a grant program, everyone focuses on the per capita share? All the universities are trying to build research strength in their particular areas of expertise and are looking for financial support from government. How do you balance that need against the need to have a strong hub?

The tension between "raising all boats" and promoting the competitiveness of one or more flagships played out in other provinces and at the federal level as well.

### FEDERAL POLICY AND PROGRAMS

What role, if any, does the federal government play in the governance of universities in Canada? As noted in chapter 2, although the provinces have constitutional responsibility for education in Canada, the federal government has long been involved in funding universities and continues to provide financial assistance to students and to fund research, owing to its jurisdiction over trade and commerce, its spending power, and its concern for general management of the economy (Bakvis and Cameron 2002). Government spending powers, which are not set out explicitly in the constitution, enable governments to spend outside their areas of jurisdiction. Since the federal government has greater fiscal capacity than the provinces, it is able to use its spending power to achieve policy objectives it could not otherwise pursue (Shanahan 2015a).

Current and former Ottawa officials interviewed spoke about jurisdictional sensitivities. A typical comment was that "over the years the federal government has been very careful to walk the line of not getting involved in the education side of the house." Another former federal official said:

We have always tried to respect the fact that universities were the creatures of the provinces and that the provinces were really different and had their own priorities. But, by the same token, we were trying to influence what was done at universities, how it was done and the impact that it had. It was kind of walking that tightrope between trying to influence without being or being seen to try to take over responsibility for something that was a provincial responsibility.

## THE EVOLUTION OF FEDERAL RESEARCH AND INNOVATION POLICY

Increased federal investment in university research beginning in the 1990s was prompted by perceptions among government officials, in Canada as in other countries, that universities could play key roles in economic development. In the words of Halliwell and Smith, "the period from 1997 to [2010] represent[ed] a major and purposeful federal reinvestment in the universities designed to enhance Canadian research capacity and to catalyze private sector innovation through R&D 'push'" (2011, 376). That reinvestment entailed a dramatic initial increase in federal funding for research (Bakvis 2008, 208). Over time, "increas[ing] proportion[s] of funding from the research councils [were] aligned with federal priority areas ... [Many programs carried] an explicit expectation of business partnerships, knowledge transfer mechanisms and the generation of economic returns" (Halliwell and Smith 2011, 384). This reflected changed federal expectations of universities. An interviewee described "a growing expectation from individuals within the federal government – both elected and non-elected officials – that the universities in particular play a more direct role in various aspects of socio-economic development," noting that this expectation had "increased in conjunction with the statements and advocacy positions of the universities themselves." All the while, federal laboratories and scientific facilities were seeing their budgets cut, and the importance of intramural research decreased relative to university research (Halliwell 2013).

There was a shift from peer review toward merit review of funding proposals. A number of former officials interviewed for this project spoke about this trend. One recalled that a granting council had begun involving people from outside the academy in review processes in the late 1970s – a novel idea at the time, and one that seriously rattled university members. That shift gathered strength with the growth in the size of research and research infrastructure projects (and the corresponding need to assess the capacity of universities and hospitals to implement them), the involvement of private sector and other partners, and interest in assessing the impact that proposed projects would have on achieving targeted outcomes (Doern, Castle, and Phillips 2016).

Along with the increase in the number and complexity of programs came a corresponding increase in regulation. One granting agency official described "a whole set of both federal and provincial regulations that universities are required by law to adhere to around research [that] have to do with everything from material-handling to protection and care for animals to data handling." Among the regulations was a tri-council code of ethics to which all university-based researchers were required to adhere. Whereas "research ethics were first a system of self-regulation arising from within the social system of science ... [in recent decades], federal requirements for the regulation of research ethics ha[d] grown via rules established first by the granting councils individually and then in the late 1990s reinforced as a regulatory regime by the granting councils collectively" (Levasseur 2009, 260). This regime was developed by agreement between the granting councils and the universities through the Association of Universities and Colleges of Canada (now Universities Canada) and implemented in stages during the late 1990s and early 2000s. The tri-council policy statement on ethical conduct of research involving humans meant that, in order to receive continued federal funding, each university would have to appoint a Research Ethics Board to review the ethical acceptability of all research involving humans conducted by their faculty, staff, or students, regardless of where the research was conducted. According to one interviewee, university presidents regarded this approach as less intrusive than the equivalent regulations in the US.

With respect to the impact of federal politics on universities in Canada, Doern, Castle, and Phillips (2016) concluded that there had been both continuities and differences across Liberal and Conservative governments and prime ministerial eras. Information obtained in interviews was consistent with this. According to a former granting agency official with many decades of experience in this policy realm,

> when you look at all those years, when we would meet with government officials and elected officials, there was never really a question about whether this [investing in university research] is something we should do or not. That was a given, and there was no argument about the need to do this. There were differences in approach – about how much to do this or that, what kinds of investments. The balancing between the basic and the more applied, the commercialization ...

When the Conservatives came to power in 2006, some within the research community feared that the new government would undo investments made under previous Liberal governments. That did not happen. The Conservatives did, though, add programs that reflected their own priorities, which included a greater focus on applied research and economic (relative to social) outcomes. A Liberal government was elected in the fall of 2015 and re-elected in 2019. At the time of the Ottawa interviews for this study in 2015, it was too early to tell whether and how its policies would differ from those of its predecessor. Overall, interviewees expected continuity – informed, perhaps, by a broader conception of the role of universities – as well as relatively more support for basic research.

## THE IMPACT OF FEDERAL POLICY AND PROGRAMS ON UNIVERSITIES

The picture that emerged from interviews and other sources was of major changes over recent decades in the nature of university-based research and the work of faculty members and others involved. Asked whether and how university research had changed, one former granting council official said:

> It's been dramatic in terms of transformation! There's no doubt whatsoever. It's hard to know where to start, because if you take a look at what was happening in 1975–77, it was investigator-driven research. There were peer review committees that were totally academic. Research was starting to evolve in Canada, but it was still a very small community. You had very little collaborative research ... So the world was very different. It was very simple in the way it was structured ... So, it has changed dramatically!

The extent and nature of the changes no doubt varied by discipline and professional field, but overall, former and current federal and granting council officials suggested that the changes in federal policy and programs described above echoed those in other jurisdictions, thus contributing to the following:

- The creation of more funding programs and opportunities for "researchers" (as faculty members engaged in research tend to be described), as well as the opportunity for those in many fields to secure funding for projects of a scale that would not have been feasible in the past.
- Incentives to formulate proposals for research that would contribute to desired outcomes (e.g., address targeted questions or needs or result in commercialization).
- Incentives to work in partnership with firms or other organizations.
- The opportunity and need to do proportionately more work in teams that cross institutional, sectoral, and international boundaries.

- More administrative complexity and accountability – time writing up proposals and agreements, getting approvals, administering projects, and completing paperwork needed for audit purposes.
- Greater competition to secure funding.

Although the federal government does not have constitutional responsibility for universities in Canada, interviews for this study and the existing literature suggest that the evolution of federal government and agency policy and programs for research in recent decades had a profound impact. In the first place, it altered the balance between and funding of research activity and educational activity at Canadian universities. Funding shifted from transfers to the provinces to spending on university research, thus increasing research capacity while passing on more of the costs of education to students and their families (Bakvis 2008, 219). Federal programs also reshaped the nature of research performed at Canadian universities, making possible projects of new magnitude in many fields. Those programs also bolstered associated university-based research capacity, mobilized research resources for targeted purposes, and forged partnerships among universities as well as between universities and other organizations. University officials interviewed spoke about the importance of the federal government's contributions and the resulting research opportunities, while noting the increasingly targeted nature of the support, the increased focus on economic outcomes, and differences in levels of support across disciplines. In the process, federal policy altered the distribution of research capacity and activity at universities across the country, thus increasing the degree of hierarchy and specialization. According to Bakvis, "the new resources and the manner in which they were allocated worked to the benefit of the major research-oriented medical-doctoral universities. The result is what some would call a two-tier or even a three-tier system" (218). The U15 group of universities, which enrolled 68 per cent of all doctoral students in the country in 2008, accounted for around 80 percent of all the external research funding received by Canadian universities (Lacroix and Maheu 2015, 226).

The actions of the federal government and its agencies gave rise to changes in institutional structure, governance, policies, and staffing. University policies with respect to research conducted at universities (e.g., scholarly integrity, human research ethics) were developed or revised to comply with granting councils' requirements. The business of major universities' boards of governors, and, in some cases, their senates or equivalents, was affected by federal initiatives. The boards appeared to be paying more attention to research due to the financial sums and risks involved, the significance of research performance for institutional reputation, and the extent of the associated compliance obligations. Academic governance bodies' roles and structures related to research appeared to be more varied. For example, at UBC, where there is a senate for each campus, the UBC Okanagan senate had a Learning and Research Committee, whereas the Vancouver campus senate did not and was described as focused primarily on educational matters. U of A's General Faculties Council had a committee on research, as did the University Assembly at UdeM, whereas at UQAM, the academic committee (commission des études) considered matters related to research but did not have a specific committee for this. At Dalhousie, research had recently been added to the mandate of one of the senate's committees.

Ottawa's actions also spawned changes in the extent and nature of administrative leadership and support for research. To enable their faculty members to succeed at securing grants and contracts, carrying out projects, and administering associated pre- and post-award processes, universities created positions for vice-presidents and associate vice-presidents of research as well as professional research managers. They also appointed staff in areas such as proposal development, research administration, contracts and agreements, internal audit and compliance, knowledge mobilization, and research communication. Deans and chairs now saw themselves as having responsibility for facilitating their colleagues' research. In addition, there were often associate deans or vice-deans with this specific responsibility. Levels of support available to researchers varied by institution, but increases in staff and other resources devoted to research administration and support were reported by interviewees at many. These resources supported faculty members as they prepared proposals, thus enhancing those proposals' prospects of success. An interviewee at one of the larger universities commented that support for "proposal development ... mean[t] requiring or assisting investigators in thinking differently about their research. There are all sorts of positions around the university now that are ... research facilitators and proposal editors or whatever." Many of the resources devoted to research administration and support were, however, devoted to compliance: "The ramp-up in terms of regulatory requirements and compliance of capability requirements has been enormous ... The reporting requirements are so much more stringent. The regularity of reporting, the audit requirements, and so forth. It's a huge impact on the institution, and not just on our time, but on researchers' time as well." Federal requirements also shaped the planning in which universities engage. Universities were required to develop strategic research plans (SRPs) in order to be eligible for funding from the Canada Foundation for Innovation. This requirement was described as pivotal and as having engendered new conversations between senior administrators and faculty members. Administrations now had a reason – indeed, a need – to formulate or formalize research priorities for their universities.

Federal investments of course generated many opportunities and challenges for faculty members and students. To degrees that varied by discipline and profession, federal investment in university-based research expanded the opportunities available to faculty members to pursue research – and, along with it, the amount of paperwork involved. Numerous university interviewees echoed the observations of federal officials about how much more time many faculty members now had to spend on developing research proposals, arranging partners, and reporting on projects. To succeed, faculty members learned to propose and conduct projects in ways that met criteria for impact, partnerships, and so on. Given the need for junior faculty members to demonstrate success in research in order to secure promotion and tenure, the impact of federal policy and programs on academic careers in many fields was strong and "très structurant" (highly structuring).

Finally, the nature and manner of federal investment in university research may have complicated relations between university administrations and faculty members, staff, and students engaged in research. On the one hand, federal investment encouraged universities to get and keep "world-class" researchers and to free them up from other responsibilities. On the other, the obligations associated with grants and agreements required universities to track and monitor compliance with financial and other requirements more actively than in the past. This amplified the role of universities as "internal regulators" (Levasseur 2009, 255) of the conduct of faculty, staff, and students involved in research.

In sum, it is clear that notwithstanding the provinces' jurisdiction over education and their role in the governance of Canada's universities, the federal government shaped universities and their activities very significantly through its policies, programs, and research spending. Ottawa's impact was felt at all levels of the institutions – from governance, planning, administration, and resource allocation to the opportunities available to individual faculty, graduate students, and staff. At the most basic level, as Lacroix and Maheu (2015) have pointed out, governments' decisions about the relative extent of support for research in government organizations, universities, and other organizations are critical in determining the capacity of universities to lead in the advancement and application of knowledge. In that respect, the federal government's privileging of universities as sites for research relative to government labs reinforced the formers' capacity, which in turn had benefits for their capacity to educate students and disseminate knowledge.

Given the federal government's strong impact on and within research-intensive universities, should it be viewed as a participant in their external governance? That depends on one's definition of governance. If one equates governance with control, no. The Public Sector Accounting Board (PSAB) of the Chartered Professional Accountants of Canada (CPAC) defines control as "the power to govern the financial and operating policies of another organization with expected benefits or the risk of loss to the government from the other organization's activities" (PSAB n.d., 8). By this definition and associated indicators, the federal government does not control universities in Canada (with a very few possible exceptions involving institutions that operate under federal legislation). The national policies, regulations, and requirements to which universities have been required to adhere were, for the most part, voluntarily agreed to by them in exchange for the opportunity to secure federal research and research infrastructure funding. That said, by a broader definition of external governance, the federal government is exercising its powers in order to induce universities and their members to contribute to its policy priorities – whether that be in the volume and nature of the research they conduct, in commercializing or mobilizing knowledge, in adhering to ethical standards in the conduct of research, or in other ways.

Federal policies and agreements in other realms besides research (e.g., trade, immigration, environment) also shape the parameters within which universities must operate. This relates, for example, to the faculty, students, and staff institutions are able to recruit, to the competition they face, and to the regulatory standards to which they must adhere. Figure 4.1 summarizes current major federal and provincial instruments affecting university governance, decision-making and activity.

The tenor of relationships between universities and the federal government seemed to differ from the one between universities and provincial governments. Doern and Stoney have characterized the former relationship as a quasi-principal/agent one because "the direction of pressure and interaction works in both directions" (2009a, 6). Our interview findings were consistent with this in that they confirmed the importance of the advocacy of key university presidents and Universities Canada in the development of federal policy and programs (Bakvis 2008; Morgan 2009; Doern, Castle, and Phillips 2016). The influence at the federal

| FEDERAL INSTRUMENTS | | PROVINCIAL INSTRUMENTS |
|---|---|---|
| • International relations and trade agreements<br>• Immigration policy<br>• Intellectual property legislation<br>• Economic and innovation policies<br>• Research and knowledge mobilization policy, programs, and funding and associated regulations (e.g., safety, ethics, animal care, equity in hiring) and reporting requirements<br>• Student financial assistance<br>• Infrastructure funding<br>• Indigenous affairs (e.g., legislation, funding, services)<br>• Tax policy/regulation of charities<br>• Regulation of electronic and other communication technologies)<br>• National security policy and programs<br>• Official language programs<br>• Transfers to provinces and associated conditions | UNIVERSITY GOVERNANCE & DECISION-MAKING | • Governing legislation (e.g. acts and charters)<br>• Appointments to governing bodies)<br>• Post-secondary legislation and regulation (e.g., degree authorization, fees, sexualized violence prevention)<br>• Public-sector legislation (e.g., access and privacy, executive compensation, accessibility, accountability requirements)<br>• General legislation (e.g., employment standards)<br>• Immigration policy (QC)<br>• Memoranda of understanding, mandate agreements, letters of expectation, etc.<br>• Funding and associated requirements (operating, capital, research, student assistance, etc.)<br>• Quality assurance (e.g., program approval and review processes)<br>• Audit and accounting regimes<br>• Policy and programs in other realms (e.g., health, economic development) |

Figure 4.1 | Major government influences on the governance of universities in Canada. *Source:* Eastman, Jones, et al. (2019, 338).

level of what Burton Clark (1986) described as "academic oligarchy" could also be seen in the roles played by former and current university leaders in the leadership of granting agencies and in science policy development. Universities appeared to chafe at increasing provincial regulation, yet they seemed to have relatively happily accommodated themselves to federal initiatives, for which their leaders were some of the principal advocates.

The federal government's actions could be seen as turning universities increasingly into sites of what Bourdieu described as "large-scale production" – by reducing opportunities for faculty members to pursue research of their choice, burdening them with paperwork, subjecting them to more administrative oversight, and/or increasing administrative staff and expenses. However, there are respects in which Ottawa's actions can also be regarded as potentially enhancing universities' capacity for knowledge production. It appeared from our interviews that the federal government, even while increasingly prioritizing economic outcomes and targeting funds to particular areas, sought to make possible original research of international calibre in the fields it funded. Among its desired outcomes were the creation of world-class research capacity, the training of highly qualified personnel, knowledge mobilization, and commercialization – in other words, complex outcomes. Federal agencies were apparently seeking to foster autonomous knowledge production, as well as forms of production subject to managerial control. By funding research of international calibre in some fields, they strengthened universities' capacity – indeed, their need – to attract top researchers and to provide the resources and conditions necessary for their work.

In contrast, some provinces appeared to look to universities for production tailored to prescribed outcomes (e.g., "job-ready" graduates, particularly in high-demand fields). One federal official recounted:

> From what I saw and discussions with my provincial colleagues – and I think this was principally on the education outcome side – there were certainly provinces where there was great desire to micromanage in a way that – and I wouldn't even hazard a guess as to whether it's appropriate or not on the education side, but it certainly didn't make sense on the research side – [for example, focusing on] the employability of graduates, [on] getting more people into discipline A as opposed to discipline B. And that would kind of slop over a little bit into "Why don't they do research into what we're interested in?" as opposed to do research in what they're excellent at.

## PROFESSIONAL AND ACCREDITING BODIES

Asked to describe the external governance of their universities, most interviewees spoke about the roles of governments – in particular, provincial governments. That said, bodies that accredit professional programs – some of which are provincial and others national in scope – were also described as playing major roles. Professional faculties and programs are prominent within the academy. A provost interviewed estimated that around 65 percent of students in degree programs at major Canadian universities would require or seek some sort of professional or other externally adjudicated credential for employment:

> At that point, then, who is really in charge of the quality of the program if the trumping agent in the quality matrix is the accrediting body? ... The hard question is to what extent the external agencies can compel the institutions to make financial decisions outside the normal academic priorities. You don't have to go even beyond medicine ... to say, it's pretty dramatic, it's unsettling, how much money gets moved in response to threats of loss of accreditation.

In some cases, program accreditation is required in order for students to practise, but in others, whether or not to seek accreditation is genuinely a matter of choice for the faculty or department. It appears that some units seek accreditation even though it shapes and constrains academic decision-making, principally because it is perceived to be advantageous for them in recruiting students as well as for students in obtaining employment. A science department chair interviewed cited the accrediting body for his discipline as an important influence on decision-making in his department even though accreditation was optional in the field. He explained, "we're going to go through our accreditation review next fall and we will make sure that we are accredited by the [Canadian accreditation body], so that we can recruit students on that basis."

Comments about the extent of accrediting bodies' influence – or, indeed, control – over academic and financial decisions were made by university officials across the country, but concern about the extent of the control exercised by professional bodies seemed to be especially great in Quebec. A number of interviewees at all levels of both case universities in Quebec expressed serious concern about intrusions into academic decision-making. It was not possible to discern whether there was greater reason for concern in Quebec or greater sensitivity to the issue within the case universities in that province.

### OTHER EXTERNAL ACTORS

Responses to our open-ended questions about the external governance of universities focused on the central role of provincial governments, touched upon the roles of the federal government and accrediting bodies, and offered less information and insight into the mechanisms by which other external actors affect university decision-making. As illustrated in figure 2.1, the latter actors are numerous. Municipal governments regulate matters such as land use. University issues are increasingly referred to and resolved by the courts. Various accounting and other bodies affect university decision-making and activity by virtue of their standard-setting and regulatory roles. Seemingly technical decisions by those bodies can have far-reaching unforeseen consequences for universities. Universities are far from unique in being subject to increased regulation. As one interviewee observed, "we are [ ] a much more regulated society."

Other sets of actors lack authority but may exercise influence. These include businesses, lenders, bond rating agencies, foundations, donors, and policy, advocacy, and interest organizations. Concern about the extent of business and donor influence on universities was expressed by some faculty and student union representatives, and by others interviewed, especially in Quebec. At UQAM in particular, defence of the university's autonomy from non-government influences – including industry and professional associations – was a major concern for many interviewees. Overall, however, the interviews did not generate sufficient systematic information to enable us to shed light on the mechanisms by which universities protect themselves from, or allow, such intrusion.

The lack of information about the roles of non-government actors in shaping university decision-making and activities represents a major lacuna; more research is needed on the roles and impact of external bodies other than senior governments on university decision-making in Canada.

### THE CASE UNIVERSITIES AS ACTORS

Universities are far from passive objects of external control and influence. On the contrary, they and their constituents engage with, and both influence and are influenced by, a plethora of actors associated with their teaching, research, and service missions.

"Provincial university" or equivalent status appeared to translate into greater than average institutional latitude and autonomy. An interviewee at U of T said:

> The province's role is relatively modest in terms of governance, at least for us ... Because this was the province's original, primary university [and is] a very clear leader, we do tend to have ... [an] ability to operate with some understanding of our unique role in the

provincial quasi-system, and as such I think our governing structure is being treated with some respect, and there is limited sign of any inclination to meddle.

Being the provincial university also appeared to carry with it expectations and obligations. Asked what was distinctive about U of A, an interviewee there said:

> Well, you have to remember that the University of Alberta was founded by the first act of the first legislature of Alberta, so we were founded as the province was being founded, and we were founded to serve the sons and daughters of Alberta, but also to be national, and to be, to as great an extent as possible, global in nature ... There are [now] twenty-six institutions in Alberta in the post-secondary sector. So when you talk about what's distinctive, we do consider ourselves and understand ourselves to be the flagship, meaning we are the largest, the oldest, and the most research-intensive, and it is our understanding that we have a specific role to play in the province because of that, that is, to advance this province.

The case universities, though subject to external forces, were also very much agents. Their presidents advocated on behalf of their individual institutions and (except in Quebec at the time of the interviews) collectively with their respective provincial governments, the federal government, and the public at large. Their government relations strategies appeared to have both common features (e.g., preservation of institutional discretion and decision-making room, expanding the overall "pie," securing additional resources for their institutions) and distinctive ones. Dalhousie's strategy, for example, appeared to comprise the following elements:

- Maintaining and insisting upon Dalhousie's right under its act to recommend board appointments to the province.
- Remaining financially sound and well governed and managed (because, as a board member explained, whereas a financially healthy institution can be master of its affairs, "a needy child" – that is, one that runs deficits and needs assistance – runs serious risk of government interference).
- Being responsive to provincial needs and priorities: "To the extent that you can be a solution for them ... they will be there to help you; you, on the other hand, need to be willing to grow in this area or that area that aligns with what they want."

- Getting ahead of issues: "Dalhousie's approach is to try to take the initiative on this – to try to take control of the agenda rather than be controlled by it."

Other case universities' government relations strategies had other emphases, reflecting their particular situations. For example, while advocating for increased provincial investment in the university sector at large, the Université de Montréal urged government to recognize the financial needs arising from its status and activities as a leading global francophone research university. For their part, UQAM's leaders were proud of its special status within the UQ and sought greater autonomy, calling publicly in 2014 for its removal from both the GRE and the UQ. Officials at U of A had been deeply concerned about a previous minister's efforts to transform Campus Alberta into "a much more ministerial-directed entity with twenty-six moving parts." The minister in question had, in the words of one interviewee:

> wanted to brand all of us under Campus Alberta with pins and logos and we would go to the world as "Campus Alberta," lowercase university of Alberta. That would be a disaster because, while we don't like rankings for all kinds of sound reasons, the world does and we would never get Campus Alberta ranked, and if you did, it wouldn't do very well. So we need an identity internationally to compete and you have to be roughly top 100 to get any attention from that peer group, and if they can't find you because you've been pushed into Campus Alberta, then quite literally they won't talk to you.

Fortunately, from the point of view of U of A, the former minister's conception of Campus Alberta had not come to fruition.

The provincial governments were preoccupied with the good of their respective provinces, whereas the universities were very much players on the national and global stages – recruiting faculty and students nationally and internationally, belonging to global and regional networks, engaged with partners around the world, and attentive to their competition and reputations across the country and abroad. To some extent, universities could compensate for provincially imposed constraints through actions at the national level (such as advocacy for federal funding) and/or the global level (such as compensating for domestic tuition fee limits by enrolling more international students). Precisely because of the general *lack* of alignment of federal and provincial policy, Canadian federalism appears to provide scope for universities to pursue their own priorities in ways they could not in a more coordinated federation or a unitary state. In this respect, federalism as practised in Canada fosters institutional autonomy and agency. It also militates against large-scale reform (Tupper 2009; Jones and Noumi 2018).

In sum, our study confirmed that the external governance of universities in Canada is a complex web. Provincial governments, with their constitutional responsibility for education, played central roles in the external governance of the case universities. Provincial policies had some common elements, but the nature of the state–university relationship varied significantly from province to province. Interviews and other sources confirmed that the federal government played a less official and visible – but nevertheless significant – role in the case universities' evolution. The influence of accrediting bodies on curriculum development, resource allocation, and standards was a subject of comment and concern. It merits further study, as do the roles of external bodies other than senior governments in shaping university decision-making and activity.

# 5

# Internal Governance

Having examined the case universities' external governance, we turn to the internal dimension – to how the six universities were organized, led, and managed at the time of the interviews and how authority was distributed and exercised within them. We start with interviewees' characterizations of universities as organizations and a high-level comparison of the case universities' governance structures. The focus then shifts to their governing bodies – their boards and senates or equivalent, their faculties, and their academic departments. Anonymized quotations give voice to interviewees and convey the flavour of their input. The universities' leadership positions, including the roles of presidents or rectors, deans, chairs, and others, are described, as is the participation of faculty members and students in governance. After a brief overview of strategic planning and budget processes, the chapter concludes with reflections on the state of the six universities' internal governance and how it supported the exercise of academic judgment while fostering institutional responsiveness to external needs and demands.

## THE CHARACTER OF UNIVERSITIES AS ORGANIZATIONS

One question we asked interviewees was whether they perceived universities as differing from other types of organizations, and if so, how. While identifying some similarities (such as the need to balance the books and to be accountable for the use of public money), interviewees at the case universities overwhelmingly described universities as highly distinctive in their missions, governance complexity, cultures, approaches to consultation and decision-making, the autonomy of professors, and other respects. Many of the features they cited corresponded squarely to Mintzberg's (1979) description of professional bureaucracy, including as it related to:

- diffuse authority levels and hierarchy,
- leaders who are not professional managers,
- academics who do not perceive themselves as employees,
- the lack of a simple measure of success such as return on investment, and
- collegiality in decision-making – a topic to which we return at the end of the chapter.

Several board members with backgrounds in other sectors commented on the distinctiveness of universities. One board chair said:

> I've never seen anything quite like a university; the complexity of the stakeholder groups is profound ... And everyone wants a say, everyone's interested, everyone wants to be part of the governance process ... To lead an institution with that complexity in stakeholder groups poses enormous challenges ... Businesses and public company boards, they are pretty straightforward: it's about ROI [return on investment] and shareholder return, and you can evaluate at every quarter when the numbers come out. You know how you are doing ... This is a completely different kettle of fish, much more complex, requires much more nourishment, and you've really got to have a lot of patience – and determination, too.

If we grant that Canadian universities as a group continue to differ from other types of corporations, how similar or different are they from one another? As noted in previous chapters, the literature portrays the university sector in Canada as relatively homogeneous. Most university officials interviewed seemed to share that view. For example, a senior official at UBC who had come from a university in another part of the country said that

> in terms of governance, there are always interesting differences, but [Canadian universities] are pretty similar in the way in which they govern themselves ... You can point to a lot of differences, but it's pretty similar overall, at least it feels that way on the ground.

The six case universities represented a small subset of Canadian universities at large. One might expect considerable commonality, at least among the five medical/doctoral institutions. What similarities and differences did we find?

## INSTITUTIONAL GOVERNANCE STRUCTURES

On one hand, there were important commonalities in the six universities' governance writ large. The fundamental principle of bicameralism – that control over the academic affairs of the university should be distinct from control over its business affairs – was reflected to different degrees and in different ways in the governance structures of all the universities. That was the case even at U of T, the only unicameral institution. An interviewee there explained: "[The governing council's] Academic Board [is the] premier board and really operating as the senate within a unicameral system ... We paid close attention ... when we worked out the allocations of responsibilities [within the governing council] to ensure that academic decision-making was influenced by academics and not by externals per se."

Each case university comprised academic faculties, centres and institutes, libraries, and "administrative" units (i.e., units performing diverse non-academic functions, from information technology to student services to physical plant maintenance to external relations). Although faculties were a recent development at UQAM and terminology varied between institutions, faculties played a central role in academic governance. They consisted principally of departments and/or schools. Notwithstanding the existence of interdisciplinary centres, institutes, units, and programs, the academic side of all six universities was organized largely along traditional disciplinary and professional lines.

At the same time, there was a great deal of diversity in the universities' institutional governance. Four of the institutions were essentially bicameral (Dal, UQAM, UBC, and U of A – the latter also possessed a large university–community liaison body mandated under provincial legislation). One university (UdeM) was tricameral, and one, unicameral. UQAM was part of the governance structure of the UQ. Several of the universities had more than one major campus, and these off-main-campus sites were aligned in different ways with their institutions' academic governance structures, in some cases being equivalent to faculties, in others having a more senior academic decision-making body.

The next sections of the chapter describe similarities and differences among the case universities as reflected in the interviews and documentary sources. The people we interviewed within universities were involved in institutional governance (academic and business), executive positions, academic administration, and student and faculty association leadership. Given the positions they occupied, the interviews shed more light on the distribution and exercise of formal institutional and academic

Table 5.1 | Composition of case universities' governing bodies

|  | Dal | U de M | UQAM | U of T[1] | U of A | UBC |
|---|---|---|---|---|---|---|
| **Board or GC[1]** | | | | | | |
| **Lay members:** | | | | | | |
| Govt-appted | 12 (44%) | 8 (33%) | 6 (38%) | 16 (32%) | 10 (48%) | 9[2] (43%) |
| Brd-appted | 3 (11%) | ≤ 4 (17%) | – | – | – | – |
| Other | – | 2 (8%) | – | – | 1 (5%) | – |
| Alumni | 4 (15%) | 2 (8%) | 1 (6%) | 8 (16%) | 2 (10%) | 22 (10%) |
| Faculty | 2 (7%) | 5 (21%) | 4 (25%) | 12 (24%) | 2 (10%) | 3 (14%) |
| Students | 3 (11%) | 2 (8%) | 2 (13%) | 8 (16%) | 3 (14%) | 3 (14%) |
| Non-academic staff | – | – | – | 2 (4%) | 1 (5%) | 2 (10%) |
| Chancellor | 1 (4%) | 1[3] | – | 1 (2%) | 1 (5%) | 1 (5%) |
| President | 1 (4%) | 1 (4%) | 1 (6%) | 1 (2%) | 1 (5%) | 1 (5%) |
| Other ex officio | 1 (4%) | – | 2 (13%) | 2 (4%) | – | – |
| Total voting members | 27 | ≤ 24 | 16 | 50 | 21 | 21 |

|  | Dal | U de M[4] | UQAM[5] | U of T[6] | U of A[7] | UBC[8] |
|---|---|---|---|---|---|---|
| **Senate or equivalent** | | | | | | |
| Faculty & librarians | 52 (67%) | 75 (62%) | 10 (46%) | 59 (48%) | / | / |
| Academic & other administrators | 16 (21%) | 24 (20%) | 3 (14%) | 31 (25%) | / | / |
| Students | 7 (9%) | 8 (7%) | 7 (32%) | 16 (13%) | / | / |
| Non-academic staff | – | 6 (5%) | 2 (9%) | 4 (3%) | / | / |
| Other | 2 (3%) | 8 (7%) | - | 13 (11%) | / | / |
| Total voting members | 77 | 121 | 22 | 123 | | |

Table 5.1 | Composition of case universities' governing bodies (*continued*)

|  | Dal | U de M[9] | UQAM | U of T[10] | U of A[11] | UBC[12] |
|---|---|---|---|---|---|---|
| Other Lay members: |  | / |  | / | / | / |
| Govt-appted |  | / |  | 7 (27%) | / | / |
| Other |  | / |  | 6 (23%) | / | / |
| Other | – | 2 (8%) | – | – | 1 (5%) | – |
| Alumni |  | / |  | 5 (19%) | / | / |
| Faculty and librarians |  | / |  | 2 (8%) | / | / |
| Academic & other administrators |  | / |  | 1 (4%) | / | / |
| Students |  | / |  | 2 (8%) | / | / |
| Non-academic staff |  | / |  | 1 (4%) | / | / |
| Other |  | / |  | 2 (8%) | / | / |
| Total voting members |  |  |  | 26 |  |  |

NOTES TO TABLE 5.1

/ = data not available
1  U of T's Governing Council.
2  Government appointed 11 members of the UBC board, 2 of whom were nominated by the alumni association.
3  At the time, the chancellor did not have a specific seat on the U de M board.
4  U de M's Assemblée universitaire.
5  UQAM's Commission des études.
6  U of T's Academic Board.
7  U of A's General Faculties Council.
8  UBC's Vancouver Senate.
9  U de M's Commission des études.
10  U of T's Business Board 2012/13.
11  U of A's Senate.
12  UBC's Okanagan Senate.

authority – that is, on governance at institutional, faculty, and departmental levels – than on the structure and functioning of inter-institutional bodies, centres, and institutes, or administrative areas of the universities.

BOARD GOVERNANCE

At the five universities with boards or equivalents, external members were in the majority (counting alumni as external), except in the case of UQAM, where the board had an internal majority. Table 5.1 shows the composition of the universities' governing bodies. As indicated in the previous chapter, the proportion of board (or, in the case of U of T, governing council) members appointed by provincial governments varied. Board members tended to represent similar major constituencies (e.g., the public, alumni, faculty, students, staff) and to include similar *ex officio* positions (e.g., chancellor, president), but there were differences in composition and structure, and the boards' roles and cultures differed as well.

*Dalhousie*

The portrait of the Dalhousie board that emerged from interviews in early 2013 was of an experienced board with a generally good relationship – and a modicum of tension – with the administration of a strong, long-standing president. As noted in previous chapters, Dalhousie was historically among the most private of the case universities. One interviewee explained that "the credibility of the board and its members is very important to external stakeholders. Our donors watch the decisions the board makes and form opinions about the confidence they have in the organization that they have invested in and or may wish to invest in in future. Being able to tell a good story from a governance point of view is really critical."

*UdeM*

The UdeM board was described as active and empowered and working closely with a strong rector. Board members depicted the board's role as one of high-level governance and oversight, including appointing, guiding, and supporting the rector. From the perspective of board members and senior administrators interviewed, the preponderance of external members on the board was appropriate and reflected good governance, in that the majority of board members were independent and brought valuable expertise to the governance of the university.

According to some faculty members and students interviewed at UdeM, the board and the university's executive had assumed more active roles relative to other bodies over time: "Les priorités sont de plus en plus définies par le haut" (Priorities are increasingly defined from above). The comments of an experienced member and observer of the provincial higher education scene suggested that the board's active role was typical of charter universities in Quebec:

> Pour moi ce qui est frappant dans l'évolution de la gouvernance dans les universités à charte, c'est la croissance du pouvoir réel exercé par le conseil d'administration. Il y a 40 ans le recteur faisait la pluie et le beau temps avec son conseil d'administration ... Aujourd'hui on peut dire que le recteur a un patron, qui est le conseil d'administration ... Le recteur [est] en sandwich entre la communauté universitaire, le sénat parfois et les groupes à l'interne à l'université et [le] conseil d'administration ... [Les membres du conseil] considèrent qu'ils ont des prérogatives et des pouvoirs d'orientation et de décision, et non pas simplement de s'assurer de trancher que les finances sont correctes. Ce n'est plus un lieu symbolique, c'est un véritable lieu d'exercice du pouvoir.
>
> [For me, what's striking about the evolution of governance in charter universities is the growth of the very real power exercised by the board. Forty years ago, the rector wielded significant influence over his board ... Today, one can say that the rector has a boss, which is the board ... The rector [is] between a rock and a hard place – between the academic community, sometimes the senate, and the internal groups at the university, on one hand, and the board, on the other ... [Board members] see themselves as having decision-making powers and prerogatives, well beyond assuring that the finances are sound. The board is no longer a symbolic body, but a real site of exercise of power.]

## UQAM

A different situation existed at UQAM, where the rector was elected and the role of the board of directors was constrained by the UQ on one hand and by the power of internal bodies and constituencies on the other. Although the board of directors was the supreme governing body at the institutional level, interviews with external members left the impression that it had relatively little decision-making room. This appeared to result from:

- the extent of government regulation – some rules applied to all universities, others were specific to the UQ;
- the roles of the UQ governing bodies and administration;
- the fact that the rector was effectively elected and sat on the board of governors of the UQ as well as on UQAM's board of directors;
- the membership of two other members of the university executive on the board of directors;
- the power of "la base" at UQAM and the ethos that initiatives should emerge "bottom-up" rather than "top-down";
- the tendency of faculty and student leaders to follow their organizations' "lignes de parti";
- the attendance of observers at board meetings; and
- the tendency of many faculty and students to regard "socio-économique" (socio-economic, i.e., external) members as "une menace qui ne devrait pas être là" [a menace that shouldn't be there] (in the words of one of those members).

One external board member interviewed indicated that the composition of the board tended to lead to a dynamic in which "on [external members] fait pencher la balance pour le pour ou le contre" (external members tip the scale for or against), rather than board members coming together to shape the strategic direction of or oversee the university.

Both UdeM and UQAM had executive committees composed of board members and chaired by the rector. At UdeM, the executive committee was responsible for matters delegated to it by the board, which, under the charter, could include all matters except the appointment of the rector. At UQAM, it was responsible under the act for the "current administration" of the university and for exercising powers delegated to it by the board of directors. It was described by a board member as "un mélange entre le conseil et un comité de direction" (a mix between a board and an executive committee). The existence of executive committees of this nature was common at Quebec universities (Quebec 2013) but not in the rest of Canada.

### U of T

Alone among the case universities, U of T was unicameral. It had a fifty-member governing council with an academic board, a business board, and a university affairs board. Of the fifty members, twenty-five came from within the university community and the other half were external. The chair and vice-chair were elected from among the sixteen government-appointed members. An interviewee described the thinking of the architect of unicameralism at U of T, former president Claude Bissell:

> The concept was that many universities with bicameral governance had a senate that was dealing with academic issues but had no particular authority over fiscal issues, or buildings, or [other things] hugely important to the academic mission. Conversely, you had business leaders and voluntary sector leaders who were appointed to boards that were often ... quite small and not very representative ... Those boards in turn had a business mandate ... that invariably extended into areas like collective bargaining, funding, budgets, and buildings, all of which were integral to the academic mission. Bissell's vision was to find a unifying structure that would provide an opportunity for the academic and operational missions to come together in one body, with separate key committees.

The unicameral model, first introduced under the U of T Act of 1971, had evolved over time and been shaped by five major reviews. The most recent had been a task force on governance initiated in 2007, the results of which included the creation of campus councils at the university's Mississauga and Scarborough campuses (University of Toronto n.d.a). In the words of one interviewee, the rationale for many of the changes had been to "very conscientiously delegate ... authority for decisions to the lowest reasonable and responsible level in governance – so that the most senior body can be freed up to do what governing boards should do."

Unicameral governance was described by most interviewees at U of T as effective, in that it avoided what they regarded as the artificial separation of academic and other matters associated with bicameralism. Some interviewees also noted that unicameralism tended to expose external members to the academic side of the university and faculty and students to the business side, resulting, "at least in some areas, [in] a greater appreciation that the governing body isn't a 'them' vs. an 'us.'"

## U of A

The board of the University of Alberta was described in interviews conducted in the spring of 2014 as increasingly active and pushing ahead with a "change agenda" focused on increasing relevance and efficiency. As noted in Chapter 5, the board chair and public members had been recruited and appointed by government, and compared to its counterparts at other case universities, the board appeared to be relatively close both to government and to the political party that had held power in the province for many decades. In response to budget cutbacks the previous year, the board chair had met with government officials "every week, every day" to secure reinvestment in the university and the sector.

The board's role on campus differed from that of its counterparts at the other case universities, in that the board seemed to take some initiatives on campus on its own behalf and to have an agenda distinct from that of the president. For example, whereas at most universities, strategic planning is led by the president, the board chair at U of A had led the comprehensive institutional planning process for 2014, meeting with every dean and conducting widespread consultations with various stakeholder groups. One board member said:

> The board has taken a very active role ... really pushing management and administration to say, you know, we just don't want you to come and tell us everything is good. We want to know how we are doing, we are here, we want to go there, how are we going to get there and how are we going measure it? And so we've been very active in that and pushing that notion.

University boards have traditionally been in the background, providing a steady hand on the tiller, guiding and supporting the administration. By contrast, the U of A board – in particular, its public members – had become more visible as a separate force. A university official said that at Alberta universities,

> the board chair is [increasingly] used as an agent of the minister to force the institutions to change ... Now the board is another constituency pushing its agenda, and we now have a very clear distinction between the public board members and the faculty, staff, and students. The public members are as aggressive right now in pushing the administration as are the faculty association and the students' unions.

All of this had changed the relationship between the board and the university's senior administration. A member of the latter said,

> I no longer assume the public members of the board are my allies, advisers, helpers; I see them as another constituency that I approach with all radar systems on full alert. And if it's the same in other institutions in Canada, then we may live to regret this because you won't

get the very best people taking these jobs. Why would you? And you begin to get the central administration whose prime directive is survival, not leading.

## UBC

In contrast, the UBC board was described during interviews in late 2013 as having a positive relationship with the administration; though built on mutual trust and confidence, it was also characterized by engagement and asking "tough questions." Depending on their backgrounds and experience, board leaders might participate in government relations, in concert with the president and other university officials, but there was no suggestion by interviewees that they were guided or directed by government, other than through policy, mandate letters, and other formal mechanisms.

### ACADEMIC GOVERNANCE

#### *Senates or Equivalent*

Each of the case universities had one or more bodies that fulfilled the traditional roles of an academic senate, but there were variations in their structure, functioning, and relationships with other internal bodies.

#### *Dalhousie*

Dalhousie's senate had been reformed in the 1990s to change it from a body consisting of all full professors and department heads into a representative body, consisting of around seventy members, including elected faculty members, elected student representatives, representatives of affiliated institutions, and senior administrators serving *ex officio*. Senate reform was said by a number of interviewees to have reduced the role of the faculty association in academic governance and to have separated academic governance from academic labour relations. One interviewee said,

> Certainly in the old days, the senate was a battleground between the DFA [Dalhousie Faculty Association] and the administration. In the pre-95 days, with 400 members and an average attendance of about 50, it was very much luck of the draw who would show up. Typically people would be lobbied to show up based on what was on the agenda. Question period was often an attempt to put

the president on the spot on various things, from the DFA. It's been an evolution since that time ... I'd say that now that type of senate is pretty much gone ... perhaps to the point where the senate is too calm at times.

The archaic statute under which Dalhousie operated sketched out in very general terms the nature of the senate's authority – "the internal regulation of Dalhousie College and University." The scope of that authority and the way it was exercised had then been delineated over time. Revisions to the Senate Constitution, approved by the senate and board in 2011 and 2012, had reduced the number of committees from thirteen to seven and introduced an attendance requirement. Student leaders were seeking greater student representation on the senate, but elections for faculty positions were relatively rare. More often, filling a vacancy "involve[d] deans finding somebody willing to sit on senate."

*UdeM*

The functions assigned to a senate at many Canadian universities were shared by two governing bodies at the U of M: the Assemblée Universitaire (university assembly) and the Commission des études (academic council).

The university assembly's functions under the charter included articulating the general principles for the orientation and development of the university and making recommendations to the board of governors on matters related to the administration and development of the university. As of fall 2014, it had around 115 members. Although the charter provided for the university assembly to be chaired by the rector or his or her designate, in practice there was also a meeting chair (*président des délibérations*) who chaired the discussions, typically a senior faculty member. An interviewee explained that the university assembly's role tended to be a catch-all:

> [Un de ses mandats est d'énoncer] les principes généraux qui président aux grandes orientations de l'université. Là on ne parle pas d'énoncer les grandes orientations, mais les "principes généraux." Mais ça c'est la théorie, parce que dans les faits ça veut tout dire et rien dire. Il y a une centaine de membres et c'est un peu là où se discute tout ou rien. Ça va du stationnement en passant par les bibliothèques. En réalité l'AU n'a pas de pouvoir sur ces choses-là.
>
> [[One of its mandates is to enunciate] the general principles that govern the university's strategic directions. Here, we are not talking about setting out the strategic directions, but rather the "general principles."

However, that's the theory. In fact, it means everything and nothing. There are a hundred members of the university assembly and it's where everything or nothing is discussed – from parking through libraries. In reality, the university assembly does not have power over those things.]

The role of the university assembly with respect to such matters was rather to make recommendations to other governing bodies or to the executive. Among the matters considered by the university assembly were the budget framework (which was provided to it for information and comment), the campus plan (which it recommended to the board of governors), and matters related to research. One interviewee explained that, although the role of the university assembly was largely consultative, there was an element of internal accountability: "le recteur doit rendre compte de plusieurs dossiers à l' Assemblée Universitaire" (the rector is accountable to the university assembly for various matters).

The level of participation in meetings was described as generally good (in part because of regulations concerning attendance), but positions for faculty members were often filled by acclamation rather than by election. In recent years, faculty members associated with the union had been playing a more active role on the body. One interviewee explained: "C'est l'association des étudiants qui nomme les représentants étudiants, mais ce n'est pas le syndicat des profs qui nomme les profs à l'assemblée. Sauf que quand le syndicat dit de voter pour un tel, c'est lui qui rentre. Le syndicat contrôle d'avantage la représentation professorale" (It's the student association that appoints the student representatives, but it's not the professors' union that appoints profs to the assembly. Except when the union says to vote for so-and-so, then that person is elected. The union has growing control of faculty representation).

The *commission des études* was responsible for coordinating instruction and for decisions concerning academic programs, including approval of new programs and the establishment of academic regulations. As of fall 2014, the *commission des études* was composed of around forty members, including the rector (as chair), all vice-rectors and deans, directors of affiliated schools, and representatives of students, professors, and sessional instructors.

## UQAM

At UQAM, a *commission des études*, chaired by the rector and composed of twenty-two members, was responsible for making recommendations to the board of directors concerning rules and procedures for teaching and research. Its membership included seven faculty members and seven students, one of each representing each faculty. Deans were observers, as were union representatives.

The *commission des études* was described as "une instance très vive" (a very lively body) in which there was a high level of participation. The student leader interviewed described it as an important body and one on which students could exert influence. As of 2013, its composition and powers were embedded in the collective agreement with the professors' union. The agreement provided that the *commission des études* would annually approve target class sizes for each department at each level. Article 7.08 specified that the seven professors elected to the *commission des études* were to include one dean or vice-dean, one director of an undergraduate program or module, one director of a department, and one director of a graduate program or research centre. The election of professors to the *commission des études* was conducted at a general assembly of the union (UQAM et Syndicat des professeurs et professeures de l'Université du Québec à Montréal 2009, 31).

## U of T

At the University of Toronto, the governing council's academic board "is our senate equivalent ... a large board with a very clear preponderance of colleagues – a substantial number of [whom] are in ... 'administrative exile,' but also many front-line faculty as well as students." The academic board's 123 members[1] met six times per year. Except in purely academic matters, its recommendations required final approval by the executive committee or the governing council itself. For instance, although the academic board established the university's annual operating budget, the budget was approved by the governing council. The academic board was described as "functioning more in a way that one would like a senate to function, but with the additional happy wrinkle that they have a line of sight ... on budgetary and operational issues."

## U of A

The University of Alberta's senior academic governance body was a 147-member general faculties council (GFC), chaired by the president. It had a complex committee structure, and most of its work was conducted in committee and forwarded to the GFC for approval. It did not have authority for budget matters, but one of its committees was briefed on the university's budget.

Although the GFC was not seen to be as active as the board in setting the direction of the university, it was described in interviews in the spring of 2014 as continuing to play an important and central – if perhaps, overly bureaucratic – role in the life of the university. Several interviewees commented that, although collegiality and shared governance had perhaps frayed somewhat in the wake of recent budget cuts, these remained a reality at U of A, and the GFC played a major role in that.

There were tensions between the GFC and the administration. Some GFC members viewed the latter as defensive and controlling – for example, they brought matters to the GFC late in the day instead of seeking early input from the GFC into proposed initiatives. Because of the proximity of government to the board, the GFC could become a place of resistance. "There are people on GFC who view GFC as an opportunity to push back against the government," said one interviewee, "while the administration worries about that causing problems." Some members of the senior administration perceived decision-making by the GFC as slow and process-heavy. The president had established a task force to look at the effectiveness of the GFC and recommend any appropriate reforms.

## UBC

The University of British Columbia had two senates – one for each campus – with a Council of Senates as a coordinating body, all chaired by the president. The senates were described as having "a fairly focused mandate" dealing primarily with curricular matters. The Council of Senates had a committee that advised the president on the development of the budget.

During interviews late in 2013, some senators expressed the view that the administration should involve the senates earlier in the process of considering major new initiatives. Most senate work was done in committee, and senate consideration of the resulting matters tended to be *pro forma*. Attempts had been made to foster discussion of "big picture items" at senate to boost interest and engagement, but "it d[id]n't really happen very well and we tended to slide back into the approvals of all the new programs and the approvals of all the new scholarships and not a lot of debate." According to interviewees, there wasn't a lot of interest among faculty members in serving on senate, because "faculty are busy," service to one's department or faculty was more highly valued than service on senate, and, finally, "things are working fairly well."

## FACULTIES

All six universities comprised disciplinary and professional faculties. Most were of long standing – indeed, some at U of M predated the founding of the university. At UQAM, though, faculties were a recent development.

Until 1997, the year that UQAM began creating faculties, all universities within the UQ had a matrix structure consisting of academic departments and modules. The modules comprised undergraduate programs and were governed by committees, which were composed of equal numbers of students and faculty, as well as of socio-economic representatives (Corbo 2012, 16; Bertand 2012, 227). The main rationale for establishing faculties was that UQAM had grown to the point that an intermediate level of coordination was needed between the central administration and the departments (Corbo 2012). The creation of faculties was described by a former dean as having had numerous benefits. By bringing cognate disciplines and professions together within faculties, it had facilitated communication, sharing of resources, creation of multidisciplinary programs, and development of new forms of research. In addition, it permitted decentralization of some administrative functions to the faculty level. (The corollary of this, described by a vice-rector interviewed, is that there was less contact between the central administration and individual faculty members and the vice-rectors' roles became more policy-oriented and strategic. Some faculty members expressed frustration at no longer being able to deal directly with the central administration.)

At the other case institutions, faculties were well-entrenched and robust. The deans we interviewed (one or two per university) were all from large departmentalized faculties, but there were variations between universities in terms of:

- the extent to which faculty governance was specified in legislation;
- the degree of homogeneity or heterogeneity in faculty governance across faculties; and
- the extent to which authority (for matters including budget and graduate studies) had been decentralized to line faculties.

The relationship between faculties and senates or equivalent could be ambiguous. A senate officer at one of the universities said:

[Faculties] are officially creatures/committees of the senate. They don't necessarily see themselves that way. Neither do we. Nor do they behave quite that way. When it comes to the approval of academic programs, it's very clear. They come to the senate through the committee structure for approval of programs. For the rest of it, I would say it's a more delicate, [a] touchier area ... Faculties think of themselves as masters of their own houses.

Faculties and departments at most of the case universities also appeared to enjoy significant autonomy from the central administration. An interviewee at the U of M commented that:

Il y a ... une forme de décentralisation du pouvoir parce que les facultés et les départements ont tous une certaine marge d'autonomie. La direction ne pourrait pas s'immiscer dans les affaires d'un département, à moins d'un enjeu très fort.
[There is ... a form of decentralization of power, because the faculties and departments all have a certain degree of autonomy. The administration couldn't interfere in a department's affairs, unless there was a very strong case for doing so.]

Strong faculties had many benefits but also costs. Interviewees at several institutions suggested that the power of faculties created siloes and rigidities, impeding interdisciplinary and multidisciplinary program development as well as student flows across faculty boundaries. Inter-faculty differences could also give rise to inequities. A graduate student leader at U of A said that "we see vastly different treatment of graduate students as employees. While we have a single collective agreement, governance cultures and work cultures are very different."

By virtue of its sheer size, its complexity, and its budget model, U of T was the most decentralized of the case universities. The role of the centre had evolved to become one of overseeing and supporting the divisions (faculties). An interviewee at U of T said that "because of our size and strength and quality, we are able to have our departments and faculties more autonomous. We cannot micromanage. It is the same internationally: The really good universities elsewhere also do not micromanage. It's just a recipe for disaster." Another senior official at U of T described its recent strategy:

We have been following a very deliberate plan of decentralization with a different central planning and coordination approach than has been the case before ... So here is the big long-term framework of the institution, now, year to year, go about your business and we will try to give you more tools to make better decisions and to be successful academically and sound fiscally ... Let's have a conversation ... where we are trying to ... not only ensure that you have the tools you need to advance your division's specific mission but ... also tap the inter-divisional opportunities and multi-divisional collaborations in teaching and research. Let's start that conversation with a view to our ability to help you with the tools that are outside the current budget envelopes such as fundraising or government relations or multi-year capital planning, where the university's borrowing capacity and its balance sheet comes into play.

The existence of strong faculties at case universities did not necessarily mean that faculty councils were active and engaged. Numerous interviewees said that faculty council meetings were generally *pro forma* and poorly attended. For example, a dean at one of the case universities said, "I have four [ ] Faculty Council meetings a year ... I have a faculty of 350 faculty members and there are probably another twenty people who can come. I struggle to get a quorum, which is forty, and I think that's not untypical."

Some deans were troubled by low participation and taking steps to increase engagement in governance, but others did not see it as signifying a problem. It could even be a sign of trust. Another dean said, "I think most faculty are perfectly fine with keeping their heads down and working on teaching and research and trusting the heads and the administration to do the best they can and when there are some tough decisions to be made they want to be informed about them in a timely fashion and help shape solutions." In the meantime, deans worked closely with associate or assistant deans and with chairs, heads or directors of departments to advance their faculties' activities.

## ACADEMIC DEPARTMENTS

Most faculties at the case universities were composed principally of academic departments based on discipline or professional specialization. Much has been written about new modes of knowledge production and the organizational mechanisms that bring people together across disciplines, professions, and organizational boundaries for that purpose. This study did not permit us to ascertain whether, or the extent to which, cross-disciplinary structures had grown at the case universities relative to discipline- or profession-based units, but it appeared that the latter continue to be the building blocks of academic governance and administration.

How departments functioned varied, partly as a function of scale. One or two chairs, heads, or directors of academic departments were interviewed at each case university. The size of their units ranged from a couple of dozen regular faculty members to about eighty. A department chair at U of T observed that flexibility is "needed in an organization of this size because the disciplines are so very different, and one size does not fit all." There was also diversity in practice and culture at the departmental level at smaller universities. That was in part a function of disciplinary cultures. A science department chair at one of the smaller institutions said of his department that "we are by far the best organized among all the departments in the faculty of science ... And in my experience, professionally, that's typical of the culture of [this discipline] ... to be just way more detailed, organized, everything is spelled out."

Some chairs or directors interviewed said that their departments had detailed governance documents; others tended to rely more on established practices. Several were in the process of creating or updating a departmental handbook.

The diversity of departmental governance practices across institutions was illustrated by examples from UQAM and U of T. A department director interviewed at UQAM, when asked how his department made decisions, said "c'est la collégialité" (it's collegial). The director was elected by the departmental assembly, a body consisting of professors and a representative of the sessional lecturers that met once a month. An executive committee, composed of professors appointed by the departmental assembly upon the recommendation of the director, considered departmental matters and made recommendations to the assembly. Decisions were made in accordance with formal procedures and minutes of meetings taken.

In contrast, the chair of a very large department at U of T described decision-making within his department as

> consultative and based on advisory committees, which, I think, is the way most Canadian universities are run. So I have an executive committee, like a cabinet, [that] consists of my associate chairs and my top administrators [and helps run the department from day to day, week to week] and an advisory committee, sort of like my parliament, it has memberships from across the different research areas of the department ... I go to the advisory committee for confirmation of policies that I want to put forward. I have them get feedback from

their groups, bring it back, let's discuss it, reformulate it if we can, we can scratch off those ideas that have no resonance with the groups. Eventually once I have good consensus there, then, when I go to the department meeting, I say, this is the way we shall be next year.

### LEADERSHIP AND ADMINISTRATION

In chapter 2, we looked at the state of the presidency – and of administration generally – at Canadian universities at large. Leadership and administration reflect and influence not only the inner workings of universities but also their place in the socio-economic order. Bourdieu perceived the educational system's relative autonomy from the state and other external forces as due largely to its self-reproductive capacity. He "point[ed] to the ... system's capacity to recruit its leadership from within its own ranks as the reason for its unusual historical continuity and stability, analogous more to the church than to business or the state" (Schwartz 1997, 206). What did we learn about the leadership and administration of the case universities?

*Presidents*

At the time of the interviews for this study, the positions of president or rector were filled by people who were academics and had previously held one or more senior administrative positions at a university. Three of the presidents had been appointed from outside their universities, three from within. None had been appointed from outside Canada.

The presidents' roles had much in common but there were differences in the processes by which they had been appointed and variations in the nature of the roles. All the presidents were members of the boards (or, in the case of U of T, governing council) of their institutions, but they played different roles in relation to the senates or equivalents. The president chaired the latter at UBC, UQAM, and U of A. At UdeM, the rector was chair of the university assembly, but in practice meetings were chaired by a delegate. At Dalhousie, the president was a member of senate but there was an elected senate chair. At the four anglophone universities, presidents were appointed by the board or governing council on the recommendation of a search committee. The presidential search processes at these universities were "closed" insofar as the names of candidates were kept confidential.

As of 2013–14, the rector of UdeM was appointed by the board after an extensive process involving the striking of a committee by the university assembly to advertise the position and seek nominations. The committee developed a list of candidates to be invited to make public presentations, invited university assembly members to rank the candidates by means of a ballot, and obtained feedback from others; a slate of candidates was then forwarded to the board by the committee. Under the university's by-laws, the board appointed one of the recommended candidates – or another individual – after consultation with the committee. On a number of occasions, the UdeM board had appointed an individual who had not received the most support in the ballot and/or from the committee, and this had engendered a perception in some quarters of the university that the board was dismissive of the university community's views. Some faculty members and students interviewed saw the process at UdeM as undemocratic compared to the one at Université Laval and the UQ, where rectors were elected. A board member said:

> Les recteurs récemment nommés n'ont pas toujours été ceux que la communauté souhaitait. On est allé chercher quelqu'un d'autre, et cela a créé beaucoup de tensions. Dans mon modèle idéal à moi, la communauté devrait reconnaître que c'est le rôle du Conseil de décider qui va diriger l'université. C'est la plus importante de nos responsabilités.
>
> [The recently appointed rectors weren't always the ones the community wanted. We went for someone else, and that created a lot of tension. In my ideal model, the community should recognize that it is the role of the board to decide who will lead the university. That is the most important of our responsibilities.]

In its rector appointment process and in numerous other respects, the UdeM appeared to be midway between governance practices in the rest of Canada and those elsewhere in francophone Quebec. A university official said:

> Dans la culture et le fonctionnement, cela nous distingue des autres universités québécoises ... Je pense qu'on est la plus canadienne des universités francophones. On est le modèle qui se rapproche le plus de ce qui se fait ailleurs au Canada. Le processus est plus participatif et on est à cheval entre ce qui se fait entre le Québec et le Canada.
>
> [In terms of culture and operation, this sets us apart from other universities in Quebec ... I think we are the most Canadian of francophone universities. Our model comes closest to what is being done elsewhere in Canada. The process is more participatory, and we straddle what is being done in Quebec and in Canada.]

At UQAM, the rector was formally appointed by the government upon the recommendation of the board of directors, but that took place after a consultation by means of a ballot of faculty members, administrators, members of the academic committee, and others. The process was described by interviewees as an election.

Consistent with Mintzberg's (1979) observations about the leadership of professional bureaucracies, the universities' presidents appeared to have less power than most corporate CEOs. One president said:

> Universities essentially consist of people who think of themselves as self-employed professionals ... Of course, they are employees, salaried employees, but they operate as if they were independent professionals. And that's a function of their recognized knowledge and expertise in the spheres in which they work. So I, as president, can tell the chemistry department to do certain things, but I can't tell the department how to teach chemistry, because I don't have a clue. I can say, "you have too few students in that class" or "you have to go through a process to do this or that." But at the end of the day they have a significant degree of autonomy because they have that expertise.

Also consistent with Mintzberg's description of professional bureaucracy, all six presidents played boundary-spanning roles. They mediated not only between the universities and external stakeholders, but also between major constituencies within the institutions, many of whose members saw the world in very different ways.

At one university, the president's role seemed to be largely external but, at the other five, it was both external and internal. Indeed, whereas a previous rector at the UdeM had introduced the practice of having deans report to a vice-president academic and provost, the rector in office in the 2010s had reverted to the model of deans reporting directly to the rector. According to one interviewee, the "provost" model had not been popular with deans, some of whom felt it distanced them from the leadership of the university. One external/internal president said: "I can't see ever leading a university like this without basically being a follower who is talking to colleagues trying to figure out where they are going, where the discipline is evolving and being attuned to academic issues and concerned about academic quality and standards. I make no apology in my view that the president should be doing both [external and internal relations]."

Even among the external/internal presidents, there appeared to be differences in the extent to which they represented the external community to the internal one or the internal community to the outside world. One anglophone president said:

> The president has a wonderful and fascinating job, but it can drive you crazy too, because the very people you are supposed to protect and celebrate and validate are people that don't understand anything [about the environment in which the university operates]. You have this bifurcated perception of the professoriate because, on one hand, you have to manage them to a purpose – and in that sense you are controlling and dictating. On the other hand, you have to recognize their total importance ... [and] you need to make sure that they are empowered to do all the things they should be doing ... You're out there as an educator, a salesman – explaining what the university actually does, why it's important. And why the university is in the best position to decide – that somebody else trying to impose goals will ultimately be counterproductive. The role of being at the interface of competing and overlapping systems is complicated. It's never unidimensional. Sometimes you have to carry the message in from outside and push it down and say, "You have to understand what these people want." And sometimes you have to go out and say, "What you're suggesting is ridiculous. You need to support us and what we are doing." There's a lot of complexity in the job.

The board-appointed rector of the UdeM was described by a faculty-level administrator as "le grand patron de l'U de M [et] ... le chef de l'université" (the top boss of the UdeM [and] ... head of the university). In comparison, the role of rector at UQAM seemed to be more that of defender of the internal space. Asked to describe the rector's role, the rector said:

> Moi je suis un recteur élu par la communauté universitaire. Je pense que la chose la plus fondamentale pour un recteur est de défendre l'autonomie de l'université et la liberté académique... Pour ce qui est du recteur, ce sont les relations avec le gouvernement et les relations avec la population en général qui définissent le lieu idéal pour défendre l'université – ce quelle est, ce qu'elle veut, ce qu'elle veut dire – et préserver son autonomie.[2]
>
> [I am a rector elected by the university community. I think the most fundamental thing for a rector is to defend the university's autonomy and academic freedom ... For the rector, it is relationships with government and with the public that present the ideal place to defend the university – what it is, what it wants, what it wants to say – and to preserve its autonomy.]

The fact that the rector of UQAM was elected – and sat on the UQ's board of governors – appeared to shape the relationship of the rector to the UQAM board. Whereas other presidents were formally accountable to the boards that had appointed them – and informally accountable to many others – the rector of UQAM seemed to be relatively more accountable to the academic community and less of an employee of the board.

### University Secretaries

At five of the six case universities, a university secretary was responsible for organizing the work of, and advising the chairs and members of, the governing bodies (however, at UBC, responsibility for governance support was divided between a number of offices). At two of the institutions, this position was of relatively recent origin, whereas at others it was long-standing. At UdeM, the position of *secrétaire général* had been created in 1877 – one year before the establishment of the forerunner of the university (Université de Montréal. n.d.).

Asked to describe the university secretary's role in governance, one said, "You are ... a connector between ... the board, the senate and the administration." Another explained that "the principal concern of the university secretary ... is to ensure that decisions are made by the right people on the basis of good, timely information and that the decision-making process is sound and free of conflict of interest." A third described the role as one of persuasion rather than authority, noting that even though the university secretary is a guardian of the rules, the principal role is to inform and advise rather than enforce *per se*. Besides lending support to governance, some of the case institutions' university secretaries were responsible for matters that might benefit from a degree of independence from senior administration, such as legal affairs, internal audit, privacy and access to information, records management, and student and faculty appeals.

### Administration

Interviewees at many of the case universities spoke about growth in "administration" and in the extent of administrative decision-making. For example, a dean at one university said:

> When I first got involved, there was one president and two vice-presidents. Now there are five vice-presidents and each of them [has] at least two associates. There are a lot more people in the senior

administration. That is a statement of fact, that is not a judgment. I think the complexity of running the university particularly within the broader context has increased massively over that time. There is absolutely no question that we need a vice-president of research whereas maybe we didn't in 1990.

Some interviewees cited external regulation as a source of increased administration. One president said:

There are 101 regulations for everything – employment relationships, health and safety, building codes, human rights, pension regulations ... This complexity has led to more professional managerial authority in universities ... So you have an administrator telling a professor, your lab has to be renovated, because the fire code requires it – or you can't treat an admin assistant like that, because it's contrary to human rights regulations – or pension rules have changed and now you have to pay for pension contributions for your research assistant from your research grant. The complexity of the university's operations and external relationships requires a managerial cadre to deal with it.

A faculty association official at another university said:

I haven't read the act recently, but I don't believe it mentions that the university administration is [a] kind of professional managerial site of authority ... but I think increasingly, and I don't mean this in a kind of polemical or ideological or critical way, I mean in a factual way, that increasingly, one of the key sites of decision-making at the university is administrative.

Committees composed largely of academic administrators were cited as playing important roles. At U of T, for example, a principals and deans group, and another that also included academic directors and chairs, were described by a senior university official as "more and more engaged in real decision-making." That seemed to be the case not only at institutional levels but also within faculties, where committees of chairs or directors chaired by deans were very active.

What was described by faculty union representatives at one university as increased administration and managerialism was perceived by senior administrators and board members at the same institution as professionalization of the administrative side of the institution, improving effectiveness and efficiency.

Notwithstanding concerns about the increase in administration and in the proportion of university employees who were not connected to the academic mission, a few interviewees identified instances of *in*sufficient administrative resources. A dean who had joined one of the case universities from a private institution in the US observed that "many of our professors and academic administrators are doing admin type of work that takes away time that they could dedicate to things that only they can do." An administrator at UQAM said that compared to other major universities, UQAM had very few professional support staff within faculties, which meant that department directors and program directors had to do a great deal of administrative work. That, coupled with decentralization of administration from the centre to faculties and from faculties to departments, was making it increasingly difficult to recruit directors.

There also appeared to be differences in the extent of senior administrative discretion among the case universities. At one end of the spectrum, UQAM was described by faculty association officials as co-managed by the administration and the union under the faculty collective agreement. Some functions performed by academic administrators at many other universities (e.g., assignment of faculty workloads; allocation of faculty positions to units; establishment of target class sizes) were carried out by academic governance bodies at various levels. On the other hand, an interviewee at U of T said: "[Many] committees [here] ... are formally advisory. They are picked by either chair, or dean, or whoever the key administrative head is. And then they advise that person ... When it works well, people feel included; when it doesn't work well, people start to point to the fact that the committees are ultimately advisory only, and they are hand-picked."

*Vice-Presidents*

Perceptions of increasing administration and administrative power notwithstanding, many vice-presidents interviewed described their roles as largely facilitative. A vice-president responsible for external relations described his role as "mediator, perhaps? My role is to make sure that the university is well served and that the donors' needs and expectations are well served." A vice-president of research said, "I'm a broker, a matchmaker." Another said, "Our function as a service unit is to support [and] advocate on behalf of researchers to further their activities. We also establish policy and take certain top-down initiatives to make things happen ... But we are service providers and we can't impose rules on the research community." Even academic vice-presidents and provosts, most of whom had line and budget authority, said that the mode in which they worked was far from "command and control." A senior official at UdeM said that faculties and other units had a high degree of autonomy and that the only real power of the executive lay in the allocation of resources. The nature of that autonomy was reflected in comments by senior officials at different universities. One said:

> La coordination de l'évaluation des programmes est institutionnelle, au niveau du vice-recteur. Mais c'est avant tout les facultés et départements qui évaluent les programmes. Donc on n'a pas de pouvoir. Par exemple nous avons un programme où le taux d'échec et d'attrition est [très haut]. Mais selon nos statuts on ne peut pas obliger le doyen à arrêter ce programme. Peut-être de manière indirecte par l'arrêt de financement ou l'arrêt de nomination de nouveau profs ... [Autre exemple:] les MOOCs [massive open online courses] se développent actuellement et si on décide d'y aller, cela sera difficile. Je ne peux pas imposer un prof ou un département de le faire. On peut stimuler mais nos gens sont assez conservateurs. Changer une méthode pédagogique [ici] c'est extrêmement difficile.
>
> [The coordination of program evaluation is institutional, at the level of the vice-president. But it is, above all, the faculties and departments that evaluate programs. So, we have no power. For example, there is a program where the failure and attrition rates are [very high]. According to our rules, we cannot force the dean to close this program. Perhaps indirectly, by stopping funding or the appointment of new professors ... [Another example:] MOOCs [massive open online courses] are currently on the rise and, if we decide to go there, it will be difficult. I can't force a professor or a department to do it. We can provide stimulus, but our people are quite conservative. Changing a teaching method [here] is extremely difficult.]

A senior official at another university said:

> [At this university, t]here is no presidential review of tenure, the tenure decision is made at the faculty level, there is no senior salary committee, there is no provostial review of increments, or PTR [progress through the ranks], or merit, these are all handled at the level of deans. As a result, the quality of the university is defined by the quality of professors and is really a sum of faculty activity. There is little the provost or the president can do.

The numbers of vice-presidents at the case universities ranged from five to seven (eight, if two campus principals at U of T were included). There were variations in the seniority of the vice-president academic or provost relative to other vice-presidents; the capacity of the former to coordinate activity across vice-presidential portfolios; whether deans reported to the vice-president academic; and the extent of the latter's responsibility for the university's budget.

The relationship of the vice-rectors' positions at UdeM and UQAM to those of the rectors differed from that of their counterparts at anglophone universities, in very different ways. At anglophone universities, the appointment of vice-presidents typically involves search committees chaired by the president, which make recommendations to the board. At UdeM, however, vice-rectors' appointments were proposed by the rector and endorsed by the university assembly before the individuals were appointed by the board. This meant the executive of the UdeM was effectively turning over on a regular basis. Although the understanding at anglophone universities is increasingly that a president needs to have confidence in his or her senior team (i.e., anyone lacking the president's confidence will leave), that is not automatic, and university senates tend not to have control over vice-presidential appointments, especially of a non-academic nature.

In contrast, at UQAM, several vice-presidents were elected and effectively had their own constituencies. As one interviewee pointed out, their election platforms and constituencies might align more or less with those of other members of the executive, sometimes necessitating a process of consensus-building at the executive level. The extent to which the board provided direction to the rector and the rector to the vice-rectors appeared to be more limited at UQAM than at other case universities.

*Deans*

The deans interviewed were all academics serving as the academic and administrative leaders of their faculties for multi-year terms. Most had been appointed as deans from within their universities but a few had come from other universities in Canada or abroad. The picture that emerged from interviews was of the deanship as a key position involving a complex balance between leadership and followership, institutional affiliation and collegial allegiance, external and internal responsiveness. With respect to that balance, a dean at UBC said, "I spend half of my time protecting faculty from the real world, the other half of my time reminding them there is a real world."

Institutions varied regarding the extent of faculty input into decanal appointments: at most of the anglophone universities, faculty members provided input to search committees, which made recommendations to the president or board. At UdeM in 2013 and at UQAM, faculty members voted as part of the appointment or reappointment of deans. However, the ballot was advisory at UdeM and the process has subsequently been changed.

A dean at U of A suggested that deans are increasingly perceived by boards and administrations as institutional actors and agents of change. He expressed concern about the expectation that

> deans come in with a vision, which then they will be evaluated on ... for the next five years. My concern about that is that, especially for someone coming from the outside, how would you know? It's so hard to know what the faculty is until you are there, but the board of governors really wants the deans to behave more as senior managers and to be much less defending their faculty.

Though typically appointed by the board or equivalent, deans did not appear to be easy to remove. A senior official at one of the universities said:

> c'est difficile de mettre un doyen ou un directeur de département à la porte. Même quand il gère mal. Surtout s'ils ont le soutien de leurs collègues ... J'ai connu une époque où [une] faculté ... était en opposition avec l'université. Dans une entreprise un directeur de service qui s'opposerait à son supérieur ne durerait pas longtemps.
>
> [it's hard to fire a dean or a department head, even if they manage their unit badly. It's especially true if they have the support of their colleagues ... There was a time here when [a] faculty [here] was in opposition to the university. In a company, a department manager who opposed their boss would not last long.]

Above and beyond variations in the way deans were appointed and reappointed, there were differences in the positions to which deans reported and in the extent of decanal involvement in institutional governance, central administration, appointment, promotion, and tenure decisions, and resource allocation.

At UQAM, where faculties were a relatively recent creation, the role of deans differed from that of their counterparts at the medical-doctoral universities. Whereas there had been a general consensus at UQAM about the need for faculties, steps to remove deans from the faculty bargaining unit had been strongly contested by the union. The role of deans had grown since the establishment of the first faculties but did not yet have the same scope of that of deans at most other universities. As of 2013, deans at UQAM did not have responsibility for the administration of faculty personnel matters (e.g., appointments, promotion, tenure), nor did they have authority to allocate positions among departments in their faculties. Asked whether deans experience tension between their responsibilities to the central administration and those to the faculty, a former dean interviewed said, "En général ça se passe assez bien, parce que le vice-recteur est aussi élu par les membres de l'université. Donc c'est nécessairement un prof qui est imputable au collège électoral" (In general, things go quite well, because the vice-rector is also elected by the university's members. So, [the vice-rector] is necessarily [also] a professor who's accountable to the electoral college). In contrast, a dean of arts at one of the anglophone universities said:

> At the end of the day – and I don't know if all our faculty members understand this – the dean is not an elected politician or advocate. I'm not elected by colleagues here in some popularity contest or some assessment of skill level or whatever. Ultimately, in terms of governance, I report to the vice-president and the president and the board ... The decisions that I have to take can be at odds with the collegial process, because technically I don't have to answer to that constituency ... I constantly move between "how to deal with the constituency" and where my real reporting relationship is, which is ultimately to the president.

In addition to variations between case universities, there were some internal differences in deans' roles. The latter seemed to vary within universities in accordance with factors such as faculty culture, governing structure, budgetary context, and extent of professional or other external outreach. Chairs also described the style of the individual dean as having an important impact on how things function within faculties. Most deans worked closely with associate and assistant deans and chairs or directors of departments, besides conducting meetings of faculty councils. At the institutional level, it was typical for universities to have some form of deans' council, chaired by the vice-president academic or the provost.

## Chairs

The manner in which department chairs were appointed varied from institution to institution and tended to reflect the processes used for more senior academic administrators. Asked what the chair's role entailed, a science chair at Dalhousie said:

> It's sort of hard to sum it up in a simple way. Basically, it involves a kind of constant oversight of the short-term functioning of the department, which often means settling personnel issues ... In the medium term, it involves determining the teaching schedules for the upcoming year, which is a huge headache every year. And in the longer term, it involves identifying and carrying out opportunities to do hires.

One of the chair's most important roles was to make sure that the department's teaching programs were delivered properly. Efforts were made to accommodate colleagues' teaching preferences to the extent possible, but:

> you know, if push comes to shove, which it occasionally does in our department, if someone says, "I'd like to teach X, it's my pet thing," and I say, "I'm really sorry, but we really have to put on these classes to meet the requirements of our degrees and if you wish to do that, it'll be an extra thing as overload, which will be unpaid ... You can do that, that's perfectly fine with me, but you must do this, because we have to put this on in order to offer our degree program." So that's in a way the glue that kind of pulls things together.

In contrast, the chair's role vis-à-vis their colleagues' research was principally one of informing, coaching, and providing feedback on performance. Other responsibilities identified by chairs at Dalhousie included preparation of the department's budget and administration of promotion and tenure processes. Chairs at other institutions also commented on their roles in hiring of contract instructors and in reviewing and following up on course evaluations ("I'm constantly reviewing what happens with student evaluation, and I talk to instructors where there appear to be problems").

The titles and roles of chairs or equivalent varied between case universities. An interviewee at UBC explained: "Here [the position] is called 'head' ... which is meant to suggest something slightly different." At the UdeM and UQAM, the title was "directeur/directrice." In addition to variations in title, the chair's position differed between universities regarding whether and how chairs were involved in annual reviews of faculty members, the number of years for which they were appointed, whether they were members of the faculty union or association (UBC: yes; U of A: yes; U of T: yes; U de M: no; UQAM: yes; Dal: yes), and whether they assigned teaching responsibilities. At UQAM, they did not: the department's executive committee prepared an annual plan for allocating workload, for approval by the departmental assembly.

Whatever these variations, chairs interviewed overwhelmingly described their power as limited. A chair of a professional department at U of T explained:

> The university is and is not a hierarchical structure, right? So I have superiors and I have subordinates, but neither the superiors give me orders nor do the subordinates listen to my orders ... And, also, in another year I am stepping down. So I can't burn my bridges with people that are going to be my colleagues next year. And so most of what we do is by example, and by influence and leaning over people to get things done, by building consensus. So I have to exercise a lot of consensus building, listening and gathering feedback and all that so as to have credible proposals that when I take [them] to the dean, I can say these are based on X, Y, Z, activities that I have done to arrive at that consensus in the department.

A counterpart at UdeM said:

> Je suis le plus petit patron, en bas de la hiérarchie des patrons ... Hormis la gestion quotidienne, [le rôle] est de voir à transmettre les orientations de l'université aux profs ou transmettre à l'administration le souhait des profs. Il y a encore cet aspect de discussion et de démocratie consultative, mais je ne décide d'à peu près rien.
>
> [I am the smallest boss, at the bottom of the hierarchy of bosses ... Apart from daily management, [the role] is to ensure that the policies of the university are communicated to the professors or that the wishes of the profs are communicated to the administration. There is still an element of discussion and consultative democracy, but I decide almost nothing.]

Notwithstanding their limited decision-making authority and need to operate by consensus-building, numerous instances were described in which chairs had exercised leadership. For example, one had worked with the department council and colleagues to draw students into gateway courses, not in response to enrolment targets, but "because, as an incoming chair, I was concerned [about] some of the patterns that I saw both in terms of what's happening with the enrolment and also in terms of the teaching behaviour of the department that I thought could be improved."

A chair interviewed at UQAM expressed the view that it was important that chairs remain within the faculty union: "On est capable de vraiment représenter le département sans avoir le sentiment d'être du côté des patrons. Ça nous donne une certaine indépendance qui permet de gérer un peu plus facilement les départements" (We can truly represent the department without feeling like we're on the side of the bosses. It gives us a certain independence, which makes it easier to manage the departments). Although directors at UdeM may have been closer to the "côté des patrons," temporary exclusion from the bargaining unit did not necessarily determine their perceptions of where their accountability lay. A director there said, "I do not consider myself a representative of the administration to the professors, but as a representative of professors to the administration ... I draw my legitimacy from the confidence my professors have in me." He was "responsible to everyone: the dean, professors and students. But only the dean can fire me." A counterpart at Dalhousie suggested that although, technically, only the dean could fire him, his colleagues could play a large role in that. "They could depose me if they wanted to, I suppose. They would just go to the dean, and say, 'Things are completely dysfunctional, this, this, and this has happened, you have to make a change.'"

Interviewees at several universities said that it was becoming increasingly difficult to recruit new chairs. A department director at UQAM said:

> Gérer un département ce n'est pas uniquement gérer de l'argent et des cours. C'est aussi la gestion des collègues – et c'est ce qui fait peur à tout le monde! ... La gestion administrative ... est [aussi] difficile ... Et ça devient de plus en plus difficile de trouver des directeurs de département, parce que le travail administratif est de plus en plus lourd.
>
> [Managing a department is not just about managing money and courses. It is also the management of colleagues – and that is what scares everyone! ... The administrative management ... is [also] difficult ... And it is becoming more and more difficult to find department directors, because the administrative workload is heavier and heavier.]

A dean at UBC expressed concern about the difficulty of the head's role from a different perspective:

> I see there is a conflict between the concept of shared academic governance and the worker–management relationship of the faculty association ... And we need to figure out how to get the heads out of the middle of so much of this. Heads are members of our faculty association, they are faculty but they end up bearing the burden of too much of the disciplinary issues. If you look at an org chart for a university on the academic side of the house, it makes no sense ...

A department head in [this faculty] might have sixty direct reports. That's just ludicrous ... It only works if all the faculty members behave in a professional manner and basically do their job with little or no supervision. And that's true in a vast majority of cases, but all it takes is one faculty member that kind of becomes a problem and all of a sudden, the head's job, which is already pretty impossible, starts to be consumed by managing this personnel problem ... It's also really uncomfortable because that person is your colleague. And increasingly I'm finding it more difficult to recruit heads into the position. Our board wants us to work more on succession planning [but, to] be blunt, sometimes, I don't want our folks to really know what's it like to be a head.

Senior officials at UBC and elsewhere recognized the challenges of the role of head or chair and were seeking to bolster support for them through means such as putting in place more training and coaching and giving them more support in the form of associate heads, professional staff, and other resources.

### FACULTY PARTICIPATION IN GOVERNANCE

Consistent with Mintzberg's (1979) observations about decision-making in professional bureaucracies, there was considerable professorial control over academic matters at the case universities, through departments, faculties, and senates. Nevertheless, according to a senior official at Dalhousie, that control was neither absolute nor assured:

Even [in the case of academic policies and regulations], increasingly, you have legal counsel drafting policy and they tell you that you can't do X or Y because of this or that legislative requirement ... Broadly speaking, the academic direction of the university still derives very substantially from academic authority. But not totally. Even in that area, there's a perception on the part of public funders that innovation has to occur and we have to make it happen. It's not acceptable from their point of view if we say "the professors have considered this and don't want to change."

Regular faculty members participated in governance at the departmental level and had opportunities to participate on faculty councils, senates, and boards. As noted above, faculty council meetings were often poorly attended, and at most of the case universities with senates, faculty members were less than keen to serve. Senior officials spoke about trying to improve the quality, import, and impact of discussion and engagement in meetings of senates, faculty councils, and other academic governance bodies.

Above and beyond opportunities to participate in governance or administration (whether they chose to pursue them or not), individual faculty members were described as having a lot of autonomy. Asked whether and in what ways universities are distinctive from other organizations, three chairs from across the country provided similar responses:

> One of the primary things [that] makes it distinctive is the place that the faculty feel they have. It's like herding cats. They don't feel themselves to be working for anyone except for themselves, so why do they need to do anything anyone tells them to do or asks them to do? They rarely see themselves as part of a community or collective. If the university tells them what to do, they think they have the right not to do it. So that extends way beyond the intellectual rights, it has to do with every single thing. And in large part, universities respect that. We govern ourselves. I am a member of the department and I will go back being a member of the department. It's a weird, unusual form of governance. No one knows where you are. My colleagues are gone or here, I assume they are doing their job, but what do I know? It's unique. (UBC)

> It always seems to me that what makes universities distinctive is that – at least in research-intensive universities like this one – professors, although we are employed to do a job as if we are in a company, in fact, we are rewarded based on things like research performance and grants. That kind of work is very individual, so the professors behave more or less like they are a collection of independent contractors, more than like they are employees of a single coherent firm. They can't really be fired for underperformance, unless the underperformance involves virtually criminal activities or something really extreme. The administration has strikingly little power over the individuals in terms of what they do with their time, whether they do it well or not. In that way, it is very different from a commercial enterprise. (Dalhousie)

> Oui je pense que les universités sont uniques dans la façon de fonctionner. La liberté de chacun des profs. Même le prof adjoint de 30 ans a une très grande autonomie pour le développement de sa recherche,

les comités qu'il accepte ou pas. Des organisations où les professionnels même avec un PhD ont cette autonomie, je n'en connais pas. Je travaille régulièrement avec les gens de l'industrie ... et je vois nos vis-à-vis dans ces compagnies-là ... Q: *Selon vous, pourquoi est-ce comme cela ?* C'est parce que l'université est une organisation où la liberté académique et la possibilité de faire quelque chose d'original [sont valorisées et] on veut laisser la possibilité à chaque individu de pouvoir développer sa créativité. Et pour pouvoir faire cela il faut laisser la marge de manoeuvre. En entreprise on veut bien que l'individu soit créatif, mais créatif uniquement dans cette direction-là. Des situations industrielles où un chercheur développe quelque chose qui fonctionne bien et le jour suivant on lui demande de passer à autre chose parce que ce projet-là est fini. À l'université le chercheur va décider de continuer ou d'arrêter. Chacun fait son propre jugement. (UdeM)

[Yes, I think universities are unique in the way they operate. The freedom of each professor. Even the thirty-year-old assistant professor has a great deal of autonomy in the development of their research, the committees they accept or not. Organizations where professionals even with a PhD have this autonomy, I do not know of any. I work regularly with people in industry ... [and], I see our counterparts in these companies ... Q: *Why do you think it is like that?* It's because the university is an organization where academic freedom and the possibility of doing something original [are valued and] we want to allow everyone to develop their creativity. To be able to do that, you must leave room for manoeuvre. In business, we want the individual to be creative, but only creative in that [specific] direction. In industrial situations, when a researcher develops something that works well, the next day, they are asked to move on because that project is finished. At the university, the researcher will decide to continue or to stop. Everyone makes their own judgment.] (UdeM)

Comments about the extent of professors' autonomy – and the challenges of "herding cats" – were also made by interviewees at other levels of administration.

What impact did faculty unions or associations have on decision-making at the case universities? All six institutions engaged in faculty collective bargaining, but at the time of the interviews for this study, U of A and U of T differed from the other four universities in that their faculty were not unionized. The case universities were not representative of Canadian universities at large in this respect.

The Association of Academic Staff of the University of Alberta (AASUA) was the largest academic staff association in Canada. It included members from seven constituencies: the academic faculty, academic librarians, administrative and professional officers, contract academic staff, faculty service officers, sessionals and other temporary staff, and trust/research academic staff. The university president was a member. Each of the seven constituencies had its own separate agreement with the university. Under the Post-secondary Learning Act, members were not unionized and were not permitted to strike.

At U of T, the faculty association represented faculty members in the negotiation of their salaries, benefits, and key academic human resource policies. The memorandum of agreement between the university and the association functioned as an agreement and could not be changed unilaterally, but the faculty association was not certified as a union under the Ontario Labour Act. According to the faculty association official interviewed, "there is not sufficient appetite for that here yet."

At the other four universities, faculty members were unionized and had the right to strike – a right they had exercised four times since unionization in 1978 at Dalhousie (Pettigrew 2012; WID ESDC 2020), three times since unionization in 1971 at UQAM (SPUQ n.d.), and once since 1975 at UdeM[3] (WID ESDC 2020; Gill 2017). No faculty strikes had taken place at UBC, where there was provision for arbitration of disputes in lieu of strike and lockout (UBCFA 2010). A director at the UdeM said that exercising the right to strike had involved a very significant cultural shift: "Quand je suis arrivé ici la notion de grève des profs était pratiquement impensable. Personne ne se posait cette question là" (When I first arrived here, the idea of a professors' strike was almost unthinkable. Nobody was asking themselves that question).

Even among the four unionized universities, the extent of the faculty's involvement in institutional decision-making through their unions varied greatly. Asked about the faculty union's influence in decision-making (other than at the bargaining table), a union official at Dalhousie said: "The only input we have as an organization is through grievances – we can grieve decisions, that's about it." In contrast, the faculty union at UQAM was described by a senior administrator as "très présent dans la gérance de l'université" (very present in the management of the university). Its power was described by a student leader as "primordial." Union representatives interviewed described the SPUQ as a partner in the co-management of the university, objecting to the term "governance" because it implied the imposition of decisions rather than participation in decisions. An article by two professors at UQAM who had served on the executive of the FQPPU explained:

Les professeurs et leur syndicat...sont plus que les gardiens [de l'autogestion à l'UQAM]. Ils sont initiateurs, sinon partie prenante, des décisions majeures et des grandes orientations de l'université. En fait, les modalités d'une gestion collégiale de l'université sont inscrites dans leur convention collective qui, plus que de garantir leurs droits individuels...leur *réserve formellement une présence et un rôle dans toutes les instances de l'université*. (Lafortune and Roy 2019, 122)

[The professors and their union ... are more than the guardians [of self-management at UQAM]. They are the initiators, if not stakeholders, of major university decisions and policies. In fact, the collegial management of the university is enshrined in their collective agreement, which, above and beyond guaranteeing their individual rights, formally reserves for them a presence and a role in all the bodies of the university.]

Besides specifying that elections to the *commission des études* and the board would be conducted at a general meeting of the union, the professors' collective agreement (2009–2013) contained provisions related to resources, including the number of professorial positions to be created each year.

At the UdeM, relations between the faculty union and the administration appeared to be poor, and union representatives said the parties had different visions of the university. They described the board as controlled by "Québec Inc." and the role of the union as now extending beyond advocacy for better compensation and work conditions to include advocating for a vision of the university embodying values of collegiality and university democracy. Like their counterparts at UQAM, they objected to the role of external members on the board and advocated that universities be governed by faculty and students.

The faculty association at UBC had been voluntarily recognized by the university as a union (UBCFA n.d.). According to one administrator interviewed, relations between the faculty union and the administration were becoming more acrimonious and issues were increasingly being resolved through arbitration.

Faculty union/association leaders seemed to share some of the concerns expressed by academic administrators about lack of faculty engagement. Those at several case universities, including UQAM, spoke about this. A faculty association official at one of the anglophone universities said:

> I want more of our colleagues to take more seriously the responsibilities [of] academics to play a meaningful role in running the

university. I think too many of us are or have become lazier or complacent, or we forgot or we never really knew what our university meant. It doesn't just mean the freedom to teach your own classes or to design your own research, it means ... to be involved in decisions about the conditions under which those things take place.

## STUDENT PARTICIPATION IN GOVERNANCE

Students participated in the governance of the case universities through membership on governing bodies and by providing advice and input, and in many other ways as well. Some of the mechanisms by which they participated were common to all six universities – for example, all had students on their boards and senates – but there were also important differences. One was in the extent to which student input came from individual students (elected directly by their peers or, in the case of advisory committees, selected by a university administrator or body) or through their associations or unions. At U of A, the student union was said to be clearly recognized as the official voice of students, whereas at some of the other universities, the voices of students other than student union representatives seemed to be relatively more important in governing bodies and other forums.

Student organizations at the case universities were all engaged in both advocacy and service provision, largely autonomous of the universities, and connected to associations at the provincial and/or national levels. However, they differed significantly in structure, responsibilities, relationships, and culture. Some of the differences were perceived to reflect differences between Quebec and the rest of Canada. According to a student leader at UdeM, "au Québec, les gens ont plus envie de s'impliquer au niveau politique dans leurs universités qu'au Canada. Dans le milieu anglophone les associations étudiantes ont l'air d'être plus des associations de service" (in Quebec, people are more interested in getting involved in their universities at the political level than in Canada. In the English-speaking academic community, student associations appear to be more like service associations).

Nevertheless, there were also significant differences both within Quebec and among case universities in the other provinces. At UBC, the student members on the board of governors and the senates were elected directly by students. Three student societies existed at the university's two campuses. The student leader interviewed at UBC said that the university recognized the student societies as independent organizations and was helpful but did not interfere. Members of the university executive and other university officials met and communicated regularly with student society leaders. The relationship between student societies and the university was described as very good at the time of the interviews: "Our attitude is, and [it's] the same with the administration, that we can get a lot more done when we are working together."

Under Alberta's Post-Secondary Learning Act, the student members on U of A's board of governors were nominated by the student societies, as were some of the student members on the general faculties council. The Students' Union (SU) and the Graduate Students' Association (GSA) were established under the PSLA as the official bodies for the administration of student affairs and the representation of students. The status of the associations in legislation was cited by student leaders interviewed as a special feature of Alberta – one that gave student bodies recognition and legitimacy. A senior university official also saw the status of the student organizations as beneficial in that it avoided splintering of the student voice: "There is order, there is discipline, and they are big enough that they have professional staff."

Student leaders at U of A were also active at the provincial level. A graduate student leader explained:

> Alberta is the only rich province where students actually have [a] very substantial say in post-secondary decision-making. By that I mean the access to government that you really only see in smaller and poorer provinces. So, my counterparts in New Brunswick, Newfoundland, Manitoba, we all have very good access. My counterparts in British Columbia complained all the time about not having access to government for the last two years. Certainly, they would not get an audience with the minister, they were lucky to get time with backbenchers. [In] Ontario, you can get time with backbenchers, but it's very hard to get time with ministers ... And in Quebec, instead of [the] brokerage politics that you see in other provinces, Quebec is much more oriented towards student protests ... After periods of major protest and concessions, student leaders and government go back to not talking to one another very much. So it's completely different from anywhere else. Sometimes my Quebec colleagues make recommendations to the rest of us, but it's difficult because we just don't work that way.

This interviewee went on to say:

> In Alberta it's not uncommon for a student union president to have an MLA or even a minister's cell phone number to go out and have

dinner or coffee, not just with backbenchers, but with ministers ... So student unions are unique here ... GSAs [graduate student associations] do not have [quite] that same level of access [as undergraduate student unions] for a couple of different reasons ... [First], we don't have the numbers of constituents that the student unions represent. So when provincial politicians think of who to talk to about issues ... they think of the student unions first ...[A]nd secondly, [graduate students] are a little too close to faculty. This isn't a province where the governing party is really friendly to academics. So graduate students are sometimes seen as, not on the dark side like critical academics, but they are [seen as] on their way.

Because of the exceptional longevity of the Progressive Conservative government in power in Alberta at the time of the interviews for this study, links appeared to have developed between it and not only university boards, but also student leadership. It was explained that:

if you are really ambitious in this province, the advice to student politicians is often to be careful not to be seen as being too close to the opposition parties ... Student politics is sort of seen as an excellent way to have that access, to build these relationships, and to go into politics after graduation. I can easily cite twenty or more current and former members of the legislative assembly here who started with student politics at one institution or another, and that's sort of the cycle.

At U of T, there were eight student members on the fifty-member governing council, elected by students, and sixteen on the 123-member academic board. According to the graduate student leader interviewed, students were seeking increased representation on its governing bodies. At the same time, the interviewee observed that "governance is one of the most difficult things to get students interested in, particularly because it is such a disempowering form of governance." Five student unions and associations represented students across U of T's three campuses.

At the UdeM, the student members of the board (two of between twenty and twenty-four members), the university assembly (at least six of well over 100 members), and the *commission des études* (four of around thirty-five members) were nominated by the student organization. Provincial legislation required universities to recognize student associations, provide them with space, and include their representatives on various councils, committees, or other bodies. The act established organizations representing university students at the level of the accredited unit (department or faculty) rather than the institutional level. At UdeM, student associations existed at the departmental level. At the institutional level, students were represented by one federated body, the FAECUM (Fédération des Associations Étudiantes du Campus de l'Université de Montréal). Representatives of FAECUM were elected from among the representatives of the eighty-two academic unit associations, the numbers of positions being prorated to the size of each association.

Departmental associations were strongly independent and affiliated with different student organizations at the provincial level. The student leader interviewed explained:

> On est représentant de toutes les associations, nonobstant leurs affiliations. Il y a une importance capitale accordée à la souveraineté locale. On ne vient pas imposer des décisions aux associations étudiantes... Sur demande d'une association locale, la fédération peut aider dans certaines initiatives. Mais en aucun cas il y a une ingérence et cela est primordial.
>
> [We represent all associations, regardless of their affiliations. Local sovereignty is of paramount importance. We do not impose decisions on student associations ... At the request of a local association, the federation can assist in certain initiatives. In no case is there any interference and that is fundamental.]

UQAM was unique among the case universities in the role that students played in governance. There was student/faculty parity on the senior academic governance body, the *commission des études*, as well as on program committees. Two students served on the sixteen-member board of directors. Although the power of students at UQAM was said to have declined since its early years, it was described by student leaders at the institutional and provincial levels as high relative to other institutions: "Il y a le plus d'implication étudiante à tous les niveaux" (there is more student involvement at all levels).

A distinctive feature of UQAM's academic regulations was the university's *règlement* no 5/section 7.9 concerning "Entente d'évaluation" for undergraduate courses. It provided that, for each course, there should be an agreement between the professor or instructor and the students regarding the number and nature of the mechanisms by which students in the course would be evaluated and the weight to be given to each. It set out a procedure whereby, within two weeks of the start of classes, an agreement would be signed by the professor or instructor and two students acting as witnesses to the students' agreement to the proposed means of evaluation. In the event of disagreements, the issue would be submitted for resolution to the director of the department offering the course. His or her decision could be appealed to the academic council.

There were seven faculty-level student associations at UQAM. Five were associated with the more militant ASSÉ (Association pour une solidarité syndicale étudiante) and two with the FEUQ (Fédération étudiante universitaire du Québec). Both of these provincial student associations have since disbanded. The student leader interviewed described the cultures of faculty-level student associations as very different in terms of "l'esprit de participation et de contestation" (the spirit of participation and contestation). The associations worked with one another and with the faculty union and other unions on a file-by-file basis. The official position of the interviewee's association was for the abolition of the rectorat. He described his association as having three mandates, which were sometimes in competition: "À la fois on essaie de défendre individuellement les étudiants dans leurs difficultés dans leur cheminement. On a un combat à l'interne de l'université et on a un combat social et politique plus large" (We try to defend individual students encountering difficulties throughout their journeys. At the same time, we engage in a fight inside the university, as well as in a broader social and political battle).

What conception (or conceptions) did interviewees have of students' relationships with the universities? A provincial official in Nova Scotia expressed the opinion that the relationship of both students and the public to universities in the province had changed over the decades:

> Before, universities were untouchable, like the public school system in Nova Scotia. It was impossible to modify anything within the university sector without the prospect of students protesting. Nobody in government wanted to touch the universities.
>
> Now, university students are different. They're pressured to make good economic decisions, they worry about what they will be able to do with their degrees, they don't have time to be on strike, and they don't want to be held hostage to any situation. Students now tend to adopt a very business-like approach of "I paid so ... [here's what I'm owed]" ... Something has fundamentally changed in terms of the relationships [of students and the public] with the universities.

The student leaders interviewed for this study did not ascribe to the view that students are customers or clients, but several said that some students at their institutions – undergraduate students, for example, or graduate students in course-based professional programs – tended to think that way. Here's what a number of student leaders across the country said about whether students at their universities regarded themselves as clients or customers:

> Pas du tout! À moins que les gens veuillent nous insulter. (UQAM) [Not at all! Unless people want to insult us].

> Students view themselves as both customers and clients because there is a sense of entitlement, where they made an investment and feel that they should get something out of it. This is particularly true at undergraduate level where there is a culture of "blame the professor for not giving you the grade that you deserve." That customer-service relationship creates a sense of entitlement that tends to lessen at the graduate level. (U of T)

> The weird thing is that it changes from faculty to faculty. A lot of it has to do how we are paid at the end of day as graduate students. In science and the applied sciences ... where students are on basic guaranteed stipends for a number of years ... the prevailing thought is that they view themselves as employees of the professors ... In the Faculty of Arts, where there is a lot of money for students but they are mainly through scholarships ... they more see themselves as patrons of the university or students of the university. So ... one side sees themselves as employees because they are paid a salary, you did have some sort of understanding at some point [of] how many hours you should be working, and the other is that "they are not paying me, so I do what I want, I am a student, a patron of the university." (UBC)

> [At a meeting with provincial student leaders] ... the minister said ... "you guys are customers, you should be dictating." OK, thanks for acknowledging that we should play a bigger role in the governance of the institutions, but we shouldn't be seeing higher education as a business–customer transaction. It should be more than that.

### STRATEGIC PLANNING

All six universities had an institutional strategic plan. Some had moved away from the preparation of detailed multi-year plans toward high-level objectives that provided a framework for planning and activity at other levels. Plans were approved by boards or equivalent, often upon the recommendation of the senate or some other major academic body. The planning process was typically led by the president or rector and separate from provincial planning processes. U of A, however, had a comprehensive institutional planning process mandated by government and led by the board chair, in addition to a vision and an action plan.

### BUDGET PROCESSES

All four anglophone universities had decentralized their budget processes to varying degrees or were in the process of doing so. Neither of the Quebec universities had done so at the time of our interviews. Dalhousie had begun to share incremental tuition fee revenue with faculties in 1989 and had refined "enrolment-based budget allocation" (ERBA) over time (Eastman 2005). Faculties were required to balance their budgets but had significant latitude for decision-making within their "envelopes." One dean said:

> Within [the] envelope [we receive], we are free to use it in the way we want to. And we are closer to the academic mission of the university than, say, the board of governors ... We can decide ... whether we want to hire people, introduce a new program, whatever we want to do we get to decide that. I think that has worked well for us. Because we can make that [decision] in a collegial way, within the faculty.

ERBA made faculty budgets highly sensitive to increases or decreases in enrolments. A dean observed that "in the end, if you're not bringing in students, you're very quickly going to lose your power, because you're going to lose your funding through the university mechanism ... It's in our interests to be offering programs that are attractive to students." A number of interviewees observed that ERBA also had costs in that it tended to diminish inter-faculty collaboration and to lead to privileging of short-term over long-term considerations.

U of T had gone furthest in decentralizing its budget. In 2002, it had adopted a modified form of responsibility-centred budgeting (RCB) for its business school, after an experiment with a form of RCB at Scarborough College in the late 1990s (Eastman 2005). In this form of budgeting, long practised by major American universities, the centre allocates revenue lines – instead of expenditure lines – to faculties. Faculties are then required to generate revenue sufficient to cover all their direct and indirect costs as well as any taxes collected by the centre for strategic institutional purposes, including cross-subsidization. U of T had subsequently extended the new budget model to other divisions in 2005–06 (Myers 2019).

Asked what governance changes, if any, had taken place over the years at U of T, a university official said that

> the singularly most significant change that I have experienced here at U of T in terms of governance and the way it feels is the new budget model, which ... – despite all of the protestations at the beginning that "nothing will really change, it's all going to be the same" – has [been] ... an enormous change ... It has and continues to fundamentally change the nature of the institution.

How had the new budged model changed U of T? We were advised that "there ... has been a massive change in the perceived strength and authority of central administration, relative to that of the academic divisions." Interviewees at divisional (faculty) and departmental levels echoed the view that the new budget model had empowered them and their colleagues:

> In our faculty, it [the new budget model] has empowered departmental chairs and directors of institutes to plan strategically ... The same is true at the faculty level, so that we have a much better sense [of our financial future] and also ability to increase the revenues, to contain costs in a way that also would benefit the local community, the local faculty. I think if the financial piece is what you are looking at in terms of the broad governance, absolutely that has transformed [governance at U of T] significantly.

The new budget model was also said to have increased transparency in a way that was beneficial, because, prior to its introduction, "everybody probably thought they were subsidizing the rest of the university."

Both U of A and UBC were moving in the same direction. A senior official at U of A suggested that one of the drivers was the need for increased transparency:

> As universities have gotten more and more complex – as governments insist on more and more reporting – ... it becomes more difficult to be transparent. So ... rank-and-file faculty members [ ] don't believe that there are the financial constraints that those at the centres believe there to be ... so I think part of the move to push down the actual cost of things is to make people realize that every decision carries with it some kind of cost.

## THE STATE OF THE UNIVERSITIES

How did the governance of the case universities align with the standard depiction of Canadian universities as homogeneous, public, secular, bicameral, unionized institutions?

### Variations in Internal Governance

All were secular, but, as described in the previous chapter, they were "public" to varying degrees. They were increasingly regulated and administered, as well as highly unionized, though faculty at two institutions were not unionized at the time of the study. Overall, there was more diversity in governance than one might expect. Even among the five medical-doctoral institutions, there were major differences in structure: one was unicameral, one tricameral, and three were essentially bicameral. UQAM remained unique in many respects, despite the forces of isomorphism.

The roles of the boards at the case universities varied. Most were traditional sources of oversight, authority, guidance, and support for the administration, but the board of U of A seemed to be evolving into a force of its own and the UQAM board seemed relatively disempowered. The roles of presidents and rectors, and of senates or equivalents, also varied. Although it is risky to generalize about large, complex institutions based on a limited number of interviews, the prevailing conception of collegiality seemed to differ from university to university, too. At UQAM, collegiality had a democratic flavour. It appeared to mean that directors, deans, vice-rectors, and others would implement their colleagues' will. An interviewee at UQAM said of academic administrators there that "en général on a le même devoir de faire ce que nos membres souhaitent" (in general, we have the same duty to fulfil our members' wishes). An interviewee at U of T suggested that collegiality had a quite different flavour there:

> I do think the governance model here, the more you start poking at it, the more you start to ask yourself, what does collegiality actually mean here? I think it can work if consultation is real, if people are made to feel included, but it's all based ultimately on norms of engagement. I think collegiality here really does mean almost the style of interpersonal interactions, that people who have authority are seen to be fair and wise.

In this view, collegiality at U of T was a function of decision-makers seeking and hearing their colleagues' views and taking those views into account in making decisions.

The comments of an administrator at the UdeM suggested that the conception of collegiality there lay somewhere between those at UQAM and U of T:

> Chez les universités et la nôtre en particulier on a un mode de fonctionnement assez collégial. On reçoit l'avis de tout le monde. On essaie de composer avec, on marche par consensus. Ce n'est pas toujours facile ... [mais, on] essaie de travailler de manière consensuelle et éclairée et on essaie d'écouter l'opinion de tout le monde, et c'est bien comme ça.
>
> [In universities – and in ours, in particular – we have a rather collegial way of operating. We receive everyone's opinion. We try to get on the same page; we work by consensus. It's not always easy ... [but, we] try to work in a consensual and informed manner and we try to listen to everyone's opinion, and that's fine.]

This version of collegiality doesn't involve following one's colleagues' wishes, or taking their views into account in making decisions, but instead, striving to obtain consensus and buy-in.

The state of relations between faculty associations and administrations varied from university to university, as did the boundaries between academic governance and faculty labour relations, even among the four universities where faculty were unionized. Academic governance and collective bargaining had long been deeply entwined at UQAM. The faculty union was described as increasingly influential in academic governance at UdeM, whereas its counterpart at Dalhousie was perceived as having become less so over time. The roles of faculty unions in institutional decision-making seemed to vary, from co-management to broad opposition to the administration to more traditional collective bargaining. The nature and extent of student participation in governance diverged substantially from campus to campus as well. Each university had its own personality and culture. An interviewee who had held senior positions at two of the anglophone case universities said: "I am amazed at how differently the universities feel, [even though] we are basically doing the same kinds of things ... This place feels different. I think it has different values and different [roots]."

## COMMONALITIES IN INTERNAL GOVERNANCE

One common feature – especially at the medical/doctoral universities – was the extent of continuity in governance. Our study involved snapshots of universities, so it did not enable us to compare them at different points in time, but interviewees described changes they had witnessed. Based on their accounts and archival sources, there was substantial stability in the governance of the universities. Major changes in the structure of some of the institutions had taken place. Some examples: the governance changes at UBC resulting from the acquisition of UBC Okanagan; the facultarization at UQAM; the decentralization of decision-making at U of T; the addition of faculties to Dalhousie; and devolution of authority for graduate programs to line faculties at some institutions. There had also been significant changes in boards' and senates' committee structures and practices. Overall, however – with the possible exception of UQAM, which had become more like other Canadian universities over time – the portrait that emerged from the interviews and other data was one of stability in institutional governance structure.

A second common feature was the involvement of people from outside the universities in the oversight and governance of their institutional and business affairs. Consistent with the Flavelle Commission's conception of bicameralism, at the medical-doctoral universities, people who were neither students nor employed by the university, including alumni, constituted the majority of voting members on the board or, in the case of U of T, the Business Board.

A third broad commonality was the primacy of regular faculty in academic governance – relative to other teachers and researchers, non-academic personnel, and others – and the extent of their autonomy. For a host of reasons, including increased regulation in society and growth in institutional complexity and administration, faculty members in Canada seemed to have less collective control over university affairs than they did, briefly, decades ago. That said, our study suggests that professors nevertheless retain a lot of autonomy in their academic work, as well as – through their departments and faculties – control over academic hiring and offerings. Notwithstanding legislative impingement and governments' accountability regimes, academic governance at the case universities appeared to remain largely in the hands of professors (including ones in administrative positions) and students.

## Mechanisms That Support Academic Judgment

All the universities had mechanisms that fostered and protected academic judgment – that is, decision-making over educational, research, and related matters based on expertise and norms in pertinent field(s) – and academic freedom. Asked how their universities fostered and protected these, interviewees cited mechanisms such as the following:

- The existence of senates or equivalents – that is, separation of control over academic matters from control over business and operational matters.
- The presence of internal members on boards of governors, which sensitized other board members to the nature of the academy.
- The power of faculties and limits on the capacity of boards and central administrations to affect their academic direction.
- Legislative, policy, and/or procedural requirements that academic program proposals and curriculum changes originate in departments and faculties rather than being imposed on them.
- Appointment procedures for professors and academic administrators that allowed for academic input or control. (This feature of universities – which Bourdieu regarded as a pillar of autonomy – was cited by relatively few interviewees, perhaps because it was taken for granted.)
- Faculty members' prerogatives under policy and/or collective agreements (including their ability to set their own research agendas, subject to availability of necessary funding, and their academic freedom) and the availability of mechanisms for seeking redress if those prerogatives were infringed.
- The willingness and capacity of faculty unions or associations to include and define academic freedom in collective agreements and to defend their members' rights.
- The roles of academic administrators at all levels in providing space for collegial discussion and decision-making.
- Understanding on the part of deans and chairs of their evolving disciplines or professions and their roles in representing their colleagues' views.
- Policies on matters such as freedom of speech and publication (e.g., avoidance of excessive delays) and commitment by administrators to enforce those policies.

- Practices such as reviews of draft research contracts for appropriate protection of rights to publish.
- Cultural norms that favour and support freedom of expression.
- Communication to external stakeholders of the value, impact, and/or relevance of what universities do, which was perceived to reinforce their autonomy and capacity to govern themselves in a collegial manner.

Interviewees within universities overwhelmingly acknowledged or affirmed the importance of academic freedom, but they expressed varied conceptions of and perspectives on it. A clear, consistent understanding of academic freedom was lacking, even among academic administrators. Different perspectives were expressed as to whether academic freedom legitimately extends to extra-curricular speech rights (i.e., the ability to criticize the university and or society) and/or expression unrelated to one's discipline or profession. Several interviewees observed that academic freedom was sometimes misconstrued. For example, a faculty-level administrator described academic freedom as an important principle, but "un concept un peu flou qu'on utilise pour toute sortes de choses – parfois pour excuser certains comportements" (a somewhat vague concept that is used for all sorts of things – sometimes to excuse certain behaviours). Another interviewee said, "Ça varie peut-être de l'interprétation d'un individu à un autre. Il y a des individus qui ont tendance à extrapoler la liberté académique très loin. La liberté académique existe dans le cadre de notre recherche et de notre enseignement, mais il y a des gens qui la transportent partout ailleurs" (The interpretation may vary from one individual to another. Some people tend to extrapolate academic freedom very far. Academic freedom exists in our research and teaching, but some people transpose it everywhere else).

A number of senior academic administrators suggested that academic freedom is more straightforward in the realm of research than in that of teaching. A provost said:

There's academic freedom around the research more than the teaching part, because we have an obligation to fulfill our contract to students to teach what we said we were going to teach – in a way that satisfies learning outcomes … The way you frame your assignments, the way you discuss it, your choice of authors, topics, sub-topics [are up to you]. Nonetheless, there's a framework under which you have an obligation … to produce this kind of learning and this kind of

students and to get them from A to B. There's certainly a fair amount of freedom there, but it's not *carte blanche*.
That was particularly the case in professional fields, but even in disciplinary ones, academic freedom in teaching was perceived to be complicated. A provost at another case university said:

> Academic freedom in teaching is an interesting combination. If I am asked to and I agree to teach a course in formal logic and I teach a course on ethics instead, I am not free to do that ... Or if I teach formal logic and I get all the proofs wrong, I am not free to do that either. But if I teach a course in ethics, and I want to focus on Hume rather than Kant within the scope of the course description, I am free to do that. But there are a lot of fences ... which academic freedom with respect to teaching is bounded by.

In other words, academic freedom in teaching is complex because professors are responsible for teaching the approved curriculum in a way that meets the standards of the discipline or profession. Collective responsibility to deliver a coherent curriculum and to ensure that students have mastered prescribed content and skills has traditionally been more pronounced in professional fields than in disciplines; however, as universities focus more on articulating and measuring desired learning outcomes in non-professional fields and designing curriculum around that, the balance may shift.

Academic freedom in research was seen by the interviewee quoted above and by others as more straightforward: "So that's easier, that's a much easier question. Because [if] you are a philosopher and you want to publish a paper on formal logic and you get all the proofs wrong, no journals will publish your paper. So we don't need university policies to come into effect ... People are free to do research on what they want." Interviewees did cite constraints on faculty members' ability to pursue their research interests, but the limits took different forms than those in the realm of teaching, for example: capacity to secure resources, merit as assessed by external peers, research priorities established by granting councils, federal tri-council ethics rules, and ultimately the fact that "you are not free to do anything that is illegal."

Above and beyond their institutional affiliations, faculty members and students at the case universities belonged to a host of disciplinary, interdisciplinary, and professional fields. Disciplines in particular tend to function as what Bourdieu described as fields of restricted cultural production; governed by norms and sanctions specific to them, such fields tend to be self-contained and unresponsive to external needs and demands (Bourdieu 1993). As evident from previous chapters, contemporary universities can no longer operate simply as agglomerations of outposts of disciplines and professions, if they ever could. They need to respond to the expectations of governments, students, other stakeholders, and the public at large in order to fulfill their missions, secure support, and obtain resources to operate. That requires collective responsiveness to stakeholders' needs.

## Mechanisms That Promote Responsiveness

Interviewees were asked by what means, if any, their universities foster responsiveness to external needs and demands. Many expressed the view that it is important that universities attend to the changing needs of students and society. Their conceptions of responsiveness were broad. Interviewees spoke about universities' roles in preparing students for employment, fostering students' intellectual, personal, and civic development, contributing to community and regional development, partnering with industry, and contributing to society through leadership in the advancement of knowledge. Asked about mechanisms that foster responsiveness, one university official said:

> We respond to our students. If our students flock into philosophy as they do, we will offer lots of philosophy courses. We will also offer Slavic studies ... and [medieval studies because we have] brilliant ... department[s,] even though those departments don't have as many students as philosophy or engineering or biosciences. We ... are committed to those disciplines. So we are responsive to a lot of things, to student demand, to being a place where research and scholarship and teaching thrives, and that means offering medieval studies, and also to government because government is both our funder but also in a democracy captures the will of the people. So there are a lot of things for us to be responsive to, and we try to be responsive to them all.

One mechanism for fostering institutional responsiveness to stakeholders' needs was the involvement of students, alumni, the public, and others in governance. One interviewee described the board of governors as "the focal point of accountability to the public." Another said "we have all the stakeholders represented in governance ... and ... ensure that all the perspectives of the broader university stakeholders are considered. And that's the most effective way to govern."

Governance guided and oversaw leadership and hierarchy, which also served to align internal activities with external needs and demands. At all but one of the case institutions, the governing body appointed a president or rector to lead the university. She or he was the head of a hierarchy of academic and other administrators and staff. Members of the academic administrative hierarchy were responsible both to the position or body above them and to their colleagues. The balance of accountability varied to some extent by institution in accordance with culture as well as appointment or election practices.

At the bottom of the academic administrative hierarchy were chairs and directors. They described their roles as consisting largely of facilitative and administrative leadership and as holding little authority. How much authority did people further up the academic administrative hierarchy have? That was not clear. It seemed to vary by university and indeed by faculty within universities. Some interviewees described "top-down" administration as increasing at their institutions, but many senior officials described their roles as largely facilitative and said they had access to very few levers of power. In general, management authority appeared to be heavily circumscribed by academic governance, collective agreements, policies, regulations, and cultural norms.

Other aspects of institutional structure that appeared to foster collective responsiveness to external needs and demands included:

- professional faculties and departments and the mechanisms that link them to their professions and those they serve, including teaching hospitals and other affiliated organizations;
- research centres and institutes;
- advisory bodies composed in whole or in part of stakeholders;
- structures such as TECEdmonton, set up at U of A to encourage and support spin-offs, and UQAM's infrastructure for collective services.

Processes that could foster responsiveness appeared to include:

- strategic planning, implementation, and follow-up (at the institutional level, for research, and in other realms);
- cyclical program reviews incorporating student and stakeholder feedback;
- mechanisms for reallocating faculty positions and other resources

("En embauchant de nouveaux profs, on change l'expertise du corps professoral et on adresse les besoins sociétaux" [In hiring new teachers, we change the expertise of the professoriate and address societal needs]);
- annual student evaluations of courses and teaching and other mechanisms for obtaining student feedback;
- processes for identifying, measuring, and improving learning outcomes;
- use of pertinent performance measures at the institutional, faculty, or unit level.

Resource requirements also encouraged or necessitated institutional responsiveness to stakeholders and market forces. Owing to the way the universities were funded, they and their units needed to recruit and enrol appropriate numbers of students. An interviewee at UBC said:

> This is a 2-billion-dollar university, with a 1.1-billion-dollar operating budget. Forty-five percent of that comes from the government, but 30 percent of it comes from domestic tuition, and going on 15 percent comes from international tuition, so the students in a modern university have as much to say as the government does ... The students bring a set of expectations. They want a great experience.

Research requires resources, and in that regard, an official at U of T said:

> There's simply not enough public money to enable us to do the research we want to do, so we're turning to other sources ... The magnitude of the scope of our engagement with the private sector [has increased] ... As we go along that path (which many people are suspicious of), we increasingly have to be clear and discriminate between what is actually research and scholarship in conjunction with private sector entities, and what are service agreements.

Fundraising was also part of the case universities' strategies and also entailed receptiveness to external interests. A dean said:

> Sometimes it is a matter of demonstrating the value of what we do and the long-term benefit. Sometimes donors want to change what you're doing. It's a very delicate balance. You have to work with that. You have to respect donor wishes, be donor-centric and at the same time make sure that the tail doesn't end up wagging the dog – that

you don't do something that goes against collegial processes or against the broader understanding of what the academy is.

Budgetary decentralization could strengthen incentives or requirements for faculties and other units to respond to the needs and demands of students, funders, and others.

Institutional history and culture were also cited as fostering responsiveness to stakeholders and society. For example, UQAM had a tradition and an ethos of social empowerment and improving access to higher education. Likewise, an interviewee said that "the University of Alberta in its founding moments was assigned the task of advancing Alberta, so we have a long experience through agriculture, energy and water, land, and having very close working relationships with major industry groups."

The desire of individual faculty members to work with external organizations and groups was also deemed important in outreach to society. Several senior administrators commented on the desirability of a broader definition of scholarship, in order to recognize and support faculty members in such activities.

Finally, regulation was cited as a means by which universities secure their members' compliance with external requirements. As an interviewee at U of T observed, "when government imposes a new requirement on universities, that requirement has to be rolled out from the centre, because if you let individual faculties and departments do it themselves, some of them will, some of them won't. So increased government regulation has increased central regulation."

*Intersecting Processes and Forces*

The portrait that emerges is of universities as places where academic judgment is exercised and encouraged at the individual, departmental, faculty, and institutional levels. Collective responsiveness to stakeholder needs and demands is fostered through a host of mechanisms, from institutional structures and culture, to planning and quality assurance processes, to financial incentives, and ultimately, regulations and administration. Unions and/or associations serve the interests of their employee or student members within and outside the institutions.

These mechanisms – for exercise of academic judgment, for collective responsiveness, for labour and student relations – combined with the great breadth of disciplines and professions represented at the case universities, made for immensely complex organizations. Complexity was a major theme at several, taking a variety of forms and giving rise to a variety of issues. Complexity made it difficult to apprehend the university as a whole. How the university works and why tended to be mysterious, even to people within it. A head at UBC alluded to this:

> I felt that when I was a faculty member, I was in a big swimming pool. Everyone else is swimming around and bumping each other. They are going in various directions, but we are basically under the water. So we see each other but we do not see above the edges of the swimming pool. And when I became a head, I would suddenly have my body in the swimming pool but I could see all around the edge of the swimming pool. And it struck me that outside there are all kinds of things that I had never noticed before. I had some vague idea, I know there is the president, but UBC is a giant place, so I had this image of cabanas, palm trees, lots of buildings out there, all the central administration was above the level of the regular swimming pool ... As a head, you are kind of half way in between. I think as a dean you maybe have your toes in the swimming pool and then it goes on from there. There is a lifeguard somewhere ...

Even at the level of governing bodies, it could be hard to attain and maintain a focus on matters of significance to the university as a whole. An official at one of the larger universities said:

> One of the governance issues that [big universities] have to confront is ... [that] the complexity tends to hang up on tiny issues, because [governing body members] can't hold on to the entirety. We will spend, and I'm not kidding, we will spend an hour debating parking rates, and we will spend five minutes approving a [multi-billion-dollar] consolidated budget. Our deliberating tribunals like academic senate and subcommittees of the board are really unable to contend with the size and magnitude of the institution we have.

Complexity also appeared to impede decisions and actions. Some commented on "over-governance" at U of T – one of the issues tackled by the recent governance review. At U of A, a number of interviewees expressed concern about the university's capacity for change. One said:

> This university is not nimble. We are like the *Titanic* and this is true probably for every university ... There's an iceberg ahead, and we are

incapable of changing course quickly ... But the reality is, until somebody has that kind of power and the ability to exercise it, and the willingness to put up the flag, we will continue in the same course we are going with just minor course corrections.

Similar comments were made by several interviewees at UdeM. The sheer complexity of the institutions – the diffusion of authority through legislation, structure, policy, collective agreements, and other mechanisms across a host of disciplines and professional fields – could lead to inertia, leaving people at many levels feeling disempowered and frustrated. Some of the case universities appeared to be tackling this by decentralizing their budgets and effectively disaggregating. In the university-as-holding-company, faculties may be more responsive, both to their disciplines or professions and to their stakeholders and environments, than a contemporary large university could ever be. The university's governance structures might look the same, but roles would have changed, as would the nature of the university.

### SUMMARY

Notwithstanding the general portrait of Canadian universities as relatively homogeneous, public universities, we saw in the previous chapter that the case universities' external governance differed substantially, even though all of them were experiencing increased government regulation. The six institutions were part of provincial higher education systems with different histories, dynamics, and characteristics. They had different relationships to the state, and some were more "public" than others.

This chapter identified both similarities and differences in their internal governance. All six universities embodied bicameral principles insofar as their governance featured – to varying degrees and in various ways – separation of institutional/business from academic governance, external oversight of institutional and business affairs, and substantial internal control over academic matters. Faculties and academic departments, organized largely along traditional disciplinary and professional lines, were the building blocks of their academic governance and administration. The universities were led by presidents or rectors, appointed or nominated by a board or equivalent, who headed up academic and non-academic administrative hierarchies. The universities all had mechanisms for fostering both the exercise of academic judgment in educational and research-related decision-making, and institutional responsiveness to external needs and demands. Overlaid on these were mechanisms for collective bargaining with faculty and staff groups over terms of employment, which could extend into tensions or conflict in other realms. All had vehicles for student participation in governance and autonomous student unions. At the same time, the six universities' internal governance exhibited diversity, too. They differed in their governance structures, the roles of governing bodies and leaders, institutional cultures, the relationship of faculty labour relations to academic governance, the nature and extent of student participation, and the extent of budgetary decentralization, and in other ways as well. Spanning myriad disciplines and professions, the case universities were immensely complex organizations, characterized by substantial stability in governance.

# 6

## Updates and Observations

The last of the interviews for this study was conducted in 2015. How has the six universities' external and internal governance changed since then? This chapter summarizes developments over the past five years as reported in publicly available sources. It begins with an overview of major changes on the external governance front – principally, in public policy. We then turn to developments in internal governance. Given the size and complexity of the case universities, no attempt is made to provide a comprehensive account of such developments. Instead, the second half of the chapter describes a series of events through which the governance of each case university evolved and/or was tested in the years since the study. This sheds light on forces for, constraints on, and dynamics of change in university governance.

### EXTERNAL GOVERNANCE

Changes in government took place in all five provinces:

*Nova Scotia*

In Nova Scotia, the NDP government in power at the time of our interviews was succeeded by a Liberal government, elected in 2013 and re-elected in 2017, and then by a Conservative government in 2021. Some of the province's universities continued to struggle financially, and several received special funding from the provincial government in order to cope. In May 2015, the province passed the Universities Accountability and Sustainability Act to make universities more financially accountable and deal with ones in financial distress (Laroche 2015). In addition to requiring additional financial reporting, the legislation established a mechanism whereby universities facing financial exigencies could restructure (Nova Scotia 2015). The legislation gave the Nova Scotia government and university boards powers to override aspects of governance and collective agreements in cases of financial exigency. Through new memoranda of agreement on funding and fees signed in 2016 and 2019, the provincial government required the implementation of stand-alone sexualized violence policies and frameworks for university–student consultation at each university (Nova Scotia 2016, Academica 2019b). At the same time, the province's fee policy allowed or encouraged Nova Scotia universities to focus even more on generating revenue by serving out-of-province and international student markets. The September 2021 mandate letter for the new Minister of Advanced Education called for "a review of all University charters and Acts, their respective governance models and structure" (Nova Scotia 2021).

## Quebec

In Quebec, the Parti Québécois government in power at the time of the interviews was succeeded in the spring of 2014 by a Liberal government. Neither it nor its successor enacted proposals for a new framework law and a Council of Universities that had emanated from the Summit on Higher Education in early 2013. Proposals for reform of the governance of Quebec universities that had been the subject of intense discussion for more than five years thus did not see the light of day.

When it came to power in 2014, the Liberal government reduced funding to universities as part of a major deficit reduction initiative. The rector of UdeM said in 2017, "The Maple Spring paralyzed everyone who criticized the underfunding of universities. No one wants to take up our cause, especially not politicians. Nobody wants to discuss funding, let alone tuition fees. These have become toxic topics" (Venne 2017a).

There was significant turnover in rectors at Quebec universities and difficulty filling their positions, particularly within the UQ (Venne 2017b). Among the reasons cited were the open nature of appointment processes, uncompetitive compensation, constrained institutional funding, and the "fact that universities and their rectors draw little sympathy from Quebec's general population" (Venne 2017b).

Bill 62 (An Act to foster adherence to State religious neutrality and to provide a framework for requests for accommodations on religious grounds) was passed in 2017. The justice minister stated that it required students to have their faces uncovered in class; however, some universities and colleges in Montreal declined to enforce this, citing other obligations and values (Canadian Press 2017). Shortly thereafter, legislation required all post-secondary institutions to develop and implement policies to prevent and combat sexual violence (*Gazette* 2019).

In 2018, a new funding policy was introduced. It increased university operating funding by over 11 percent in the first year, reduced the number of factors in the calculation of institutions' grants (from 538 to 107), and tied part of their funding to the attainment of targets. The new policy deregulated fees for some non-Quebec students and enabled universities to keep international student tuition fees. It also required that salary increases for rectors be limited to rates in the public and para-public sectors (Venne 2018).

The Liberal government was succeeded later in 2018 by the centre-right Coalition Avenir Québec. In 2019, the new government, having campaigned on a commitment to reduce immigration to Quebec, announced modifications to a fast-track immigration program for foreign students and temporary workers. After a backlash from business, the university sector, and students, the government suspended the changes (CBC 2019). As of spring 2019, partial provincial reinvestment in Quebec's universities and colleges was reflected in an increase of 9.6 percent over ten years in budgeted transfers to institutions – more than in any other province.

In 2020, Quebec's chief scientist led broad consultations on the future of the province's universities. The resulting report contained twelve recommendations addressed to government, universities, and other stakeholders, including improved base funding, simpler and more effective data collection, greater interdisciplinarity and social engagement, and the promulgation by government of an official statement recognizing the role of universities and affirming the centrality of academic freedom and institutional autonomy (Quebec 2021a). In response to the report, the minister struck an independent commission on the recognition of academic freedom in the university milieu, charged with making recommendations to governments and universities (Quebec 2021b).

The establishment of the commission reflected the Quebec government's concern about the manner in which several universities had responded to complaints about speech by professors and other instructors that was perceived by many students and others as unacceptable. Among the instances was one at the University of Ottawa in the fall of 2021, in which use of a term by a professor in the course of a class discussion resulted in complaints from students, a backlash on social media, demands for "zero tolerance" speech policies, criticism of the professor's conduct by the dean and president, and her temporary suspension

(Yakabuski 2020). This and other controversies, including at Concordia University and McGill University, stirred debate in the academic community and received a great deal of media attention in Quebec.

In December 2021, the commission on academic freedom recommended to the government that it pass legislation: defining the mission of the university; identifying university autonomy and academic freedom as essential elements of that mission; and requiring each institution to adopt a policy on academic freedom and a committee to guide its oversight (Quebec 2021c, 62). The commission opined that "[L]es salles de cours ne peuvent pas êtres considérées comme des 'espaces sécuritaires' (safe spaces), en particulier lorsque ce concept est défini par l'existence et l'entretien d'un environnement exempt de toute confrontation d'idées ou de remises en question" (63) (classrooms cannot be considered 'safe spaces,' particularly when this concept is defined by the existence and maintenance of an environment exempt from the confrontation of ideas or questioning).

In sum, developments beginning in the second half of the decade in Quebec included renewed consultations, restoration of public funding, expansion of scope for universities to generate revenue from international markets, additional regulation of executive compensation, measures reflecting and addressing socio-cultural issues, and, in April 2022, legislation to remedy perceived failure on the part of universities to protect academic freedom.

*Ontario*

In Ontario, the Liberal government in power at the time of our interviews was re-elected in 2014 and defeated in 2018 by the Progressive Conservative Party, which formed a majority government. The change in government was accompanied by significant changes in policy, including:

- withdrawal of support for a newly established, but not yet operational, francophone university in Ontario (however, the provincial government subsequently reconsidered this decision [Doucet 2019]);
- a requirement that post-secondary institutions in Ontario adopt and implement policies on free speech, consistent with the University of Chicago's Statement of Principles on Free Expression;
- a 10 percent reduction in tuition fees (other than for international students and full-cost recovery programs), announced in January 2019 and coupled with replacement of a "free" tuition program for low-income students introduced by the previous government with grants and loans (Academica 2019a); and

- a "Student Choice Initiative" – a policy that classified non-tuition fees as either essential or non-essential and that required universities to enable students to opt out of non-essential fees, including fees for activities such as student newspapers, campus food banks, and student clubs.

The Canadian Federation of Students and a university-level student union successfully challenged the Student Choice Initiative in court. In November 2019, a Divisional Court ruled that the policy exceeded the government's jurisdiction and intruded on the autonomy of universities and student governments. The court found that

> [8] Universities are private, autonomous, self-governing institutions. They are "publicly assisted" but not publicly owned or operated. For more than 100 years, Ontario has had a legalized policy of non-interference in university affairs, reflected in private legislative Acts conferring on university governing councils and senates the authority and responsibility to manage university affairs. There is no statutory authority authorizing Cabinet or the Minister to interfere in the internal affairs of universities generally, or in the relations between universities and student associations specifically. (Ontario Superior Court Divisional Court 2019)

The provincial government appealed this ruling, arguing that "attaching conditions to government grants in no way interferes with university autonomy and independence. Universities remain free to exercise their independence and autonomy through the choice to accept public funding, subject to whatever conditions are attached" (Friesen 2019). In 2021, the Ontario Court of Appeal dismissed the appeal, ruling that the government's ancillary fee framework could not be imposed by executive authority and that its implementation would have required changes to universities' legislation (Court of Appeal for Ontario, 2021).

Additional policy developments accompanied the new government's first budget. There was a provision to prevent professors from drawing pensions and salary simultaneously, which the Ontario Confederation of University Faculty Associations characterized as "a direct attack on collective bargaining" (OCUFA 2019). In addition, there was an announcement that 25 percent of university funding would be tied to performance outcomes beginning in 2021, increasing to up to 60 percent in 2024–25 (Usher 2019j). However, the implementation of performance-based funding in Ontario was postponed in the spring of 2020 because of uncertainty caused by the COVID-19 pandemic (Friesen 2020b).

In February 2021, Laurentian University in Sudbury announced that it was seeking creditor protection under the federal Companies' Creditors Arrangement Act (CCCA), having accumulated more than $90 million in debt. The university had approached the Ontario government in December 2020 asking for $100 million to fund restructuring and continuing operations. Having declined the government's offer to provide $12 million to finance operations until the end of March, pending an independent review of its finances, Laurentian declared insolvency (Jeffords 2021). As part of a restructuring process under the CCCA, the university terminated fifty-eight undergraduate programs and eleven graduate programs, with the approval of its senate (Ontario Superior Court of Justice 2021, 60). It also terminated the employment of 83 professors and 42 staff members, declared another 27 full-time faculty positions redundant, reduced continuing faculty members' salaries by 5 percent, and ended its relationship with three federated universities (Ontario Superior Court of Justice 2021; Yakabuski 2021). These measures, unprecedented in Canada, caused damage to affected students, faculty, staff, and communities and sent shockwaves across Northern Ontario, francophone Canada, and the university community at large. Questions abounded regarding why and when the university's finances had disintegrated, who was responsible, and how the board of governors and the administration had let it happen. It is too early to predict what impact creditor-driven restructuring will have on the university's future. In the meantime, events at Laurentian have highlighted the consequences of a lack of rigorous, ongoing board financial oversight and challenged long-standing assumptions about the employment security of professors and the continuance of normal institutional and academic governance processes.

On the public policy front, Ontario thus witnessed intensification of financial pressures on universities, a major initiative by government to harness them to performance goals, and a novel response by one university to financial contingency. Numerous provincial measures might be regarded either as correcting perceived deficiencies in universities' governance (e.g., in their capacity to control non-tuition fees or senior professors' compensation or to support freedom of expression) or as measures intended to garner political support from people skeptical of universities, professors, and students.

## Alberta

After more than forty years of Progressive Conservative government in Alberta, the New Democratic Party won the May 2015 provincial election, forming a majority government. In November the provincial government announced a review of the province's agencies, boards, and commissions, including universities and colleges (CBC 2015). Early in 2016, it implemented a new process for appointing board members and declined to renew the appointments of existing university and college board members, citing the need for greater diversity (Alberta 2016, 741). On the financial front, the provincial government introduced a tuition freeze and increased operating funding to post-secondary institutions in real terms while investing generously in capital projects (Usher 2016a).

In early 2017 the government passed Bill 7, An Act to Enhance Post-Secondary Academic Bargaining, which amended the Post-Secondary Learning Act and the Labour Relations Code to bring faculty members and other university staff under the latter. In introducing the legislation, the minister cited the need to comply with a recent Supreme Court of Canada decision confirming Canadian workers' right to strike while maintaining essential public services. The effect was to extend the right to strike to academic staff associations and graduate student associations and to create post-doctoral fellows associations with the right to strike (Alberta 2017b). Section 58.3(2) of the Labour Relations Code henceforth stated: "(2) The academic staff association of a public post-secondary institution is deemed to be a trade union for the purposes of acting as bargaining agent for the public post-secondary institution's academic staff members" (Alberta 2017a, 3). In other words, academic staff in Alberta had just been unionized without voting for certification.

In the spring of 2018, the province introduced a Post-Secondary Compensation Regulation that set maximum base salaries for executives, brought pensions and benefits in line with those in the public service, and required universities to submit compensation plans to government. It provided for five levels of maximum base salary, reflecting the scale of the institutions. The minister said, "For too long, executive salaries have been left unchecked and this led to compensation packages that were out of touch with those in the broader public sector and with the expectations of everyday Albertans" (Graney 2018).

Later in 2018, the government introduced legislation to amend the Post-Secondary Learning Act to cap average tuition fees across all programs at a university to annual increases consistent with the consumer price index. The regulations also "gave the minister authority over mandatory non-instructional fees" and required that any new such fees be approved by students (Kaiser 2018).

In the April 2019 provincial election, the NDP was defeated by the United Conservative Party, which formed a majority government. The new Minister of Advanced Education announced in April that post-secondary institutions would be required to adopt free speech policies based on the University of Chicago principles (Graney 2019). In August, the government announced a series of appointments to university and other boards. According to a newspaper article, "the government cleaned house at the province's largest post-secondary institutions, replacing the top bosses at the University of Alberta and the University of Calgary, along with the board chairs of seven other colleges and universities. A number of those board chairs had been appointed by the NDP and were midway through their terms" (Giovannetti 2019). In response to criticism from the NDP, the premier's spokesperson said, "the previous government made appointments based on its priorities and mandate, and it is reasonable for us to do the same" (Giovannetti 2019).

Also in August 2019, the government received the report and recommendations of a Blue Ribbon Panel on Alberta's Finances (the MacKinnon Panel). It found that spending far exceeded depressed resource revenues and that "without decisive action, the province faces year after year of deficits and an ever-increasing debt" (Alberta 2019, 4). Alberta had outspent the average of the other provinces over a twenty-five-year period, but "in some key areas, in spite of the higher level of funding, the results are no better and, in some cases, worse than in other provinces" (4). The panel concluded that Alberta should reduce spending and focus on getting results. It recommended that the government:

- set goals for the post-secondary system after consultation with stakeholders;
- lift the tuition freeze and work with stakeholders to achieve a revenue mix, like BC and Ontario;
- assess the financial viability of the province's post-secondary institutions and "move quickly to address the future of post-secondary institutions not viable in future funding scenarios" (6);
- adopt a funding model linked to outcomes; and
- "assess whether the current governance model can address the challenges facing post-secondary institutions in Alberta by exploring alternative models used in the rest of Canada and in other jurisdictions"(42).

When interviewed following the release of the report, the minister said that "the conclusion that the MacKinnon Panel Report makes is that ... we have one of the most expensive post-secondary systems in the entire country and the outcomes don't appear to be matching that investment" (Academica 2019c).

In its first budget, tabled in October 2019, the UCP government announced a reduction in post-secondary funding of 5 percent in 2019. The percentage reduction would vary by institution: for the University of Alberta and the University of Calgary, it would be 6.9 percent. Tuition fees would be permitted to rise 7 percent per year at the institutional level for the next three years (Frangou 2019).

Along with freezing hiring, hosting, and travel, the minister asked institutions in January 2020 to defer expenditures until after the end of the budget year to the extent possible and to submit monthly financial reports (Bennett 2020). With the Alberta economy in dire straits, the province's 2020 budget included a further annual reduction of 6.3 percent in post-secondary funding (Johnson 2020). This was part of a plan to reduce such funding by 20 percent over three years. The extent of the funding cuts varied by institution. U of A and two colleges received the deepest reductions – 9 percent from 2019–20 to 2020–21 (French 2020).

In April 2021, the provincial government released a ten-year strategy for post-secondary education. The report stated with respect to governance that "many stakeholders have encouraged Alberta's government to review its relationship with institutions and explore options to reduce red tape, so post-secondary institutions can more freely innovate, and generate their own revenue sources. As a result, government will explore a new relationship with an initial group of institutions to consider removing controls and further reducing red tape" (Alberta 2021, 30). To this end, the government would "explore amending the current composition of boards of governors so government no longer appoints a majority of the members at certain institutions" (30). One month later, Alberta responded to mounting concern in Canada about the implications for national security and human rights of research collaboration with Chinese partners, by ordering the province's four major universities to suspend the pursuit of partnerships with individuals and organizations linked to the Chinese government or the Chinese Communist Party (Chase and Fife 2021).

In sum, Alberta witnessed developments that included post-election changes in university board leadership and membership, sometimes abrupt; unionization of university faculty and staff by government; relative generosity in public funding succeeded by deep restraint;

policy-borrowing (e.g., on free speech); and continued tendency on the part of the state to treat universities like government agencies, followed by the prospect of more autonomy and independent board governance, for some, in the interests of innovation and improved performance.

## British Columbia

The governing Liberal Party won a plurality of seats in the 2017 provincial election but did not achieve a majority. The NDP subsequently formed government with the support of another party. The new government did not display the single-minded focus of its predecessor on preparing graduates for jobs, but the principal mechanisms for government oversight of the post-secondary sector – the accountability framework, mandate letters, budget framework, tuition regulation – remained in place. All board members were required to sign their university's mandate letter "to acknowledge government's direction to [their] organization" (British Columbia 2019).

In the fall of 2018, the government quietly removed a section from the University Act (s. 23(1)(g)), introduced by a previous Liberal government in 2012, that prevented faculty or staff members who were members of their unions' executives or bargaining teams from serving on university boards (British Columbia n.d.).

The Minister of Advanced Education gave high priority to preventing and responding to sexualized violence; it also implemented the UN Declaration on the Rights of Indigenous Peoples and the Calls to Action of the Truth and Reconciliation Commission, as well as measures to improve access to post-secondary education and mental health care on campuses. Universities' mandate letters referenced these priorities while continuing to emphasize the expansion of programs aligned with labour demand, compliance with a cap on fee increases, and meeting financial targets such as "maintaining balanced or surplus financial results" (British Columbia 2019).

## Ottawa

Recent years also witnessed developments in policy and programs at the federal level that affect universities. The Truth and Reconciliation Commission of Canada, established in 2008 as part of the Indian Residential Schools Settlement Agreement, issued a report in June 2015 that concluded: "Much of the current state of troubled relations between Aboriginal and non-Aboriginal Canadians is attributable to educational institutions and what they have taught, or failed to teach, over many generations. Despite this history – or, perhaps more correctly, because of its potential – the Truth and Reconciliation Commission (TRC) believes that education is also the key to reconciliation" (TRC 2015a, 117). The goals of the commission's ninety-four calls to action included "eliminat[ing] educational and employment gaps between Aboriginal and non-Aboriginal Canadians" (224). The same report made targeted recommendations to post-secondary institutions and professional faculties.

A Liberal government was elected in the fall of 2015 and re-elected in 2019 and 2021, forming a minority government. The government identified reconciliation with Indigenous peoples as a top priority and passed legislation to implement the UN Declaration on the Rights of Indigenous Peoples. However, tangible results to date have been few (Papillon 2020).

The federal government made a major investment in university and college infrastructure in 2016–17, but total granting council funding remained relatively constant in real terms between 2005–06 and 2016–17 (Usher 2019k, 42–4). A Fundamental Science Review that made far-reaching recommendations in 2017 led to some additional investment in 2018 and to regularization of funding for the Canada Foundation for Innovation (Sa 2019a).

New equity provisions were added to the Canada Research Chairs (CRC) program (Sa 2019b). In 2006 the CRC program had reached a settlement with a group of academics who had filed a complaint with the Canadian Human Rights Commission concerning underrepresentation of equity groups. In 2017, the 2006 Settlement Agreement was made a federal court order (Canada Research Chairs Program 2019). By the end of 2017, universities wishing to participate in the CRC program were required to submit equity action plans to address the underrepresentation of chair holders in four designated groups (Shen 2018). The CRC program entered into a mediation process with the plaintiffs and the human rights commission concerning changes to the settlement agreement. The outcome involved increasing institutional targets for representation of women, visible minorities, persons with disabilities, and Indigenous peoples to reflect representation within the Canadian population by the end of a ten-year period, rather than representation within pools of academics available for hiring (Hannay 2019). In 2019, 33.5 percent of Canada Research Chairs were women, 15.9 percent were "visible minorities," 1.6 percent were people with a disability, and 2.1 percent were Indigenous; by 2029, 50.9 percent of chairs are to be awarded to women, 22 percent to visible minorities, 7.5 percent to people with disabilities, and 4.9 percent to Indigenous scholars (Hannay 2019).

Meanwhile, stepping briefly into provincial jurisdiction, the federal Minister for Women and Gender Equality struck an advisory committee to develop a national framework that would hold universities and colleges accountable for addressing sexualized violence on campuses. The 2018 federal budget had committed $5.5 million over five years to the development of a framework for preventing and addressing gender-based violence at post-secondary institutions. Ottawa also indicated that beginning in 2019, it would withdraw funding from institutions that did not implement "best practices." Ontario, Quebec, BC, and Manitoba already had legislation requiring universities to implement policies to combat sexualized violence (Bresge 2019).

In 2021 the federal government followed Alberta's initiative to limit research collaboration with China by requiring researchers who were applying for grants from the Natural Sciences and Engineering Research Council (NSERC) to complete national security risk assessments for work involving foreign researchers or organizations. Projects deemed to involve significant risk would be reviewed by security officials and scientists and, if found to involve excessive risk, would not be funded. Some commentators characterized the new measures as long overdue; others expressed concern that they would lead to discrimination against students and faculty members of Chinese nationality or origin (Chase 2021), undermine universities' efforts to be open and inclusive, and have a chilling effect on research (Parsons 2021).

Our study and the above provincial updates encompassed five of ten provinces accounting for 88 percent of the Canadian population (Statistics Canada 2020b) and 91 percent of university students (Statistics Canada 2020c). Governance arrangements and trends in other parts of the country may be different. Further study will be needed to ascertain whether similar patterns prevail in other provinces and the territories. Nevertheless, what can be gleaned from these updates?

Recent years have witnessed changes in government in all five provinces, but the extent of associated policy change has varied. In some jurisdictions, there has been substantial continuity; in others, there has been significant change and even effective policy reversal. Constraints on universities' decision-making are intensifying in all five provinces as well as at the federal level. Initiatives like Ontario's free speech policy requirement have increased the likelihood that the courts will come to regard universities as agents of government, leading to further reduction in their autonomy and increased litigation and associated costs (Dea 2020a). That said, changes in institutional decision-making scope have not been unidirectional. A handful of legislative and regulatory measures – for example, the return of more control over international student fees to universities in Quebec – might be said to have expanded or partly restored university powers. Most significant in this respect would be budgetary deconsolidation and more independent board governance for major universities in Alberta, signaling provincial recognition of the detrimental effect of excessive regulation on universities' performance and a major change in the state-university relationship in that province.

Many government initiatives were prompted by universities' perceived shortcomings – perceptions that universities had, for example, failed to stop sexualized violence, ignored risks associated with international research collaboration, failed to control executive or faculty compensation, or permitted unwarranted restrictions on free expression. The possibility of legislation on academic freedom in Quebec is deeply ironic in that it would involve state intervention in order to uphold a fundamental value that universities are expected to uphold. Such legislation, while potentially beneficial for the academic mission, would entail a reduction in university autonomy in that individual universities would have less scope to balance academic freedom against other considerations. In some of these instances, politicians were responding to the concerns of university constituents, including faculty members and student groups. In others, they appeared to be responding to other stakeholders' concerns and/or exploiting populist sentiment in society at large.

There were instances of government micromanagement of universities and numerous examples of policy diffusion/borrowing, both across provinces and from abroad. Sometimes borrowing took place among governments of a similar political stripe (e.g., with respect to free speech and voluntary student unionism); in other instances, it crossed political lines. For example, steps by the federal and provincial governments to require universities to tackle sexualized violence appeared to cross party lines as a reaction to public outrage, in Canada and abroad, over sexual violence on campuses and in society at large.

For universities, responding to government policy initiatives required funding, staffing, additional policies and procedures, and education – in sum, more administration. Insofar as even the most worthy objectives – to support students experiencing mental illness, for example, or to address sexualized violence – represent expansion of universities' missions to make up for deficiencies in the health and justice systems available to all Canadians, some of the initiatives also raised questions about socio-economic equity.

As noted in Chapter 5, the flavour of policy often varies between governments of different political stripes, an example being the emphasis placed on social equity relative to the economy. Recently, differences in flavour appear to have become magnified. Harking back to Newman's classification of government intrusions into university affairs as bureaucratic, political, or ideological, instances of political and ideological uses of government power appear to be on the rise. When provincial governments engage in this, it increases the likelihood that successor governments of a different political stripe will reverse course. This is difficult for universities, particularly if they are enmeshed with government. When federal and provincial governments simultaneously pursue policies of a different political and/or ideological hue, the implications for universities are even more fraught.

Depending on whether and how the performance-based funding arrangements announced by several provinces are implemented, they could represent a major shift in the way universities are funded in Canada. Lang identified a number of reasons why early performance funding arrangements in Canada and the United States tended to be ineffective, including mismatch with universities' long production cycles and uncertainty about the future. He found that the previous performance funding cum performance indicators program in Ontario had changed four times in eight years (Lang 2016a, 6). Insofar as indicators are political, they are unlikely to be stable.

Stability is also important in board leadership. It is natural that governments consider appointments through different lenses and that they bring legitimate policy considerations to the process. That said, the abruptness of the changes in university board membership in Alberta gives one pause. Effective governance requires deep knowledge of and credibility within a university, and abrupt changes in board membership can deprive an institution of such governance.

On the external front, recent years have also witnessed more exposure of universities to markets, especially the international student market, as well as court decisions that either protect or constrain universities' decision-making jurisdiction.

Between government policy and regulation, court decisions, and collective agreements, at a certain point one might ask, what is left for governing bodies to decide? We will return to that question in the final chapter.

### INTERNAL GOVERNANCE

What developments have taken place in the internal governance of universities in Canada since the mid-2010s?

Universities' activities have of course been reshaped dramatically by the coronavirus pandemic (see below). A number of other recent governance and leadership challenges have also been common to all or almost all Canadian universities. All universities were called upon to respond to the findings and calls to action of the TRC. According to a 2017 Universities Canada survey, 71 percent of universities were working to include Indigenous representation within their governance and/or leadership structures, two-thirds were incorporating Indigenous knowledge and protocols in teaching and research, 78 percent were promoting intercultural awareness and competency, and 69 percent were reaching out to prospective Indigenous students (Universities Canada 2017). All or almost all universities have also responded to student, public, and governmental concern about sexualized violence and rising rates of mental illness on campuses. Many institutions were faced with campaigns by student organizations and groups to divest investments in fossil fuels.

These instances involve external actors but also have internal roots. Many universities had already begun to address the issues involved, and many university constituents were and still are strong advocates for change. Truth and reconciliation, prevention of sexualized violence, youth mental health, carbon neutrality, combating and preventing racism – these and other goals entail massive changes and thus sweeping institutional agendas. Most require the investment of substantial resources – for leadership and staff, policy and program development and implementation, education, monitoring, and reporting – as well as widespread collaboration and cultural, attitudinal, and behavioural reform. External and internal stakeholders expect universities and university leaders to deliver progress on these agendas in the context of decreasing real public funding, diminishing institutional autonomy, increasing social polarization, and high levels of organizational complexity, unionization, and professorial autonomy (see previous chapters).

The case universities (indeed, all universities) have been grappling with the above issues. What developments in internal governance were specific to them? Given that governance involves a multitude of processes at many levels, this chapter does not purport to provide a comprehensive account. Instead, it describes a series of events since the interviews, over the course of which the governance of each case university was tested, based on institutional documents, media reports, and other sources. These vignettes allow us to enter into processes and events within the six universities as their administrations and governing bodies sought to initiate change or responded to incidents and pressure for change.

## Dalhousie

Dalhousie's tenth president stepped down in 2013 after eighteen years in office. His successor, appointed from outside the university, initiated the development of an updated strategic direction document that set out numerous objectives, one of which was to foster a collegial culture grounded in diversity and inclusiveness (McNutt 2019). In December 2014, sexist, misogynistic, and homophobic posts on a Facebook site belonging to a group of senior male dentistry students came to light. Some of the posts focused on women in their class (Backhouse, Iyer, and McRae 2015, 4). As internal processes began to unfold in response to a complaint, the story was picked up by the media. A subsequent external report commissioned by the university described what happened:

> The Faculty of Dentistry and the University came under heavy fire as traumatized students, worried parents, and an outraged public demanded action, demanded names, demanded expulsions and resignations, and above all, demanded answers ...
>
> Reporters chased both female and male students, as well as some of their families and neighbours, to ask for comments. They followed them from school to their homes and workplaces. Students were harassed on social media. Day after day, the scandal dominated the front pages of newspapers, and was the lead story on radio, TV, and internet news across the country. An online petition to expel the students picked up over a thousand signatures in an afternoon, forty thousand within a week, and fifty thousand by mid-January. A #dalhateswomen Twitter campaign amassed more than 60,000 tweets. (Backhouse, Iyer, and McRae 2015, 4)

Views differed on campus and beyond regarding the appropriateness of the restorative justice process put in place by the university. There were protests on campus, online campaigns, and calls for the president to resign (Backhouse, Iyer, and McRae 2015, 16). The senate discussed and tabled a motion that would have pre-empted an academic standards committee within the Faculty of Dentistry from adjudicating the behaviour of the students (Backhouse, Iyer, and McRae 2015, 20). The restorative justice process took five months, concluding with the release of a public report by the facilitators late in May (Backhouse, Iyer, and McRae 2015, 22). The dental class of 2015 graduated in the spring (Mackinnon 2018, 34).

Table 6.1 | Updated institutional overview chart[1]

| University | UBC | U of A | U of T | U de M[2] | U de M[3] | UQAM | Dal |
|---|---|---|---|---|---|---|---|
| Total 2019–20 enrolment[4] | 61,547 | 39,938 | 92,000 | 46,899 | 69,911 | 38,017 | 19,645 |
| % enrolment change since 2013–14 | +6.1% | +5.9% | +9% | −0.2% | +4% | −9.6% | +5.9% |
| % graduate | 19 [18] | 21 [20] | 22 [19] | 28 [25] | 27 [25] | 21 [17] | 23 [21] |
| % international | 26[5] [19] | 23[6] [17] | 23[7] [15] | 22[8] [10] | — | 11[9] [8] | 24[10] [14.5] |
| faculties & equivalents # | 16[11] [17] | 18[12] [18] | 17[13] [18] | 13[14] [16] | 15 [18] | 7 [7] | 12 [12] |
| FT teaching staff 2018-19[15] | 2,847 | 1,629 | 2,718 | 1,428 | 1,977 | 1,110 | 972 |
| % change since 2013–14 | +2.8 | −2.0% | +0.2% | — | — | +1.1% | +3.2% |
| FT teaching staff 2018–19 excluding med & dent[15] | 2,202 | 1,443 | 2,508 | 936 | 1,485 | — | 672 |
| % change since 2013–14 | +6.5% | −0.6% | +11.8% | — | — | — | +6.2% |
| research $ per faculty member 2018[16] | $261.7 [$235.9] | $235.9 [$248.2] | $407.7 [$467.3] | — | $278.0 [$281.0] | $64.3 [$65.6] | $123.2 [$139.1] |

Table 6.1 | Updated institutional overview chart (continued)

| University | UBC | U of A | U of T | U de M² | U de M³ | UQAM | Dal |
|---|---|---|---|---|---|---|---|
| total income 2018-19[17] | 2,903,707 | 2,051,154 | 4,217,414 | 1,381,151 | 1,847,227 | 549,886 | 824,654 |
| % change since 2013-14 | +26% | +7.8% | +17.3% | +8.2 | +12.5% | +7.5% | +24.4% |
| general operating income 2013-14[17] | 1,610,079 | 1,206,003 | 2,651,128 | 786,800 | 1,083,401 | 423,149 | 521,634 |
| % change since 2013-14 | +33.6% | +13.6% | +37.8% | +9.4% | +12.2% | +6.3% | +16.5% |
| % from govt[18] | 39% [49.7] | 56.5% [56.6] | 25.8% [34.6] | 68.9% [71.2] | 67.5% [70.1] | 72.4% [72.6] | 43.4% [46.5] |
| % from tuition & fees[19] | 50.5% [39.5] | 29.3% [28.5] | 68.3% [58.5] | 20.3% [19.1] | 23.3% [20.8] | 24.0% [23.2] | 42.3% [37.5] |
| endowment net asset balances 2019[20] | 1,065,839 | 1,432,304 | 2,593,176 | 345,691 | 380,535 | 0 | 512,887 |
| % change since 2013-14 | +29.0% | +44.1% | +37.9% | +25.0% | +22.7% | – | +36.3% |
| *Maclean's*[21] ranking 2020 | 3[2] | 5[5] | 2[3] | 10[12] | – | 11²²[13] | 8[6] |
| ARWU²³ ranking 2019 national | 2[2] | 5[5-6] | 1[1] | 6-9[5-6] | – | 21[19-23] | 10-12[8-16] |
| ARWU²³ ranking 2019 international | 35[40] | 101-150 [101-150] | 24[28] | 151-200 [101-150] | – | 601-700 [401-500] | 201-300 [201-300] |

## NOTES TO TABLE 6.1

1. Figures in square brackets are for 2013/14.
2. Without affiliated institutions.
3. With affiliated institutions (École des hautes études commerciales [HEC] and École Polytechnique).
4. Universities Canada (2019b).
5. From 2018/19 data. UBC (2019).
6. From 2018/19 data. University of Alberta (2019b).
7. From 2018/19 data. University of Toronto (2019b).
8. Université de Montréal (n.d.d.).
9. UQAM (n.d.b.).
10. Dalhousie University (2019c).
11. UBC Office of the Senate. There were 12 faculties at UBC Vancouver and 6 at UBC Okanagan in 2019, including two dual faculties. In 2013, there was only one dual faculty.
12. U of A (n.d.).
13. U of T (2019c).
14. U de M (2019b).
15. Statistics Canada (2020d).
16. RE$EARCH Infosource.com (2019).
17. In thousands of dollars. Canadian Association of University Business Officers. Financial Information of Universities and Colleges. Fiscal year ended 2019.
18. Percentage of general operating income from government. CAUBO. FIUC 2018–19.
19. Percentage of general operating income from tuition and other fees. CAUBO. FIUC 2018–19.
20. Net asset balances in the endowment fund, end of fiscal year 2018–19. CAUBO. FIUC 2018–19.
21. *Maclean's* (2019a, 2019b).
22. UQAM was ranked in the Maclean's comprehensive category of universities, whereas the other universities were ranked in the medical/doctoral category.
23. Shanghai Rankings (n.d.b.).

The president appointed an expert external task force to conduct an independent examination of the events. Their appointment was endorsed by the senate (Backhouse, Iyer, and McRae 2015, 2). Their report described the events and "the breadth and depth of the harm [the] events caused" (5). Based on meetings with around 150 students, faculty, staff, administrators, and members of the broader community, as well as written submissions and analyses of university policies, they identified themes such as a culture within the faculty that permitted incidents of sexism, misogyny, homophobia, and racism, and distrust of the university's response to reports of discrimination. The task force identified education and research as keys to significant and lasting change (3) and recommended training and diversification of members of all levels of the university (81).

These events gave additional impetus and import to the work of a committee struck previously to advance the university's strategic goals related to diversity and inclusiveness. That committee made far-reaching recommendations (Dalhousie University 2015). An institutional equity, diversity, and inclusion strategy embodying many of its recommendations was launched in spring 2017 (Dalhousie University 2019a, 22).

Among the outcomes of all this work were educational sessions for members of the board, the senate, and the senior administration (Dalhousie 2019b), revisions to the board appointment process (Dalhousie University 2017, 9), and a 2017 change in the Senate Constitution to modify and diversify the senate's membership. In early 2018, the university restricted recruitment for the position of vice-provost (Student Affairs) to racially visible persons and Aboriginal people (Bundale 2018). Developments in governance included revision of the board's committee structure in July 2016 (Dalhousie University 2016, 5) and updating of board processes and by-laws.

Dalhousie's governance continued to exhibit structural stability, notwithstanding incremental change in senate composition and governance processes. The controversy at the Faculty of Dentistry highlighted institutional complexity (e.g., overlapping policies and institutional/faculty mechanisms), divergence of views, the impact of social media, and forces for change, as well as some of the processes by which these occur. Here, a response to incidents of sexism, misogyny, and homophobia evolved through various processes into a broader institutional effort to increase diversity and inclusion.

What of Dalhousie's evolution on other fronts? The updated Institutional Overview Chart (table 6.1) shows changes in enrolments, faculty structure, faculty numbers, income and assets, sponsored research, and rankings.

## The Université de Montréal

In 2015, UdeM's charter began to undergo revision for the first time in fifty years. Late that year, the administration presented a discussion document titled "Réflexions sur la transformation de l'Université de Montréal" (Reflections on the Transformation of the Univerity of Montreal) to the university assembly, launching a broad process of consultation. An external agency was engaged to help facilitate the consultations and produce a report (Université de Montréal and Institut du Nouveau Monde 2016).

The Syndicat général des professeurs et professeures de l'Université de Montréal (SGPUM) lodged a complaint with the Tribunal administratif du travail alleging that, in launching a process of institutional transformation, the university had contravened its faculty collective agreement and the jurisdiction of the university assembly. The union called for a boycott of the consultation process (Orfali 2016b, A3). *Le Devoir* reported:

> Recours devant les tribunaux, appels au boycottage, craintes de disparition de certaines facultés: un ambitieux projet de transformation institutionnelle piloté par le recteur de l'Université de Montréal crée bien des flammèches au sein de la maison d'enseignement du Mont Royal. (Orfali 2016b, A3).
>
> [Recourse to the courts, calls for boycott, fears of the disappearance of certain faculties: an ambitious institutional transformation project led by the rector of the Université de Montréal sparks tensions within the educational institution on Mount Royal.]

The consultation process nevertheless proceeded, with almost 4,400 individuals and associations providing some form of input. The report on the consultations stated that:

> Les enjeux relatifs à la gouvernance et à la gestion administrative sont [parmi] ceux ... qui préoccupent les participants ... Les répondants au sondage appuient fortement une amélioration de l'efficacité des processus administratifs (96%), de rendre plus rapide la prise de décision (93%), l'allègement de la structure organisationnelle (90%), la collaboration entre les employés de différentes unités (90%) et la collégialité dans la prise de décision (87%) ...
> La multiplication des niveaux hiérarchiques, l'éloignement des décideurs par rapport à la réalité quotidienne ... le travail en silos, la lourdeur et la lenteur administrative, la bureaucratie, la rigidité, la

compétence (ou l'incompétence) des gestionnaires, ont été montrés du doigt comme des facteurs d'inefficacité et d'insatisfaction, voire de démobilisation.

Un répondant a comparé le fonctionnement de l'Université à celui du Vatican. (Université de Montréal 2016a, 21)

[Governance and administrative management issues are [among] those ... of concern to participants ... The survey respondents strongly support improving the efficiency of administrative processes (96%), the speed of decision-making (93%), the streamlining of the organizational structure (90%), collaboration among employees in different units (90%) and collegiality in decision-making (87%) ...

Proliferation of hierarchical levels, distance between decision-makers and daily reality ..., "silo" mentality, cumbersome and slow administration, bureaucracy, rigidity, managerial competence (or incompetence), were pointed out as factors of inefficiency, dissatisfaction, and even, demobilization.

One respondent compared the functioning of the University to that of the Vatican.]

Key takeaways from the consultative forums included the desirability of reducing administrative complexity; increasing transparency; fostering dialogue with external and internal constituencies; encouraging participation and "le bottom-up"; and re-equilibrating the size of faculties and schools (Université de Montréal 2016a, 21).

In his annual address of December 2016, the rector identified three priorities for improvement arising from the consultations, one of which was to "repenser comment on fait les choses, ce qui engage nos processus et notre gouvernance" (rethink how we do things, which involves our processes and our governance) (Université de Montréal 2016b, 5). The rector said this would involve updating the charter and that amendments had been approved by the *conseil* (board) and soon would be discussed by the university assembly and the National Assembly.

The university's website listed the three main objectives of the reform as follows:

1 S'ouvrir au monde extérieur, en faisant une plus large place à ses diplômés dans ses différentes instances [To open up to the outside world and accord more space to our graduates in our various bodies]
2 Préciser le rôle des instances dans le fonctionnement général d'une université moderne comme la nôtre [To specify the role of

decision-making bodies in the general functioning of a modern university like ours]
3 Optimiser le recrutement des officiers (recteur, vice-recteurs, doyens) en revoyant le processus de nomination de manière à la fois à assurer une plus grande collégialité et à préserver la confidentialité des candidatures pendant l'essentiel de l'évaluation des dossiers des candidats. Par sa durée et son caractère public, le processus actuel tend à décourager les candidatures de l'extérieur, privant l'UdeM de l'apport de nouveaux talents et d'idées neuves. Nous sommes à contre-courant des grandes universités de recherche [To optimize the recruitment of senior officials (rector, vice-rector, deans) by reviewing the appointment process so as to both ensure greater collegiality and preserve candidate confidentiality during the evaluation of their files. By its length and its public nature, the current process tends to discourage applications from external candidates, depriving the Université de Montréal of new talents and new ideas. We are doing the opposite of top research universities] (Université de Montréal n.d.a.)

Early in the new year of 2017, *Le Devoir* reported that:

Un ambitieux projet de refonte de la gouvernance de l'Université de Montréal ... provoque de la grogne au sein de la communauté universitaire ... Des professeurs craignent que l'Université se mette au service des entreprises, au détriment de la liberté intellectuelle des professeurs et des étudiants ... Autre source d'inquiétude chez les professeurs, la Charte précise que les doyens des facultés "relèveraient du recteur ou de la personne que ce dernier désigne," ce qui fait craindre pour la liberté au sein de l'établissement.
En entrevue au *Devoir*, le recteur Guy Breton a déploré l'opposition de groupes qui ne daignent même pas participer aux consultations ... "On veut faire une place beaucoup plus importante à nos diplômés et aux nouvelles catégories d'employés dans nos instances," dit-il. (Fortier 2017b, A1)
[An ambitious project to overhaul the governance of the Université de Montréal ... provokes discontent within the university community ... Some professors fear that the University will put itself in the service of companies, at the expense of the intellectual freedom of professors and students ... Another source of concern among

professors is that the Charter would specify that faculty deans "would be accountable to the rector or the person designated by the latter," which raises fears for freedom within the establishment.

In an interview with *Le Devoir*, President Guy Breton deplored the opposition of groups that don't even deign to participate in the consultations ... "We want to give a much more important place to our graduates and to new categories of employee in our decision-making bodies," he said.]

The rector expressed the hope that a private member's bill would be submitted to the National Assembly by 7 February, and passed before the end of the session in June – well in advance of an election foreseen for the fall of 2018.

On 26 January 2017, an open letter signed by thirty-two members of the Faculty of Law appeared in *La Presse* stating that "le projet de loi élaboré par la direction de l'Université de Montréal afin de reconfigurer radicalement sa loi constitutive et de redéfinir la vocation même de cette institution a été unanimement dénoncé par l'assemblée de la faculté de droit de l'U deM" (The bill put forward by the administration of the Université de Montréal in order to radically reconfigure its constitutive law and to redefine the very mission of this institution has been unanimously denounced by the assembly of Université de Montréal's Law Faculty). The letter stated that the reform would take power away from internal bodies and centralize it in the hands of a body or bodies dominated by external actors. It concluded that "une université n'est pas une institution facile à gouverner ... Mais le projet de loi – mis de l'avant sans explications, en dehors de tout processus de concertation – maquille, sous des dehors liés à la gouvernance, une volonté de brider l'autonomie des professeurs, de leurs doyens, des étudiants et du personnel" (a university is not an easy institution to govern ... But the bill – put forward without explanation, without any concertation process – disguises, under pretenses linked to governance, an intention to restrict the autonomy of professors, their deans, students, and staff) (Leclair et al. 2017). *Le Devoir* reported that:

> aux prises avec un barrage de questions des professeurs, le recteur de l'Université de Montréal a mis de l'eau dans son vin et présenté lundi une version amendée de son projet de réforme de la gouvernance de l'établissement ... Il affirme être convaincu que ce compromis répond aux inquiétudes soulevées au cours des derniers jours par la communauté universitaire ... "Je répète, personne ne va y perdre. On vient

renforcer l'autogestion de l'université, je veux qu'on se gère nous-mêmes," a déclaré le recteur durant une réunion houleuse de l'assemblée universitaire. (Fortier 2017c, A3)

[Faced with a barrage of questions from professors, the rector of the Université de Montréal adopted a more mellow stance and presented, on Monday, an amended version of his project to reform the governance of the establishment ... He said he is convinced that this compromise addresses the concerns brought up in recent days by the university community ... "I repeat, no one is going to lose. We are reinforcing the self-governance of the university, I want us to govern ourselves," declared the rector during an acrimonious meeting of the university assembly.]

The university assembly met on 23 January, 30 January, and 6 February to discuss the proposed amendments. At the meeting on the thirtieth, it rejected a motion by several members of the Faculty of Law to strike a committee to assess the difficulties associated with the current charter – a motion that would have suspended the amendment process (Université de Montréal 2017a). Twenty-seven of the 116 members of the university assembly boycotted the 6 February meeting to protest the process (Fortier 2017d, A4). Despite concerns and criticisms of the process and, in particular, the time frame, the university assembly proceeded to discuss the amendments one by one. After lengthy discussion and debate, a number of amendments were recommended to the *conseil* (Université de Montréal 2017b). The assembly tasked a committee with analyzing the dozen outstanding amendments and reporting back in April (Université de Montréal 2017c). The assembly continued its discussions on 20 February, notwithstanding a continuing boycott by some of its members. With respect to the powers of deans, the board had agreed to revert to pre-existing language in response to concerns that a proposed amendment would have reduced their autonomy (Université de Montréal 2017c).

The university assembly spent the day of April 10 considering the committee's report on outstanding amendments. Some members left the meeting at its outset to express their continued opposition to the project, but a quorum was achieved. The items that received the most attention in the course of the discussions were the appointment process for the rector and the composition of the university assembly (Université de Montréal 2017d). With respect to the former, the assembly rejected a proposal by student members that an electoral college be created, as existed at a number of other Quebec universities (Université de Montréal 2017d).

On 15 May the university assembly completed its consideration of the charter amendments. "Au cours de six séances, dont plusieurs intensives, l'Assemblée universitaire a recommandé, toujours à l'unanimité ou par une forte majorité des voix, toutes les dispositions de la Charte appelées à être modifiées, recommandations qui ont par la suite été entérinées par le Conseil de l'Université" (Over the course of six sessions, several of which were intensive, the University Assembly recommended, unanimously or by a strong majority of voices, all the charter provisions to be modified, recommendations which were subsequently ratified by the University Board) (Université de Montréal 2018).

Early in the fall of 2017, a bill to modify the charter was submitted to the National Assembly. On 6 December 2017 the university's chancellor, rector, and secretary general met with the parliamentary commission on culture and education to speak to it. The documents presented included a resolution of support from the university assembly (Université de Montréal 2017e).

The university's chancellor had championed the reforms embodied in Bill 234 in an article published in *Le Devoir* on 18 November 2017. Besides outlining the rationale for the reforms and rebutting continuing criticisms, the chancellor noted that one aspect of the bill would replace, with a new mechanism, an obsolete process whereby faculty members accused of sexual harassment were judged by peers. This would help combat sexualized violence – a major recent issue on campus (Roy 2017).

Several days later, the executive of the university's faculty union (SGPUM) responded with an item in the same newspaper titled "Les erreurs manifestes de la chancelière de l'Université de Montréal" (The manifest errors of the chancellor of the Université de Montréal) (Comtois et al. 2017). Taking issue with the chancellor's characterization of the spirit of the reforms as modern, democratic, and respectful of collegiality, they maintained that "[en] réalité, le projet de loi 234 fait le contraire et consacre l'établissement d'une chaîne de commandement verticale, centralisatrice et autoritaire" (in reality, Bill 234 does the opposite and establishes a vertical, centralizing, and authoritarian chain of command). The reform project was described as "dénoncé vigoureusement par les représentants de l'ensemble des professeurs d'université du Québec et du Canada" (vigorously denounced by the representatives of all university professors in Quebec and in Canada). Besides addressing numerous perceived errors, inexactitudes, and omissions, the authors described the chancellor's characterization of the bill as a means of improving the handling of harassment complaints as politically motivated misuse of a key social priority to justify an authoritarian project – and an attempt to discredit professors.

That was followed a week later by a piece signed by the executive of the student union (FAECUM), which stated:

> Depuis les débuts du projet de modification de la charte de l'Université de Montréal, le Syndicat général des professeurs et des professeures de l'Université de Montréal (SGPUM) s'est évertué à travers les pages de ce quotidien à dépeindre ce projet comme un véritable coup d'État. Pour y arriver, les membres de l'exécutif du SGPUM n'ont pas hésité, à travers des entrevues, des lettres ouvertes et des communiqués de presse, à utiliser des exagérations, des demi-vérités et parfois même des mensonges.
>
> Alors que le débat faisait rage entre le SGPUM et l'administration de l'Université de Montréal dans l'espace public, la communauté étudiante s'est tenue à l'écart. Cependant, nous considérons qu'avec sa lettre ouverte publiée le 23 novembre dernier, l'exécutif du SGPUM a dépassé les limites de la mauvaise foi et les faits se doivent d'être rétablis. (FAECUM 2017)
>
> [Since the beginning of the project to modify the charter of the Université de Montréal, the General Union of Professors of the Université de Montréal has striven through the pages of this newspaper to depict this project as a veritable coup d'état. To achieve this, the members of the SGPUM executive did not hesitate, through interviews, open letters, and press releases, to use exaggerations, half-truths and sometimes even lies.
>
> While the debate raged between the SGPUM and the administration of the Université de Montréal in the public space, the student community stood aside. However, we consider that, with its open letter published on 23 November, the SGPUM executive has exceeded the limits of bad faith and the facts must be re-established.] (FAECUM 2017)

The authors accused the faculty union of misrepresenting the process for adjudicating sexual harassment complaints, maintaining that

> sur les faits, c'est bel et bien la chancelière qui a raison. À l'Université de Montréal, lorsqu'une plainte formelle est déposée pour harcèlement ou inconduite sexuelle contre un membre du corps professoral, cette dernière est traitée aux termes du Règlement disciplinaire concernant les membres du personnel enseignant, et donc ... elle est jugée par un comité formé de 3 personnes professeures de carrière dont une exerçant des fonctions d'officière. Bref, dans l'état actuel des choses, "des chums jugent des chums" (FAECUM 2017).

[On the facts, it is indeed the chancellor who is right. At the Université de Montréal, when a formal complaint is filed for harassment or sexual misconduct against a faculty member, the latter is dealt with under the terms of the Disciplinary Regulations for members of the teaching staff and therefore ... it is judged by a committee composed of three career professors, one of whom is fulfilling the functions of an official. In short, in the current state of things, "chums judge chums."] (FAECUM 2017)

Shortly thereafter, the president of the university's sessional instructors' union, representing around 2,500 members teaching roughly half of the university's undergraduate courses, publicly characterized the proposed charter amendments as "ouvr[ant] la porte à une représentation (la nôtre et celle d'autres groupes) nettement plus équitable dans les instances" (opening the door to a much more equitable representation [of our and other groups] on decision-making bodies) (Verge 2017).

Study of Bill 234 by the National Assembly's parliamentary commission on culture and education began on 6 December and continued on 7 and 8 December, 8 and 13 February, and 22 March (Quebec National Assembly 2018). The commission heard from nineteen groups, including parties from the university and the Confederation of National Trade Unions (CSN), the FQPPU, and the CAUT. The commission recommended several amendments. One responded to concerns expressed by the SGPUM and allied groups by stipulating that a provision in the faculty collective agreement requiring the faculty union's consent for changes to the discipline process remain in effect for the duration of the collective agreement (Kempeneers 2019, 141).

The National Assembly considered the legislation on 27 March 2018; it was passed unanimously. The new charter came into effect six months later (Université de Montréal 2018).

Work on the revision of the statutes continued in 2018. They were approved by the board late in the summer, except for a clause related to discipline. More than one hundred articles of the statutes were revised (Université de Montréal 2019). The changes resulting from charter reform and statutory revision included the following:

- Reduction in the number of government-appointed members of the board from eight to two and increases in the numbers of students, alumni, and others, for an overall increase in the proportion of internal members from 33 to 42 percent (Université de Montréal n.d.b).

- Some changes to the composition of the university assembly, including the addition of a number of alumni (Université de Montréal n.d.c).
- Expansion of the role of the *commission des études* to include coordination of research and instruction.
- Changes in the process for appointing the rector, including:
  ○ an increase in the size of appointment committees for the rector from eleven to seventeen, including a sessional instructor, an alumna/us, a staff member, and representatives of affiliated schools, as well as professors and others; and
  ○ maintenance of confidentiality concerning the identity of candidates until later in the process and the elimination of indicative ballots of the university assembly.
- Similar changes in the appointment process for deans.
- Greater flexibility in the composition and functioning of faculty councils and departmental bodies (Université de Montréal 2019).

Meanwhile, the university struggled to develop a policy on sexualized violence before the 1 January 2019 deadline prescribed by the Quebec legislation. The leaders of the university, the faculty union, and students were unable to reach consensus on the process for judging professors accused of sexualized violence. In October the FAECUM launched the campaign "l'Omertà UdeM," which denounced the existing discipline process – characterizing it as long, opaque, and inequitable for students – as well as "l'impunité des profs en matière de violences sexuelles" (the impunity of professors in matters of sexual violence) (FAECUM 2018). The president of the faculty union accused the administration of intimidation and indicated that the union would take legal action against the university for defamation, deterioration of the work environment, and denial of the right to association. Radio Canada reported that "l'Université de Montréal se déchire au sujet des violences sexuelles" (the University of Montreal is tearing itself apart on the subject of sexual violence) (Gerbet 2018).

Among the six case universities, it was UdeM's governance structure that changed most significantly in the five years following the study. Modifications to the charter first proposed with the *conseil*'s approval were strongly contested, significantly modified, and ultimately approved. In the process, pre-existing divisions within the university deepened and new ones developed.

With respect to the characteristics of the case universities identified in Chapter 6, UdeM's governance was certainly complex. Indeed, one of the reasons presented for the changes was to simplify processes and increase transparency. Also visible were tensions between external responsiveness and the traditional exercise of academic judgment. The rationale for the reforms included increasing the university's responsiveness to the external environment through additional alumni representation on governing bodies, while increasing autonomy from government. Perhaps in part because of the intersection of governance reform with student and societal outrage over sexualized violence, the faculty union's opposition to measures that included increased roles for students, sessionals, and others came to be portrayed and perceived as self-serving.

As a result of governance reform, the number of faculties at UdeM decreased by one, with the transformation of the former Faculty of Theology into an institute. Changes in enrolments, faculty numbers, revenues, rankings, and other dimensions of UdeM are shown in table 6.1.

*The Université du Québec à Montréal*

At UQAM, major governance change was broached in recent years but was not enacted. After the Liberals defeated the Parti Québécois government in 2014, students at UQAM mobilized against government austerity measures and staged numerous protests and other events. The disruption of a career session for students early in 2015 prompted fourteen political science professors to note in an open letter that "for a few years now, our university has fallen prey to the actions of a minority: courses stopped by self-proclaimed, sometimes masked, commandos, intimidations, harassment, shoving, acts of vandalism and ransacking, disruptions of meetings and conferences, repeated strikes" (Hamilton 2015).

In a subsequent letter, published in *Le Devoir*, the rector maintained that the characterizations of UQAM prompted by the professors' letter – as a "champ de bataille" (battlefield), "université assiégée" (besieged university), "règne des anarchistes, des barbares et des sauvages" (reign of anarchists, barbarians, and savages), "climat de peur" (climate of fear), and so on – did not reflect the daily reality of the university's 44,000 students and unfairly tarnished its reputation. The rector nevertheless wrote: "L'UQAM déplore avec force de tels comportements et condamne catégoriquement toute forme de pratiques militantes qui s'appuient sur le vandalisme, la violence ou l'intimidation" (UQAM strongly deplores such behaviours and categorically condemns all forms of militant practice that rely on vandalism, violence, or intimidation) (Proulx 2015).

Student strikes and other disruptions in the spring of 2015 were followed by a drop of 10.8 percent in undergraduate enrolment in the fall

(Fortier 2016a). The loss in revenue from reduced enrolment, coupled with public funding constraints, necessitated operating budget cuts of $24.5 million in 2015–16 (Daoust-Boisvert and Fortier 2016). Collective bargaining was very difficult. The rector said in an interview:

> Quand on est dans une situation où la vie universitaire est difficile parce qu'on ne dispose plus des ressources dont on aurait besoin, ça crée des insatisfactions. Un groupe est insatisfait, l'autre le devient, ces choses-là se mettent à interagir et, à un moment donné, pouf! Ça saute. (Daoust-Boisvert and Fortier 2016)
> [When we are in a situation where university life is difficult because we no longer have the resources we need, it creates dissatisfaction. One group is dissatisfied, another becomes dissatisfied, these things start to interact and, at some point, bang! It explodes.]

A sociology professor at UQAM took issue with the argument that lack of resources accounted for the difficulties at the university. In an opinion piece, he outlined the university's history and governance, explaining that:

> les universités sont dans nos sociétés les institutions les plus auto-gérées. Mais l'UQAM est, parmi les universités, l'université la plus autogérée. Jusqu'à tout récemment, lorsqu'il y avait grève des professeurs, tous les professeurs, doyens y compris, étaient en grève, à l'exception des trois ou quatre vice-recteurs et du recteur. Ici, quand la base s'impose, il n'y a littéralement plus personne au sommet pour répondre. (Thériault 2016).
> [Universities are the most self-governed institutions in our societies, but UQAM is the most self-governed university among the universities. Until very recently, when there was a professors' strike, all professors, including deans, were on strike except for two or three vice-rectors and the rector. Here, when *la base* acts, there is literally no one at the top to respond.]

He argued that the university had functioned successfully with a combination of faculty self-governance and union militantism while it was growing but that, with recent enrolment declines, "the institution is in peril":

> Un syndicalisme de combat tant chez les étudiants que chez les professeurs s'est installé, plus virulent que jamais …

Comment gérer une université où le nombre de professeurs, la moyenne cible d'étudiants par cours, les permanences, promotions, les dégrèvements d'enseignement et les principales instances sont aux mains d'un syndicat qui, au moment d'une crise interne, se comporte comme s'il faisait face à un patron du XIXe siècle?

Une institution autogérée exige un syndicalisme de coopération, et non un syndicalisme de combat... Car c'est finalement contre elle-même que l'UQAM autogérée se bat. (Thériault 2016)

[A combative syndicalism has taken hold among students and professors alike, and is more virulent than ever. How to manage a university where the number of professors, the target average number of students per course, tenure, promotions, teaching release and the main decision-making bodies are in the hands of a union that, at a time of internal crisis, behaves as if it were facing a nineteenth-century boss? A self-governed institution requires cooperative syndicalism, not combative syndicalism ... Because it's ultimately against itself that the self-governed UQAM is fighting.]

Early in 2016, the École des sciences de la gestion (ESG), UQAM's management school, threatened to separate from the university (Daoust-Boisvert and Fortier 2016). The school accounted for around 14,000 of UQAM's 42,000 students (Orfali 2016a). Having advocated for budgetary decentralization within the university for some time without success (UQAM 2016), the school's dean announced publicly that he would hold a referendum on whether ESG should become an independent institution (Fortier 2016a). The rector expressed willingness to discuss the possibility of more autonomy for the school (Fortier 2016a), but he and the board chair told the dean he should conduct himself as a "membre de l'équipe de direction de l'institution" (a member of the institution's senior management team) and do nothing that would harm the university (Fortier 2016b). By early the following week, seventy-one professors had signed an open letter denouncing the suppression of freedom of expression at UQAM: "[La direction de l'UQAM semble] considérer le doyen comme un simple employé, comme l'exécutant de la volonté du conseil d'administration de l'UQAM ... Au contraire, le doyen est le porteur de l'expression et de la volonté d'une communauté de 16 000 personnes qui l'ont choisi et élu; il est notre porte-parole" (The senior administration of UQAM seems to consider the dean like a simple employee, as the executor of the will of the board of UQAM ... On the contrary, the dean is the bearer of the expression and the will of a community of 16,000 people who have chosen and elected him; he is our spokesperson) (Fortier 2016c).

The university engaged two external consultants – both academics who had also served as senior public servants and senior university officials – to identify models of decentralization at other universities, assess the situation at UQAM, consult, identify options, and make recommendations. They met around one hundred people at UQAM and also interviewed pertinent officials at several other Quebec universities. In their September 2016 report, Dandurand and Tremblay commented on UQAM's strengths, including the renown of many of its professors, its engagement with civil society, its commitment to extending access to higher education, and its attachment to values of collegiality, accessibility, and interdisciplinarity. They also identified issues, including these:

- "Une facultarisation inachevée" – incomplete creation of faculties (Dandurand and Tremblay 2016, 5);
- Varied conceptions of collegiality, including as "un modèle ... qui relègue les cadres académiques, y compris les cadres supérieurs, à un rôle de porte-parole des volontés des unités de base" (a model ... that relegates academic administrators, including senior ones, to a role of spokesperson for the wishes of lower-level academic units) (6). The authors characterized this conception of collegiality as incompatible with managerial accountability and oblivious to possible conflicts of interest.
- The heaviness of structures. The authors observed that policies, collective agreements and administrative practices had evolved through "sedimentation" (8). They pointed to confusion about roles and responsibilities, lack of trust, and rigidity in decision-making.
- Very serious financial challenges, including the need to reduce a significant operating deficit and eliminate an accumulated deficit of around $200 million (9).

The authors deemed budgetary decentralization a plausible strategy for addressing these challenges, although community members' views on it were mixed (10). The report proposed a set of goals, values, and principles that could inform the process and described what the roles of various bodies would be. The intended result would be to give faculties more autonomy while maintaining a meaningful role for central bodies and improving the health of UQAM's culture, finances, and reputation.

The consultants' report was submitted to the board in September 2016, and the rector invited feedback. Its recommendations were welcomed enthusiastically by the ESG and by deans generally (Lafortune and Roy 2019, 129). The Syndicat des professeurs et professeures de l'Université du Québec a Montréal (SPUQ) demanded and obtained extension of the deadline for feedback and embarked on a process of analysis and consultation. Lafortune and Roy – professors at UQAM, both of whom had served as president of the FQPPU – subsequently wrote that

> la conception de l'université qui se dégage du Rapport est très éloignée, voire à l'opposé, du mode de fonctionnement de l'UQAM. Il propose, en effet, une organisation asymétrique qui concentre les décisions et les ressources dans les facultés, affaiblit le pouvoir de la Commission des études ... mais qui renforce le pouvoir de la haute direction. Cela va évidemment à l'encontre des principes d'autogestion, de collégialité, et d'autonomie départementale. (128)

[The conception of the university that emerges from the Report is very far, if not the opposite, from the way UQAM operates. It proposes, as a matter of fact, an asymmetric organization that concentrates decisions and resources in the faculties, and weakens the power of the academic council, but that reinforces the power of senior management. This obviously goes against the principles of self-management, collegiality, and departmental autonomy.]

Resolutions passed by the council of the SPUQ rejected the proposed budget model, the report's conception of collegiality, and any weakening of the powers of departmental assemblies, program committees, and the *commission des études*. The union council's resolutions were taken up by numerous departmental assemblies (130–1). When consultations wound up in March 2017, the report was effectively shelved. Lafortune and Roy explained that "un tout autre débat s'amorcera avec la course au rectorat qui suivra, puisque tous les candidats au poste, dont deux doyens qui s'y étaient pourtant montres favorables, se dissocieront du Rapport" (a whole other debate would begin with the race for the rector's position that was about to begin, since all the candidates for the position, including two deans who had once seemed favourable to it, would dissociate themselves from the Report) (132).

These events were part of a larger trajectory. As described in chapter 5, UQAM had begun creating faculties and delegating power to them in the late 1990s as part of a broader process of institutional transformation (125). ESG – established in 1992 – and other faculties naturally sought more power and control over resources. From the point of view of the dean of ESG in the mid-2010s, the extent of central control prevented the school from competing successfully with business schools across the province and around the world. Events surrounding the dean's perceived ultimatum illustrated the tensions between the desire of faculties for greater control over resources and the university's centralized governance model. With the help of external consultants, the university was able to arrive at a path toward further decentralization that won the support of deans. Ultimately, however, the fact that the rector is elected at UQAM put an end to the prospect of further change.

### University of Toronto

Like its counterparts across the country, U of T experienced an increase in students' need for mental-health-related services in recent years and invested more in student support (Lorinc 2019). The 2014–15 report of the university's ombudsperson identified the need for a policy "to establish the way in which student conduct that gives rise to concern should be addressed within the institution when mental illness is known or believed to be involved" (University of Toronto 2015, 6). The report noted that the two existing university policies pertaining to this situation were codes of conduct for dealing with alleged academic or non-academic offences. For example, the Code of Student Conduct addressed behaviour by students "that jeopardizes the good order and proper functioning of the academic and non-academic programs and activities of the University or its divisions, that endangers the health, safety, rights or property of its members or visitors, or that adversely affects the property of the University or bodies related to it, where such conduct is not, for the University's defined purposes, adequately regulated by civil and criminal law" (5–6). Neither this code nor the one pertaining to academic matters contained provisions for handling incidents involving students who had or appeared to have a mental illness.

Regardless of the lack of a suitable policy, the university had developed a mechanism for working with individual students on a case-by-case basis. The administrative response to the ombudsperson's previous annual report stated that

> on occasion, where accommodative approaches prove unsuccessful, and where the Code of Student Conduct is clearly inappropriate ... the University Administration ... acts unilaterally pursuant to Bill 168 [on workplace violence and harassment] to protect the safety of its staff and students by excluding a person from campus. In every case where mental health issues are involved, this includes ongoing

efforts to engage with the student's mental health professionals or other experts, and other supports, so as to do whatever is reasonably possible to permit a safe resumption of studies. (6–7)

The ombudperson's annual report called for the governing council to approve a policy to guide these activities and provide for oversight. It articulated principles to inform the new policy, including the following: the right to personal autonomy, written records of agreement to accommodation or limitations on conduct, procedural fairness, clarity regarding decision-making and personnel involved in case management, availability of an avenue of appeal (including representation by legal counsel), inclusion of a return-to-campus procedure, and annual statistical reporting to the University Appeals Board (8).

The vice-provost (Students) reported to the University Affairs Board (UAB) in May and June of 2017 on the development of the policy, and a draft policy was presented to the UAB for information and discussion at the beginning of October. The vice-provost explained that the policy was intended

> to provide a mechanism whereby a student may be placed on a mandatory leave of absence where, due primarily to mental health considerations, the student posed a risk of serious harm to themselves or others, or the significant impairment of the educational experience of others, or was otherwise unable to pursue their education at the University. It would apply to circumstances where accommodations and/or supportive resources had not been successful or were not feasible. (University of Toronto 2017a, 2)

The president of the U of T Students' Union (UTSU) expressed overall support for the draft policy, while raising several questions and potential concerns.

In the wake of the public release of the draft policy, many students mobilized to express their concerns. A member of the UTSU board of directors wrote in the student newspaper, *The Varsity*, that the proposed policy "gives U of T administrators unprecedented power to unilaterally place students with mental health issues on an involuntary leave of absence. This power can be invoked in virtually any situation where a student is struggling, academically or personally ... This policy has drawn the ire of students, mental health awareness groups, and campus organizers" (Huntelar 2017). The author of the article encouraged students to register to speak at upcoming meetings of the UAB and the academic board (AB), to provide input to the administration, and to participate in a Facebook group that was being organized to share concerns and collective responses (Huntelar 2017).

Prior to their late November meetings, both boards received more requests to speak than could be granted. The president of UTSU continued to express general support for the policy, but other students – including representatives of the Graduate Students Union and Students for Barrier Free Access – expressed opposition. Concerns included that that the policy did not meet the university's human rights responsibilities and that existing accommodations and supports and the proposed appeals process were inadequate. The Vice-Provost (Students) reiterated the purpose and scope of the draft policy and indicated that refinements had been and were being made in response to ongoing consultations and feedback (University of Toronto 2017b, 4–5; 2017c, 4–5).

In mid-December 2017, staff of the Ontario Human Rights Commission (OHRC) met with staff from the provost's office and expressed concern about the policy. At the end of January, the OHRC's chief commissioner wrote to the chair of the governing council recommending that the draft policy not be approved in its current form:

> In our view, the *Policy* falls short of meeting the duty to accommodate under the *Code* ...
>
> Given the negative impact of being placed on a leave and losing access to education, student services, and housing, the University must be able to demonstrate that the *Policy* and its application is *bona fide* and accommodates students with mental health disabilities to the point of undue hardship ... As you are aware, undue hardship can only be established due to excessive cost or significant health and safety risk. In rare situations, where a student with a disability poses a health and safety risk to themselves or to others, it is open to the education provider to argue that accommodating the student would cause undue hardship. In extremely rare cases, this will be clear – such as where the risk to others is imminent and serious. Otherwise, before undue hardship can be determined, education providers must evaluate the seriousness of the risk *after* accommodation has been provided and *after* other measures to manage inappropriate behaviour and reduce risk have been taken. (Mandhane 2018)

The same letter identified a number of specific concerns about matters such as the prospect of withdrawal of services from students in crisis. It concluded this way: "While we acknowledge the challenge of meeting human rights obligations while addressing behaviour[s] that present health and safety risks on campus, we are concerned that the *Policy* does not strike an appropriate balance. We urge the University Affairs Board to delay approval of the *Policy* until human rights concerns are addressed" (Mandhane 2018).

The draft policy, which had already been approved by the academic board on 25 January 2018, was withdrawn from the UAB agenda. The vice-provost (Students) indicated that the university was confident that the proposed policy was compliant with the Human Rights Code, that a number of points raised by the commissioner, as well as in feedback from students, faculty, and staff, had been reflected in the current draft, and that additional time would be taken to consider comments and feedback. The UTSU president expressed opposition to the policy, citing previous concerns. Other students also expressed concerns and called for increased university support for mental health (University of Toronto 2018c).

In April 2018, a revised draft of the policy was released and feedback was sought from students, faculty, and staff through various means, including an online form. The revised policy was passed by the UAB on 24 May 2018. At the academic board meeting the following week, some students called for continued consultation; others articulated objections, including concern for racialized students, lack of safe spaces for students in need, lack of consideration of Indigenous perspectives, and that decisions would be made under the policy by individuals without medical qualifications. After a lengthy discussion, a motion to defer consideration of the policy failed and the academic board recommended the policy to the governing council for approval (University of Toronto 2018d).

Prior to the governing council meeting in June, student unions released a joint statement declaring that the policy discriminated against those with mental health issues (Rizza 2018). At the meeting, the provost again acknowledged that the policy had elicited strong views and noted that a number of changes had been made over the course of eighteen months of consultations, including amplification of the supports that would be available to students in need. The chairs of the UAB and the AB reported on their respective boards' consideration of the policy; both said they were recommending the policy for approval. Students invited to speak called for further consultation or expressed continuing concerns. The university ombudsperson and a number of administrators spoke in favour of the policy. After a lengthy discussion, a motion to refer the policy back failed and the university-mandated leave of absence policy was approved (University of Toronto 2018b). About forty students chanted outside the meeting in protest (Rizza 2018).

In spite of statements from the administration that the new policy would be used only in rare cases in which a student was a serious threat to themselves or others, some students leaders (and others) continued to perceive and describe the policy as a barrier to students seeking mental health services. Calls to improve services continued.

In the wake of a March 2019 suicide at a building that had been the site of two previous incidents, students held a silent protest outside the president's office; they also protested outside a meeting of the business board (D'Sa 2019). According to *The Varsity*,

> [two] U of T students ... delivered stinging rebukes of the university's mental health resources during the meeting ... [One] told the board that "the university is ignoring the needs of students in a blatant attempt to take the onus off of its administration for our mental health, safety, and well-being." [She] criticized long delays in mental health services, a lack of 24-hour support, unaccountable professors, and "deeply problematic and retraumatizing" counselling as unacceptable given the university's "recklessly dangerous" competitive environment. (Takagi and Teoh 2019)

During an interview after the meeting, the president was asked whether the university was in any way culpable for the suicides that had taken place on campus. "We know that these are adults," he replied, "and we have to provide every opportunity for them to seek the kind of services they require. But it's a shared responsibility: families, friends, society more broadly, as well as the individuals involved. It's part of a much broader conversation, a much broader effort" (Takagi and Teoh 2019).

At the end of March, the president issued a public letter to students, faculty, and staff that outlined a four-part plan of action, which included the striking of a Task Force on Student Mental Health, chaired by the dean of medicine, to review mental health supports and services for students at U of T, in consultation with students, student groups, and other stakeholders (University of Toronto n.d.b).

New student groups sprang up to advocate for change and improved access to mental health resources (Lorinc 2019). Some criticized the thirteen-member task force and called for its dissolution on grounds such as lack of transparency, diversity, and accountability (Carty 2019a). A report prepared by a group of student activists, *Nothing About Us Without Us*, said:

Many of us believe that the University's administration has played a significant role in not only the creation of conditions which cultivate and normalize mental illness, but also in the creation of inadequate if not entirely nonexistent supports for said mental illness ... While we recognize that [the lack of needed supports] is, in part, because of understandable mistakes, intricacies, and factors that are external to the University, we also recognize that this phenomenon is at least equal parts a direct result of **negligence** as well as the **ongoing suppression of critical voices** at this institution. (*Nothing About Us Without Us* 2019, 3; bold type in document)

Further protests followed another student suicide in September 2019 (Warren 2019). After a meeting of the academic board was disrupted on 3 October 2019, representatives of several student groups were invited to address questions to the president and the vice-provost (Students). The questions included, "How do you sleep at night?" (Takagi 2019). Protests continued outside October's governing council meeting. Among the protesters' demands was the repeal of the mandated leave policy (Carty 2019b).

In January 2020, the report of the Task Force on Student Mental Health was made public along with an administrative response accepting all the task force's recommendations. With respect to mental health services, the report stated:

Student mental health concerns present on a continuum from mild/moderate ... to more severe mental illness, which requires more intense clinical resources. There are expectations in our community that the University should provide mental health services at all points of this continuum ...

Balancing expectations with regard to the types of services and programming that should reasonably be situated in an institution of higher education, like the University of Toronto, versus in clinical settings is an enormous challenge. We do not believe it is practical to expect that the University will reach a point where all immediate, long-term, and/or complex cases of mental illness can be managed internally. However, we believe that frustration, confusion, and misconceptions about services and care could be mitigated with enhanced communication and awareness-raising about the options for students along the continuum of care. (University of Toronto 2019, 6)

Besides making recommendations with respect to student mental health service delivery, coordination, space, and partnerships with other organizations, the task force noted that the university's "culture of excellence" could lead to intense competition and negatively affect some students' well-being. It recommended that U of T expand its notion of excellence to include wellness and update its mission statement or institutional priorities to include wellness as a core value. With respect to the mandated leave policy, it noted that there remained "real philosophical differences within our community over the policy's goals" (University of Toronto 2019, 22). It recommended continued education concerning the policy's intent and scope as well as robust ongoing review.

According to *The Varsity*, student groups' reaction to the report was "cautiously optimistic," notwithstanding continued opposition to the mandated leave policy (Carty 2020).

The above account illustrates the processes by which U of T's governance and administration responded to a perceived policy gap and, more broadly, to the need and demand for more mental health services and supports for students. Although this is an issue on campuses across the country, it had a particular flavour at U of T because of the university's academic culture and standards, its program profile, the structure of its campuses, and the demographics of its students. Forces at work in this case included not only the expectations of students and student leaders but also those of parents and alumni, advocacy organizations, community leaders and others, the jurisdiction of the Ontario Human Rights Commission, and the capacities of organizations in the health sector. Demands for more mental health services and supports for university students spring partly from the inadequacy of those available to Canadians and young Canadians more broadly. In responding to those demands, the university sought to define what was within its mission and what is or should be the responsibility of other sectors of society.

## *The University of Alberta*

In the spring of 2018, faced with a $14 million structural deficit and $157 million in accumulated operating budget debt, the U of A administration submitted to its board of governors for approval a budget entailing reductions of 4 percent in units' budgets, increases of 3 percent in international student fees and 4 percent in residence fees, and hikes in the cost of students' meal plans. The provincial government had increased the university's grant by 2 percent while freezing tuition fees for domestic students and providing funding for tuition backfill (Bailey 2018). In mid-March, around six hundred students protested the fee increases (Mastel 2018), and at the board meeting two days later, a number of student board members spoke against the proposed fee increases. After a lengthy discussion, the board approved the budget (University of Alberta 2018a, 6–10).

The *Edmonton Journal* reported that Alberta's Minister of Advanced Education "slammed" the board's decision and "said there is no reason for the U of A's budget cut." The minister also took aim at the university president and his compensation: "It's concerning to me to see the president lining his own pockets while he's cutting money being spent on classrooms and students" (E. Graney 2018).

The chair of the U of A board issued a statement defending the board's budget decision, outlining the rationale for it, and indicating that the university compensated its executive competitively (Ramsay 2018). The CBC reported that "[Minister] Schmidt said he is looking at what options he has to deal with the situation. The chairs of boards at colleges and universities report directly to the minister, so Schmidt said he plans to have a discussion with [board chair] Phair" (Bellefontaine 2018). The minister said the university should look for savings in administration (E. Graney 2018). He indicated he would bring in legislation to regulate international tuition fees and that the government was reviewing salaries paid by agencies, boards, and commissions (Bellefontaine 2018).

At the end of March, students continued to protest the fee increases. Hundreds attended an annual winter forum held by the president, interrupting his presentation with chants of "Let us speak!" The student union president urged the board to rescind the fee hikes (McLean 2018). Asked by a reporter early in April whether the university would revisit the budget, the president said that fee levels could be considered for the next budget the following year (McEwan 2018). The board chair met with the premier and reiterated that the board would not reopen the 2018–19 budget (University of Alberta 2018d).

Meanwhile, U of A had announced the names of those who would be receiving honorary degrees at its spring convocation. Canadian universities have been recognizing exceptional people through the award of honorary degrees since the early 1800s (Rancic 2019). At most Canadian universities, an honorary degrees committee invites members of the community to nominate candidates, considers nominees in relation to the institution's particular criteria, and makes recommendations to the academic senate or another governing body (Rancic 2019). If the offer of a degree is accepted, arrangements are made for the individual to receive it at an upcoming convocation ceremony. Depending on the number of degrees approved and honorands' schedules, there may be an interval between the decision to award the degree and the date it is bestowed.

At U of A, decisions about who will receive honorary degrees are made by a committee of the senate, which is not an academic senate, but rather a large university/community liaison body mandated by the province's Post-Secondary Learning Act. The act provides that each university have a senate, the purpose of which is "to inquire into any matter that might benefit the university and enhance its position in the community" (Alberta 2003, s. 13(1)). The senate is chaired by the chancellor and consists of university officials; appointed representatives of deans, the board, the general faculties council, students, staff, and alumni; and members of the public, in addition to thirty members elected by the senate to represent geographical areas and groups and organizations within the province. The origins of U of A's Senate in this form can be traced back to 1941, when the university's pre-existing senate voted narrowly not to grant an honorary degree to the province's premier (Macleod 2008, 124). That was followed by legislation that transformed the senate into a mechanism for community involvement, increased the power of the board of governors, and assigned responsibility for most academic matters to a general faculties council (138).

The list of U of A's thirteen spring 2018 honorands included prominent environmentalist David Suzuki, a strong critic of the oil and gas industry. At a time when the province's economy was struggling, Suzuki had spoken out against a major pipeline project regarded as a beacon of hope by many Albertans (Issawi 2018). The university was honouring Suzuki "for contributions to public understanding of science and the environment" (Weber 2018).

The backlash was prompt and furious. Alumni, donors, industry leaders, and many others called upon the university to reverse the decision and threatened to withhold donations and support (Bennett 2018). A Calgary tax law firm announced it was cancelling a donation of $100,000 to the law school (Fung 2018). Full-page advertisements appeared in Edmonton and Calgary newspapers calling for U of A to reverse the decision (Kent 2018). Petitions circulated online, including one launched by the United Conservative Party (Ross 2018). UCP leader Jason Kenney said that Suzuki "makes millions defaming the livelihood of hundreds of thousands of Albertans" and that his "extreme" views made the decision to honour him an insult to the people of the province (Ross 2018).

The U of A Students' Union announced it had received the tax law firm's gift and would welcome other redirected donations (University of

Alberta Student Union 2018). The dean of engineering posted a statement: "It truly saddens me to know that many of you are, as am I, left feeling that one of Alberta's most favoured children, the University of Alberta, has betrayed you by choosing to confer this honorary degree" (University of Alberta 2018b). The dean of business likewise posted a message in which he "apologize[d] most deeply and sincerely to our alumni and supporters who understandably feel disappointed and betrayed by this situation" (University of Alberta 2018c). An industry advocacy group, Rally for Resources, began organizing a protest on campus on the day Suzuki was to receive the honorary degree (Ross 2018).

While acknowledging that Suzuki was a controversial figure in Alberta, the university's president said in a statement, "we will stand by our decision because our reputation as a university – an institution founded on the principles of freedom of inquiry, academic integrity, and independence – depends on it" (Fung 2018). In the face of all the outrage and calls for U of A to reverse its decision, he said that "the university must give people the space and support they need to think independently without fear of external control or reprisal" (Fung 2018).

Asked what she thought of the university's decision to award an honorary degree to Suzuki, Alberta premier Rachel Notley said: "I'm not a big fan of this decision … If I'd been on the [university] senate, I wouldn't personally have voted for it. It struck me as being a bit tone deaf, but academic independence, university independence is important. So they have made that decision, they will defend that decision and that's the way it should work" (Bennett 2018).

At the convocation ceremony on 7 June 2018, David Suzuki received his honorary degree. He addressed the graduating science students and others assembled. Some audience members remained seated but others gave him a standing ovation (Weber 2018).

Over a period of less than four months, the U of A had withstood strong pressure to reverse two decisions. In the first instance, pressure from student leaders and the minister to rescind fee increases; in the second, pressure not only from alumni, donors, industry, politicians, and many others, but also from people within the university critical of the senate's decision. The NDP government subsequently rolled back and capped executive compensation, and the university reviewed its process for awarding honorary degrees. The resulting report confirmed many elements of the process. It added more vetting and consultation, including regarding the scheduling of the conferral of individual degrees, but it also confirmed the senate committee's authority and rejected a suggested principle of "no harm." On that subject, the report concluded that "it is not possible to manage all conceivable sources of harm, particularly since not all stakeholders would agree on the same definition of harm or damage to the university. Some degree of controversy in the awarding of honorary degrees is inevitable from time to time" (University of Alberta 2019, 24–5).

What do these two episodes involving the U of A add to previous findings? The first set of events is consistent with the observation that provincial governments are seeking greater control over university decisions. The minister's attacks on the competence of the board and the integrity of the president are an example of what Newman (1987) characterized as political intrusion, insofar as they sought to garner political support by characterizing those parties as deficient, self-interested, and even corrupt. Perhaps ironically, university autonomy was threatened by the minister in the first series of events but defended by the premier in the second.

Both series of events illustrate the permeability of institutional boundaries: the minister joined students in opposing a board decision in the first instance; deans and others within U of A added their voices to external criticism in the second. The force of that criticism – and the extent to which many Albertans felt betrayed by the university's decision to award the honorary degree – attested to the U of A's importance in the province and its place in people's hearts. In both cases, some stakeholders had difficulty grasping that, important as their support, funding, or oversight might be, a university is and must be beyond their control.

*The University of British Columbia*

In August 2015, UBC announced that its thirteenth president had resigned after only one year in office. Questions abounded. The university and the president had signed a non-disclosure agreement, so reasons were not provided despite calls for transparency. A professor specializing in leadership, gender, and diversity suggested on social media that the president had lost his job because he "lost the masculinity contest," "wasn't tall or physically imposing," and was "the first brown man to be the university's president" (MacKinnon 2018, 7). The board chair, who had funded the professorship held by the professor in question, called her to discuss her comments. She also received a call from a member of the dean's office of her faculty expressing concern about the impact of her comments. The UBC faculty association alleged that this breached her academic freedom, as well as numerous university policies. UBC and the faculty association engaged Lynn Smith, a former judge and UBC law dean, to investigate the matter.

She concluded that "UBC failed in its obligation to protect and support [the professor's] academic freedom. The Collective Agreement Preamble creates a positive obligation to support and protect academic freedom. Through the combined acts and omissions of [the board chair], [individuals in the business school], and others, UBC as an institution failed to meet that obligation" (Smith 2015, 3).

Smith found that neither the board chair nor the individuals in the business school had infringed any provisions of the collective agreement or university policies (3–4), but that "there were some errors of judgment" (6). The board chair resigned. The faculty association invited its members to declare non-confidence in the board; they did so in a ballot in which around 25 percent of them voted (Mackinnon 2018, 18).

Meanwhile, former UBC president Martha Piper agreed to return to UBC to serve as president while a search was conducted. As president, she assumed the chair of senate. At the senate's October meeting, she outlined Smith's findings, said that the administration had accepted them, and outlined steps it would take to ensure that academic freedom was safeguarded at UBC. In the course of the ensuing discussion, it was noted that UBC had one definition of academic freedom in its collective agreement and another in its calendar. Senate members spoke about differences between freedom of expression and academic freedom, expert commentary and personal opinion, traditional scholarly communication and social media, and other complexities (Vancouver Senate, 2015, 2–3). Near the end of the meeting, one member provided notice of a motion to be placed on the next agenda. The motion called upon the president to invite the board and the former president to renegotiate the terms of his resignation so that both parties could "speak fully to the reasons for his resignation." The mover of the motion suggested that transparency would reduce speculation and calm concerns; others expressed the view that it would intensify the continuing turmoil. After vigorous debate, the motion failed (Vancouver Senate, 2015, 10).

Magnified by intense media focus on UBC, other challenges ensued. Early in 2016, an article in the *Vancouver Sun* described UBC's centennial year as an *annus horribilis*:

> The University of British Columbia – beset by a sex scandal, secret meetings, protests by faculty and more – has been struggling in what should be its celebratory centennial year. The [year] began with the sudden departure of its new president last summer, but has continued with allegations of interference in academic freedom, the resignation of the board of governors' chair and the inadvertent release

of documents that breached privacy rules. Several students alleged inexcusable delays in investigating sexual assaults and other students protested a lack of transparency and respect in how the university decided against divesting in fossil fuels ... Earlier this month, more than 500 professors signed a petition expressing lack of confidence in the school's board.

The university is operating in a power vacuum. It has an interim president, interim provost, new board chair, new vice-president of external relations and a chancellor who has been there less than two years. The school must find a new president, one capable of both healing the rifts on campus and carrying the university forward. (Sherlock 2016)

There were calls from the faculty association and various commentators for a governance review, prior to the search for a new president. The Ministry of Advanced Education said it did not intend to undertake such a review and that it did not have a role in the selection of the next president (Sherlock 2016).

The professor at the centre of the academic freedom complaint was elected to the presidential search committee but subsequently resigned because of lack of confidence in the committee (Mackinnon 2018, 18). In spite of this and other challenges, the committee completed the search and made a recommendation that was approved by the board. UBC's new president was installed in November 2016.

A premature presidential departure inevitably sends waves through a university community. In this case, it spiralled into events that shook the board and led to sustained media hyper-coverage of anything newsworthy at UBC. As Lynn Smith observed, "sometimes several relatively small mistakes can lead to a failure of the larger system" (Smith 2015, 6). In this instance, there was "a cascading series of events in which there were some errors of judgment ... and some unlucky circumstances" (6–7). The first key point of failure identified by Smith was that the board chair and the chancellor had not involved academic leaders in work on communications related to the president's resignation, so "no-one thought to advise [the board chair] against telephoning [the professor] when he said that he intended to do so" (7).

Events at UBC speak to the fragility of university governance and leadership and the very small margin of error in an era of divergent expectations, social media, and readiness on the part of internal and external constituencies to rally their members in response to university or board actions. They also attest to the lack of a clear collective conception of what academic freedom is, what it isn't, and what is necessary to protect it – notwithstanding definitions embedded in collective agreements and university policy.

## CANADIAN UNIVERSITIES' 2020 PANDEMIC RESPONSE

Late in the second week of March 2020, Canadian universities quickly moved instruction online in response to the COVID-19 pandemic. According to Usher, by 16 March there had been "a 90%+ shutdown of Canadian PSE classes, and it mostly happened in the space of about five hours on Friday" (Usher 2020a). The Universities Canada website reported that universities were "following the directives of public health agencies and taking strong measures to facilitate social distancing while continuing to provide essential supports for students" (Universities Canada n.d.).

Professors and instructors across the country scrambled to figure out how to provide the remainder of their courses remotely. Amid extraordinary travel conditions, many students studying at universities far from their homes struggled to pack up and get home. The demands on university IT systems and staff went through the roof. Universities closed libraries, residences, most services, and many buildings. Student services, graduate supervision, office operations, administrative processes – and a host of meetings – moved online. Social distancing measures were put in place for staff and researchers whose work required them to continue to come to campus. Almost overnight, most began working from home. Universities also assumed other roles, including sourcing and donating medical supplies and initiating and intensifying research to help combat the pandemic and its consequences (Universities Canada 2020b).

Some faculty associations expressed concern that universities' decisions to cancel classes and move instruction online were inconsistent with academic freedom (Dea 2020b). What advice did the Canadian Association of University Teachers give its members about this? The last question on its Q&A, "COVID-19 and the Academic Workplace," at the end of March 2020, was this: "Our institution is modifying academic policies without due regard to principles of shared governance. How should we respond?" The answer read in part:

> The seriousness of the current situation demands appropriate flexibility in light of some need for expedited institutional responses and the likelihood that meetings of Senate and other large governance bodies are not possible. However, the approval of any modifications

to academic policy should remain the purview of academic governance bodies, consistent with principles of shared governance ... In no case should administration assume final authority for academic decisions using the current situation as justification. (CAUT 2020a)

At the time of writing it is far too early to assess the implications of the pandemic on university governance in Canada, though it is already clear that the impact has been complex and multifaceted. Future research will need to consider whether the necessary prioritization of public health requirements in response to the pandemic will have continuing implications for institutional decision processes.

### SUMMARY

The provincial and federal updates at the beginning of this chapter largely confirmed the finding of the case study reported in Chapter 5 – that governments are controlling and regulating universities in Canada to a greater degree. Those updates and the ensuing institutional ones included instances of government intrusion or micromanagement, as well as several instances in which politicians sought to rally support through criticism of, or initiatives aimed at, universities or university constituencies. That said, the sketches also revealed instances in which provincial governments respected or reinforced university autonomy. The Quebec national assembly reduced the number of government appointees on the UdeM board from eight to two (Table 7.2 provides updated information about the composition of the case universities' governing bodies). The governments of British Columbia, Alberta, and Nova Scotia did not intervene when furor erupted on campuses within their jurisdictions, despite calls to do so.

The institutional updates illustrated the porosity of institutional boundaries and the readiness of people and groups within universities to join with outside allies to advance common causes – from prevention of sexualized violence, to improved services for students with mental illness, to maintenance of faculty prerogatives, to support for the oil and gas industry. It is evident that issues that arise at universities can arouse passions on the part of students, faculty, and citizens at large, fuelled by social and other media – passions that can be tapped for a variety of ends.

In chapter 5, the universities' internal governance structures were characterized as generally stable and as so complex as to potentially impede change. The institutional updates provided in this chapter provide two additional overarching insights.

First, they show that, stable as governance structures may have been, what went on within them was far from tranquil. At different points over the past six years, five of the six case universities found themselves in turmoil in the course of the events described above. In the course of most of those events, the universities' boards and senates or equivalent backed the university's president through action or inaction. In the case of UBC, it was a parting of ways between the board and a president that precipitated further upheaval.

As noted in chapter 2, presidential leadership failures have become much more common in Canada. Although one of the six case universities experienced this, they appear to have fared or performed better than the norm in this respect. That said, it is evident from these accounts that expectations of universities are diverse and forceful and that the margin for error or perceived error in leadership roles at all levels is very narrow.

Three of the vignettes illustrated the complex roles of deans as linchpins between their faculties, professions, and broader constituencies on one hand, and their universities' governance and administration on the other. Sometimes they align themselves with the former, sometimes with the latter. In three of the six series of events, a faculty union acted as a sort of opposition to the university's board and/or administration.

A second overarching insight is that the stability and complexity of institutional governance – the overlap of mechanisms for institutional responsiveness, protection of academic judgment, and representation of constituents' interests – did not preclude change. Our dives into the internal dynamics of the universities revealed instances when:

- a university responded to internal and external reaction to unacceptable student behaviour and the way the university had handled it by investigating the causes and developing and implementing a strategy for broad institutional change (Dalhousie);
- a board and administration initiated, modified with input from an academic governance body and others, and, ultimately, secured approval for significant changes in governance, in the face of strong opposition (UdeM); and
- a university developed, modified, and implemented a new policy in the face of significant student opposition and ultimately revisited the issues at stake and adopted a broader strategy (U of T).

At the same time, the sketches demonstrated that forces for change can be resisted, insofar as there were instances of a university community choosing not to proceed further on a previously initiated path of decentralization (UQAM); a university's governing bodies and leadership resisting external and internal pressure to rescind decisions (U of A); and a university managing to keep its governance intact in the face of abrupt changes in institutional and board leadership and associated disruption and controversy (UBC).

Canadian universities' responses to the pandemic that began in 2020, which reshaped university education across the country in a matter of days, demonstrated unequivocally that universities can change fast in a crisis – as fast or faster than many other organizations. As this manuscript was being finalized in the summer of 2021, most Canadian universities were planning for a return to in-person activities that fall. It remains to be seen what enduring governance and other changes will result from the pandemic and how much need and capacity there is for further change. We return to that question in the final chapter of this book, informed by a look at how universities and university governance in Canada compare with universities elsewhere in the world.

Table 6.2 | Update on composition of case universities' governing bodies

| | Dal 2014 | Dal 2020 | U de M 2014 | U de M 2020 | UQAM 2014 | UQAM 2020 | U of T[1] 2014 | U of T[1] 2020 | U of A 2014 | U of A 2020 | UBC 2014 | UBC 2020 |
|---|---|---|---|---|---|---|---|---|---|---|---|---|
| Board or GC[1] Lay members: | | | | | | | | | | | | |
| Govt-apptd | 12 (44%) | 12 (44%) | 8 (33%) | 2 (8%) | 6 (38%) | 6 (38%) | 16 (32%) | 16 (32%) | 10 (48%) | 10 (48%) | 9[2] (43%) | 9[2] (43%) |
| Brd-apptd | 3 (11%) | 3 (11%) | ≤4 (17%) | ≤5 (21%) | — | — | — | — | — | — | — | — |
| Other | — | — | 2 (8%) | — | — | — | — | — | 1 (5%) | 1 (5%) | — | — |
| Alumni | 4 (15%) | 4 (15%) | 2 (8%) | 4 (17%) | 1 (6%) | 1 (6%) | 8 (16%) | 8 (16%) | 2 (10%) | 2 (10%) | 2[2] (10%) | 2[2] (10%) |
| Faculty | 2 (7%) | 2 (7%) | 5 (21%) | 5 (21%) | 4 (25%) | 4 (25%) | 12 (24%) | 12 (24%) | 2 (10%) | 2 (10%) | 3 (14%) | 3 (14%) |
| Students | 3 (11%) | 3 (11%) | 2 (8%) | 3 (13%) | 2 (13%) | 2 (13%) | 8 (16%) | 8 (16%) | 3 (14%) | 3 (14%) | 3 (14%) | 3 (14%) |
| Non-academic staff | — | — | — | 1 (4%) | — | — | 2 (4%) | 2 (4%) | 1 (5%) | 1 (5%) | 2 (10%) | 2 (10%) |
| Chancellor | 1 (4%) | 1 (4%) | 1 | 1 (4%) | — | — | 1 (2%) | 1 (2%) | 1 (5%) | 1 (5%) | 1 (5%) | 1 (5%) |
| President | 1 (4%) | 1 (4%) | 1 (4%) | 1 (4%) | 1 (6%) | 1 (6%) | 1 (2%) | 1 (2%) | 1 (5%) | 1 (5%) | 1 (5%) | 1 (5%) |
| Other ex officio | 1 (4%) | 1 (4%) | — | 2 (8%) | 2 (13%) | 2 (13%) | 2 (4%) | 2 (4%) | — | — | — | — |
| Total voting members | 27 | 27 | ≤24 | ≤24 | 16 | 16 | 50 | 50 | 21 | 21 | 21 | 21 |

| | Dal 2014 | Dal 2020 | U de M[3] 2014 | U de M[3] 2020 | UQAM[4] 2014 | UQAM[4] 2020 | U of T[5] 2014 | U of T[5] 2020 | U of A[6] 2014 | U of A[6] 2020 | UBC[7] 2014 | UBC[7] 2020 |
|---|---|---|---|---|---|---|---|---|---|---|---|---|
| Senate or equivalent | | | | | | | | | | | | |
| Faculty & librarians | 52 (67%) | 65 (67%) | 75 (62%) | 78 (64%) | 10 (46%) | 10 (46%) | 59 (48%) | 56 (49%) | / | 63 (40%) | / | 37 (42%) |
| Academic & other administrators | 16 (21%) | 20 (21%) | 24 (20%) | 21 (17%) | 3 (14%) | 3 (14%) | 31 (25%) | 30 (26%) | / | 30 (19%) | / | 16 (18%) |
| Students | 7 (9%) | 11 (11%) | 8 (7%) | 8 (7%) | 7 (32%) | 7 (32%) | 16 (13%) | 16 (14%) | / | 60 (38%) | / | 18 (21%) |
| Non-academic staff | – | – | 6 (5%) | 8 (7%) | 2 (9%) | 2 (9%) | 4 (3%) | 4 (4%) | / | 5 (3%) | / | – |
| Other | 2 (3%) | 1 (1%) | 8 (7%) | 7 (6%) | – | – | 13 (11%) | 9 (8%) | / | 1 (1%) | / | 17 (19%) |
| Total voting members | 77 | 97 | 121 | 122 | 22 | 22 | 123 | 115 | / | 159 | / | 88 |

Table 6.2 | (continued)

| | Dal 2014 | Dal 2020 | U de M[8] 2014 | U de M[8] 2020 | UQAM 2014 | UQAM 2020 | U of T[9] 2014 | U of T[9] 2020 | U of A[10] 2014 | U of A[10] 2020 | UBC[11] 2014 | UBC[11] 2020 |
|---|---|---|---|---|---|---|---|---|---|---|---|---|
| Other | | | | | | | | | | | | |
| Lay members: | | | | | | | | | | | | |
| Govt-appted | | | | | | | 7 (27%) | 7 (23%) | | 9 (15%) | | |
| Other | | | | | | | 6 (23%) | 6 (19%) | | 32 (52%) | | |
| Alumni | | | | | | | 5 (19%) | 5 (16%) | | 4 (7%) | | – |
| Faculty and librarians | | | / | 5 (14%) | | | 2 (8%) | 2 (7%) | / | 3 (5%) | | 30 (49%) |
| Academic & other administrators | | | / | 21 (57%) | | | 1 (4%) | 4 (13%) | / | 6 (10%) | | 14 (23%) |
| Students | | | / | 4 (11%) | | | 2 (8%) | 2 (7%) | / | 5 (8%) | | 14 (23%) |
| Non-academic staff | | | / | 3 (8%) | | | 1 (4%) | 2 (7%) | / | 2 (3%) | | |
| Other | | | / | 4 (11%) | | | 2 (8%) | 2 (7%) | / | 1 (2%) | | 3 (5%) |
| Total voting members | | | | 37 | | | 26 | <= 31 | / | 62 | | 61 |

## NOTES TO TABLE 6.2

1 U of T's Governing Council.
2 Government appointed 11 members of the UBC board, 2 of whom were nominated by the alumni association.
3 U de M's Assemblée universitaire.
4 UQAM's Commission des études.
5 U of T's Academic Board.
6 U of A's General Faculties Council.
7 UBC's Vancouver Senate.
8 U de M's Commission des études.
9 U of T's Business Board 2012/13, 2020.
10 U of A's Senate.
11 UBC's Okanagan Senate.

PART THREE

# Global Context and Reflections

7

# Governing Universities: The International Context

How does the governance of Canadian universities compare with that of universities in other parts of the world? This chapter begins by sketching out broad trends on the international scene, as identified in recent literature. It then describes how universities are governed in three Anglo-American jurisdictions with which Canada is often compared (the UK, Australia, and the US), France, and China, and how their governance has evolved in recent years. The chapter concludes with reflections on the potential relevance of these models to Canada and a look at university governance in this country in the global context.

## INTERNATIONAL THEMES AND TRENDS

Estimates of the number of universities in the world vary widely. According to the World Higher Education Database, there were around 11,000 institutions called "university" in 2019 (WHED n.d.). By another recent estimate, there were more than 20,000 universities – and 200 million university students – in 2020 (Altbach and de Wit 2020).

Because universities are creatures of their environments, they differ greatly in size, composition, program breadth and depth, accessibility, clientele, delivery models, financing, culture, autonomy, assets, reputation, and a host of other respects. They are nestled within higher education systems that vary in composition (e.g., in terms of the additional presence of colleges or technical schools). They articulate with secondary schools in different ways and provide varied paths to tertiary education. The sheer number of universities and their diversity caution against generalization. Nevertheless, a few overarching themes stand out.

Universities and governments around the world face common challenges. Unit or per student costs rise faster than inflation (Altbach, Reisberg, and Rumbley 2009, 76). The demand for higher education has increased relentlessly and government revenues can rarely keep up with it (68).

Until well into the twentieth century, higher education was largely public in terms of legal status, finances, and external governance and had become increasingly so over time (80). In recent decades, governments have responded to the challenges just noted by spreading funding to expanding public institutions more thinly, by permitting or requiring universities to rely more heavily on fees and other private sources of funding, and/or by relying on private and for-profit institutions to meet the increased demand for higher education. The growth of private institutions, both not-for-profit and for-profit, has been most pronounced in developing and post-communist countries (80). It is anticipated that the economic consequences of the pandemic that began in 2020 will further tighten public funding, particularly in low-income countries (Altbach and de Wit 2020).

In recent decades, the challenges experienced by states in financing higher education and research, coupled with their desire to capitalize on the role of universities in the global knowledge economy, have prompted widespread restructuring, especially in traditionally state-centric jurisdictions. "University governance structures are in a constant process of transition and adaptation to respond to external pressures in a way we have not seen before" (Shattock 2014a, 12). Countries across Europe have witnessed far-reaching reforms of both external and internal governance, as have Japan and many others. In contrast, "in the UK and Australia the role of government in matters of internal university governance has been much more nuanced, while in the U.S. it has been non-existent" (5).

In many European countries, the state has "stepped back" – that is, it has sought to give universities more autonomy and introduced more competition among them in order to promote excellence, innovation, and responsiveness to industry and other stakeholders. The European Commission has urged governments to make universities "*autonomous and responsible* in order to encourage innovation and assist change" (8). At the same time, governments of what Marginson and Carnoy (2018) described as "limited liberal" states have sought more control over the behaviour and outputs of their traditionally rather autonomous universities through regulation and market-like mechanisms. Governments of all types have employed regulation, incentives, accountability mechanisms, quality assurance regimes, and sanctions to steer universities and other higher education institutions (Austin and Jones 2016, 85). The result appears to have been a degree of convergence in external governance: "Countries seemingly are converging towards what seems to have become a universal trend but they are coming from different directions. State-centric countries are moving towards more market-based approaches to governing but with the state maintaining some level of oversight, and noninterventionist countries are imposing more government controls while encouraging more corporatized and market-based approaches" (Austin and Jones 2016, 119).

What about *internal* governance? One broad trend has been growth in university administration at the expense of collegial governance and professorial autonomy. In their 2009 report for UNESCO, Altbach, Reisberg, and Rumbley (2009) wrote:

> In years past, even if academics were not well paid, they held a good deal of autonomy and control over their teaching and research as well as their time. This situation has changed in many academic systems and institutions ... Universities have ... become much more bureaucratic as they have grown and become more accountable to external authorities ... The power of the professors, once dominant and sometimes used by them to resist change, has declined in the age of accountability and bureaucracy. The pendulum of authority in higher education has swung from the academics to managers and bureaucrats. (93)

With respect to the state of the academic profession globally, they observe that "the growing tension between enrolment demand, constrained budgets, and greater accountability has resulted in a discouraging environment for the academic profession worldwide ... Like higher education generally and largely as a result of massification, the academic profession has become differentiated and segmented ... The full-time professoriate is in retreat" (80–90). In many parts of the world, academic salaries have not kept up with compensation for other highly trained professionals, so "it is no longer possible to lure the best minds to academe" (92). A study of professorial compensation in twenty-eight countries found that in fewer than half was it "possible for most full-time academic staff to live comfortably on their base salary" (Altbach, Reisberg, and Pacheco 2012, 11). Around the world, greater numbers of fixed-contract academic staff, part-time and full-time, have been hired, even in countries with traditions of civil service appointments or tenure-track hiring (6).

What about students?

> Major shifts have occurred in the size, demographic makeup, needs, aspirations, and expectations of the student population across the globe, [which has] exerted significant pressure on individual

institutions and entire systems of higher education in many countries. Efforts to respond to new student realities have resulted in a wide range of institutional and systemic adjustments that have changed – and continue to change – the size, shape, and very nature of higher education ... Where progress toward broader social inclusiveness has occurred, diversification of the student body has placed a complex new set of demands on higher education institutions and systems around the world. Central to this discussion is the need to reconsider the fundamental questions of what is taught, when, and how, and what constitutes quality in higher education. (Altbach, Reisberg, and Rumbley 2009, 100)

Beneath the surface of these global phenomena, national patterns are discernable. Nation-states played key roles in the evolution of universities and university systems. Globalization notwithstanding, they retain great influence on universities' governance, financing, and activities. How are universities governed, externally and internally, in other jurisdictions?

## The United Kingdom

The UK epitomizes the "limited liberal" (Marginson and Carnoy 2018) conception of the role of the state, insofar as "its universities were historically never part of the state, their staff were never civil servants, [and] the degrees awarded were awarded on the authority of the university itself, which selected its own students, appointed its own staff, created its own degree programs, owned its own buildings and issued its own set of accounts" (Shattock 2014b, 128).

Government began funding universities on an ongoing basis in the late nineteenth century and established a University Grants Committee (UGC) in 1919. Between 1919 and 1939, around one third of university funding came from the state, one third from tuition fees, and one third from endowments, local grants, and other sources. After the Second World War, the state became the principal funder; by 1949–50 the share of university funding provided by the UGC had reached 80 percent (129). The system remains overwhelmingly public today, although a for-profit sector has emerged in recent years with government encouragement (Scott 2019, 68).

With respect to internal governance, the traditional bicameral governance model, to which Oxford and Cambridge have always been exceptions, consisted of a governing body with an external majority, chaired by an external member, and a senate composed of members of the academic community, usually senior ones (Shattock 2014b, 127). As in Canada, the governing body was responsible for financial and business matters, and the senate for academic governance, and universities were composed of faculties and academic departments. Vice-chancellors were typically appointed by the governing body on the recommendation of a joint committee of the board and senate (127). When, in the second half of the twentieth century, the state took responsibility for funding universities, senates and vice-chancellors gained power relative to councils, which had previously played key roles in fundraising (129). The "golden age ... for the academic control of university governance" in the UK came to an end with cuts in government funding in the 1980s (132). A series of reports recommended strengthening the power of governing bodies and transforming vice-chancellors from academic leaders into CEOs. The importance of senates declined, "partly because the demands of the external environment and the speed with which events move require a background knowledge of detail that can only be reliably acquired through day to day familiarity, and partly because the increasingly regulatory environment puts a greater priority on interpretation than on policy formulation" (136).

The late twentieth century witnessed widespread restructuring of academic units, driven in part by competition for funding. A cyclical Research Assessment Exercise (RAE), initiated in the 1980s by the UK Funding Councils, was employed to allocate block grant research funding to universities, based largely on peer review (Barker 2007). Every few years, each "unit of assessment" – that is, each subject/disciplinary area of each university, often corresponding to a school or department – was required to provide data on research output per named faculty member during the period in question, as well as information about all academic and support staff, students involved in research, external research funding, and other matters. The assessments done by peer review panels – of which there were sixty-nine in 2001 – resulted in ratings of the research quality of each unit. This, besides serving as the basis for block grants to universities, had great reputational impact. The RAE quickly became "a dominant phenomenon for UK universities, which devote[d] huge resources toward managing their strategies towards it and managing it" (3).

There was extensive restructuring of academic units: between 1993 and 2002, 74 percent of the eighty-one institutions examined in one study restructured faculties and departments (Hogan 2005, ctd by Shattock 2014b, 137). The restructuring involved measures such as reducing the number of faculties, abolishing faculties in favour of colleges whose heads were imbued with budgetary powers, and merging departments into larger units. Of the seventy-two universities in a second study, 65 percent engaged in major restructuring between 2002 and 2007. According to Shattock, "invariably, restructuring has been a top down rather than a bottom up process, and a major consequence has been to reduce academic staff participation in institutional governance" (137).

In recent decades the autonomy of universities in the UK has become increasingly constrained by legislation, regulation, audit and accountability measures, and the requirements of research councils and other funding bodies. The 2017 Higher Education and Research Act gave the secretary of state the power to strip universities of degree-granting powers granted under royal charter (Scott 2019, 69). In 2014 the RAE was succeeded by a Research Excellence Framework (REF) involving expert panels for thirty-four subject areas; these panels assess quality of outputs, impact, and the research environment. In some fields the process relies more heavily on metrics than did the RAE. According to one critic, the process continues to have

> many unforeseen negative consequences including a huge drain on the time of academics who serve on REF panels, a need for more administrators, and a distortion of incentives that has led to a focus on the production of "world-leading research" and a consequent devaluation of more specialised research activities, and of teaching. HEIs now spend literally years not just on the REF itself but on "mock REFs" ... By definition, not everyone can be "world leading," yet those who are not producing 3* and 4* papers are made to feel that their work has no value. (Bishop 2020)

An Office for Students (OfS), established in 2018 as the principal regulator of the higher education sector, "hold[s] universities to account for the quality of teaching they provide [and has] an explicit legal duty to promote choice and consider the student, employer and taxpayer interests." It "play[s] a central role in pressing institutions to respect student's rights and comply with consumer law consistently across the sector" (UK Department for Education 2018). A Teaching Excellence Framework (TEF) measures student satisfaction, entry grades, and employment outcomes (Scott 2019, 70). According to Bishop, the TEF "relies on inappropriate statistical analysis of indirect, invalid proxy measures of teaching quality [and] then proceeds to turn these into a three-point scale [institutional rating] of gold, silver and bronze" (Bishop 2020).

Notwithstanding the quality assessment regimes in place for instruction and research and other forms of regulation, universities in the UK appear to remain highly autonomous by European standards. According to the European Universities Association's (EUA) most recent indicators, they ranked first in organizational autonomy and third in financial, staffing, and academic autonomy among twenty-nine countries (Pruvot and Estermann 2017).

Increased regulation has been accompanied by market-like competition (Scott 2019, 86). The way universities in England are funded has been transformed. Beginning in 2010, in lieu of direct public operating funding, universities' teaching budgets were to be "covered almost entirely by tuition fees funded by the state against loans repayable by students" (Shattock 2014b, 130). That might have been expected to strengthen the role of governing bodies, but according to Shattock, it instead bolstered the power of executive groups (140). A "management class" has arisen in UK higher education (Scott 2019, 82). Vice-chancellors are regarded as CEOs and are compensated as such. The tradition of part-time rotating pro-vice-chancellors and deans has disappeared at most universities (74). In Shattock's words, "universities have become 'managed' institutions and managed from the top down rather than managed collaboratively in a shared governance model" (142).

Academic salaries at most universities are set through collective bargaining between the University and College Union (UCU) and an employers' association (Scott 2019, 84). The abolition of tenure in 1987 did not significantly affect security of employment for previously eligible categories of academic staff (76), but recent decades have seen increased differentiation between research career and teaching career paths, greater impact of market factors on compensation, and growth in non-traditional fixed-contract teaching and research roles. The academic profession is now characterized by "increasing inequality of rewards and promotion prospects" (85). Levels of unionization remain relatively high, but in Scott's estimation, the power and influence of unions has declined over time (78–9).

Universities in the UK belong to and advocate for their respective interests through several "mission groups," the most prominent of which is the Russell Group of research-intensive universities (68). In the most research-intensive universities, the level of academic participation in governance is much higher than in most teaching-oriented institutions (Shattock 2014b, 138). Collegiality continues to exist in modified form at the former institutions, but, in general, "the trend is away from the traditional to a more authoritarian and hierarchical model in policy-making and overall to a more atomised and disenfranchised staff" (143).

## Australia

Like Canada, Australia is both a former British colony and a federation in which education is legally a state rather than a federal responsibility. In Australia, however, the national government has played a dominant role in higher education policy, funding, and regulation for more than sixty years (Marginson 2018a, 127). The national government shapes higher education though its spending power (142), but states have retained responsibility for university legislation, including the composition of governing bodies (McInnis 2006). They also take some initiatives related to universities, such as making investments in research, besides being responsible for regional economic development, land use, municipal services, public safety, and other matters (Marginson 2018a, 129).

As in Canada, the higher education sector is relatively homogeneous, dominated by thirty-seven largely public comprehensive universities (128). Public research universities provide mass tertiary education. The middle layer of universities is very substantial and accounts for a significant proportion of research conducted, as well as instruction offered (130).

In the 1980s, governance of Australia's university system remained largely collegial and funding was allocated through a buffer body (Baird 2014, 146). The current shape of the system arose from a major reform enacted between 1987 and 1992 that created a Unified National System through mergers, institutional upgrades, and incentives for increased enrolment. Expansion of participation was financed in part by tuition loans repayable through taxation on an income-contingent basis (Marginson 2018a, 147). Fees for domestic students were regulated; those for international students were not (148). International education was encouraged, and it thrived as an economic sector. The national government introduced measures to ensure quality and protect international students (Baird 2014, 148). The impact of international rankings in shaping universities' behaviour was reinforced. As a result, "while the autonomy of Australian universities from government is comparatively high, their freedom to act is increasingly moulded and conditioned by extra-university laws, government controls on student fees, other gatekeepers, regulation, scrutiny of decisions and by market forces" (149).

The distribution of constitutional authority within the Australian federation and the formal autonomy of universities notwithstanding, the national government attached conditions to grants and negotiated undertakings with individual universities, besides establishing tuition fees, reporting requirements, scholarship arrangements, enrolment levels, conditions for recruiting international students, and "performance-based instruments for shaping academic practices" (Marginson 2018a, 154).

A Tertiary Education Quality and Standards Agency was established in 2011 to register institutions, accredit courses of study, and set standards across the higher education sector (155). The roles of professional and accreditation bodies and their influence on university activities have also grown, in part because of a move to national regulation of health professions (Baird 2014, 148).

Though relatively homogeneous, Australian universities vary in research intensity, reputation, disciplinary breadth, extent of offshore operations, and other respects. The Group of Eight research universities advocates for the interests of its members separately from the wider body, Universities Australia, and the former group has managed to retain greater autonomy for its members (Baird 2014).

Australian universities are "similar to British universities in their disciplinary groupings, organizational cultures, academic career structures, modes of governance and university–state relations" (Marginson 2018a, 138). Governing bodies, sometimes chaired by a chancellor, typically consist of *ex officio* members, a small number of elected internal members, and members appointed by the minister or the governing body itself (Baird 2014, 150). In recent decades, boards have decreased in size. They are increasingly expected to function as corporate boards, providing external accountability and strong oversight of management (150–3). In 2004, National Governance Protocols for Higher Education specified the responsibilities of a governing board and that a majority of board members must be independent (McInnis 2006). Those protocols were subsequently replaced by a voluntary code (Baird 2014, 150). Some states have passed legislation regarding the composition and size of university boards. Overall, boards are subject to extensive scrutiny by external regulatory and investigative bodies (Baird 2014). Owing to their international involvements, Australian universities are experienced in the governance and management of partnerships. Networked governance, by contract and multiparty arrangements, is extensive (153–7).

Academic governance is usually the responsibility of an academic board or senate, the powers of which derive from legislation. That body is chaired by the vice-chancellor or an elected chair. Over time, academic governance bodies have tended to become marginalized and the scope of their deliberations has narrowed from broader institutional matters to teaching, research, and academic quality assurance (Baird 2014; Rowlands 2017).

Since the turn of the century, Australian universities have been characterized by strong chief executive authority, powerful senior executive groups, and appointed heads of department responsible for managing their units (Baird 2014, 154). Increasing numbers of executive leaders have non-academic backgrounds (McInnis 2006, 122). The "scholar-dean" has been replaced by the "manager-dean" (De Boer et al. 2010, ctd by Baird 2014, 154). There is ongoing leadership and management training for "academic middle managers" (154).

Academics continue to be highly unionized compared to their private sector counterparts (Baird 2014, 158), but neither academic nor student unions wield the influence they once did (147). There has been significant casualization of academic staff (155). The number of casual academic staff grew 125 percent over two decades (Welch 2012, 66). With regard to students, their formal participation and influence in governance has diminished (Baird 2014, 155) even as their importance as clients has increased.

In sum, the result of centralized federalism, national policy and regulation, and market competition has been that Australian universities operate as "a heavily regulated quasi-market sector" (Baird 2014, 145). "Executive leaders are animated by drives for status, revenues and global impact. There are established product formats in research and proxy forms in relation to education, such as student satisfaction and graduate employment rates. The international student market sharpens commercial skills ... Correspondingly, the downsides of markets are more fully apparent: inhibited cooperation between faculty and between institutions, hyper-accountability and a frenetic performance regime probably inimical to deeper creativity" (Marginson 2018a, 166).

## The United States

Like Australia and Canada, the United States is a federation in which higher education is a state responsibility. As in Canada (but unlike Australia), the federal government's role is limited. It includes funding research and student scholarships and loans, as well as regulation related to the environment, non-discrimination, immigration, and other matters (Dill 2014, 166). Eligibility for student financial support is tied to a regional system of voluntary accreditation of institutions, itself increasingly influenced by federal regulation (166). For their students to be eligible for federal financial assistance, universities and colleges must report and disclose a wide range of information about institutional characteristics and student outcomes (Kelchen 2018, 46).

In contrast to Australia and Canada, universities in the United States are highly diverse in mission, financing, and delivery models. There are private universities and public universities as well as a large for-profit sector. The private sector includes a broad spectrum, from world-leading research universities to small colleges. The structure of public university systems varies from state to state. The rise of mass for-profit higher education is a relatively recent development, involving a rapid increase in enrolments beginning in the late 1990s (Antonio, Carnoy, and Nelson 2018, 50).

With regard to internal governance, the "American principle of academic organisation" is one in which "ultimate control of a higher education institution rests with an external board rather than with the faculty" and in which "institutions with active administrations" (Dill 2014, 166) compete in national and international markets. The nature of boards varies depending on whether the institution is public, private not-for-profit, or private for-profit.

During the nineteenth and early twentieth centuries, the governance of public higher education was decentralized. Boards governed their institutions and insulated them from state governments (Antonio, Carnoy, and Nelson 2018, 68). The twentieth century saw a trend toward centralization at the system or state level. Whereas only eighteen states had a statewide governing or coordinating board in 1940 (Kelchen 2018, 72), all did by 1979 (Antonio, Carnoy, and Nelson 2018, 69).

Public institutions may be governed by institutional-level or system-level boards. The majority of the members of these boards, the average size of which is twelve, are political appointments. A survey published in 2010 reported that 77 percent of trustees were appointed by the state governor, but some were elected (Kelchen 2018, 134–5). Nearly two thirds of board members were in business or professional fields other than education. States where board members were appointed varied in the extent and nature of the processes for vetting candidates (136). In 2010, half of all public college boards had at least one voting student member, 13 percent had at least one voting faculty member, and 7 percent had at least one voting staff member (Schwartz 2010a, ctd by Kelchen 2018, 137).

In recent decades, "trends toward centralized coordination, performance measurement, and increasing regulatory authority of the state have raised concerns that extensive accountability expectations threaten the autonomy of public higher education institutions" (Dee 2006, 136). Public governing boards have also become increasingly politicized (Mortimer and Sathre 2006, 82). According to Usher, "we are increasingly seeing state boards (often entirely made up of government appointees) acting like appendages of the Governor's office, which makes them hyper-partisan" (Usher 2016b). Sunshine laws in some states limit boards' capacity to examine alternatives and build consensus (Mortimer and Sathre 2006, 90). A 2013 survey found that only 20 percent of presidents of four-year public colleges were very confident that their boards governed well, compared to 45 percent of presidents of four-year private colleges (Kelchen 2018, 137).

Relative to their public counterparts, the boards of private institutions are larger and more varied in structure (138). According to a 2016 Association of Governing Boards publication, the average size was twenty-nine members (138). Private boards tend to be self-perpetuating (i.e., to appoint their own members), though some alumni are elected or serve by virtue of their roles in alumni associations. Many private institutions require board members to contribute money as well as time. Board membership often includes major donors. In 2010, 8.5 per cent of private colleges had at least one voting student member, 14.9 per cent had a voting faculty member, and 19.5 per cent had a voting staff member (Schwartz 2010b cited by Kelchen 2018, 138). Presidents were rarely voting members of boards in the public sector but served on 61 percent of private boards (Dill 2014, 172).

Boards of publicly traded for-profit colleges resemble corporate boards. In 2009, the typical size was nine members. Whereas board members of public and private not-for-profit institutions are typically volunteers, the median for-profit board member was paid more than US$100,000 in 2009 (Field and Fain 2011, ctd by Kelchen 2018, 141). Of the 294 research and doctoral universities in the US in 2013, 175 were public and 119 were private not-for-profit (Finkelstein 2019, 222).

As noted in chapter 2, American university boards were historically very powerful, but presidents, and subsequently professors, gained influence within these institutions over the course of the twentieth century. In 1966 the American Association of University Professors, the American Council on Education, and the Association of Governing Boards issued a joint Statement on Government of Colleges and Universities that set out the American model of "shared governance." The faculty was to have primary responsibility for subject matter, curriculum, methods of instruction, research, faculty status, and some aspects of student life. Finances were the responsibility of the board and the administration. Areas of shared responsibility included strategic planning and priority-setting, budgeting, and selection of the president (Dill 2014, 171). According to Kelchen, "shared governance ... has traditionally been fairly strong at most public and private non-profit colleges" (2018, 143). A number of studies over the decades suggested that the extent of faculty input into institutional decisions was greater in research-intensive universities and in liberal arts colleges than in other types of institutions, many of which tended to operate in a more top-down mode, although a 2007–8 survey suggested these differences may have diminished (Dill 2014, 174-176). At for-profit institutions, faculty members – generally teaching syllabi developed by others, on part-time or limited-term contracts – have little or no role in governance (Finkelstein 2019, 239).

Ninety percent of institutions responding to a 2009 survey indicated they had a faculty senate. Unlike in Canada, where senates typically exist under and derive authority from charter legislation, senates in the US frequently operate under the authority of the board. Responses to the 2009 survey suggested that the influence of senates varies. Thirteen percent of institutional leaders (board chairs, presidents, and provosts) characterized their institution's senate as "policy-making," 59 percent as "policy-influencing," and 29 percent as "advisory" (Schwartz, Skinner, and Bowen 2009, ctd by Kelchen 2018, 143).

The American academic department has traditionally been a powerful mechanism for professional control of academic matters – one that has avoided the excessive personal authority characteristic of European chair systems (Dill 2014, 174; Finkelstein 2019, 224). Relative to their European counterparts, faculty members in the US have enjoyed an "extraordinary degree of professional autonomy ... in their teaching and research from government/state control" (238).

What about executive leadership? Historically, American university presidents had much more power than university leaders in Europe. According to Duderstadt and Womack (2003), today's presidents "are less visible and authoritative than in earlier times" (136). The president's role varies depending on whether the institution is public, private not-for-profit, or private for-profit. Presidents of for-profits are "basically operational managers ... [whose] first accountability is managing the bottom line ... as a result [of which], the academic voice at the top of these companies is silent, or at best a whisper" (Ruch 2001, 116). The roles of presidents of private and public universities include academic leadership, but the presidents of private institutions tend to have more authority (Shaw 1998, 45). In contrast, leading a major public university involves "a mismatch between responsibility and authority" such that "many people, including university presidents, have become convinced that the contemporary public university is basically unmanageable and unleadable" (Duderstadt and Womack 2003, 137).

The turn of the century witnessed a trend toward hiring presidents from outside the higher education sector, particularly in the private not-for-profit and for-profit sectors. The percentage of such presidents increased from 10 percent in 1986, to 13 percent in 2006, to 20 percent in 2011, before declining to 15 percent in 2016 (Galiardi et al. 2017; Corrigan 2002, ctd by Kelchen 2018, 142). The tenure of presidents fell from 8.5 years in 2006 to 6.5 years in 2016 and was even shorter at public four-year institutions (Galgiardi et al. 2017, ctd by Kelchen 2018, 141). According to Duderstadt and Womack (2003), the average tenure for presidents of major public universities was about five years. "[This] reflect[s] the serious challenges and stresses faced by universities, which all too frequently destabilize their leadership. The contentious politics on college campuses, from students to faculty to governing boards, coupled with external pressures exerted by state and federal governments, alumni, sports fans, the media, and the public at large, all make the public university presidency a very hazardous profession these days" (132).

With respect to the employment status of faculty, 26 percent of full-time and 21 percent of part-time faculty were unionized in the US in 2012, with the percentage of full-time faculty who were unionized ranging from 60 percent at community colleges to 3 percent at private, non-profit colleges (Kelchen 2018, 145). The great majority of unionized faculty are in the public sector, owing to a 1980 Supreme Court decision that deemed full-time tenured faculty at private colleges to be part of management owing to their roles in shared governance (146). Unionized faculty are concentrated in a small number of states, including California, New York, Illinois, New Jersey, and Washington (Finkelstein 2019, 231).

In recent decades, full-time tenured and tenure-track faculty across the United States have increasingly been replaced by full- or part-time faculty on contracts. The shift away from tenure-track appointments began in the late 1980s (234). The percentage of tenure-track and tenured faculty (on a head count basis) fell from 50 percent in 1993 to 35 percent in 2013 at private research universities and from 62 percent to 49 percent at public research universities (Finkelstein et al. 2016, ctd by Kelchen 2018, 144). "Off-track" appointments tend to involve teaching, research, or service (rather than the integration of the three) and to include marginal or no involvement in academic governance (Finkelstein 2019, 235).

The academic profession in the US has become fragmented along lines such as institutional sector and type, labour market (full-time tenure-track vs contingent), and disciplinary field (235). Most research in the country is conducted outside universities, so there are good opportunities in industry and government for people with doctorates in the sciences, business, and professional fields. Universities need to offer competitive conditions of employment in order to retain academics in these areas. In contrast, faculty in the humanities and many social sciences, for whom there is less market demand, tend not to be as highly compensated, to face higher teaching loads and reduced access to resources, and to be proportionately more reliant on fixed-term contracts (235). "The members of campus communities are increasingly fragmented and isolated from each other as well as distanced from their own administrators [] not to mention the members of their governing board" (Ramaley 2006, 159).

Faculty members at for-profit institutions are overwhelmingly part-time (Finkelstein 2019, 234) "at-will employees like everybody else" (Ruch 2001, 112), and "are viewed by the business side as being delivery people, as in delivery of the curriculum" (118). Driving these phenomena are long-term trends in financing. Until the middle of the nineteenth century, funding for universities was almost exclusively private, consisting of tuition, gifts, and contributions by foundations. A few state institutions were established at the end of the eighteenth century, but it was not until the 1860s that federal legislation brought a substantial public sector into being (Antonio, Carnoy, and Nelson 2018, 41). Public universities were funded primarily by state and local governments but also to varying extents by tuition. Beginning in the 1980s, it became increasingly difficult for states to fund the rising costs of higher education (71). "States ... mov[ed] away from their traditional roles as 'owners-operators' of public institutions ... [toward] selective subsidy of institutions ... linked to a narrower definition of how postsecondary education contributes to the public good" (McGuinness 2002, ctd by Longanecker 2006, 96). Tuition fees rose at public as well as private institutions, the for-profit sector blossomed, and federal student loans multiplied in volume, effectively making the federal government "the banker of the higher education system" (Antonio, Carnoy, and Nelson 2018, 39). The rise in tuition fees and student debt generated enormous social and political pressure to protect "consumers" (Finkelstein 2019, 240), and the federal government responded by attaching additional institutional accountability measures (including ratings on affordability, student completion rates, and graduate earnings) to eligibility for student financial aid (Antonio, Carnoy, and Nelson 2018, 91).

Gallup began measuring Americans' trust in higher education in 2015. Between 2015 and 2018, the percentage of American adults who said they had "a great deal" or "quite a lot" of confidence in higher education dropped from 57 percent to 48 percent. The drop was 17 percent among Republicans and 6 percent among Democrats. As of 2018, there was a gap of 23 percent between Republicans and Democrats in their confidence in higher education, compared to a 12 percent gap in 2015: "Higher education has clearly become more politicized in Americans' eyes" (J. Jones, 2018). Carey (2019) has observed that

> as the American electorate becomes ever-more efficiently divided into ideologically coherent political parties, every major issue of public concern becomes another front in the partisan forever war. [To date, s]tate university systems have mostly avoided that fate, held steady by history, tradition, cultural commitments, and a bipartisan faith in the economic value of learning and knowledge production.
>
> Now tectonic political pressures are threatening to overwhelm that consensus ... Propaganda outlets like Fox News have turned difficult campus free-speech debates into a nightly drumbeat of manufactured outrage against colleges and universities. Liberal professors are indoctrinating the youth, the true fascists are in the lecture hall, and so on. The anger builds, and soon the academy becomes the enemy and the other.

States' policies reflect this. Whereas California, New York, Maryland, and Massachusetts reinvested in higher education in the decade leading up to 2018, Arizona, Louisiana, Oklahoma, Alaska, and Alabama cut funding for higher education by 35 percent or more (Carey 2019). Increased politicization is also apparent at the federal level, as illustrated by an executive order on "Combating Race and Sex Stereotyping" issued by the then US president in 2020, prohibiting federal contractors and grantees, including universities, from using "divisive" concepts, such as the existence of systemic racism, in workplace training (O'Malley 2020).

*France*

The classic Continental European model of university governance provided strong roles for both the state and the academic profession. The state regulated and funded universities and exercised extensive bureaucratic control over higher education. At the same time, it traditionally "protected the autonomy of the university as a social institution, academic freedom as well as academic self-governance, and [delegated] substantial matters ... to academics within a broad state framework" (Enders, de Boer, and Weyer 2013, 7). Relative to their Anglo-American counterparts, European universities were weak and "bottom-heavy" and had little capacity for collective action (8). National higher education systems were characterized by "vast heterogeneity and virtual incompatibility with regard to financing, curricula, rights and obligations, as well as systems of regulation and coordination" (Dobbins and Knill 2014, 5).

By the late twentieth century, "higher education had become bigger, more expensive, less elitist, politically more visible, and economically more strategic" (Enders et al. 2013, 8). Sluggish economic growth in a highly competitive global knowledge economy, troubling university showings in international rankings, demographic pressures, and other forces came together to prompt change (Dobbins and Knill 2014). Most European systems had by then undergone a degree of reform, but the launching of the Bologna Process in 1999 stimulated diffusion of new models across the continent (4). While the European Union had taken steps to promote cooperation and student mobility, the Bologna Declaration – an initiative of university leaders and member-states – went much further, creating a common degree structure (6–8).

Europe also witnessed far-reaching national reforms of higher education. Many involved a shift from state control to state supervision, as well as specification of outputs in lieu of process controls, stimulation of market-like competition, and efforts to strengthen universities and make them more autonomous (Enders et al. 2013, 8). Although many of the major tenets of reform were similar across Europe, national higher education systems, rooted in unique historical, institutional, and cultural contexts, naturally "digested" them differently (Dobbins and Knill 2014, 2). As in many other realms, the results of reforms did not necessarily align with policy-makers' intentions (Dobbins and Knill 2014).

The European University Association began collecting data on university autonomy in 2007 and subsequently conducted three studies intended to measure and track the extent of the autonomy of public universities in Europe. The 2017 report found that there had been an overall increase in participation of external members in governing bodies, that most universities were free to decide on their internal academic structures and to create legal entities, and that executive leaders were typically chosen by the institution (with external validation in about half the systems) (Pruvot and Estermann 2017, 53). Increases in some measures of autonomy had, however, been coupled with countervailing developments. In Hungary, the state had reasserted control over universities. In other jurisdictions, implementation of decentralization had faltered, funding was insufficient for universities to self-actualize, or increases in formal autonomy had been counteracted by increases in accountability requirements (57). Overall, the report concluded, "there is no uniform trend towards university autonomy in Europe" (5).

France has traditionally been characterized by very strong state control over higher education (Dobbins and Knill 2014, 38). The autonomy of early French universities was greatly reduced by the emergence of the nation-state. Under various monarchs, national rules were established for matters such as curriculum content, examination procedures, and academics' professional status (Musselin 2004, 9). "French universities became de facto appendages of the state" (Dobbins and Knill 2014, 53).

During the French Revolution, university corporations and faculties were abolished. In 1806, Napoleon established the Imperial University – a centralized, national system of higher education, delivered through faculties (Musselin 2004, 10) – described by some as the first centralized national system of university education in the world (Carpentier 2019, 21). Pre-existing institutions such as the Collège de France retained mandates for research. Specialized institutions (*grandes écoles*) were created to educate a national elite (Dobbins and Knill 2014, 53). Faculties provided open access to standardized academic programs to all high school graduates, embodying a principle of equality for citizens across France, whereas the *grandes écoles* were highly selective. Higher education in France was thus characterized by the "seemingly paradoxical co-existence of the deeply rooted principle of égalité and the de facto elitist character of numerous aspects of the system" (55–6). This model of higher education provision – by faculties operating under a central national authority on one hand, and *grandes écoles* on the other, separated from research – remained in place for more than 160 years (Musselin 2004).

The system was unable to cope with postwar enrolment growth, and in 1968 the Loi Faure abolished the faculties and re-created universities. It prescribed that the universities be governed jointly by students, administrative staff, and teachers, with involvement from external stakeholders (35). Musselin wrote that

> the Loi Faure has been criticized often and by many: for shattering the collegial model and thereby disincorporating professorial power; for setting up a system where the electoral modes and composition of university decision-making bodies made them vulnerable to politicization; for reconstituting the old faculties within "incomplete" universities ... and for the new basic university component it created, the Unité d'Enseignement et de Recherche or UER ... It cannot be denied, however, that the law of 1968 returned universities to French higher education after nearly 200 years of absence. (32)

During the 1970s, university governing bodies became highly politicized – "councils were often transformed into general assemblies and verbal sparring in the pursuit of particularist and category interests won out over concerted solution-seeking and reconciling of differences" (Musselin 2004, 36). According to Musselin, who began studying them at that time, by the 1980s, universities had descended into anomie (37). In spite of the Loi Faure and subsequent legislation, French universities remained for many years weak in their capacity for collective action. A turning point identified by Musselin was the implementation in the 1990s of multi-year contracts between the ministry and universities (4). This "a permis aux universités ... de se penser comme des collectifs" (permitted universities to think of themselves as collectives) and "a renforcé le sentiment d'appartenance des universitaires à leur établissement" (reinforced academics' sense of belonging to their institutions) (Musselin 2019a, 42).

In France, government policy with respect to higher education and research has traditionally been formulated with the involvement of influential academics, who provide advice and input and/or move in and out of ministry and broader government roles (48). By the turn of the century, French policy-makers, who had tended to view higher education through a national lens, began to take a broader perspective. The poor showing of French universities in international rankings ignited further pressure for reform (Dobbins and Knill 2014, 62). Recent decades have seen far-reaching state-driven changes.

One thread of reform was to increase the strength of universities relative to other actors within the higher education system and give them more control over their affairs. The Loi relative aux libertés et responsabilités des universités (LRU) of 2007 enabled universities to select their own faculty members, allocate lump-sum budgets, and decide which programs to offer (subject to ministry accreditation), besides increasing the power of presidents within the institutions. Faculty members remained civil servants, and their remuneration remained tied to national scales, but universities were permitted to provide discretionary salary adjustments (Jones and Finkelstein 2019, 267). Control of student admissions and tuition fee levels, which remain low by international standards, remains with government (Musselin 2019a, 45). In spite of measures to increase their autonomy, French universities continue to rank low among their European counterparts on the EUA's indicators. As of 2017, France ranked twentieth out of twenty-nine among the European countries in terms of universities' organizational autonomy, twenty-fourth out of twenty-nine in financial autonomy, and twenty-seventh out of twenty-nine in both staffing and academic autonomy (Pruvot and Estermann 2017).

Other threads of recent reforms were to increase competition in higher education and research and to reconnect the two realms. State initiatives to concentrate resources and improve performance included a shift from recurrent to competitive allocation of research funding, partial performance funding of universities, and major "excellence" initiatives. The principle of equivalence among and within universities gave way to differentiation based on competition (Musselin 2019b, 20–3).

Finally, there was extensive restructuring of institutions. Ten new universities were created between 2009 and 2019, through mergers of twenty-eight pre-existing institutions (7). In an effort to bring universities, *grandes écoles*, and research organizations together to form world-class research universities, a series of measures encouraged them to amalgamate or form consortia. Indeed, a 2013 (Fioroso) law required institutions to join larger territorial groupings (27). These tended to adopt additional layers of administration and governance on top of existing ones (34). There are more than 70 universities in France, more than 220 *grandes écoles*, and a variety of other higher education institutions (Musselin 2019a, 46; Lacroix and Maheu 2015, 166). The universities account for around 63 percent of students (Musselin 2019a, 45). As of 2009, government grants accounted for 91 percent of universities' operating budgets (Lacroix and Maheu 2015, 179).

How are contemporary French universities governed internally? In addition to creating university councils, the Loi Faure of 1968 provided for a central scientific council at the institutional level, as well as UER-level bodies (Musselin 2019b, 128–9). A series of reforms over the years modified structures, composition, and terminology (129). Under the Loi Savary of 1984, the university council (*conseil d'université*) became a *conseil d'administration* (241) (i.e., a board). Subsequent legislation reduced the size of boards and provided for academic councils (129).

University presidents are elected by an absolute majority of the members of their boards (Lacroix and Maheu 2015, 188). French universities have administrative structures consisting of elected presidents, vice-presidents, and *chargés de mission* (project officers) charged with policy, on one hand, and directors-general, to whom report directors of services, on the other. According to Musselin (2019b), the result of this dual hierarchy tends to be tension between the political and administrative branches, the creation of silos, and multiplication of positions (108–11). Overall, the effect of legislative reforms and budget reductions has been to centralize university decision-making and administration (141–2).

Quality assessment mechanisms and measures to foster competition in pursuit of excellence have increased the pressure on faculty members to publish and the extent of internal differentiation within universities (62).

Continuing university faculty positions are of two major types: *maîtres de conferences* and professors. To become a *maître de conference*, a person with a doctorate must be qualified by the pertinent disciplinary committee of the National Council of Universities (Musselin 2019a, 51). In 2014 there were 36,555 *maîtres de conferences* and 20,353 professors (49). Unlike in tenure-track models, promotion to professor is possible only if there are vacancies, so many people remain *maître de conference* until they retire (49). Starting salaries for *maîtres de conferences* are not attractive – only 1.4 times higher than the French minimum wage (52). Since 2000, the number of temporary academic positions has increased. As in other countries, these positions are precarious, poorly paid, and less prestigious (59).

On both the external and the internal fronts, university governance in France has undergone massive reform in recent decades. Prompted by perceptions that French universities were not performing well, reforms have changed a standardized national system into one that is more institutionally differentiated and competitive. Is it time for the pendulum to swing back? With respect to that prospect, Musselin (2019b) wrote:

> Le nombre toujours croissants d'étudiants, leurs profils de plus en plus variés, les besoins multiples en qualifications que réclame le marché du travail questionnent depuis déjà longtemps le maintien d'un paysage peu différencié. Par le passé, le refus de répondre aux évolutions de la société a couté cher au système universitaire, car toutes les activités qu'il n'a pas voulu intégrer se sont développées à l'extérieur, au sein d'établissements – grandes écoles et organismes de recherche – qui se sont engouffrés dans l'espace laissé libre. Aujourd'hui, encore plus qu'hier, vouloir maintenir un système universitaire basé sur une équivalence nationale des institutions, des formations et des personnels…est irréaliste.
>
> Si les universités ne parviennent pas à offrir, en qualité et en quantité, des parcours qui correspondent aux attentes des étudiants et de leurs parents et soient en phase avec les besoins de la société, on continuera à voir les bacheliers qui en ont les moyens se tourner vers les très nombreuses formations privées et payantes crées au cours des dernières années. (38–9)
>
> [The ever-increasing number of students, their increasingly varied profiles, and the multiplying qualifications demanded by the labour market have long called into question the preservation of a relatively undifferentiated landscape. In the past, refusal to respond to the evolution of society has cost the university system dearly, because all

the activities that it did not want to take on were developed outside the universities, within institutions – the *grandes écoles* and research organizations – which rushed into this vacant space. Today, even more than yesterday, wanting to maintain a university system based on national equivalence of institutions, educational programs, and staff ... is unrealistic.

If universities fail to offer, in quality and quantity, courses that meet the expectations of students and their parents and are in line with the needs of society, we will continue to see students with the means to do so turn to the many private and revenue-producing programs created in recent years.]

*China*

In China, an imperial examination system began to emerge around 400 CE, reached its full form under the Tang dynasty (618–907 CE), and, during the Song dynasty (960–1279), "crystallized into patterns that were to last right up to 1911" (Hayhoe 1996, 10). It consisted of a complex set of institutions that "made possible a 'ladder of success' through a series of examinations, culminating in the palace examination in the presence of the emperor himself" (9–10). The system was "clearly an arm of the state for the recruitment and training of civil officials" (11). Whereas the universities that emerged in Europe during the period of the Song dynasty consisted of faculties, the imperial examination system was based on an integrated canon of texts (10). In contrast to the European guild of scholars (*universitas*), which acquired a measure of autonomy from both church and state, Chinese scholar-officials were intimately linked to the state, holding "a scholarly monopoly over the imperial bureaucracy ... predicated on their loyalty to the emperor and the classical texts" (11).

While European academics sought to advance knowledge through disputation and theory, Chinese intellectual development was oriented to practise insofar as "the highest knowledge could only be tested by scholar-officials through its use in the practice of government" (12) – knowledge in the service of power.

Coexisting with and complementing the imperial examination system were *shuyuan* – "scholarly societies or academies, that were often financially independent through bequests of land, and usually headed by one great scholar, who attracted disciples and colleagues through the virtuosity of his scholarship" (10). According to Hayhoe, the *shuyuan* ... were characterized by an autonomy both fragile and fragmented. Having nothing equivalent to the papal charters to protect their institutional development, their rise and decline often reflected the fate of particular scholars and the groups of disciples around them ... In some periods, they were ruthlessly suppressed on the grounds that they were subversive to imperial authority. In other periods they were successfully coopted into the service of the imperial examination system ... In contrast to the broadly based autonomy of the European university, [there were] patterns of a scholarly monopoly of empire at one pole of Chinese scholarship, and a fragile and fragmented autonomy at the other pole. (11)

In contrast to India, China was never colonized extensively by European powers (4). However, it was subject to inroads and periods of domination (15) and was forced in the late nineteenth century to open up to the West. Over the next half-century "[a] wide range of models or types of higher education institutions were introduced, some through initiatives taken by foreign missionaries or governments, others through efforts undertaken by individual Chinese scholars and successive Chinese regimes" (18). China drew upon the Japanese university system, itself influenced by the German model as well as American examples (Yan and Mao 2019, 172–3). The forerunner of Tianjin University was the first university to be established, in 1895; Jiaotong University's predecessor was founded in 1896 and the Imperial University (Peking University) in 1898 (Hayhoe 1996, 3).

After the creation of the People's Republic of China in 1949, China adopted the Soviet model of higher education. Pre-existing private colleges and universities were closed or transformed into public institutions (Yan and Mao 2019, 173). Most institutions reported to the national government and followed a unified curriculum. "Higher education was a state apparatus for producing the human resources needed for planned accelerated industrialization" (Wang and Yang 2018, 419). Institutions were all publicly owned and operated, students did not pay fees, and graduates were assigned to jobs. Academic staff positions offered life employment and comprehensive benefits (Wang and Jones 2020, 2). "The central intellectual institution, People's University, held a position that enabled it to dominate and regulate all teaching and research in the social sciences, to educate or re-educate all leading cadres [in crucial fields] ... and finally to train an army of political instructors whose task was to ensure absolute intellectual orthodoxy throughout the university community" (Hayhoe 1996, 20).

During the Cultural Revolution of 1966–76, the higher education sector was "more or less dismantled" (Wang 2010, 479). According to Hayhoe (1996), the force of this dismantling was in part a reaction to Soviet social imperialism (20). The subsequent rebuilding of the higher education sector included reintroduction of a nationwide college entrance examination system in 1977 (Wang and Yang 2018, 430).

In Marginson and Conroy's terms, modern China epitomizes the "comprehensive state" in which "government exercises authority in a holistic manner" and takes "responsibility for the prosperity, health and orderly functioning of society and economy" (Marginson and Carnoy 2018, 9). Although such states may embody sophisticated forms of devolution, authority derives from the centre. The extent of subsidiary actors' autonomy, including university autonomy, tends to be "shaped from above and [to] evolve largely through politics and policy rather than the legal framework" (9).

China is not a federal state *per se*, but rather a "regionally decentralized authoritarian system" under the leadership of the Communist Party of China (Wang and Yang 2018, 409). It features political centralization and central control of leadership appointments, coupled with economic and administrative decentralization (Xu 2011, ctd by Wang and Yang 2018, 412).

Wang and Yang have characterized the reforms of the early 1980s as a shift from a "control-all" strategy to a "commanding heights" strategy (419). While devolving authority for mass higher education to lower levels of government, the central government retained control over top universities and over key mechanisms and resources, including policy, institutional and program accreditation, enrolment levels and procedures, student financial aid, and research funding (419). At the same time, China drew upon American and European university models (Yan and Mao 2019, 173).

The late 1990s saw the advent of mass higher education. Regions were encouraged to expand access by launching new institutions funded through fees (Wang and Yang 2018, 433). The number of universities and colleges increased from approximately 1,100 in 2000 to 2,491 in 2013 (433). The number of undergraduate and junior college students increased from approximately 3.4 million in 1998 to 22.3 million in 2010 (Yan and Mao 2019, 182). At the same time, the central government implemented a number of excellence initiatives (e.g., Project 211 in 1995, Project 985 in 1998, and the "double world class" initiative in 2015) to develop world-class public universities and to make China a world power in higher education by 2050 (Wang and Jones 2020, 4). These initiatives included programs to recruit distinguished academics from abroad. Collaboration with foreign scholars and recruitment of foreign students were both encouraged. The number of international students in China reached around 500,000 in 2019 (Huang 2020b). Performance indicators became increasingly important in the allocation of funding (Wang 2010, 489). The wave of reforms gave rise to mergers involving more than six hundred higher education institutions, resulting in the creation of more comprehensive universities (Yan and Mao 2019, 186).

The system has four tiers: (1) public universities directly under the Ministry of Education and other line ministries, "Project 211" institutions, and leading public provincial institutions; (2) public institutions affiliated with other central bodies or with provincial governments; (3) four-year private or public institutions; and (4) three-year public or private vocational colleges (Wang and Yang 2018, 427). Each year, the Ministry of Education, in consultation with provincial education departments, establishes enrolment quotas and the sequence in which tiers of institutions will admit students, based largely on results in the national entrance examinations. This enables national universities to consistently admit the top students (430). Per student expenditure varies by institutional tier, and the gap has grown in recent decades (427). Faculty members at national universities receive much more research funding and have access to better facilities, resources, and opportunities than their counterparts at provincial universities (Yan and Mao 2019, 187).

The Ministry of Education oversees the governance of the seventy-three national universities, and other line ministries and central agencies oversee another forty institutions. Regional four-year public institutions are under the jurisdiction of provincial departments of education, and many three-year vocational institutions are affiliated with local governments (Wang and Yang 2018, 443). Provincial institutions are more dependent on tuition fees than national ones (Yan and Mao 2019, 186).

The exercise of central authority – and, hence, the extent of local autonomy – tends to wax and wane in China (Marginson and Conroy 2018, 10). The term "university autonomy" first emerged in academic vocabulary in the late 1970s (Long and Liu 2006, ctd by Wang 2010, 479). A 1985 Communist Party policy granted universities a measure of autonomy in academic, personnel, and financial matters (479). The 1985 *Decision on the Reform of the Educational System* stated that "the core part of the current higher education reforms is to change the central government's tight control over institutions, to improve institutional autonomy ... so that institutions can build up their closer links to industry and other sectors, and foster their initiatives and capacity to meet economic and social needs" (Guo 1995, 69, ctd by Yang, Vidovich, and Currie 2007, 579).

In the wake of the Tiananmen Square Massacre of 1989, however, university presidents were put under the leadership of the Communist Party Committee in order to strengthen ideological control (Wang 2010, 480). Regulations introduced in 1992 and 1993 gave institutions greater control over curriculum, new undergraduate programs, personnel management, budgetary matters, admission of self-funded overseas students, and other matters. The 1998 Higher Education Law (revised in 2015) set out areas in which institutions would have jurisdiction (Yang, Vidovich, and Currie 2007). A 2000 measure gave universities further autonomy in personnel matters (Wang and Jones 2020, 7). Managers and academics at two Nanjing universities interviewed in 2003–04 reported that both institutional and individual autonomy had increased significantly over the previous two decades (Yang, Vidovich, and Currie 2007). That said, "implementing the law has been challenging, and autonomy is restricted in practice" (Yan and Mao 2019, 181).

According to Wang (2010), elite institutions tend to have more autonomy than those in other tiers (490). As of 2008, private colleges appeared to have more autonomy from senior levels of government than their public counterparts, but they were also subject to constraints imposed by local governments, in addition to facing increased party control (485).

How are Chinese universities governed internally? The university's administrative structure typically exists in parallel with a Communist Party hierarchy – the former headed by the president, the latter by the party secretary. A party committee makes major academic, personnel, and financial decisions, including the appointment of deans and department heads, while an administrative committee attends to routine matters (Yan and Mao 2019, 180). Party groups also exist at faculty and departmental levels (Wang 2010, 489).

Presidents and party secretaries within public universities are appointed by government and the Communist Party (483). According to Wang, "senior administrators in public HEIs ... see themselves as government officials ... [and] university presidency is viewed as a stepping stone to a further political career by many presidents, especially those in top universities" (487). In the realm of personnel, "in effect, the central authority has maintained direct control over hiring and firing decisions in the universities" (Wang and Yang 2018, 426).

A regulation promulgated by the Ministry of Education in 2014 required all universities to establish academic committees to exercise jurisdiction over academic affairs (Wang and Jones 2020, 8). That said, few faculty members participate in university governance and those who do tend to be senior (Yan and Mao 2019, 179–81).

The shift away from public funding of non-elite institutions in recent decades has made institutions more dependent on tuition fees and other sources of revenue, including provision of adult and continuing education, consultancy, and university-related businesses. Decisions about academic program offerings are now influenced to a greater degree by market considerations, and differentials have emerged across disciplines in faculty compensation (187).

Faculty recruitment and hiring takes place at the institutional level (178). Employment conditions of faculty vary between the public and the private sector. Although faculty of public universities are not civil servants, their employment is subject to more government regulation and is relatively secure (176). Faculty members in the private sector are more likely to be evaluated by administrators (189) and to be dismissed for poor performance (Wang 2010, 484). As in many other systems, the qualifications required for faculty positions and the balance between teaching and research vary greatly by institutional tier (Yan and Mao 2019, 176–7). Beginning in 2003, many top-tier universities adopted "up or out" tenure-track systems (Wang and Jones 2020, 3).

The *Teacher's Law* (1993) bestows rights upon teachers, including university teachers. These rights include experimenting in teaching, conducting research, expressing ideas and opinions, and providing proposals for improving teaching and administration (Yan and Mao 2019, 181). They do not include academic freedom, that is, the right to advance and disseminate knowledge without constraint other than the law. In practice, such rights are limited by official ideology. The resulting constraints impinge more on faculty in the social sciences and humanities than on their colleagues in STEM fields (181).

Under the presidency of Xi Jinping, ideological control of universities and society at large has intensified. In 2014, the State Council and the Communist Party Central Committee issued an opinion on strengthening ideological education in universities, including tightening of party control, strengthening political training for faculty, and standardization of textbooks (Minzner 2019). In early 2015 the official Xinhua News Agency reported that the minister of education had met with university presidents to urge tightening of control over books that spread

"Western values" and avoidance of comments that "defame the rule of the Communist Party, smear socialism or violate the constitution and laws" (Yeung 2015). Many universities revised their curricula to put Xi Jinping Thought at the centre. Mandatory ideology classes for students were updated to more fully reflect its tenets (Shepherd 2018). In 2019 the charters of several top Chinese universities, including Fudan University, Nanjing University, and Renmin University, were revised by the Ministry of Education to emphasize the leadership of the Communist Party. For example, a reference to "academic independence and freedom of thought" in the charter of Fudan University in Shanghai was removed. As of early 2020, the process of charter revisions was expected to continue (Sharma 2020).

In sum, recent decades have witnessed significant decentralization and marketization of Chinese higher education, but the national government retains a high degree of policy and political control over universities. As Wang and Yang (2018) observed, "the commanding heights strategy is more than a convenient higher education policy; it is part of the system of political rule in China" (450). Increased digital monitoring and surveillance of citizens in China (*The Economist* 2016, 2018) intensified during the coronavirus pandemic and may strengthen the degree of state control over students, faculty, staff, and administrators.

Achievements resulting from the reforms launched in the early 1980s have been many. Access to higher education has increased dramatically. Research has multiplied in quantity and quality. According to the US National Science Foundation's *2018 Science and Engineering Indicators*, China accounted for 18.6 percent of the publications in Elsevier's Scopus database in 2016, surpassing the US to become the largest source of research papers in the world (Huang 2020a). World-class Chinese universities have been created and have moved rapidly up the international rankings. Chinese universities and academics became valued partners around the world. Eight countries involved in China's Belt and Road initiative[1] increased their collaborative research with China by over 100 percent from 2013 to 2017, while India and Russia did so by more than 90 percent (Baker 2019). There have of course been downsides – increase in low-quality degree programs, regional disparities, academic misconduct, publication of poor-quality papers, neglect and/or suppression of work in non-STEM fields, discrepancies between remuneration of foreign and Chinese academics, and so on. Overall, however, the reforms of the last four decades "must be reckoned wholly successful" (Marginson 2019). The governance of higher education is a key element of China's resurgence and ascendancy.

## CANADA IN THE GLOBAL CONTEXT

This brief look at university governance in other parts of the world suggests that many of the trends observed in Canada reflect global developments – from increased regulation, accountability, and competition to more pronounced institutional hierarchies. On some dimensions of higher education – for example, accessibility – Canada appears to be ahead of many other countries, whereas on others, it lags, for better or for worse.

As of the mid to late 2010s, post-secondary education in Canada remained relatively well-funded overall (Jones and Noumi 2018, 100). Usher concluded, based on 2016–17 data, that "Every single Canadian province has public spending on post-secondary education which is higher than the OECD average, and they combine that with substantial private funding. The result is that there is no EU country where total funding to post-secondary institutions is as high as the *poorest* Canadian province" (Usher 2019d).

Both overall levels of post-secondary funding and the relative proportion of public and private funding vary from province to province. According to Usher (2019d), "from a funding perspective, Canada is very much a place of two solitudes. One is Ontario, which has a funding system almost identical to the United States, and the other is the rest of the country, [which] ... combines European levels of public funding ... with Japanese levels of private financing."

The data on which Usher's analysis were based are post-secondary – that is, for universities *and* colleges – but Canada's total expenditures on "long-cycle" tertiary institutions per full-time equivalent student were also among the highest of countries within the OECD in 2016 (OECD 2019, C1). According to Usher (2019f), Canada was second among major OECD countries in expenditure per long-cycle/university student as well as first among major developed countries in expenditure per short-cycle/college student that year.

Whereas the US, China, and a host of other countries have seen increases in private provision, higher education in Canada remains overwhelmingly public, even as the proportion of revenue from private sources has risen. As explained in chapter 2, much of the recent increase in private funding has come from international student fees. The number of international post-secondary students in Canada rose from fewer than 40,000 in the late 1990s to more than 245,000 in 2016–17, making up 14 percent of all university enrolments (Usher 2019k, 21). The university sector is financially dependent on the continued enrolment of international students, though less so than its counterparts in Australia and the UK, which are even more dependent on international enrolments and the associated revenues (OECD 2018, B61). In the wake of the coronavirus pandemic, Australian universities cut more than 17,000 part-time and full-time jobs as a result of the decline in international student enrolments and other factors (Maslen 2021).

Turning from financing to external governance, an obvious point of comparison is other federal countries. Since the Second World War, national-level governments in federal systems have tended to assume greater power over higher education and to act as "modernizing and reforming" agents through investments in infrastructure, human capital development, and advanced research (Marginson and Conroy 2018, 32). In Canada, that tendency has been severely constrained by the constitutional division of powers, the resistance of Quebec and other provinces to federal intrusion, and relatively balanced fiscal federalism (Capano 2015). Based on a survey of nine national systems, including the US, Australia, and China, Marginson and Conroy (2018) described Canada as second (after Germany) "closest to a healthy, stable balance between national and state/provincial government – a balance not fraught by federal fiscal overhang or free-wheeling national interventions" (34). They observed that "both [Canada and Germany] have a healthy broad-based capacity, high participation (especially in Canada), very strong research university sectors, good second sectors (especially in Germany) and mass higher education of adequate quality" (34).

What about institutional autonomy? As noted in chapter 2, Canadian universities have traditionally been regarded as highly autonomous by international standards. Over the years, various studies have sought to measure the degree of autonomy available to universities in different jurisdictions. Studies in which Canada and/or Quebec have been included (e.g., Richardson and Fielden 1997; Anderson and Johnson 1998; Jamet 2014; Lacroix and Maheu 2015) all found Canadian universities to be relatively autonomous from government. Cameron concluded his 1991 book on universities, government, and public policy in Canada with the observation that "provincial policy has been remarkably respectful of institutional autonomy. Universities have nowhere in Canada become mere agents of provincial governments, and there is no indication that any province seriously intends to have it otherwise" (446).

Our case study and subsequent developments suggest that has changed. Although the extent of institutional autonomy varies across the country, every university in our study was experiencing increased requirements for accountability and greater pressure to respond to government priorities. Their governing bodies' jurisdictions were increasingly constrained. In this respect, Canada appears to be part of the broader phenomenon described above whereby higher education in limited liberal states is converging in terms of autonomy with systems in state-centric jurisdictions. In Canada, as in other Anglo-American countries, the state is exerting greater control, even while governments in traditionally state-centric jurisdictions "step back" to varying degrees and attempt to undo the damage inflicted by excessive prior state control.

At the same time, the relatively balanced nature of Canadian federalism and lack of intergovernmental coordination appear to give universities in Canada a degree of freedom not available to their counterparts in many federations or unitary states. Relative to their Australian counterparts, Marginson (2018b) characterized "Canadian universities, funded by province as well as nation, [as] hav[ing] more generous financing and a healthier decentralized university autonomy" (165). Furthermore, universities in Canada have to date also been relatively free from regulation of quality and performance. Unlike their counterparts in many other countries, they continue to be largely responsible, individually or (in some provinces) collectively, for governance of quality. They have not been subject to the powerful quality assurance regimes in place in the UK and Australia, nor to institutional accreditation as practised in the US. Although announcements with respect to performance funding in Ontario and Alberta could be harbingers of change, until now "generally speaking provincial governments, unlike in other Western countries, have not developed a strong policy based on the assessment of institutional performance" (Capano 2015, 116–17).

In the realm of internal governance, universities in Canada have to date been spared the government-directed reform and restructuring experienced by their counterparts in France and many other state-centric countries. Nor have they been subject to the types of government policies and/or quality assurance regimes that triggered widespread mergers and institutionally led restructuring of universities in Australia and the UK. The overall structural stability seen in our case study appears to be unusual, if not exceptional.

Overall, the internal governance of Canadian universities is more similar to that of universities in the UK, Australia, and the US than to that of universities in France, Europe, or Asia. That said, there are significant differences, even with the US, with which board governance in Canada evolved in parallel.

Relative to American institutions, Canadian universities are arguably situated at an intermediate point (varying by province and institution) between private universities (where boards are self-perpetuating) and public ones (where state governors appoint more than three-quarters of board members) (Schwartz 2010, ctd by Kelchen 2018, 134). Although provincial appointments account for a significant proportion of board members in Canada, there has to date been less political influence on boards in Canada than has been observed recently in many American public systems. As seen in the case study, many provincial governments appoint board members from lists of candidates proposed by universities themselves based on their competency needs. Affiliation with the party in power has been a factor in such appointments (Mackinnon 2014, 93), but at least until recently, most provinces did not purge university boards of their predecessors' appointees. Appointees of different governments tended to work together with one another and with members representing other constituencies in a non-partisan way (Usher 2016b). In some American states, by contrast, boards of public institutions have been politicized to the point that presidents can become political casualties (Duderstadt and Womack 2003, 144).

Another important difference between boards in Canada and those in the US – in both the private and the public university sectors – is that faculty, students, and staff play a greater role on boards in Canada. In that respect, Canadian boards are more similar to governing bodies in Australia and the UK. In Australia, the proportion of external board members has grown over time, "boards are [increasingly] dominated by corporate norms" (Baird 2014, 160), and there has been a shift away from "the idea of [the board] as a legislative or deliberative body devised to represent the university to itself and its community" (Marginson and Considine 2000, 103). As noted in Chapter 3, concerns about corporatization of boards are also common in Canada. The governing boards of the universities involved in our case study were far from behaving like corporate boards, but they had been influenced by governance "best practices" originating in the private sector.

Concerns about the state of academic senates in Canada appear to mirror those of scholars and commentators, not only in Anglo-American countries, but around the world. At the sub-institutional level, there may be a more nuanced story. At the case universities, there was more continuity in academic governance structure than there has been in Australia and the UK. Faculty and departmental structures at the six universities appeared to be quite stable and, at the majority of institutions, powerful, in contrast to their counterparts in Australia where there has been "a discernable decline in the role of the academic disciplines in governance" (Marginson and Considine 2000, 10). Canada appears to be more like the US, where discipline-based academic departments, which also "typically operate on principles of collegiality through consensus" (Jones and Finkelstein 2019, 268), are strong and well-entrenched (Duderstadt and Womack 2003, 188).

What about executive leadership? Governments in traditionally state-centric countries sought to empower universities and their executives, while relatively strong executive leadership in the UK and Australia became still more powerful. In their 2000 book *The Enterprise University*, Marginson and Considine identified "a new kind of executive power" (9), characterized by "a certain *will to power*, expressed as a singularity, a solo purpose, and a relative detachment from the institutional structures around them" (75). A decade and a half later, Baird (2014) wrote that "the authority of vice-chancellors [has] continued to strengthen" (154). Likewise, in the UK, "vice-chancellors [are] now firmly regarded as chief executives (and rewarded as such)" (Scott 2019, 74). As noted earlier in this chapter, private university presidents in the US have more authority than their public counterparts. With respect to presidential power, Canadian universities again appear to be in an intermediate position relative to US public and private institutions – leaning, to degrees that vary by province, toward the public side. Our case study suggested that presidents' roles vary but that overall, Canadian ones lack the authority of their Australian, British, and private US counterparts.

With regard to compensation, the average total annual remuneration of university and college leaders in 2014–15 was $860,000 for Australian vice-chancellors, $685,000 for private US institutions, $600,000 for public US institutions, $495,000 for those in the UK, $340,000 for those in New Zealand, and $300,000 for those in Canada,[2] all in Australian dollars (Kniest 2017). Looking only at elite mission groups, average total annual remuneration for 2014–15 (again, in Australian dollars) was $1,060,000 for vice-chancellors of Australian "Group of Eight" universities, $670,000 for vice-chancellors of UK's Russell Group universities, and $440,000 for presidents of U15 institutions in Canada (Kniest 2017). Since 2015, provinces have placed more constraints on executive compensation.

In the US, the UK, and Australia – as in Canada – the tenure of university presidents has declined over the decades and there are "concerns about increased turnover, lack of leadership continuity and reduced experience among presidents" (Turpin, De Decker, and Boyd 2014). If Canadian university presidents are perhaps less CEO-like than their counterparts in the UK and Australia in terms of authority and compensation, that may in part be a reflection of less managerialism at all levels of Canadian universities. Boyko and Jones (2010) studied the roles of deans and chairs at Canadian universities and did not find the degree of change reported in other jurisdictions. Based on analysis of institutional documents and collective agreements of thirty Canadian universities, they concluded that "the formal roles and responsibilities of chairs and deans have not changed dramatically in recent years ... One key factor that may be playing a role in discouraging large-scale change in the roles of chairs and deans in Canadian universities is faculty unionization" (21–2).

This finding of relative role stability is consistent with observations from our case study that chairs functioned as academic team leaders entrusted with limited degrees of authority. The study and subsequent updates showed that, although deans are board-appointed senior university administrators, they are strongly connected to their faculties, disciplines or professions, and associated communities – and far from creatures of the president or the board. In contrast, Australia has seen the rise of "executive deans" who "no longer enjoy an authority derived from a wide base in the traditional disciplines" (Marginson and Considine 2000, 80), and in the UK, what were previously decanal positions have "become answerable to the chief executive not to the faculty or the academic community" (Shattock 2014b, 140). Usher commented that

> when it comes to management, North American universities are quite different than, say, Australian and UK ones. To over-generalize only a little bit, we only manage the institutions; they also manage the academics. In our universities, the non-academic bits are organized along standard 21st century Weberian organizational lines, while the academic bits are organized like something between a jazz band (when they work well) and a riot. One side has oversight, goals and hierarchical accountability, the other side is governed largely by professional norms and not much else ... In Australia and the UK, [department chairs] do, in fact, act like managers. In North America they do not.

In Usher's (2018c) view, the North American approach "works a lot of the time, in the sense that it produces decent outcomes such as valuable research, well-educated students, etc. ... It works to the extent that small groups of professors organized in departments are respectful, diligent, collegial, and team-oriented. To the extent they are not, it delivers bad outcomes." More specifically, lack of management at the departmental level can lead to inequity in workloads among department members and failure to provide students with coherent curricula:

In the UK when they use the word "course," they mean "a course of studies" or what we would call "a programme" ... Individual courses are simply building blocks to a collective whole. To us, individual courses belong to individual professors ... A curriculum in our world is often nothing more than a collection of buckets to be filled to different levels ... Now it's not impossible to create a more structured curriculum in our current manager-less departments ... And in some high-functioning departments, that does happen. But for the most part it doesn't. (Usher 2018c)

What is the state of the faculty in Canada relative to other parts of the world? Whereas in most countries, "the full-time professoriate is in retreat" (Altbach, Reisberg, and Rumbley 2009, 90), "Canadian universities (and, perhaps more importantly, faculty unions) have continued to protect the full-time, tenure-stream professoriate" (Jones 2019, 257). In the US, more than half of new, full-time faculty appointments over the past twenty years have been off the tenure track (Finkelstein 2019, 234). In Canada, the number of full-time, tenure-stream faculty increased from 34,000 in 2002 (Jones 2019, 257) to approximately 46,000 in 2017–18 (Usher 2019k, 26).

In Canada – as in Germany, the UK, the US, France, and Japan – "professional autonomy for those on permanent appointments is high, as is academic freedom" (Jones and Finkelstein 2019, 268). Our case study suggested that professors at major Canadian universities retain substantial autonomy in their work. Faculty members may no longer have the degree of power within Canadian universities that they possessed early in the second half of the twentieth century, but they have been subject neither to major government-imposed governance restructuring nor to universal performance assessment/quality assurance, and they continue to have substantial input into both governance and leadership. Their terms and conditions of employment and other prerogatives have been bolstered by near-universal faculty unionization (Jones and Weinrib 2012, 84).

Canadian professors work hard – according to a 2007 survey for the Changing Academic Profession project, an average of 50.7 hours per week, which is longer than in any other country surveyed except South Korea (Karram Stephenson et al. 2017, 32). According to Glen A. Jones (2013), the overall findings of the 2007 survey suggested that Canadian professors are "hardworking, productive scholars who have the institutional resources necessary to do their work" (78).

With regard to remuneration, "comparative international studies of faculty have found that average faculty salaries in Canada are quite high" (Jones 2019, 249). Since 2014–15, average faculty salaries have declined in real terms, particularly for full professors, owing to smaller salary settlements and the stabilization of retirement age in the wake of the abolition of mandatory retirement (Usher 2020b). Looking at 2018–19 data, Usher found that average salaries at doctoral universities in Canada were comparable with those at public American doctoral universities but lagged those at private universities, especially at the full professor level. In contrast, at comprehensive/master's and baccalaureate level institutions, Canadian salaries were 25 to 40 percent higher than for equivalent public institutions in the US, and 15 to 35 percent higher than at equivalent private ones, depending on the rank. Usher attributed this in part to the extent of faculty unionization in Canada, which tends to level salaries within and across institutions (Usher 2020b).

Widespread faculty unionization in Canada also appears to have "had a homogenizing influence on academic career pathways" (Jones 2019, 261), resulting in less differentiation in compensation, workload, and mission between institutions than is seen in many other countries. That said, as noted in chapter 6, enrolments have increased faster than the number of regular faculty, so Canadian universities rely increasingly on other categories of academic staff, including continuing teaching-stream positions and sessional lecturers. That, coupled with the creation of various kinds of research chairs, has led to more differentiation of academic work over time, albeit less than is now seen in the US, the UK, and China (Jones and Finkelstein 2019, 269).

In the Canadian context, faculty collective agreements tend to specify not only terms and conditions of employment, narrowly defined, but also the processes whereby decisions are made about matters ranging from academic appointments, to teaching assessment, to restructuring of units for financial reasons – and the precise roles of university bodies, officials, and members in those processes.

What about students? As Altbach and colleagues (2009) observed, "shifts ... in the size, demographic makeup, needs, aspirations, and expectations of the student population across the globe ... have changed – and continue to change – the size, shape, and very nature of higher education" (100). Canada is characterized by high levels of post-secondary accessibility (Jones and Noumi 2018). Students entering universities are both more numerous and increasingly diverse. Whereas 27 percent of Canadians aged fifteen to twenty-four described themselves as belonging to a "visible minority" in the 2016 census, 44 percent of students entering university in September 2018 did so in response to a Canadian University Survey Consortium survey (Usher 2019h). The percentage of students self-identifying as having a disability reached 24 percent (Usher 2019h). As seen in earlier chapters, diversification has raised the profile and urgency of issues of equity and diversity in governance, both in academic settings and on campuses more broadly.

In the UK and Australia, focus on students as customers has increased since the 1990s. In the UK, higher tuition fees, competition to recruit students, and a plethora of survey and other tools have led to increased emphasis on student satisfaction, a more corporate approach to management of teaching, and expansion of student service personnel and roles (Scott 2019, 86). In Australia, the influence of students in governance is said to have declined, even as competition to recruit students increasingly drives institutional behaviour (Baird 2014, 155). The US has long been known as "a market place where students and their parents as 'consumers' have shopped around for the best post-secondary values available" (Finkelstein 2019, 225). Recent years have also witnessed a "new 'In Loco Parentis' ... driven by tuition-payers' expectations, colleges' concerns about legal liability, shifting cultural and social norms, and an evolving understanding of human development" (Patel 2019).

Many of these developments are also evident in Canada – in universities' branding and recruitment activities, in increased attention to student experience and learning outcomes, and in the expansion of student services and supports. That said, our case study suggested that students continue to have significant input into decision-making at some universities and that many student leaders resist and object to characterizations of students as customers or clients.

Can other national systems offer insights for Canada? Absolutely. Several of those we've looked at embody models to which this country may be catching up. In the recent past, Canada has been known to lag other Anglo-American jurisdictions in higher education policy and dynamics. In their influential 1997 book *Academic Capitalism*, Slaughter and Leslie analyzed developments in Australia, the UK, the US, and Canada. They concluded that "only three of the four countries successfully developed national higher education and R&D policies that promoted academic capitalism. The exception was Canada" (214).

In contrast to the other three jurisdictions, Canadian higher education continued to feature "high student subsidy, basic or 'curiosity-driven' research, and faculty and institutional autonomy" (214). Ten years later, Metcalfe re-examined questions explored by Slaughter and Leslie based on newly available data. She found that Canada had moved along the same path as the other countries (Metcalfe 2010, 490). Overall, provincial governments had decreased the public share of higher education funding and encouraged private revenue generation. The federal government had become more strategic and targeted in the deployment of research funding and secured increased accountability from universities for research performance and commercialization (509). In these and other respects, rather than being an exception, Canada had lagged other Anglo-American countries.

Canadian governments also followed the paths blazed by Australia and the UK in promoting increased institutional reliance on international student fees. If international student mobility rebounds after the current pandemic, Canadian universities may become even more dependent on the international student market to sustain their operations. The Canadian population is aging, health is competing with education for public dollars, and governments may find themselves in dire financial straits in the post-pandemic era. Informed commentators have long expected public funding for universities in Canada to continue to decline in real terms per student (e.g., Fallis 2007, 165). If governments need to ratchet back expenditures post-pandemic, universities will be unable to rely on robust public funding over the medium term. Increased reliance on fees, both domestic and international, and other private sources of revenue may be necessary to stave off decline in academic and institutional capacity and quality. In this scenario, evolution toward the more corporate models seen in England and Australia may be the way of the future in the Canadian university world, perhaps accompanied by greater labour-management conflict.

The United States also offers useful lessons. Canadian policy-makers have learned from American approaches to issues ranging from sexualized violence to performance funding to free speech on campus. Universities in this country have adopted responsibility centre budgeting, enrolment management techniques, and the National Survey on Student Engagement from their American counterparts. Above and beyond specific policy ideas and management techniques, the US may offer larger lessons, both positive and negative.

One is a cautionary tale about public trust. In response to a 2018 Pew Research Center survey, 61 percent of Americans said that higher education in the United States is going in the wrong direction. Respondents with a bachelor's degree and those who had attended but not completed college were even more likely to say so (64 percent and 67 percent, respectively). What's wrong with American higher education? The views of Republicans and Democrats differ; overall, however, 84 percent of respondents cited high tuition costs, 65 percent said students were not getting the skills they need for employment, 54 percent said that universities and colleges were too concerned about protecting students from views they might find offensive, and 50 percent said that professors brought their political and social views into the classroom (A. Brown 2018). Loss of trust is linked to political polarization in the United States (J. Jones 2018). Populism and polarization have also emerged in Canada (Marchand, Dubé, and Breau 2020). If these grow, Canadians' trust in universities can be expected to decline. Universities in some or all provinces may experience what has happened to their public counterparts in many American states.

What about France? Does its university system offer guidance for Canada? According to Lacroix and Maheu, no. They concluded their survey of the university system in France with the observation that "the history of French universities is long, but riddled with events that have hobbled their development. These events have limited their ability to engage and perform as key actors in the scientific and academic world of the twentieth century ... [Recent developments and reforms] fail to undo the many constraints that are deeply rooted in their history" (Lacroix and Maheu 2015, 193–4).

Even a scholar who is deeply appreciative of the strengths of French universities suggests that Canadian universities may not have a lot to learn from that quarter. Based on almost forty years of study of higher education in France and other countries, Musselin (2019b) offered proposals regarding the external and internal governance of French universities. They included: coordination of higher education and research by national or regional agencies (instead of site-based higher education conglomerates); multi-year contracts between government and universities to increase university autonomy and diversity (much like strategic mandate agreements with multi-year budget allocations); raising and regulating tuition fees; replacing dual policy and administrative university hierarchies with integrated academic administrative structures, as in Anglo-American countries; and, finally, adopting bicameral governance structures, like the ones found in Canada and Germany (Musselin 2019b). In other words, Musselin recommends that French universities move toward governance models more like those that exist in Canada.

China embodies a fundamentally different relationship between the university and the state than that in Canada and other Anglo-American countries. The Chinese model is highly relevant because it shows that advancement of knowledge is perfectly possible in many fields without university autonomy or academic freedom. Given China's status as a – perhaps soon, *the* – global superpower and the achievements of Chinese universities, universities in other countries may move toward that model.

They might do so in order to retain access to Chinese students, researchers, universities, investment, or government favour, as universities in Australia, the UK, the US., Canada, and many other countries have been accused of doing. They might gravitate toward the Chinese model because authoritarian government is gaining legitimacy in democratic or formerly democratic states or because the public and governments have ceased to believe in universities' broader roles, including as places for free inquiry, social criticism, and preservation of knowledge.

Alternatively, universities in Canada and other countries could find themselves cut off from China. With the recent increase in tensions between it and other powers, forceful concerns have been expressed in the US, Australia, the UK, and Canada that research collaboration with Chinese researchers undermines national security, intellectual property, privacy, economic competitiveness, and human rights. As seen in the previous chapter, the Alberta and Canadian governments recently introduced measures intended to mitigate these risks. Concerns have been expressed about the role of Chinese embassies in coordinating and monitoring the activities of Chinese students on Western campuses (Ross 2019a, 2019b). A 2020 report by a coalition of human rights groups led by Amnesty International Canada stated that "academic freedom and freedom of expression of university students in Canada speaking out on China has been increasingly stifled, as many individuals fear that Chinese governments or consular agents are monitoring their speech or their activities" (Fife and Chase 2020, A8). The report called for Ottawa to initiate a public inquiry and set up an office to collect complaints of intimidation and refer them to the police. In 2019, the Australian government struck a task force that issued a set of guidelines to counter foreign interference in the university sector (Ross 2019c). Owing to the importance of technological leadership for global supremacy, "campus laboratories aren't just hotspots for international collaboration. They're seen by some U.S. officials as battlegrounds" (Ellis and Gluckman 2019). Universities find themselves caught up in a 'new Cold War' between the US and China that threatens to end free exchange and mobility and to separate universities into camps (Marginson 2019).

In a third scenario, universities in Canada and other countries would retain their traditional modes of governance while remaining engaged with China. Success would involve figuring out how to do so without compromising their fundamental values and broader roles. Now that governments in Canada have become more active in this policy arena, it is not clear how realistic this scenario is or how much latitude universities will have.

It appears from the above survey that Canadian universities are recognizably part of the Anglo-American world, notwithstanding the distinctiveness of Quebec universities. Like their British, Australian, and American counterparts, universities in Canada are formerly highly autonomous institutions, now subject to increasing regulation and marketization. The evolution of their internal governance is also consistent with numerous Anglo-American trends. At the same time, Canadian universities are arguably still somewhat less corporate than British and Australian ones and less subject to politicization and bureaucratization than public American universities in many states. As universities in the Western tradition, they embody a fundamentally different model of governance than that which exists in China. Differences in conceptions of universities will complicate the future of global higher education and research, whether it amounts to "a new Cold War," rapprochement in governance, or respectful mutual engagement.

# 8

## Concluding Reflections and Advice

In earlier chapters, we delved into the history and status of universities and university governance in Canada, the governance of six major universities, recent policy developments in five provinces, and the governance of universities abroad. We now return to the question we raised earlier: is university governance in Canada fit for the twenty-first century?

We will look at possible directions for reform and what reform could entail. We will consider whether university governance in Canada could be improved without legislative change. The chapter does not prescribe or propose specific reforms, but it does venture merrily into the normative realm and concludes with reflections addressed to major players in university governance. Those reflections are informed by the case studies, literature, and other material and also by the experience of some of the authors in university governance and administration and public administration. The views expressed are not necessarily shared by all members of the research team.

Looking back in time, we saw small guilds of masters, or masters and students, carve out space for teaching and learning at the intersection between church and state in Europe. At different times and to different degrees, their universities became part of national systems. We observed that, as a former British colony, Canada is among the countries in which universities were traditionally relatively autonomous. Owing to federalism and the pattern of colonization, the state/university relationship varied substantially across the country. The provincial higher education systems that emerged in the 1960s continue to have different personalities, and the Quebec system is especially distinctive.

Like their American counterparts, Canadian university boards and presidents traditionally had substantial authority over their institutions. While many institutions were originally private, over the course of the twentieth century they became largely public in finance, perception, and, ultimately, control. During a brief period of relatively plentiful resources in the 1960s and 1970s, academic governance bodies and internal constituencies gained influence relative to boards and administration. The onset of public sector fiscal constraint led over time to greater state control and marketization. Universities that had been professional bureaucracies – veering toward organized anarchies in their research functions – became more bureaucratized, corporatized, and unionized. As seen from the case study, major universities spanning the disciplines and professions became organizations of immense complexity.

How can such organizations move forward? How can they deliver on their missions? How can they, in Ashby's words, "sustain the ideal which gave [them] birth and [be] sufficiently responsive to remain relevant to the society which supports [them]?" (1966, 3). Hierarchy doesn't tend to work well in universities (Musselin 2019b). At the same time, multiversities are too large and fragmented to advance by virtue of good leadership and shared goals and values, as might be possible at smaller institutions. As a result, some are decentralizing their budgets and, effectively, their governance.

Even before the pandemic began in 2020, university governance and leadership in Canada were under significant stress. Boards were increasingly constrained in their decision-making by governments and were more frequently in the news because of controversy, conflict, and real or perceived missteps. Among university presidents, turnover and premature departures had been increasing. Some senates were becoming forums for the voices of faculty unions. Student, faculty, and other university-based advocacy groups were sometimes enlisting allies outside the institutions – and ultimately, governments – to effect change within.

Early in the pandemic, universities reorganized their educational and service activities quickly and dramatically in order to protect public health. The rapid pace and sweeping nature of the changes inevitably gave rise to additional issues and stresses. The Ontario Confederation of University Faculty Associations (OCUFA), for example, expressed concern that "some administrations are forgoing their responsibility to respect the shared governance structures of their institutions and, instead, are making academic decisions without the involvement of senates and academic councils or proper consultation with faculty" (OCUFA 2020). Student unions called for reductions in tuition fees and expressed concerns about the quality of remote learning (Friesen 2020a; CAUT 2020b). The use of proctoring software raised concerns about surveillance and digital racism (Friesen 2020c). Another legacy of the pandemic may be exacerbation of the financial challenges facing universities over the medium term. Even if international student enrolments rebound fully once the coronavirus is under control, public operating funding may be scarce. Long before the pandemic, knowledgeable observers predicted that universities would continue to trail health and other priorities in the competition for public spending. In the current context, it is an open question whether current levels of support will be maintained, crucial as that is. The pandemic has brought to light other compelling social needs and caused governments to incur massive deficits. They will eventually need to ratchet back expenditures while attending to other priorities. Universities may feel the pinch.

Public sector fiscal restraint in the 1970s led to a deterioration in the quality of universities as places to learn and work and to almost universal unionization of faculty and staff. What might result from intense financial pressure now? It might well be increased dependence on fees and other private sources of revenue, continued reliance on technology, and further corporatization, perhaps coupled with increased labour relations strife.

In these circumstances, will the governance of Canadian universities enable them to deliver on their missions? If change is in order, what should be the direction of reform? There are three broad possibilities. Clark's famous triangle (1983) does not capture all the complexities of contemporary higher education systems (Cantwell, Pinheiro, and Kwiek 2018, 71), but it remains powerful and useful. It depicts university activities as being coordinated by the state, by the market, by an academic oligarchy, or a combination of the three. National systems vary in their locations within this triangle. Forty years ago, Clark (1983) located Canada near the middle, "close to Britain ... with a somewhat weaker tradition of oligarchical influence" (144). He characterized state influence as greatest in Quebec and Alberta (144). Since then, Canadian universities have moved closer to both the state and the market. In which direction should they evolve now?

Shifting even closer to the state would not be wise. Given the increase in state control of Canadian universities in recent decades, we risk replicating the conditions that came to plague European universities and led governments there to "step back." State control did not work well in Europe, even in countries where senior academics played influential roles in policy-making, as in France. In Canada, where relations between provincial ministries and universities tend to be characterized by mutual incomprehension, state control is even less likely to succeed. Many provincial governments lack the capacity to provide effective direction to higher education and research. Even if they all possessed such capacity, strong state control by ten separate provinces and three territories would create a dysfunctional patchwork. Moreover, as shown by the examples of numerous American states, governments today may not be good partners for universities.

What about greater proximity to the market? That may come about of its own accord. If public funding for universities continues to decrease, Canadian universities may come to look more like those in Australia, the UK, and the US. As those examples show, there tends to be a cost to that in terms of public service and public trust.

Academic oligarchy is associated with European chair systems in which senior academics were very powerful, but it is sometimes understood more broadly as academic self-governance (Dobbins and Knill 2014, 39–40). It relies heavily on peer mechanisms and collegial control and tends to be unresponsive to demands for utility, applicability, and economic or social benefits (40). It is less formally organized and less client-oriented than professional bureaucracy.

Academic oligarchy in the broader sense has declined since the 1970s in Canada and around the world. More proximity to that pole would be attractive to some, perhaps many, professors, but the model is far from democratic or inclusive. It would be less responsive to the needs and desires of most current students, including in terms of outcomes related to employment. Given the sums of public money invested in universities in Canada, no government in Canada is likely to buy it.

In sum, the directions in external governance reform that appear possible (more state control and/or more market control) are not particularly desirable. In the international context, Canadian universities seem to be quite well-situated in relation to state, market, and academic oligarchy. Regular faculty members are relatively prioritized and well-remunerated. They continue to have a lot of individual autonomy. Disciplines and professions continue to be strong – perhaps, overly strong – forces within institutions and systems. Students have a voice in governance, as well as through markets, and governments prioritize accessibility. Universities themselves are situated in an intermediate space, with sufficient distance from all three poles that local agency is possible, not only at the institutional level within national and provincial systems, but also within institutions.

What about internal governance structures? The brief review of other models in the previous chapter suggests that there is no obvious better model. In the late twentieth century, the elite American research university was the model to which institutions in many parts of the world aspired and gravitated. It may have lost its lustre but it has not yet been superseded. China's universities have made immense strides in recent decades, but aspects of their governance are at odds with Western traditions, so Chinese models are unlikely to be embraced here. Furthermore, Canada's bicameral arrangements have merits. Ideally, they endow a university with a governing body that represents the public interest and is capable of overseeing a large, complex organization, as well as an academic governance body composed largely of academics (including ones in term administrative positions) and students. Though often imperfect in practice, it is a model capable of securing public trust.

That said, there are many specific ways in which the Canadian model could be reformed. One would be to tackle the relative lack of institutional diversity. As seen earlier, the Canadian university sector is regarded in the international context "as relatively homogeneous and based on a common institutional form" (G. Jones 2018, 107). Isomorphism is a problem around the world, but in Canada, it has arguably been exacerbated by federal policy, which has tilted almost all institutions' priorities toward research (Tupper 2009, 56) and near universal faculty unionization. Those factors taken together have tended to homogenize the terms and conditions of academic employment (G. Jones 2019, 261). Provincial governments can – and, to varying extents, do – encourage institutional differentiation by means including legislation, funding policy, and mandate agreements; however, as seen in Chapter 3, there have been calls to go further. Clark, Trick, and van Loon (2011) advocated that Ontario establish undergraduate teaching-oriented universities. The 1996 Royal Commission on Aboriginal Peoples (RCAP) recommended that First Nations, Inuit, and Métis leaders, in collaboration with the federal government, establish a university under Aboriginal control, consisting of a network of institutions and programs (RCAP 1996, vol. 3, 492–5). Stonechild (2006) called for the federal government to "enact[] legislation that will empower Aboriginal higher education institutions with the benefit of permanent funding" (138) – a call reinforced by Article 14 of the UN Declaration on the Rights of Indigenous Peoples, which recognizes their "right to establish and control their educational systems" (Hannah and Stack 2015). Yet another possible approach to increasing institutional diversity would be for the federal government to more expressly follow the lead of other national governments in implementing "excellence initiatives" that explicitly target top-tier research universities. That would increase *de facto* differentiation even if it did not increase statutory diversity of mission.

Another possible reform would be to change the balance between external and internal members of university boards. The extent to which lay people should be involved in institutional-level governance has been a topic of broad discussion in Europe, where it tends to be a relatively recent phenomenon, and as seen in earlier chapters it remains a subject of debate in Quebec. English Canada, in having external members constitute the majority of board members, embodies the model toward which many traditionally state-centric jurisdictions have moved or are moving. Given that the purpose of boards is to represent the public interest – and given the extent of provincial funding of universities in Canada – most governments are unlikely to entrust greater roles in universities' governance to people employed in or served by them, notwithstanding calls for this by some faculty and student organizations. That said, provinces could move in the opposite direction. They could either increase the relative proportion of external members over time, as happened in Australia, or adopt the practice of most American universities and eschew student, faculty, and staff membership altogether.

Would that be a good idea? Not necessarily. The typical reason cited for the dearth of faculty members, students, and staff on American boards is that their presence would be inconsistent with fiduciary responsibility (Association of Governing Boards 2017, 1) – in particular, it would engender conflicts of interest. The latter can be avoided or addressed by means of procedures applicable to all board members. An argument *for* the presence of internal members on boards is simply that understanding universities is crucial for effective governance of them, just as is true in business, health, the arts, and other sectors. External members of university boards often arrive with little knowledge or experience of university matters. The result can be ill-informed actions and overreliance on senior management (Shattock 2014b, 140). Duderstadt and Womack suggested as a partial remedy in the US context the appointment of active or retired presidents, senior administrators, or eminent faculty members from other institutions (Duderstadt and Womack 2003, 175). Yet even they acknowledged that the appointment of faculty members to boards, while controversial, might be a valid option if there is a "clear sense of accountability and liability in such an appointment ... so that the faculty board members would not simply become advocates for the faculty position but would be responsible to the entire institution" (176).

Being "responsible to the entire institution" is not easy for board members, particularly for elected ones. Just as provincially appointed members are not on boards to be the voice of government, elected faculty, staff, and students are not there to represent their constituencies' interests or to be the voices of their associations or unions. All are there to make decisions in the best interests of the university as a whole. In the case of internal members, not all their colleagues or fellow students or staff understand that. At some universities, faculty and staff members step out of their unions while serving on the board, but that requirement is far from universal. For faculty, staff, and student board members who also serve on the executives or boards of their unions or associations, conflict of interest is unavoidable. Even those who don't wear multiple hats may be subject to immense pressure, as well as – in an era in which meetings may be recorded and posted on the internet – to ridicule or censure for how they have voted or what they have said or not said.

In sum, there are arguments for the presence of student, faculty, and staff members on boards, even though it raises difficulties and complications. For it to work, however, all board members must avoid conflicts of interest and be committed to acting in the best interests of the university.

Another prominent topic is the weakness of academic governance bodies – a prominent theme in the literature and commentary, both international and Canadian. The senates or equivalent bodies of some of the case universities in our study were described as playing important roles, but we also heard many concerns. Would unicameralism be a more effective form of governance? Interviews suggested it works reasonably well at the University of Toronto. Would it work elsewhere? That is not clear. It may be not unicameralism *per se* that makes U of T work, but the governance culture at U of T that makes unicameralism work. Back in the 1960s, Duff and Berdahl rejected unicameralism as an option for Canadian universities on the grounds that academic matters might tend to be neglected (Cameron 1991, 305). Nevertheless, now that it has evolved and been tested over decades at U of T, it could be an option for other institutions and jurisdictions to consider.

U of T is one of very few Canadian universities where faculty members are not unionized. Near universal faculty unionization is one of the distinctive features of universities in this country. What are its benefits and costs? Faculty unionization no doubt accounts in large part for the healthy level of investment in professorial positions in Canada, relative to other countries. Given that the decentralized nature of universities can easily produce unfair employment outcomes, unionization also has important benefits in terms of equity, standardization, and procedural fairness. To the extent that faculty unions tend to act as "oppositions" to administrations, it no doubt keeps the latter on their toes – at least as far as faculty members' interests are concerned.

That said, faculty unionization also has significant drawbacks. First, since collective bargaining is an adversarial process, it is in a union's interests at the bargaining table – and, ultimately, in the economic interests of its members – that faculty members be disenchanted or angry with the administration. There is therefore an incentive for unions to ramp up the rhetoric and to convince their members that the administration or the board are self-serving, incompetent, and/or enemies of academics and academic values, particularly in the lead-up to collective bargaining. Economic issues tend not to be sufficient to rile up academic troops, so recourse is often made to broader values and issues. Since vertical communication in universities tends to be poor (Musselin 2019b) and many professors experience frustration and stress, the result can easily be a faculty that is alienated from or hostile to "administration." Collective spirit and governance functions are undermined. Unionized environments also tend to be characterized by tension between the faculty member's role as a professional and their role as an employee. When unions expand collective bargaining to encompass matters that might be considered elements of academic self-governance, the result is to emphasize the employee role and to reduce both the authority of academic self-governance and the professional autonomy of the professoriate. A final major disadvantage of unionized collective bargaining is of course that when it leads to strikes or threats of strikes, students are hurt.

If the results of faculty unionization have been a mixed bag, should universities – or governments – seek to roll back the clock? Realistically, no. Some may wish it were possible, but faculty unionization is now a deeply entrenched feature of higher education in Canada. Furthermore, as Cameron pointed out decades ago, "to contemplate legislation depriving faculty members of rights already obtained would be to contemplate political interference that would certainly be divisive and would probably be unconstitutional" (Cameron 1991, 448).

That said, a worthwhile avenue for legislative reform would be to separate governance from collective bargaining, as proposed by MacKinnon (2014). The two processes are fundamentally different. Governance concerns "the means by which order is created in the academy to achieve the goals of educating, researching, and providing service to multiple publics" (Austin and Jones 2016, 2). Collective bargaining is "the process whereby an employer and a trade union seek to negotiate a collective agreement" – "a document recording the terms and conditions of employment and the rights and duties of the employer, trade union and employees in a bargaining unit" (Carter et al. 2002, 43). In practice, as seen in earlier chapters, institutional governance and faculty collective bargaining can become intertwined. UQAM was notable among the case universities in this respect. The CAUT advocates that the roles of boards and senates be circumscribed through collective bargaining. Provincial governments that think otherwise could consider legislation to establish the boundaries between governance and collective bargaining on terms and conditions of employment. According to MacKinnon, such legislation would "emphasize that 'terms and conditions of employment' open to collective bargaining must be construed so as to leave unhindered the legislature's prerogative to provide for the statutory authority of boards, senates and their responsible officers" (MacKinnon 2014, 110). In other words, it would prevent universities from giving away powers bestowed on their governing bodies and officials by provincial legislation. Whether or not provincial governments will do this may be a function of their relationships with organized labour.

What other changes in governance might provinces and universities consider? The possibilities are endless. Even if the ratio of external members to internal members on boards does not change, the proportion of alumni to other external members, or of board-appointed to government-appointed members, or the ratio of students to faculty and staff, or the balance between regular faculty members and other categories of teaching and/or research staff, could. As people who are "independent" of the university but connected to it and its students, alumni can play an invaluable role in institutional governance. Changes in the composition of academic governance bodies, and in the powers and responsibilities of bodies and actors in governance at different levels, might be contemplated as well.

As noted in previous chapters, many universities are seeking to increase diversity and, in particular, Indigenous participation in governance. The discovery of unmarked graves at many former residential schools in 2021 underscored hard truths about Canadian history, exacerbated survivors' pain, and reignited calls for change. Renewed protests and actions against anti-Black and anti-Asian racism can also be expected to give further impetus to universities' equity and inclusion initiatives. More complex and challenging than increasing the number of Indigenous and racialized people engaged in governance are Indigenization – that is, incorporation of Indigenous knowledge, world views, and perspectives (Lavallee 2020, 130) – and decolonization, in the sense of putting an end to ongoing colonization "[and] divesting of power back ... so that self-determination is fully realized" (Cote-Meek 2020, xvi). Cote-Meek and Moeke-Pickering (2020), Lavallee (2020), Moeke-Pickering (2020), Kuokkanen (2007), and others have suggested measures for effecting change; but insofar as neocolonial universities are hierarchical institutions, organized and driven by disciplines and professions, decolonization and Indigenization may ultimately, as Lavallee suggests, represent "an unrealistic and impossible condition" (Lavallee 2020, 123). Nevertheless, given the vital importance of further progress toward those goals, how and to what extent they can be achieved within existing universities will in all likelihood remain a focus of attention.

Another major avenue for reform would be to move away from organizing departments, faculties, and representation on academic governance bodies based on disciplines and professions. The roles of disciplinary departments and groupings in many systems have weakened, yet those in Canada and the US remain strong. Writing about the trend toward cross-disciplinary organization in Australia, Marginson and Considine (2000) suggested that much is lost when disciplines are superseded as a basis for organizing universities – that the effect (and perhaps the intent) of such changes is to strengthen executive power at the expense of academic considerations and voices. On the other hand, disciplinary and professional units can create silos and impede cross-institutional collaboration. Disciplines and professions structure and validate knowledge and "consolidate certain ways of looking at the world while excluding others" (Kuokkanen 2007, 14). Duderstadt and Womack (2003) are among those who argue that "departmental structures ... pose a major impediment to change. They maintain a disciplinary focus that is increasingly orthogonal to the rapid pace of intellectual change ... They also perpetuate practices of selecting, evaluating and rewarding people which hinder the development of a more cohesive university community capable of serving a rapidly changing world" (188).

Canadian universities already make extensive use of centres and institutes and have units focused on area of study (e.g. environmental studies, gender studies) as well as ones organized along disciplinary and professional lines. Should they go even further and begin to phase out disciplinary departments? Even if universities wish to restructure professional schools, the structures of the latter are not within their control, insofar as they are driven by accreditation bodies and requirements. According to Duderstadt and Womack, "universities need to understand better just how restrictive these accreditation requirements are and, if they are found to be too constraining, work with peer institutions to modify them" (189) – a daunting task.

In sum, there are myriad possible directions for governance reform. The considerations involved are complex, the interests varied, the issues contested, and the potential consequences profound. In MacKinnon's view, "this is not internal work for the universities themselves" (2018, 119). Insofar as universities are publicly mandated and funded and serve a larger societal purpose, that is undoubtedly true. MacKinnon has called for "a new commission for the[] study and determination" of these issues – "a blue ribbon panel ... consisting of members well versed in governance including a former university president ... and a senior representative of Canadian provincial governments who can assist in ensuring that legislative changes recommended by the panel are acted upon by them" (119). The Flavelle Commission, the Parent Commission, and the Duff–Berdahl Commission were turning points in university governance in Canada and in Quebec. Should a new commission be established?

A new commission might well generate fresh insights, but there are grounds for caution. It is far from certain that any recommended changes would be implemented on a national or even broad interprovincial scale. Owing to the constitutional division of powers, university governance reform in Canada does not take place at the flip of a switch. As seen earlier, in most provinces, universities have individual acts; only Alberta and BC have omnibus university legislation. Thus, reform would have to take place institution by institution in some provinces, and province by province in others, unless all provinces decided to move to omnibus acts. In the latter event, a great deal of institutional diversity and personality would be lost. How would the provinces react to a commission? Quebec might well be skeptical of a national exercise – and it might not be alone.

The conditions surrounding the establishment of the Flavelle, Parent, and Duff-Berdahl Commissions differed from today's in several material ways. For one thing, professors' relationships to universities and university presidents were different. The forerunner of Universities Canada, the National Conference of Canadian Universities, included both senior administrators and faculty members (Cameron 1991, 31). The Canadian Association of University Teachers co-sponsored the Duff-Berdahl Commission with a predecessor of Universities Canada – something difficult to imagine today. At present, there are entrenched differences between Universities Canada and CAUT on many issues. A new commission could give rise to a bunfight between the two organizations, thus increasing tensions on campuses, putting student leaders in a difficult position, generating unfortunate press, and ultimately damaging the reputation of universities and undermining public trust.

When the Flavelle Commission was established, the governance of U of T had been in dire straits for many years. The same was true of education in Quebec in the early 1960s. By the time Duff and Berdahl began their work, governance arrangements in English Canada were clearly out of step with the times. The current state of university governance in Canada may not yet be bad enough for stakeholders to agree on and be prepared to embrace fundamental change.

A final major reason to hesitate in establishing a new commission is that the socio-political environment may not be conducive to such an exercise. When such commissions were established in the past, Canadians were optimistic that universities and the knowledge they generated would contribute to the public good. The Flavelle Commission described the university as "an institution of the highest importance, at once to the intellectual life of the nation, and to its progress in the practical sciences needed to open to its youth the golden opportunities of an age of scientific achievement" (Royal Commission on the University of Toronto 1906, viii). The (Massey) Royal Commission on National Development in the Arts, Letters, and Sciences, established in 1949, argued that universities "serve the national cause in so many ways, direct and indirect, that theirs must be regarded as the finest of contributions to national strength and unity" (Cameron 1991, 47). By the mid-1950s, "the idea was rapidly taking hold [among Canadians] that universities and a university education represented an almost certain path to economic growth and individual prosperity" (66–7). In the current era of employment precarity, however, doubts have grown about the value of university education, coupled with growing skepticism and distrust in many quarters – including quarters of universities – of science, expertise, and the quest for understanding (Fallis 2007). The COVID-19 pandemic may have reinforced or restored the legitimacy of science in some quarters, but the "post-truth" society still has many adherents.

Populism has emerged in many parts of the world, fuelled by economic and other grievances. Although global inequality has diminished in recent decades, within-country inequality has increased in most leading economies. In these jurisdictions, a "new, more unequal and polarized geography of prosperity and opportunity has … been accompanied by a rise in regional resentment and much greater polarization of political attitudes and voting behavior" (Marchand, Dubé, and Breau 2020, 2). In some countries, populist politicians have risen to power by stoking people's anger.

Populism has long been a contested concept (Weyland 2001), but broadly speaking, it involves juxtaposing the will of the "real people" against the interests of self-serving elites and "others" (Neuman 2020). Once in power, populists, whether of the right or the left, often set out to undermine or dismantle institutions and bodies that constrain the implementation of "the people's" will (Neuman 2020). Although populism has not yet flourished in Canada to the same extent as in the US and some other countries, the threat of the "populist wrecking ball" (Webber 2020, 9) – and the gravity of the issues that propel it – should not be dismissed. Insofar as universities are part of the privileged, cosmopolitan, connected, global community from which many are excluded, they can be targets. Populism, and reactions to it, could exacerbate the external risks facing universities as identified in earlier chapters, including these:

- Policy whiplash (i.e., initiatives taken by one government being reversed by a successor of a different political stripe).
- Politicization of university boards and even leadership.
- Use of universities as political punching-bags, with a resulting loss of legitimacy and public trust.
- Risk of precipitous legislative change in the interests of clearing away complex academic governance mechanisms to make universities more responsive to the will of governments, the people, the labour market, and/or students.

In his review of international trends in university governance, Shattock (2014c) wrote that "where ... the state has introduced governance reforms through legislation, the reform has been imposed largely on the states' terms and in furtherance of state objectives" (184). The objectives of a populist provincial government might well differ from those of many other stakeholders.

Given the uncertain benefits as well as the risks associated with opening up the Pandora's box of far-reaching legislative change, can university governance in Canada be improved without legislation? Undoubtedly. Many universities' governing bodies now exercise much less authority than is granted to them under their institutions' acts, so university autonomy would increase if governments wound back regulation and allowed them to operate consistent with their legislation. Improvements are also possible without legislation on the internal front. Previous chapters cited many examples of changes carried out by universities. Legislating reform of governance structures is not the only – and may not be the best – way of achieving change in universities. Austin and Jones (2016) observe that "there is a clear relationship between structures and human agency ... [but] there is [also] a human-social element that is at the heart of governance and the way governing instruments function" (57).

Based on the contents of previous chapters, how could we improve the practice of governance within existing legislation? This chapter provides no prescriptions, but – in the belief that changes in perspective and practice could improve universities' capacities to fulfill their missions – it offers reflections and gentle words of advice to individuals about to step into roles in external and internal governance.

One such imaginary person is a provincial public servant about to take up a position in a higher education ministry. She has worked in other branches of government but knows little about higher education and how universities operate. Given the opportunity, what information and insights might we offer?

## TO A PROVINCIAL PUBLIC SERVANT

Universities in the Anglo-American world have traditionally operated at arm's length from governments. Autonomy has been identified as a factor in university performance. The level of institutional autonomy varies from province to province. Overall, Canada has been at a place on the spectrum of state control toward which many European and other countries have moved or are moving. Those governments have been trying to break the habit of micromanaging universities. If provincial governments continue to increase the degree to which Canadian universities are regulated, they may end up replicating the problems that led European governments to "step back."

Universities are expensive and can behave as if entitled. Provincial policy and regulation are definitely needed. They have no doubt saved universities in Canada from some of the mistakes of their counterparts in the US, Australia, and the UK. That said, overregulation "costs money, stifles creativity and diversity, defeats effective administration and, at its extremes, intrudes upon academic freedom" (Sloan Commission, ctd in Newman 1987, 24). It also undermines the capacity of universities to respond to their many constituencies and to carry out their missions.

Government is a key stakeholder, but it is not the *shareholder*. It represents the democratic will, has legislative and regulatory power, and is a major funder – all of which must be respected. But universities are accountable to others besides government. They are accountable to their students, to alumni, donors, and partners, and to local communities, and they are obligated to serve national and many other needs. At the same time, they are required to keep up with knowledge and contribute to its advancement. They and their members need space to do that. Experience in Europe, the US, and elsewhere has shown that overregulation deprives universities of initiative as well as the capacity for responsiveness and innovation – qualities you in government want in universities.

Governments cannot regulate or micromanage universities to success. As the Flavelle Commission realized more than a hundred years ago, the state simply cannot run universities effectively. When governments intervene in university affairs, they invite backlash; when they require universities to behave like arms of government – in personnel, finance, accountability, and a host of other matters – it undermines morale and performance. Governments need good boards to oversee and govern universities effectively, and those boards in turn need good presidents.

What makes a good board? Prominent among the many factors are the expertise, experience, and commitment of members. To govern a major university well, a board must bring together diverse expertise, experience, and identities, including people with senior governance and leadership experience in large, complex organizations (Duderstadt and Womack 2003, 176). A board needs members who believe in the power of higher education and are willing to provide large amounts of their time for free. If qualified candidates think they can affect the future of a university and its students, they may be willing to make that commitment. If, however, board decision-making room has shrunk to almost nothing, or if it or its members' contributions are devalued by actors within or outside the university, they're much less likely to do so. In those circumstances, boards become populated by people with less than optimal qualifications and experience. They overlook things and make mistakes, so governments feel impelled to intrude even more, setting in motion a vicious circle.

So, set the broad policy framework while avoiding excessive bureaucratic intrusion, unwarranted attacks on universities, and politicization of boards. Respect the contributions of board members. Recognize that boards know their competency needs best. If your provincial government appoints members to university boards, consider entrusting that power to boards or committing to appoint based on their reasoned recommendations. Expect board members, once appointed, to govern within the policy framework and mechanisms established by government, but don't expect them to take direction from you, because that would be inconsistent with their responsibilities. Recognize that stability in governance is crucial.

The academic aspects of university governance may be unfamiliar to you. The cumulative result of professors' academic freedom, student activism, and universities' roles as forums for criticism may not endear them to you and others in government! Ill-informed, misguided, and unfair as commentary emanating from universities may sometimes seem (and be), keep in mind that these freedoms have made possible Western universities' contributions through the ages. Chinese universities have recently made great strides without them, but it would be premature to conclude that they are superfluous.

Anglo-American governance models have yet to be superseded. Shattock (2014c) has suggested that Europe and Japan – seeking to emulate the successes of Anglo-American universities – should bear in mind that the "characteristics of the best universities [include] characteristics that governments find it easy to forget: the importance of academic participation in governance ('shared governance'), the continued priority in decision-making being given to academic values and the need to convince by argument in an academic community rather than by fiat or the exercise of executive power" (197). It is something for governments in the Anglo-American world to bear in mind too.

If autonomy is desirable, should provincial governments encourage universities to become more private and more corporate, rather than integrating them increasingly into the state? As seen in chapter 2, the public share of university funding in Canada has already declined. Owing to the massive costs incurred by governments during the current pandemic, austerity is on the horizon. Further privatization may follow. Would the resulting corporatization be better than bureaucratization? Not necessarily. The top research universities in almost all countries are public (Altbach and Salmi 2011, 27). Only in the US do private institutions dominate the top tier of universities (Altbach, Reisberg, and Rumbley 2009, 84). In that country and many others, private institutions – in particular, for-profit ones – are also prominent in the bottom tier. Privatization tends to detract from research universities' performance of their core missions (Altbach and Salmi 2011, 27). In Latin America and some other parts of the world, there are "semi-elite" private institutions, but most private and for-profit higher education is "demand-absorbing" – that is, it serves students who aren't able to gain admission to other institutions (Altbach, Reisberg, and Rumbley 2009, 85). For-profit institutions have much narrower missions, which don't include research or other functions that contribute to local, regional, or national needs and goals. Though privatization has been a trend in much of the world (Altbach, Reisberg, and Rumbley, 2009, 87), delivering on a public mission ultimately requires public dollars.

## TO A FEDERAL PUBLIC SERVANT

Stepping into a university-related role in a federal department or granting council for the first time, you may be pleased to discover that Ottawa's relationship with universities is less problematic and more pleasant than those between universities and provincial government. That is basically because it's not up to Ottawa to ensure that universities meet the needs of students, employers, and myriad others in return for the operating funding they receive. The federal government can be a fun uncle or aunt rather than a stern parent. University leaders tend to be grateful for Ottawa's investments, its broader perspectives, and its support. They and others have at times advocated for a larger federal role. Given the dynamics of Canadian federalism, it is not likely the provinces will cede much more ground.

Intergovernmental coordination on files related to universities has been lacking. This has had consequences for universities and for students and probably accounts in part for the notoriously bad state of Canadian university data. Lack of coordination is evident even in the realm of international education, which both levels of government recognize is an important contributor to human capital, economic, and other public policy goals (Tamtik, Trilokekar, and Jones 2020).

The federal government has played a vital – and largely unheralded – role in lifting the quality and capacity of Canadian universities. That said, unilateral federal action often has unintended consequences. Federal investment in university research beginning in the late 1990s, important as it was, had the effect of further separating research from education. Coupled with changes in transfer payments, it undermined the quality of undergraduate education – presumably, not an intended outcome. It would behoove federal officials to think through the implications of actions within Ottawa's realms for universities' educational missions, even if ongoing coordination with the provinces is not possible.

It would also be wise to avoid getting drawn into provincial jurisdiction. It is certainly within the purview of federal departments or agencies to set criteria for research funding, but when they attach to those criteria measures pertaining to broad institutional employment practices or measures to combat sexualized violence, that is an intrusion on provincial jurisdiction. It is one thing for universities to cope with the lack of coordination between two, or three, levels of government, each acting within its own sphere of authority. It's another matter to cope with two or more masters acting at odds in the same policy area. Given that higher education is, in Harmsen and Tupper's charming term, "an active policy community" (2017, 22), there will often be voices and groups encouraging the federal government to step in to counteract or shape provincial and/or institutional decisions. Notwithstanding the short-term political benefits, it is ultimately wise to resist.

Respecting constitutional boundaries will become even more important if Canadians become more polarized. Previous chapters included examples of changes in the ideological flavour of provincial higher education policy linked to changes in government. Depending on the extent of the change in policy direction, the whiplash for universities can be serious. It would be even more counterproductive if universities were to become sites for playing out of political differences between federal and provincial governments.

## TO UNIVERSITIES AND THEIR MEMBERS

Universities bring together people of different ages, educational attainments, personal and socio-economic characteristics, nationalities, and beliefs, in many different roles. The following reflections are offered to all of you in the naive belief that there are some things that unite you. The first few reflections are about how universities will respond to the likely scarcity of resources in coming years and the potential results of their choices. We then turn to the prospect of increased competition and stratification of institutions and the implications of this for equity and diversity. The nature of universities' missions and the risks of mission creep are briefly considered. Finally, we contemplate the sad state of understanding of academic freedom in this country. The assumption underlying all these reflections is that, in coming years, the challenges of responding simultaneously to academic competition, market demands, and social needs will become even greater.

If, as anticipated, public funding is scarce, your university may try to generate additional revenue through education, research, or other activities, to the extent permitted by governments. The dangers of commercialization identified by Bok (2003), Fallis (2007), MacKinnon (2014), CAUT (2013), and many others are real. Ensuring that revenue generation does not subvert the university is a major challenge for governance and leadership. There are many who object to seeking additional revenue even though the goal is to sustain activities and employment rather than to generate profit. But the alternative to compensating for decreased public funding through revenue generation is cost reduction, which is also not pretty.

Like their counterparts in many other systems (Altbach, Reisberg, and Rumbley 2009), Canadian universities are not good at strategic cost reduction. Austerity tends to involve layoffs of non-academic and contract instructional staff, hiring freezes, increases in class sizes, other reductions in educational quality, elimination of non-teaching budgets, lack of resources for new activities and initiatives, recriminations, and labour strife. It deprives students of the quality of education they should receive, young people wanting to join the academic profession of the opportunity to do so, precariously employed instructors of work and income, and continuing faculty and staff of the resources they require to do their work creatively and well. Putting courses on line does not in itself save money. Different approaches to cost reduction, including broad rethinking of programs and workloads, are possible but have not been common in the past.

Insofar as universities ignore market demands they could legitimately and effectively serve, they open up opportunities for other types of providers, not-for-profit and for-profit, domestic and international. That is not a bad thing, but it is a consideration. French universities illustrate what happens when public institutions are not sufficiently responsive – governments allow or encourage other options, and students with the means go elsewhere (Musselin 2019b, 39). In the past, provincial governments tightly controlled the authority to grant degrees or to use the term "university," but in recent years, several have supported the creation of private universities, both not-for-profit and for-profit (G. Jones 2018, 216). Meanwhile, foreign institutions are offeringg programs in Canada, both in person and online. The private sector in this country remains small (216), but its future growth cannot be ruled out. Furthermore, students who do not find the type or quality of program they are seeking in Canada and who can afford to go abroad will do so, while their less privileged counterparts make do. Canadian universities need to continue to respond to students' expectations and needs. From a financial and an employment perspective, as well as a moral one, it is the right thing to do.

Admittedly, to the extent that universities focus on revenue generation – and that governments require, encourage, or permit them to do so – increased competition and further stratification will result. That is typical of mature high-participation systems (Cantwell, Pinheiro, and Kwiek 2018). Massification increases social inclusion, but in the absence of countervailing government policy, it also leads to increased competition and stratification between institutions and individuals (Marginson 2018b). In that scenario, "elite institutions become more elite. They are more contested, more difficult to enter, and more subject to middle class capture" (Marginson 2018c, 34). World-class universities and their closest imitators become a "modern aristocracy peeling away from the rest" (Marginson 2018b, 169). Socio-economic status increasingly determines opportunities and outcomes. "Unequally ranked and valued students are matched with 'appropriate' unequally valued educational opportunity and the unequal social outcomes that follow" (Cantwell and Marginson 2018, 148). Those who do not go to university or college end up even more disadvantaged, because "once the higher education experience becomes normal the penalties of exclusion are profound" (Marginson 2018a, 9). Universities thus join the ranks of institutions that foster inequality.

That scenario is not inevitable. The OECD (2017) has found that "education policies and educational institutions and actors play a central role in mitigating the gap between socio-economically advantaged and disadvantaged students" (77). Governments and universities can stem or counteract the tendency of high-participation systems to increase social inequality over time (Marginson 2018b, 170).

How are Canadian governments and universities doing in this respect? Although Canadian universities have become more stratified and increasingly dependent on private funding in recent years, they appear to provide relatively healthy accessibility to educational quality. With respect to the education system as a whole, Canada is among a group of four countries that performed above the OECD average on nine of eleven of the OECD's equity indicators (the others being Australia, Finland, and Sweden). Four other countries – Estonia, Japan, Korea, and the Netherlands – outperformed on nine of ten indicators (OECD 2017, 35). In Canada, good higher education is broadly accessible. Although stratification and tuition fees are higher than in Nordic countries, "the lower tier institutions have better quality and standing than their counterparts in most other countries, and there is a large number of high-quality research universities relative to country size" (Marginson 2018b, 179). A recent Statistics Canada report indicated that the higher education participation of students from lower socio-economic backgrounds improved between 2001 and 2014 in relative terms (G. Jones 2018, 223). According to Jones (2018), provincial governments have succeeded in expanding overall participation, but some groups (such as Black students and some recent immigrant populations) have been left behind. Those left behind include Indigenous people, for whom participation and completion rates remain much lower than for other Canadians (G. Jones 2018, 222). A major caveat is that "the lack of national data makes it impossible to … actually understand who is being left behind in terms of access, the magnitude of the problem, and whether specific policy initiatives are being successful in addressing these problems" (G. Jones 2018, 224).

Even if the data confirm that Canadian universities are relatively accessible, continued attention to equity on the part of both governments and universities is crucial. Economic inequality in Canada has grown. Since the mid-1990s, it has increased by 11 percent – more than five times higher than the OECD average country increase of 2 percent (Marchand,

Dubé, and Breau 2020, 20). Although the overall level of inequality in this country is just above the average among nineteen OECD countries, it grew relatively rapidly from 1990 to the late 2000s (3).

What might "working harder" to maintain or improve equality of opportunity involve for universities? A recent Universities Canada report found that 70 percent of universities had or were developing an equity, diversity, and inclusion plan but that much remains to be done, including increasing numbers of underrepresented people in senior leadership positions and improving institutional governance, cultures, policies, plans, and data (Universities Canada 2019c, 38–9). Reconciliation with Indigenous peoples is very much an unfinished project. Recent worldwide protests against anti-Black and other forms of racism provide impetus for additional measures to increase equity, diversity, and inclusion. Student financial assistance and other forms of support for low-income students are more important than ever, given that one way to combat populism is to combat economic inequality (Webber 2020, 17).

Expecting Canadian universities to maintain or improve accessibility, even if and as they become more dependent on private funding, may admittedly not be realistic. Significant external latitude on fees, internal cross-subsidization, and/or philanthropy would be involved. At some point, institutional financing no doubt circumscribes mission. That said, the reward for success is public trust. By reaffirming and realizing their public missions, universities could not only avoid fuelling inequity and its consequences but also protect their autonomy.

At the same time, universities would be well-advised to resist pressure to further broaden their missions. The multiversity began taking on additional roles more than half a century ago. For decades, scholars and commentators have been writing about the resulting problems, including lack of unifying vision, competing purposes and power bases, and mission drift (Fallis 2007, 49). The "disaggregative effect" (Shils 1992) of forces operating on and within universities is now even more pronounced. A plethora of functions makes it difficult for members of universities to see – and feel they are part of – the collective mission.

Canadian universities are now under pressure to compensate for deficiencies in other sectors – for the dearth of mental health care available to young Canadians, for example, and for failures in the way the police and the justice system respond to sexualized violence. Expecting universities to fill such gaps is natural, but problematic. Students from middle- and upper-income families remain far more likely to attend university than students of lower socio-economic status (G. Jones 2018, 223), so it is not equitable to provide "solutions" within universities. Mission creep detracts from universities' core activities. The *principal* role of universities is not to provide their students with services or recourse that should be provided by other sectors to all people, but to give their students access to the higher education that will best prepare them for life and work. What that looks like of course varies from university to university, program to program, cohort to cohort.

Precisely because the students who attend U of T differ from those who attend U of A or UdeM, universities' missions are specific. The same is true of their research, their contributions to regional development and local communities, and their other roles: all are a function of their environments and capacities. That being the case, it behooves not only governments but also universities and their members to be mindful of homogenizing forces. What francophone New Brunswick needs from a university is obviously different from what southern Ontario or northern BC needs. It is by continuing to focus on their particular missions, notwithstanding all the pressure and incentives to move up the reputational hierarchy, that universities actualize them.

What balance should a university strike between education, research, and service? Between in-person and virtual education? Between transmitting cultural heritage and preparing students for employment? Between education of young people and lifelong learning? The answers are in large part a function of mission. Maintaining mission focus has implications not only for boards, senates, and presidents but also for faculty and administrators, who are under pressure to meet external standards and norms, and some of whom may pine to join a "better" department or institution.

Ideally, governance is structured and practised so as to enable the university to fulfill its particular purpose. The university has a well-defined mission, smart, knowledgeable, capable, committed faculty and staff, good leadership, administration, and governance, sound policy, priorities, and plans, adequate resources – and, crucially, it gives people agency. Just as universities need space to fulfill their missions, faculty, administrators, staff, and students need space to carry out theirs in creative ways. As seen in previous chapters, universities have for a host of reasons become increasingly regulated and managed spaces. The volume of new policies, procedures, incentives, accountability requirements, and initiatives can sap capacity for creative collaboration and action. The result can be loss of morale, decreased effectiveness, and increased frustration and resentment. The lesson for boards, administrations, and indeed senates is that less policy and procedure is often more.

There are also implications for faculty, students, and staff – and their unions and associations. When university members call upon governments to enact change at universities, they invite further inroads into institutional autonomy. When they call upon administrations to fix problems through policy or procedure, they invite further reduction of university members' latitude and discretion. By negotiating ever more detailed collective agreements, unions and administrations likewise further restrict flexibility.

What about academic freedom? A clear, consistent understanding of it is evidently lacking. Academic freedom was described by many interviewees as very important but also a bit ambiguous – "un concept un peu flou." Is that a problem? On one hand, ambiguity and different understandings are not surprising, given the diversity of academic and professional fields represented within universities, the different definitions put forward by the CAUT and Universities Canada, and divergent understandings of what is acceptable speech. On the other hand, can university members expect governments, other stakeholders, the media, and the public to understand and support academic freedom if they themselves don't know what it is or can't agree on why it's essential?

The confusion may arise in part because many universities and faculty associations have negotiated collective agreement provisions that do not differentiate between academic freedom and freedoms of intramural and extramural expression. Academic freedom, narrowly defined, is "the freedom of professors to teach their subjects, carry out research, and publish its results, subject to professionally sanctioned limits" (Horn 1999, x). Almost everyone can get behind that. It is self-evident that professors need freedom in teaching and research in order to advance and disseminate knowledge. That's the case whether they support or want to overthrow the existing intellectual and socio-economic order. It is also recognized that academic freedom is subject to professional norms (against, for example, plagiarism or the mischaracterization of results) and, in the case of teaching, to the governance and administrative processes by which programs are approved and delivered. In other words, academic freedom doesn't mean one can teach what one wants or when one wants; rather, it is subject to program and curriculum approval, assignment of teaching responsibilities, and course scheduling. Likewise, academic freedom doesn't guarantee funding for the research one wants to pursue.

Freedom of extramural expression, by contrast, refers to professors' rights "to speak outside their own disciplines and expertise on matters of public concern" (Barendt 2010, 13). Intramural speech rights give professors freedom to criticize their universities without repercussions

(18). Given the confusion about academic freedom in Canada – and rising threats to it around the world – a positive step would be to differentiate between these sets of rights while explaining and affirming the importance of all three. Intramural and extramural speech rights support and reinforce academic freedom. Universities grant all three to faculty members for excellent reasons. Differentiating between them may increase internal understanding of what they are and why they are important, enable university members to rally in support of academic freedom, and, very crucially, bolster public understanding of and support for that freedom at a time when it is threatened in many parts of the globe (Scholars at Risk 2019). Clarifying what academic freedom means in Canada and why it's important may enable Canadian universities to join those in other countries in efforts to sustain academic freedom and freedom of expression while respecting other knowledge traditions and university systems.

The above reflections are intended for all university members. The pages that follow offer thoughts and advice to members of specific bodies and groups within universities. Insofar as those thoughts are informed by the case study, it is worth recalling that the universities involved in it were not representative of Canadian universities at large – most being older, larger, more research-intensive, and more multifaceted that the rest. The case study suggested that a new approach to internal governance – the university as holding company – has emerged among such universities in Canada and may reinforce differentiation between medical-doctoral institutions and other universities. The role of the "centre" is likely to be quite different at smaller institutions, which may have greater capacity for collective action. If the trend toward responsibility-centred budgeting and management remains restricted to major anglophone research universities, it may also reinforce differences in university governance between Quebec and the rest of Canada. Above and beyond budget models, many other factors – including an institution's age, size, program depth, and breadth – affect the nature of a university, the experiences of those within it, what they can achieve together, and the means by which they can do so, which is something to bear in mind in assessing the applicability of the following reflections to one's situation.

## TO AN INCOMING EXTERNAL BOARD MEMBER

If you are about to join a university board, news of the erosion of board jurisdiction may give you pause. In light of the extent of government regulation on one hand, and the authority that boards have delegated through policy and collective agreements on the other, how much is left for boards to decide? Can they and their members make a difference, or have they become just another layer in complex, interwoven higher education systems? Given the time commitment involved, the levels of scrutiny and criticism boards receive, and the inevitable tension and conflict, is volunteering on a university board something a qualified person should be prepared to do?

If you believe in the importance of higher education and research for students and society, yes! There is no substitute for boards as custodians of Canadian universities. Boards would be wise to keep an eye on their jurisdiction as well as that of senates and other bodies within their institutions. They are unlikely to succeed in demanding or seizing decision-making room back. They can, however, work with presidents and third parties to make governments aware of the risks of current trends and consider very carefully any further internal delegation. By governing well and making good decisions, they can protect institutional autonomy and agency.

A board's relationship to the provincial government is complex and varies from province to province and indeed university to university. The board is accountable to the province in many ways and has ultimate responsibility for institutional compliance. That said, the board's first loyalty and responsibility is to the university, so it and its members don't "take direction."

Also complex are the university's internal workings. If you are new to the university environment, you may be surprised to discover that hierarchy doesn't work very well. The president does not have the power of a typical CEO. That being so, it is inappropriate for the board to expect her or him to effect change in the way or to the degree a corporate counterpart could. Line authority is attenuated, and policies, rules, and procedures are of limited effectiveness. They may weed out the bad (possibly with considerable pushback and mind-boggling process), but they are not sufficient to bring about the good. For that, you need a culture of aspiration, encouragement, and recognition.

If your university is on a good trajectory, the president can work with internal and external stakeholders to build upon that. If it is not on a good trajectory, it is unfortunately unrealistic to expect a president to single-handedly change the course. Such a correction may be possible, but given the strength of the currents, it is not appropriate, nor is it fair, to expect a president to turn the ship around.

Prominent among the reasons why is the extent of professors' autonomy. Tenured and tenure-track professors remain at the core of the academic profession and of universities in Canada. Use of the term "professor" seems to have diminished in recent years, in favour of "faculty member" or "researcher" or "instructor"; but if you think of the people involved as professors and professionals, rather than as employees or workers, it will give you a more accurate picture of their roles and how the university works.

At most Canadian universities, there are professors, as well as one or more students and staff members, on the board. You may not be used to the presence of elected constituent members on boards. There can be a tendency to regard them as a separate class of member. Some committees of your board are probably composed solely of external members, in order to avoid conflict of interest and ensure independence in decision-making. Internal members are nevertheless full board members. The knowledge and experience that faculty, student, and staff members bring to the board's work enable it to fulfill its role more effectively than it otherwise could. So listen carefully to their voices and respect their roles.

Be prepared to commit a lot of time to the board and for the fact that its culture may differ from those of other boards or organizations you know. Get as much orientation, formal and informal, as you can, and pay attention to board rules and procedures. Think through and disclose any potential conflicts of interest.

You can expect the board's role to become more important in coming years. As an independent member of a university board, you can play an important role in this. Forces gathering on the global, national, and provincial political scenes may buffet universities and potentially drive them off course. Boards may be called upon to affirm key values or defend members of their institutions from inappropriate criticism, whether the target is the president, the senate, the student union, a faculty member, or the board itself.

In a turbulent environment, the board can help the university stay the course by cleaving to the mission and making decisions in that light. Know what your university is called upon to do, whom it serves, and how it does so. That's not static, of course – it evolves. But if your board is competent and committed and makes sound decisions guided by deep connection to the mission, those decisions will ultimately win respect and serve the university and society well.

### TO AN INCOMING INTERNAL BOARD MEMBER

Participating in board discussions can initially be intimidating, especially for student members. It is important that you express your views (and the rationale for them), even if – perhaps, especially if – they diverge from those of other members. It is because you bring a different perspective that your contribution is so valuable to the board. Don't be deterred from expressing your reasoned position on an issue for fear of the reaction of other board members or criticism from people outside the board.

Some external members believe that internal ones are fundamentally unable to act in the university's best interests because, as employees or students, they have a personal stake in it. In this view, there are two classes of board members: independent ones and internal ones, who are inherently conflicted. Don't give credence to that perception! Be scrupulous about disclosing and avoiding any possible conflict of interest or apprehension of bias. If you are employed by the university, you'll no doubt find that the work of the board is organized in such a way that you do not participate in consideration of matters affecting your terms of employment, but potential grounds for concern extend beyond that. If you were involved in an early stage of development of a proposal coming to the board, say so. Do likewise if approval of an item would disproportionately benefit a unit or group to which you belong or if you might appear to be biased. Questions of conflict of interest and bias are often not clear-cut. If you are unsure about whether something could be problematic, consider contacting the chair or secretary in advance to talk it through. Depending on the circumstances, you may or may not be precluded from participating in discussion or voting on an issue. Whatever the case, your conscientiousness will be respected. If you are a member of a student union or a faculty or staff association that has taken a position on an issue before the board, acknowledge that – and make it clear that it doesn't determine your views. Above all, demonstrate through your actions that you think, speak, and vote in the best interests of the university as a whole, rather than as a representative of a constituency. You can – and, indeed, should – convey to other board members the perspective of your constituency, but as a board member you have undertaken to advance the collective interest.

So, expect to be treated as a full board member. And, in turn, respect other board members. Your responsibility, like theirs, is to the university. That can be tough. Following the board's procedures may require you to behave in ways that are at odds with the openness with which you would normally communicate with colleagues or fellow students, who expect you to be their advocate and ally on the board. It can be difficult to keep their trust while maintaining the level of trust within the board that it needs to function effectively.

# Concluding Reflections and Advice

## TO AN INCOMING SENATE MEMBER

It is academic governance that distinguishes universities from other organizations. The university's commitment to academic self-government at the institutional level is embodied in the senate. To the extent that there is continuity in governance between the medieval university and those of today, it revolves around deciding what will be taught and learned, establishing criteria for admission, assessment, and awarding of degrees, and forging the academic direction of the university. Today, matters involving rapidly changing learning technology, internationalization, decolonialization and inclusion, and other contemporary issues also feature within many senates' mandates. It is up to senates to approve and encourage innovations while sustaining academic standards and values. The most effective senates provide useful guidance to presidents, provosts, and deans while holding them informally accountable. To succeed in all these purposes, senates need informed, independent, academic and student voices, as well as *ex officio* members who participate actively and take academic governance seriously.

The senate, like the board, is a governing body – in this case concerned largely with strategic academic direction, policy, approvals, and oversight. However, most of the creative initiative originates in other quarters of the university. Just as with boards, there is inevitably a fair bit of housekeeping, as well as a crucial accountability function. That doesn't mean senate members should act like the opposition in a parliamentary system. To the extent they do at your institution, your senate has lost its way. Rather, it means the senate is a forum where there is rigorous consideration of proposals, rooted in institutional mission, direction, and values, and where the president, provost, and others report on the university's progress in its academic mission and receive feedback, critical comment, and support.

Serving on senate and its committees involves significant time and effort, but it is a very important form of university citizenship. You learn about the university as a whole and can participate in shaping its academic direction. Just as with boards, rigour, respect, and recognition of collective commitment to the mission are key.

For senates, even more than for boards, it is crucial to understand faculties' aspirations and program, research, and service profiles. Given the current structure of Canadian universities, it is principally through faculties that they fulfill their academic missions. Senates' relationships to faculties can be ambiguous. It can suit deans and faculties to duck the limelight. But in order to govern well, boards and senates, as well as administrations, need to understand faculties' aspirations and plans, how they are doing, and how proposed measures will affect them.

## TO AN INCOMING PRESIDENT

There are numerous sources of advice for new presidents of which you can avail yourself. Courses and workshops, as well as counsel from experienced peers, cover a great deal of territory, including governance. Here is an additional thought for you.

There is a natural tendency for a president, in interactions with governing bodies – in particular, with the board – to portray things as a little more neat and under control than they in fact are. Universities are inherently unruly places. They are both living and learning communities – places where people not only learn, teach, conduct research, and do other types of work, but also eat, sleep, meet, socialize, participate in big events, exercise, play sports, party, get happy, get depressed, and occasionally get suicidal or violent. In normal times, universities are communities of thousands or tens of thousands of people from across the country and around the world, most of whom are young. Though increasingly buttoned-down, universities remain characterized by high levels of openness, debate, and individual freedom. All that makes great things possible, but it also means a lot can go very badly wrong.

Given boards' current preoccupation with mitigating risk, it is understandable for a president to downplay the possibilities involved. After all, if board members fully understood the reality, they might be tempted to regulate or intervene in deeply counterproductive ways! That said, glossing over potential disarray can mislead board members about the nature of the university and the situations you face. It can give them an illusory sense of control and calm. Protecting them from complexities and realities can leave them blindsided when things go off the rails, as they inevitably will. Perhaps most importantly, it can reduce their ability to help and guide you.

So, be prepared to let board members into your world. Share some of your anxieties with them. Prepare the board for the fact that bad things will happen. Encourage it to prepare for governing when they do. That level of candour is obviously only possible if you can talk with your board colleagues in confidence and if you have reason to trust them – important, but not universal, characteristics of university boards.

What about the senate? Senate members understand the university environment – or, more accurately, their quarters of the university – better than most external board members. You may nevertheless feel inclined to portray things as more certain than they in fact are in the senate context as well. After all, presidents are expected to lead – to bring about progress. Acknowledging uncertainty can call progress into question. It can provide fodder for naysaying and resistance to change. At the same time, too rosy a portrait invites skepticism and absolves others of responsibility. Openness and frankness are better. Just as with boards, whether or not they are possible depends on the nature of your senate. If, when you walk into senate, there is an atmosphere of mutual respect – of being in it together, notwithstanding the breadth of fields, constituencies, and perspectives – your university is in a good place.

Whether within the board or the senate, expanding opportunities for authentic exchange and for framed discussion of strategic issues and options undoubtedly entails risks. The pay-off can be new insights and ideas and enhanced trust.

### TO AN INCOMING DEAN, CHAIR, OR DIRECTOR

What you'll be doing is typically described as "administration," but that doesn't do justice to the amount of judgment involved. External board members often refer to it as "management," but that overstates the degree of control available to you. Your colleagues no doubt cringe at the word "leadership," but a good measure of that is called for.

If your university is a well-functioning one, you have space to work with your colleagues, staff and students to make good things happen. Collegiality and similar forms of governance tend not to work well in large organizational settings (Fairtlough 2005). It is at levels like yours that people can accomplish things in a collegial manner (Fallis 2007). Your work won't be easy. Your colleagues' autonomy, the pull of sub-disciplinary and professional forces, reputational pressures, interpersonal dynamics, and union/management issues may make it difficult to get (and keep) people moving forward. In most units, however, the proportion of people who want to accomplish things together outweighs those who don't. If you keep people focused on what your department is there for and what it wants to do and be, you can channel that energy.

Take all the training you can get, network with experienced administrators and peers, and find sources of sound institutional advice. Tough cases may keep you awake at night. They may sap your energy and your soul. As Mintzberg (1979) observed long ago, professional bureaucracies don't deal well with professionals who are incompetent or unconscientious (374). The same is true of those who are troubled. And the amount of process involved is now immense. Getting people on board with new technology, policy, or initiatives can be daunting. Mental illness on the part of students, faculty, or staff can pose very complicated issues. People will come to you for help with all sorts of things. Keep an eye on the ratio of time spent dealing with problems to time spent on what you or your faculty or department wants to achieve.

Finally, take care of yourself – and try to have some fun! Your colleagues and "the administration" obviously have confidence in you. The opportunity to work with smart, creative people in a university environment offers lots to be envied and enjoyed.

## TO A NEWLY APPOINTED FACULTY MEMBER

If it's anything like the six universities we studied, your university doesn't run like a typical corporation! As a faculty member, you will have much more autonomy in your work than most people in corporate settings. You and your colleagues also have extensive control over curriculum, faculty appointments, and academic standards, as well as substantial input into leadership – so you'll be involved in governance even if you don't serve on your faculty council, senate, or board.

Just as governments in Canada need boards, so do you! The alternative is to be run by the provincial ministry responsible for higher education. That is not a pretty picture, because many government officials lack understanding of or affinity for universities, the way they operate, and what they do. The public sector is organized for program delivery aligned with government objectives. Its design and practice are not intended to prioritize and foster academic judgment in order to advance knowledge and educate current and future generations.

For that, you need universities – and good presidents, provosts, and deans. At the present time, most Canadian university presidents are academics. If you think it's important that universities continue to be led by academics, support good administrators at all levels of yours. If you are fortunate to have a great chair or dean, support them and encourage them to consider future administrative roles. It's a big sacrifice because it takes so much time away from research, teaching, and other pursuits – and a lot of those roles can be brutal. But good academic administrative leaders are badly needed and many can find "administration" rewarding, especially if they are recognized and supported.

What about you? How should you conduct yourself and expect to be treated? Although Mintzberg (1979) characterized universities as professional bureaucracies, Canadian professors have never constituted a profession in the sense that doctors and lawyers do (MacKinnon 2014). In recent decades, professors have come to be treated less as professionals and more as employees. Some now perceive themselves as "academic workers." How is that working?

Most faculties and departments function well, some superbly. There are, however, many exceptions – ones in which some or all members no longer behave according to shared professional norms or in pursuit of shared goals, but resist collaboration, supervision, let alone direction. The result is often tension, conflict, and dysfunction. Instead of being a positive, collegial place, the department becomes a miserable place, not only for affected faculty members but also for staff and students, particularly graduate students. The ensuing mediation processes, complaints, investigations, and/or grievances often fail to correct the problems. These situations reveal the extent to which replacement of professional bureaucracy by very partially managed academic spaces is not working.

What can you do to avoid this? Reclaim professional space! Behave – and expect to be treated – as a professional, by people in administrative positions, by your colleagues, and by your students. The professional conception of your role is truer to the reality than either the worker/employee or the customer service provider depiction. As a professor, you have prerogatives and responsibilities that most employees do not, because of your connection to a body of knowledge. That is why professors are involved in the governance of their universities, and it is that which engenders public trust – the belief that what a professor says about a topic in their area is based on their knowledge and expertise rather than on commercial or other personal interests, the administration's views, or the position of their union. A professor's responsibility to participate in governance may not have been covered in your doctoral program, in your orientation to your university or faculty, or in meetings of your department or faculty association, but it is nevertheless fundamentally important. Re-emphasizing the professional dimension of the "academic profession" can only reinforce institutional governance and public trust.

Recognize that as a professor, you have a lot of autonomy and power to affect others. Also, that a lot is expected of you, not only by your university and the academic reward system but by the public at large, as well. In a recent survey, young Canadians were invited to identify which of eight possible careers provided the best path for making the world a better place (respondents were invited to select up to three.) At the top of the resulting list were scientist (picked by 38%) and teacher or professor (selected by 32%) (Environics 2021). That finding speaks to the accomplishments and impact of your colleagues, to the respect in which they are held, and to what you can achieve.

### TO OTHER UNIVERSITY PERSONNEL

People other than academic administrators and professors are vital to universities' educational, research, and service missions and deliver significant portions of the curriculum at many institutions. That said, if you are taking up a position at a university that doesn't involve a tenured or tenure-track academic appointment, your opportunities to participate in governance will be significantly fewer. The number of positions on governance bodies for which you are eligible varies by university, but they tend to be few, whether you are in a contract teaching or research role, in a staff position within an academic unit, or in an administrative or support unit. In these roles are many unsung heroes responsible for delivering a large portion of the university's offerings and enabling it to function, but because the governance structure prioritizes professors' academic judgment and participation, there are proportionately less opportunities for involvement.

If you are joining the university in a non-academic role from a professional or executive position in another sector, you may find it disconcerting not to be part of the academic mainstream and to have less voice in institutional decision-making. We hope any initial disappointment is outweighed by the pleasure of working in a university environment. In the meantime, don't assume that what worked in your previous organization will work in this context. Pause to absorb and appreciate the academic mission and to take stock of how your role and functions can best support it.

The day may be approaching when regular faculty, other teachers and researchers, administrators, and staff work together in very different constellations. In the meantime, find out what roles in governance exist for people in your position and consider standing for election or nominating a co-worker. There may also be opportunities for you to serve on planning, advisory, or search committees outside the formal governance setting and to learn, engage, and contribute in that way.

### TO AN INCOMING STUDENT

The roles of students have evolved greatly over time. In the middle ages, students governed a number of universities. At others, they were essentially apprenticed to masters. By early in the twentieth century, the relationship of universities in North America to students was *in loco parentis* – in the place of the parent. That changed with the enrolment of veterans after the Second World War, student activism in the 1960s, and the reduction of the legal age of majority in the early 1970s (Bégin-Caouette and Jones 2014, 413). By then, university students in Canada were regarded as adults and student unions had become independent of universities.

Several developments since then may be reshaping students' roles. One is financial. In 1979–80, tuition fees accounted for less than 10 percent of Canadian universities' total income; by 2014–15, they constituted 25 percent (Usher 2017b). By 2017–18, tuition and other fees represented 44.5 percent of the general operating income of Canadian universities – and 57 percent of that of Ontario universities (CAUBO 2019). Have students become clients or, indeed, consumers? Student leaders interviewed for our case study did not agree with that characterization, but several acknowledged that some students see themselves that way.

Other factors potentially shaping students' experience and roles within universities are massification, increased institutional preoccupation with risk, and the need to accommodate and support more students with mental illness. The combination of these forces could prompt Canadian universities to reassume more paternalistic roles, like some American counterparts. Would that be a good thing?

On balance, probably not. Recognition of students as responsible adults enabled students to participate fully in university governance and run autonomous student organizations. Being treated as less than adult could diminish their voices. And though being a client or a customer makes one's expectations count, it does not confer rights to participate in governance.

The shift to online instruction resulting from the current pandemic has highlighted for many students the value of the human, of personal connections, of community. When you arrive at university, do so as an adult participant rather than as a customer, a client, or a minor. Come eager to learn, connect with others, and participate in the life of the university – ready to take responsibility for yourself and your education, and to support the education of others, expecting the university to be responsive to your needs and expectations while knowing that what you get out of it will be a function of your goals and efforts.

Think about participating in the university's governance. You can make a difference and, in the process, you'll learn a lot and gain invaluable skills and experience.

## POSTSCRIPT

Between the time of writing and when you read this, Canadian universities will have begun to grasp how different the post-pandemic or ongoing pandemic era is from prior times. A return to "normal" is highly unlikely. Even if the coronavirus is snuffed out, the pace of climate change, biodiversity loss, technological change, economic restructuring, and associated social and political dislocation – coupled with the mismatch between the severity of global problems and the capacity for global public governance – will present people, governments, and organizations – including universities – with ongoing challenges.

Will universities rise to these challenges and continue to be vital sites of learning and sources of knowledge in centuries to come? To what extent will their intellectual energy illuminate and help address the critical issues confronting this and future generations?

The jury is out.

On one hand, there are reasons for skepticism about universities' contributions and prospects. Some have to do with their motivation and capacity to act purposefully for the greater good. If, as Bourdieu thought, universities and their members are driven by the need and desire to accumulate intellectual, reputational, and/or financial capital in order to maintain their positions or move up in their fields, universities will respond to evolving global issues only to the extent that states and other actors structure fields of production in ways that induce or require them to do so. As long as nation-states predominate, that is unlikely.

Furthermore, universities' pre-eminence as sites of knowledge production and dissemination is far from assured. This is an era of discontinuous change. New ways of learning and mobilizing knowledge are required, and this threatens the authority of the holders of knowledge and those in power (Handy 1989). As present-day holders and validators of knowledge, universities may or may not succeed in reinventing themselves to serve current and future generations. Many forces could interfere with their ability to do so – from political and bureaucratic constraints, to revenue generation pressures, to the power of disciplines, to traditions of neutrality, to internal fragmentation and proceduralism.

In high-participation systems like Canada's, the role of norms and culture within universities has diminished. Policies, rules, and procedures abound. Government control, market-like incentives, management, and collective bargaining have all increased but do not work very well. Universities are becoming more like other organizations, but – owing to the poor fit between their new characteristics and their underpinnings – less than functional ones. They risk becoming less responsive to both the world of knowledge and the societies that support them.

On the other hand, there are grounds for optimism about universities' future contributions. Universities have a long history of resilience and great capacity for adaptation and innovation. They have prospered globally and play central roles in many societies. As the pace of economic and labour market disruption increases, they can enable future generations to prepare – and current ones to retool – for new forms of work in emerging fields. They can partner or lead in the advancement of knowledge in critical areas. They can help their students learn to cope with and surmount individual and collective challenges. With their networks of alumni and partners across the world, they could be models of globally connected, locally responsive organizations acting in the greater good.

Relative to their counterparts in many countries, Canadian universities are well-equipped to do so. They and their members continue to have room for agency and creativity. They have dedicated alumni, strong partners, sound leadership, and adequate overall financing. Faculty, students, and staff possess immense talent, knowledge, and energy. Communities from coast to coast remain staunchly attached to their institutions. And, crucially, universities in this country continue to enjoy public trust; in the 2021 Environics survey cited above, young Canadians expressed high (42 percent) or medium (36 percent) confidence in universities and colleges (Environics 2021). In a 2022 Nanos survey that explored confidence in institutions, Canadians ranked universities and colleges as the top major contributors to Canada being a better country (with a mean ranking of 7.3 on a scale of zero to ten), relative to institutions including the health care system (mean of 7.1), the Supreme Court (6.5), charities (6.5), arts and cultural organizations (6.3), and the House of Commons (5.6) (Nanos 2022). That institutions of higher education in this country enjoy this level of public confidence is a tribute to the work of their members at all levels. It is vital that universities live up to this trust.

What is necessary for them to continue to fulfill their missions and the public's expectations? There are both external and internal requirements. Externally, governments need to commit to a sound overall level of funding and an appropriate balance of public and private financing, so as to avoid the perils seen in other jurisdictions of the under-funded, over-regulated public institution on one hand, and the market-driven corporate university on the other. Governments should also pay greater attention to autonomy as a necessary ingredient of university effectiveness. They should establish broad, stable policy frameworks within their jurisdictions and then "step back," entrusting boards to govern and universities to chart their own paths.

Universities and their members also need to step up to the plate, in radical awareness that there is no such thing as entitlement and that in return for society's support, the university must serve its needs. Not societal needs in the abstract, but the needs of each university's particular students and stakeholders. A university's leaders and governing body members must have a deep grasp of its mission, a clear-eyed view of its capacities, opportunities, and responsibilities, and an acute understanding of what these imply for its strategy and activities at this juncture in human history. Universities must foster and protect academic values and practices while developing and demonstrating greater capacity to collaborate across disciplinary, employment, and institutional boundaries to meet students' and societal needs. In Bourdieu's terms, neither retreating into restricted cultural production nor moving deeper into mass production will suffice. High standards of governance and conduct and collective ambition at all levels will be called for.

At present, most universities provide orientation sessions for board and senate members, but many faculty members, administrators, staff – and students – have little understanding of the distinctive nature of universities and university governance, of the missions of their institutions, of the importance of good governance, and of the significance and nuances of academic freedom and freedom of expression. Relative to corporate governance or public administration, university governance is underresearched. Lack of understanding and appreciation of the distinctive features of university governance may have contributed to the adoption of practices from other sectors that are ineffective or counterproductive in a university context. There is much to learn about how universities govern themselves and how they can better do so. While continuing to learn from other sectors, it is time to stop regarding the governance of universities as derivative or peripheral and to start treating it as an important sphere of its own.

Given the decentralized nature of Canadian universities, "top-down" approaches to future challenges are unlikely to be fully successful. Faculty, student, and staff input and buy-in will be important. Although professors and other professionals have traditionally resisted substantive leadership and coordination, that may be changing. According to Hoffman (2021), "a new generation of scholars is emerging ... with a strong desire to make a difference in the real world" (x). Faculty members at large may come to realize that in a time of momentous global changes, the pursuit and dissemination of knowledge is more essential than ever. Invigorated by the opportunity to participate in this splendid mission, they may find renewed purpose and seek and support leadership and new forms of coordination. Universities and their members may ask themselves – or ask themselves anew – how effectively are we – in this university, faculty, or department – educating our students for the world in which they will live? Are our offerings optimal, in light of the state of knowledge in our fields, our students' employment, health, and life prospects, our strengths and capabilities, and the resources available to us? Unsure, they may ask their alumni and other stakeholders, across town and around the world. We hope they take to heart what they hear, bring their collective intelligence to bear, and act by enlisting people, knowledge, experiential opportunities, resources, technology, and partners in new ways to serve the rapidly evolving needs of their students, their publics and the planet.

Galvanized, purposeful, and endowed with proper latitude and support, Canadian universities can continue to fulfill their distinctive missions amidst the turbulence of this century. As they respond to the needs of their particular students and stakeholders, they will change. There may be more divergence in their relative emphasis on education, research and service, in the content and delivery of their programs, in the nature of their research, scholarship and related activities, and in the ways in which they engage with communities. Subject to the future of nation-states and federalism, some institutions may evolve into global entities, whereas others remain resolutely province-based or local. They may deploy human and artificial intelligence, and configure physical and virtual campuses, in distinctive ways. Additional Indigenous universities may come into being, and some neocolonial ones, rooted in disciplines and professions, may open up to other ways of organizing and mobilizing knowledge. Guided by their missions and mindful of their responsibilities to current and future generations, Canada's universities can thrive and contribute throughout this century, in ways both old and new.

# Notes

## INTRODUCTION

1 We are far from alone in applying Bourdieu's concepts to the study of university governance in order to understand this notion of relative autonomy within university decision-making. Detailed discussions of Bourdieu's theories in relation to university governance can be found in Rowlands's studies of academic governance in Australia (2015, 2018), and Zhuang and Liu's (2020) analysis of university governance in China. Naidoo (2003) notes that universities at the top of the status hierarchy, such as the highly ranked research universities included in our study, may find it easier to maintain this relative autonomy compared to other universities.

## CHAPTER ONE

1 At the time of Confederation, McGill was essentially a private, non-denominational university, even though its board was dominated by Protestants (Jones 1996, 341).
2 *Maclean's* magazine, which issues annual rankings of Canadian universities, assigns universities to three categories: primarily undergraduate; comprehensive (having a wide range of undergraduate, graduate, and professional programs and significant research activity), and medical/doctoral (having medical schools and a wide range of doctoral and other programs and research).
3 The Canadian Information Centre for International Credentials (CICIC) is a unit of the Council of Ministers of Education of Canada, established in 1990 after Canada signed the UNESCO Convention on the Recognition of

Studies, Diplomas and Degrees (CICIC 2020a). It defines a "recognized" university as a university given authority to grant degrees, diplomas, and other credentials by a public or private act of the provincial/territorial legislature or through a government-mandated quality assurance mechanism (CICIC 2020b).
4 Michael Skolnik, email message to primary author, 1 September 2020.
5 In this calculation of the percentage of members of the UBC board appointed by government, two alumni association nominees appointed by government are included among the government appointees.
6 In 2021, the Alberta government announced plans to deconsolidate certain institutions (see Chapter 6).
7 Universities Canada's criteria for membership include: possession of degree-granting authority; vesting of authority over academic programs in an elected body representative of academic staff; an independent board of governors or equivalent body; an appropriate mission statement and goals; university-level academic programs; a record of research; commitments to academic freedom and to equity and human rights; not-for profit status; and many other considerations (Universities Canada n.d.).

CHAPTER TWO

1 Organizational autonomy reflects factors such as who controls executive appointments and appointments of external members to governing bodies and whether universities have the capacity to establish internal structures and external entities. Financial autonomy reflects the length and type of public funding and whether institutions can borrow, retain surplus, and set tuition fees. Staffing autonomy is about institutional latitude in the appointment, compensation, and promotion of senior administrators and faculty. Academic autonomy is about factors like capacity to select students, determine enrolment levels, introduce new programs, determine program content, and select quality assurance mechanisms.
2 Glen Jones, correspondence with Julia Eastman, 25 October 2019.
3 Harvard College and William and Mary College.
4 The report did not include separate data for universities.
5 Several factors may account for the extent of the difference in the estimates of the time board members devoted to their work in 1995 and 2009 (e.g., difference in numbers of respondents, interprovincial variations, and whether the estimates applied to all or only external board members).

6 The differences between Paul's findings and those of the Universities Canada survey may be attributable in part to the fact that his sample did not include some newer universities or institutions that were subsets of larger universities (Paul, 2015, 30).

## CHAPTER THREE

1 Data from 2013 are used in this chapter as its purpose is to portray the case universities as they were at the time of interviews for the study.
2 These and other rankings have methodological problems and their legitimacy is disputed, but they have a great deal of influence on the actions of universities, governments, students, and university partners.
3 The FAECUM did not represent students in continuing studies.
4 The senate's members included the chancellor, the president, the chairman of the board, the deputy minister of education, deans of faculties, one elected member of each faculty, heads of affiliated colleges, ten members elected by the convocation, and other members.

## CHAPTER FIVE

1 The members of the Academic Board included fifty-seven elected teaching staff, thirty-one academic administrators serving *ex officio*, sixteen students, and six lay members of governing council.
2 The attribution of this quotation was approved by the interviewee in February 2020.
3 There was also a strike by clinical instructors in veterinary medicine at the University of Montreal in 2016 (WID ESDC 2020; Fortier 2017a).

## CHAPTER SEVEN

1 The Belt and Road Initiative is "China's signature…foreign policy" which aims to link China to other parts of the world through interconnected infrastructure and economic corridors (Ziegler 2020).
2 The Canadian figures may be somewhat understated because the data included the salaries of a few presidents who had served less than a complete year (Usher 2017a).

# References

Academica. 2019a. "ON government axes free tuition for low-income students, reduces overall tuition, mandatory fees." *Top Ten*, 18 January. https://www.academica.ca/topten/20190118.
– 2019b. "NS universities address research, health initiatives, tuition caps with new agreement." *Top Ten*, 17 September. https://www.academica.ca/topten/20190917.
– 2019c. "Further findings from AB report on PSE finances raise concerns about higher ed budget constraints, low enrolment." *Top Ten*, 18 September. https://www.academica.ca/top-ten/further-findings-ab-report-pse-finances-raise-concerns-about-higher-ed-budget-constraints.
ACHA (American College Health Association). 2016. "Canadian Reference Group Executive Summary Spring 2016." Hanover: American College Health Association. https://www.acha.org/documents/ncha/NCHA-II%20SPRING%202016%20CANADIAN%20REFERENCE%20GROUP%20EXECUTIVE%20SUMMARY.pdf.
Alberta. 2003. Post-Secondary Learning Act. Statutes of Alberta, Ch. P-19.5. http://www.qp.alberta.ca/documents/Acts/p19p5.pdf.
– 2021. *Alberta 2030: Building skills for jobs*. Advanced Education. April 2021.
Alberta. Enterprise and Advanced Education. *Guidelines for board of governors members: an introduction to board governance at Alberta's public post-secondary institutions*. April 2013. http://advancededucation.alberta.ca/media/383000/board%20manual%20complete%20-%202013-05-22.pdf.
– 2016. Alberta Hansard, 21 April. Legislative Assembly of Alberta, 29th Legislature. https://docs.assembly.ab.ca/LADDAR_files/docs/hansards/han/legislature_29/session_2/20160421_1330_01_han.pdf.
– 2017a. Bill 7: An Act to Enhance Post-secondary Academic Bargaining. Legislative Assembly, 29th Legislature, 3rd Session. https://www.assembly.

ab.ca//LADDAR_files/docs/bills/bill/ legislature_29/session_3/20170302_bill-007.pdf.
– 2017b. Legislation to enhance post-secondary bargaining. 9 April. https://www.alberta.ca/release.cfm?xID=46623B1F8E03E-D9 B9-01DE-91CB7D37A8102C34.
– 2019. *Report and Recommendations: Blue Ribbon Panel on Alberta's Finances.* August. Edmonton. https://open.alberta.ca/dataset/081ba7 4d-95c8-43ab-9097-cef17a9fb59c/resource/257f040a-2645-49e7-b40b-462e4b5c059c/download/blue-ribbon-panel-report.pdf.
Alberta Learning. 2002. *Campus Alberta: A Policy Framework.* Edmonton. https://open.alberta.ca/publications/0778513513.
Algoma University. 2020. Board of Governors By-Laws 7.3. https://algomau.ca/wp-content/uploads/2020/08/Algoma-University-By-laws-Version-7.3-July-31-2020-Reformatted.pdf.
Alliance of Canadian Comprehensive Research Universities. n.d. "Our members." http://www.accru.ca/about/our-members/.
Altbach, Philip. 2011. "The Past, Present, and Future of the Research University." In *The Road to Academic Excellence: The Making of World-Class Research Universities*, edited by Philip Altbach and Jamil Salmi, 11–29. Washington, DC: World Bank.
Altbach, Philip, and Hans de Wit. 2020. "Post Pandemic Outlook for HE Is Bleakest for the Poorest." *University World News*, 4 April. https://www.universityworldnews.com/post.php?story=20200402152914362.
Altbach, Philip, Liz Reisberg, and Iván Pacheco. 2012. "Academic Remuneration and Contracts: Global Trends and Realities." In *Paying the Professoriate: A Global Comparison of Compensation and Contracts*, edited by Philip Altbach, Liz Reisberg, Maria Yudkevich, Gregory Androushchak, and Iván Pacheco, 3–20. New York: Routledge.
Altbach, Philip, Liz Reisberg, and Laura Rumbley. 2009. *Trends in Global Higher Education: Tracking an Academic Revolution — a Report Prepared for the UNESCO 2009 World Conference on Higher Education.* Paris: UNESCO. ED.2009/Conf.402/inf.5.
Altbach, Philip, and Jamil Salmi. 2011. "The Road to Academic Excellence: Lessons of Experience." In *The Road to Academic Excellence: The Making of World-Class Research Universities*, edited by Philip Altbach and Jamil Salmi, 323–42. Washington, DC: World Bank.
Anderson, Don, and Richard Johnson. 1998. *University Autonomy in Twenty Countries.* Canberra: Department of Employment, Education, Training, and Youth Affairs.
Andrews, Michael B., Edward A. Holdaway, and Gordon L. Mowat. 1997. "Post-Secondary Education in Alberta Since 1945." In *Higher Education in*

*Canada: Different Systems, Different Perspectives*, edited by Glen Jones, 59–91. New York: Garland.

Anisef, Paul, Paul Axelrod, and J. Lennards. 2012. "Universities in Canada (Canadian Universites)." In *Canadian Encyclopedia*. Last modified July 20, 2015. https://www.thecanadianencyclopedia.ca/en/article/university.

Antonio, Anthony Lising, Martin Carnoy, and Chelsea Rose Nelson. 2018. "The United States of America: Changes and Challenges in a Highly Decentralized System." In *Higher Education in Federal Countries: A Comparative Study*, edited by Martin Carnoy, Isak Froumin, Oleg Leshukov, and Simon Marginson, 37–95. New Delhi: Sage.

ARWU (Academic Ranking of World Universities). 2013. "Academic Ranking of World Universities 2013." http://www.shanghairanking.com/ARWU2013.html.

Ashby, Eric. 1966. *Universities: British, Indian, African: A Study in the Ecology of Higher Education*. Cambridge, MA: Harvard University Press.

Association of Accrediting Agencies of Canada. n.d. https://aaac.ca/english/about-us/members.php#close. Accessed 29 July 2021.

Association of Governing Boards. 2017. *AGB Board of Directors' Statement on Shared Governance*. Washington, DC: Association of Governing Boards.

AUCC (Association of Universities and Colleges of Canada). 2013. *2013 preliminary full-time and part-time enrolment at AUCC member institutions*. http://www.aucc.ca/canadian-universities/facts-and-stats/enrolment-by-university.

Audet, Louis-Philippe. 1970. "Society and Education in New France." In *Canadian Education: A History*, edited by J. Donald Wilson, and Robert M. Stamp, and Louise-Philippe Audet. Toronto: Prentice-Hall.

Austin, Ian, and Glen Jones. 2016. *Governance of Higher Education: Global Perspectives, Theories, and Practices*. New York: Routledge.

Backhouse, Constance, Nitya Iyer, and Donald McRae. 2015. *Report of the Task Force on Misogyny, Sexism, and Homophobia in Dalhousie University Faculty of Dentistry*. Halifax: Dalhousie University. https://cdn.dal.ca/content/dam/dalhousie/pdf/cultureofrespect/DalhousieDentistry-TaskForceReport-June2015.pdf.

Bailey, Anne. 2018. "Budget 2018–19: FAQs." *The Quad* (blog), 28 March. https://blog.ualberta.ca/budget-2018-19-faqs-16343ad13ae.

Baird, Jeanette. 2014. "Influences on Australian University Governance." In *International Trends in University Governance: Autonomy, Self-Government and the Distribution of Authority*, edited by Michael Shattock, 145–63. Oxford: Routledge.

Baker, Ronald. 1997. "Prince Edward Island." In *Higher Education in Canada: Different Systems, Different Perspectives*, edited by Glen Jones, 246–58. New York: Garland.

Baker, Simon. 2019. "Is China's Belt and Road Initiative Boosting Academic Links?" *Times Higher Education*, 1 May. https://www.timeshighereducation.com/news/chinas-belt-and-road-initiative-boosting-academic-links.

Bakvis, Herman. 2008. "The Knowledge Economy and Post-Secondary Education: Federalism in Search of a Metaphor." In *Canadian Federalism: Performance, Effectiveness, and Legitimacy*, edited by Herman Bakvis and Grace Skogstad, 2nd ed. Toronto: Oxford University Press.

Bakvis, Herman, and David M. Cameron. 2002. "Old Wine in New Bottles: Post-Secondary Education and the Social Union." In *Building the Social Union: Perspectives, Directions, and Challenges*, edited by Tom McIntosh. Regina: University of Regina Press.

Banks, Kerry. 2019. "Major International Survey Will Shine a Spotlight on the Academic Profession." *University Affairs*, 30 July. https://www.universityaffairs.ca/news/news-article/major-international-survey-will-shine-a-spotlight-on-the-academic-profession.

Barendt, Eric. 2010. *Academic Freedom and the Law: A Comparative Study*. Portland: Hart.

Barker, Katherine. 2007. "The UK Research Assessment Exercise: The Evolution of a National Research Evaluation System." *Research Evaluation* 16(1): 3–12.

Bégin-Caouette, Olivier, and Glen A. Jones. 2014. "Student Organizations in Canada and Quebec's 'Maple Spring.'" *Studies in Higher Education* 39(3): 412–25.

Bégin-Caouette, Olivier, Glen A. Jones, G. Karram Stephenson, and A. Scott Metcalfe. 2021. "Canada: The Role of the University Sector in National Research and Development." In *Universities in the Knowledge Society: The Nexus of National Systems of Innovation and Higher Education*, edited by Timo Aarrevaara, Martin Finkelstein, Glen A. Jones, and Jisun Jung. New York: Springer.

Bégin-Caouette, Olivier, Claude Trottier, Julia Eastman, Glen A. Jones, Christian Noumi, and Sharon X. Li. 2018. "Analyse de la gouvernance systémique des universités au Québec et comparisons avec quatre autres provinces canadiennes." *Canadian Journal of Higher Education* 48(3): 1–22. http://journals.sfu.ca/cjhe/index.php/cjhe/article/view/188233.

Bellefontaine, Michelle. 2018. "U of A president should cut pay before charging students more, minister says." *CBC News*, 19 March. https://www.cbc.ca/news/canada/edmonton/alberta-university-salaries-tuition-fees-david-turpin-marlin-schmidt-1.4583539?%27.

Bennett, Dean. 2018. "Notley disagrees with University of Alberta honorary degree for David Suzuki." *Globe and Mail*, 25 April. https://www.theglobeandmail.com/canada/article-notley-disagrees-with-university-of-alberta-honorary-degree-for-david.

– 2020. "Alberta says universities over-budget; need to freeze travel, hiring, hosting." CBC News, 16 January. https://www.cbc.ca/news/canada/edmonton/alberta-university-funding-freeze-1.5429317.

Bertrand, Denis. 2012. "Les principaux attributs de l'Université du Québec à Montréal." In *Les universités nouvelles: Enjeux et perspectives*, edited by Lyse Roy and Yves Gingras, 213–36. Québec: Presses de l'Université du Québec.

Bindon, Kathryn, and Paul Wilson. 1997. "Newfoundland: More Canadian Than British, but Longer Getting There." In *Higher Education in Canada: Different Systems, Different Perspectives*, edited by Glen Jones, 259–83. New York: Garland.

Bishop, Dorothy. 2020. "Now is a good time for the UK to ditch the REF and the TEF." *Times Higher Education*, 24 March. https://www.timeshighereducation.com/blog/now-good-time-uk-ditch-ref-and-tef.

Bissell, Claude. 1974. *Halfway Up Parnassus: A Personal Account of the University of Toronto 1932–1971*. Toronto: University of Toronto Press.

Bissonnette, Lise, and John R. Porter. 2013. *Rapport du Chantier sur une loi-cadre des universités*. Quebec: Ministère de l'Enseignement supérieur, de la Recherche, de la Science et de la Technologie.

Bizier, Helene-Andrée. 1993. *L'Université de Montréal: La quête du savoir*. Montreal: Libre Expression.

Bok, Derek. 2003. *Universities in the Marketplace*. Princeton: Princeton University Press.

Bourdieu, Pierre. 1986. "The Forms of Capital." In *Handbook of Theory and Research for the Sociology of Education*, edited by John G. Richardson, 241–58. New York: Greenwood Press.

– 1993. "The Market of Symbolic Goods." In *The Field of Cultural Production: Essays on Art and Literature*, edited by Randal Johnson, 112–293. New York: Columbia University Press.

Bowen, Howard. 1980. *The Costs of Higher Education: How Much Do Colleges and Universities Spend per Student and How Much Should They Spend?* San Francisco: Jossey-Bass.

Boyko, L., and Glen Jones. 2010. "The Roles and Responsibilities of Middle Management (Chairs and Deans) in Canadian Universities." In *The Changing Dynamics of Higher Education*, edited by Lynn Meek, Leo Geodegebuure, Rui Santiago, and Teresa Carvalho, 83–102. Dordrecht: Springer.

Bradshaw, Patricia, and Christopher Fredette. 2009. "Academic Governance of Universities: Reflections of a Senate Chair on Moving from Theory to Practice and Back." *Journal of Management Inquiry* 18(2): 123–33.

Bresge, Adina. 2019. "Federal minister meets with committee to develop national approach to campus violence." *Toronto Star*, 16 January. https://

www.thestar.com/news/canada/2019/01/16/minister-meets-with-committee-to-develop-national-approach-to-campus-violence.html.

British Columbia. n.d. '"Point in time" Act Content: University Act [RSBC 1996] Chapter 468. Victoria. http://www.bclaws.ca/civix/document/id/complete/statreg/96468_pit#pit38.

– 2019. *Mandate letter: University of British Columbia*. Victoria: Ministry of Advanced Education. https://www2.gov.bc.ca/assets/gov/education/post-secondary-education/institution-resources-administration/mandate-letters/mandate-ubc.pdf.

Brown, Anna. 2018. "Most Americans Say Higher Ed Is Heading in Wrong Direction, but Partisans Disagree on Why." *Pew Research*, 26 July. https://www.pewresearch.org/fact-tank/2018/07/26/most-americans-say-higher-ed-is-heading-in-wrong-direction-but-partisans-disagree-on-why.

Brown, Sheila A. 1997. "New Brunswick." In *Higher Education in Canada: Different Systems, Different Perspectives*, edited by Glen Jones, 189–219. New York: Garland.

Bruneau, William. 2012. "Professors in Their Places: Governance in Canadian Higher Education." In *University Governance and Reform: Policy, Fads, and Experience in International Perspective*, edited by Hans Schuetze, William Bruneau, and Garnet Grosjean, 47–62. New York: Palgrave Macmillan.

Bundale, Brett. 2018. "Dalhousie University only looking at 'racially visible' or Indigenous candidates for VP position." *National Post*, 13 February. https://nationalpost.com/news/canada/dal-restricts-search-for-new-vp-to-racially-visible-indigenous-candidates.

Cafley, Julie M. 2015. "Leadership in Higher Education: Case Study Research of Canadian University Presidents with Unfinished Mandates." PhD diss., University of Ottawa.

Cai, Yuzhuo. 2019. "University Mergers in China." In *Mergers in Higher Education: Practices and Policies*, edited by Leon Cremonini, Saeed Paivandi, and Kishore Mahendra Joshi, 127–46. New Delhi: Studera Press.

Cameron, David M. 1991. *More Than an Academic Question: Universities, Government, and Public Policy in Canada*. Halifax: Institute for Research on Public Policy.

– 2002. "The Challenge of Change: Canadian Universities in the 21st Century." *Canadian Public Administration* 45(2): 145–74.

Canada Research Chairs Program. 2019. "Open Letter to University Presidents and Vice-Presidents from the Canada Research Chairs Program: 2019 Addendum to the 2006 Canadian Human Rights Settlement Agreement." 31 July. Program Updates. https://www.chairs-chaires.gc.ca/program-programme/2019_open_letter-eng.aspx.

Canadian Encyclopedia. 2019. "British Columbia." https://www.thecanadianencyclopedia.ca/en/article/british-columbia#History/survey-post-secondary-students-reconsidering-fall-semester-plans-wake-covid-19.

*Canadian Federation of Students v. Ontario* [2021] ONSC 6658. DC 279/19 20191121. Ontario Superior Court of Justice – Divisional Court.

Canadian Press. 2017. "Bill 62: Universities hesitant to force students from classes." *The Gazette* (Montreal), 25 October. https://montrealgazette.com/news/local-news/bill-62-universities-hesitant-to-force-students-from-classes.

Cantwell, Brendan, and Simon Marginson. 2018. "Vertical Stratification." In *High Participation Systems of Higher Education*, edited by Brendan Cantwell, Simon Marginson, and Anna Smolentseva, 125–50. Oxford: Oxford University Press.

Cantwell, Brendan, Rómulo Pinheiro, and Marek Kwiek. 2018. "Governance." In *High Participation Systems of Higher Education*, edited by Brendan Cantwell, Simon Marginson, and Anna Smolentseva, 68–93. Oxford: Oxford University Press.

Capano, Giliberto. 2015. "Federal Strategies for Changing the Governance of Higher Education: Australia, Canada, and Germany." In *Varieties of Governance: Dynamics, Strategies, Capacities*, edited by Giliberto Capano, Michael Howlett, and M. Ramesh, 103–30. Basingstoke: Palgrave Macmillan.

Cappon, Paul. 2014. "Think Nationally, Act Locally: A Pan-Canadian Strategy for Education and Training." *Canadian Council of Chief Executives*, 4 July. https://thebusinesscouncil.ca/report/think-nationally-act-locally-a-pan-canadian-strategy-for-education-and-training.

Carey, Kevin. 2019. "How Higher Education Became a Pawn in the Partisan Forever War." *Chronicle of Higher Education*, 9 July. https://www.chronicle.com/article/how-higher-education-became-a-pawn-in-the-partisan-forever-war.

Carpentier, Vincent. 2019. "Le financement et la transformation des logiques, des espaces et des contours de l'expansion des systèmes d'enseignement supérieur." In *De l'administration à la gouvernance: progrès ou recul?*, edited by Louis Demers, Jean Bernatichez, and Michel Umbriaco, 13–34. Quebec: Presses de l'Université du Québec.

Carter, Donald D., Geoffrey England, Brian Etherington, and Gilles Trudeau. 2002. *Labour Law in Canada*, 5th ed. The Hague: Kluwer Law International.

Carty, Hannah. 2019a. "The breakdown: The presidential and provostial task force on student mental health." *The Varsity*, 8 September. https://thevarsity.ca/2019/09/08/the-breakdown-the-presidential-provostial-task-force-on-student-mental-health.

– 2019b. "Mental health dominates first Governing Council meeting of the year." *The Varsity*, 27 October. https://thevarsity.ca/2019/10/27/mental-health-dominates-first-governing-council-meeting-of-the-year.
– 2020. "'Cautiously optimistic': Student groups commend direction of mental health task force report, call for more action." *The Varsity*, 26 January. https://thevarsity.ca/2020/01/26/cautiously-optimistic-student-groups-commend-direction-of-mental-health-task-force-report-call-for-more-action.
CAUBO (Canadian Association of University Business Officers). 2014. *Financial Information of Universities and Colleges 2012–13.* Ottawa.
– 2015. *Financial Information of Universities and Colleges 2013–14.* Ottawa.
– 2019. *Financial Information of Universities and Colleges 2017–2018.* Ottawa.
CAUT (Canadian Association of University Teachers). n.d. "Shared governance." Campaigns. https://www.caut.ca/campaigns/shared-governance.
– 2009. Report of the CAUT ad hoc advisory committee on governance. Ottawa. https://www.caut.ca/docs/default-source/reports/report-of-the-caut-ad-hoc-advisory-committee-on-governance-%28nov-2009%29.pdf?sfvrsn=0.
– 2013. *Open for Business: On What Terms?* Ottawa. https://www.caut.ca/sites/default/files/open-for-business-nov-2013.pdf.
– 2018. CAUT *Report on Board of Governors Structures at Thirty-One Canadian Universities.* Ottawa. https://www.caut.ca/sites/default/files/caut-report-board-of-governors-structures-at-thirty-one-canadian-universities_2018-05.pdf.
– 2019. CAUT *Policy Statement on Governance.* https://www.caut.ca/about-us/caut-policy/lists/caut-policy-statements/policy-statement-on-governance.
– 2020a. "COVID-19 and the Academic Workplace: Questions and Answers." https://www.caut.ca/content/covid-19-and-academic-workplace-questions-answers#15.
– 2020b. "Survey: Post-secondary students reconsidering fall semester plans in wake of COVID-19." *The Latest*, 12 May 2022. https://www.caut.ca/latest/2020/05/survey-post-secondary-students-reconsidering-fall-semester-plans-wake-covid-19.
CBC. 2015. "NDP launch review of 300 Alberta agencies, boards, and commissions." *CBC News*, 6 November. https://www.cbc.ca/news/canada/edmonton/ndp-launch-review-of-300-alberta-agencies-boards-and-commissions-1.3306945.

– 2019. "Quebec government suspends controversial immigration reforms." CBC News, 8 November. https://www.cbc.ca/news/canada/montreal/peq-restrictions-on-hold-quebec-1.5353991?cmp=rss.

Chan, Y. Lilian, and A. William Richardson. 2012. "Board Governance in Canadian Universities." *Accounting Perspectives* 11(1): 31–55.

Charbonneau, Léo. 2014. "Charte des valeurs québécoises: le débat fait rage. " *University Affairs*, 29 January 2014. http://www.affairesuniversitaires.ca/opinion/en-marge/charte-des-valeurs-quebecoises-le-debat-fait-rage.

Chase, Steven. 2021. "Ottawa's screening for research funding could lead to 'racial profiling': academics" *The Globe and Mail*. 2 August 2021, A3.

Chase, Steven and Robert Fife. 2021. "Alberta orders universities to curb research ties with China". *The Globe and Mail*. 24 May 2021, 1.

Christie, Brian D. 1997. "Higher Education in Nova Scotia: Where past is more than prologue." In *Higher Education in Canada: Different Systems, Different Perspectives*, edited by Glen Jones, 222–43. New York: Garland.

CICIC (Canadian Information Centre for International Credentials). n.d. "Directory of Educational Institutions in Canada." https://www.cicic.ca/868/search_the_directory_of_educational_institutions_in_canada.canada.

– 2020a. "About CICIC." https://www.cicic.ca.

– 2020b. "Find an educational institution." https://www.cicic.ca/871/read_more_information_about_the_directory_of_educational_institutions_in_canada.canada.

Clark, Burton R. 1983. *The Higher Education System: Academic Organization in Cross-National Perspective*. Berkeley: University of California Press.

– 1986. *The Higher Education System: Academic Organization in Cross-National Perspective*. Berkeley: University of California Press.

Clark, Howard C. 2003. *Growth and Governance of Canadian Universities: An Insider's View*. Vancouver: UBC Press.

Clark, Ian D., Greg Moran, Michael Skolnik, and David Trick. 2009. *Academic Transformation: The Forces Reshaping Higher Education in Ontario*. Montreal and Kingston: McGill–Queen's University Press.

Clark, Ian D., David Trick, and Richard van Loon. 2011. *Academic Reform: Policy Options for Improving the Quality and Cost-Effectiveness of Undergraduate Education in Ontario*. Montreal and Kingston: McGill-Queen's University Press.

Cobban, Allan B. 1975. *The Medieval Universities: Their Development and Organization*. London: Methuen.

– 1992. "Universities: 1100–1500." In *The Encyclopedia of Higher Education*, vol. 1, edited by Burton R. Clark and Guy R. Neave, 1245–51. Oxford: Pergamon Press.

Comtois, Philippe, Jean-Sébastien Fallu, Audrey Laplante, Mélanie Laroche, Guylaine Le Dorze, Laurent McFalls, Jean Portuguese, and Éric Troncyet. 2017. "Les erreurs manifestes de la chancelière de l'Université de Montréal." *Le Devoir*, 23 November. https://www.ledevoir.com/opinion/idees/513651/reforme-de-la-charte-de-l-universite-de-montreal-les-erreurs-manifestes-de-la-chanceliere.

Connell, George. 1987. "Renewal 1987: A Discussion Paper on the Nature and Role of the University of Toronto." Toronto: University of Toronto Governing Council.

Corbo, Claude. 2012. "'L'UQAM a 40 ans: encore une université nouvelle?" In *Les universités nouvelles: Enjeux et perspectives*, edited by Lyse Roy and Yves Gingras, 9–22. Quebec: Presses de l'Université du Québec.

Coté, James E., and Anton Allahar. 2007. *Ivory Tower Blues: A University System in Crisis*. Toronto: University of Toronto Press.

Cote-Meek, Sheila. 2020. "Introduction – From Colonized Classrooms to Transformational Change in the Academy: We Can and Must Do Better!" In *Decolonizing and Indigenizing Education in Canada*, edited by Sheila Cote-Meek and Taima Moeke-Pickering, xi–xxiii. Toronto: Canadian Scholars Press.

Cote-Meek, Sheila, and Taima Moeke-Pickering. 2020. *Decolonizing and Indigenizing Education in Canada*. Toronto: Canadian Scholars.

Council of Ontario Universities. 2012. "Interprovincial Comparison of University Revenue" Working Paper." https://cou.ca/wp-content/uploads/2012/06/COU-Interprovincial-Comparison-University-Revenue.pdf.

Court of Appeal for Ontario. 2021. Canadian Federation of Students v. Ontario (Colleges and Universities), 2021 ONCA 553 DATE: 20210804 DOCKET: C68262.

CREPUQ (Conférence des recteurs et principaux des universités du Québec). 2011. *Assurance qualité: l'expérience du système universitaire québécois et ses perspectives d'avenir*. Brief presented to the Conseil supérieur de l'éducation as part of its consultation on quality assurance. http://www.crepuq.qc.ca/IMG/pdf/CREPUQ_Memoire_assurance_qualite_29novembre2011.pdf.

Cribb, Robert, Noella Ovid, David Lao, and Blair Bigham. 2017. "Demand for youth mental health services is exploding. How universities and businesses are scrambling to react." *Toronto Star*, 29 May. https://www.thestar.com/news/canada/2017/05/29/youth-mental-health-demand-is-exploding-how-universities-and-business-are-scrambling-to-react.html.

CUSC (Canadian University Survey Consortium). 2019. "2019 CUSC Survey of First-Year Students." https://cusc-ccreu.ca/?page_id=32&lang=en.

D'Sa, Premila. 2019. "Students protest for better mental health services at University of Toronto following suicide on campus." *Toronto Star*, 18 March. https://www.thestar.com/news/gta/2019/03/18/students-protest-for-better-mental-health-services-at-university-of-toronto-following-suicide-on-campus.html.

Dalhousie University. 2013. "100 days of Listening Final Report." https://issuu.com/dalhousieuniversity/docs/100days-report-01-full-dec23.

– 2015. *Belong: Supporting an Inclusive and Diverse University*. Halifax. https://cdn.dal.ca/content/dam/dalhousie/pdf/about/Strategic-Planning/dalhousie_belong_report.PDF.lt_fo5db60d1e03d8cb96ce3e1597faecdc.res/dalhousie_belong_report.PDF.

– 2016. 28 June 2016 Board of Governors Minutes. Archives and Special Collections, Dalhousie University.

– 2017. 18 April 2017 Board of Governors Minutes. Archives and Special Collections, Dalhousie University.

– 2019a. *Dalhousie University Strategic Direction 2015-2018: Year 5 Progress Report, June 2019*. Halifax.

– 2019b. "5.0 Infrastructure and Support." https://www.dal.ca/about-dal/leadership-and-vision/dalforward/strategic-direction/infrastructure-and-support.html.

– 2019c. "Dalhousie University (Excluding King's) 2019/2020 Enrolment Statistics – Enrolment by Faculty and Permanent Residence (Headcounts)." 1 December 2019. https://cdn.dal.ca/content/dam/dalhousie/pdf/dept/oiar/Public_Reports_and_Data/Enrollment/2019/PermRes_2019.pdf.

Dandurand, Louise, and Hélène P. Tremblay. 2016. *Rapport sur la décentralisation organisationnelle et budgétaire à l'UQAM*. Montreal: Université du Québec à Montréal. https://rectorat.uqam.ca/wp-content/uploads/sites/16/2016/12/rapport-decentralisation-27septembre.pdf.

Daoust-Boisvert, Amélie, and Marco Fortier. 2016. "Les coupes affectent la paix sociale, dit le recteur." *Le Devoir*, 12 March. https://www.ledevoir.com/societe/education/465325/les-coupes-compromettent-la-paix-sociale-dit-l-uqam.

Darling, Alexander, Martin England, Daniel Lang, and Rosanne Lopers-Sweetman. 1989. "Autonomy and Control: A University Funding Formula as an Instrument of Public Policy." *Higher Education* 18: 559–83.

Davis, Brent. 2015. "Governance and administration of post-secondary institutions." In *Handbook of Canadian Higher Education Law*, edited by Teresa Shanahan, Michelle Nilson and Li-Jeen Broshko, 57–78. Montreal & Kingston: McGill-Queen's University Press.

Dea, Shannon. 2020a. "From pining to a saw-off: Campus free speech news as we begin 2020." *University Affairs*, 30 January. https://www.university

affairs.ca/opinion/dispatches-academic-freedom/from-pining-to-a-saw-off-campus-free-speech-news-as-we-begin-2020.

– 2020b. "Academic freedom in the time of coronavirus." *University Affairs*, 13 March. https://www.universityaffairs.ca/opinion/dispatches-academic-freedom/academic-freedom-in-the-time-of-coronovirus.

Dee, Jay. 2006. "Institutional Autonomy and State-Level Accountability." In *Governance and the Public Good*, edited by William Tierney, 133–55. Albany: SUNY Press.

Demers, Louis. 2019. "De l'administration à la gouvernance des universités: l'administration des universités jusqu'aux années 1980." In *De l'administration à la gouvernance des universités: progress ou recul? L'experience du Québec*, edited by Louis Demers, Jean Bernatchez, and Michael Umbriaco, 35–46. Quebec: Presses de l'Université du Québec.

Demers, Louis, Jean Bernatchez, and Michael Umbriaco. 2019. "Introduction." In *De l'administration à la gouvernance des universités: progress ou recul? L'experience du Québec*, edited by Demers, Bernatchez, and Umbriaco, 1–9. Quebec: Presses de l'Université du Québec.

Dennison, John D. 1997. "Higher Education in British Columbia, 1945–1995: Opportunity and Diversity." In *Higher Education in Canada: Different Systems, Different Perspectives*, edited by Glen Jones, 31–58. New York: Garland.

Dickason, Olive, and William Newbigging. 2019. *Indigenous Peoples within Canada: A Concise History*, 4th ed. Oxford: Oxford University Press.

Dill, David D. 2014. "Academic Governance in the US: Implications of a 'Commons' Perspective." In *International Trends in University Governance: Autonomy, Self-Government, and the Distribution of Authority*, edited by Michael Shattock, 165–83. Oxford: Routledge.

Diversity Institute. 2020. "Diversity Leads: Diverse Representation in Leadership: A Review of Eight Canadian Cities." https://www.ryerson.ca/diversity/reports/DiversityLeads_2020_Canada.pdf.

Dobbins, Michael, and Christopher Knill. 2014. *Higher Education Governance and Policy Change in Western Europe*. Basingstoke: Palgrave Macmillan.

Doern, G. Bruce, David Castle, and Peter W.B. Phillips. 2016. *Canadian Science, Technology, and Innovation Policy: The Innovation Economy and Society Nexus*. Montreal and Kingston: McGill-Queen's University Press.

Doern, G. Bruce, and Christopher Stoney. 2009a. "Federal Research and Innovation Policies and Canadian Universities: A Framework for Analysis." In *Research and Innovation Policy: Changing Federal Government–University Relations*, edited by G. Bruce Doern and Christopher Stoney, 3–34. Toronto: University of Toronto Press.

– 2009b. "Conclusions: Changing Symbiotic Research Relationships: Conflict and Compromise." In *Research and Innovation Policy: Changing Federal*

*Government–University Relations*, edited by Doern and Stoney, 288–324. Toronto: University of Toronto Press.

Donald, Janet G. 1997. "Higher Education in Quebec: 1945–1995." In *Higher Education in Canada: Different Systems, Different Perspectives*, edited by Glen Jones, 161–88. New York and London: Garland.

Dorais, Léo. 2002. "Universités nouvelles, nouvelle université." In *L'idée d'université: une anthologie des débats sur l'enseignement supérieur au Québec de 1770 à 1970*, edited by Claude Corbo and Marie Ouellon, 351–58. Montréal: Presses de l'Université de Montreal.

Doucet, Théodore. 2019. "There's light at the end of the tunnel for Ontario's French-language university." *University Affairs*, 16 October. https://www.universityaffairs.ca/news/news-article/theres-light-at-the-end-of-the-tunnel-for-ontarios-french-language-university.

Duderstadt, James J., and Farris W. Womack. 2003. *Beyond the Crossroads: The Future of the Public University in America*. Baltimore: Johns Hopkins University Press.

Duff, James, and Robert Berdahl. 1966. *University Government in Canada: Report of a Commisssion Sponsored by the Canadian Association of University Teachers and the Association of Universities and Colleges of Canada*. Toronto: University of Toronto Press.

Dwyer, Mary. 2018. "National survey of student engagement: Results for Canadian universities." *Maclean's*, 21 December. https://www.macleans.ca/education/national-survey-of-student-engagement-results-for-canadian-universities.

Eastman, Julia. 2005. "The Revenue Generation Strategies of Four Canadian Universities: A Comparative Analysis." PhD diss., University of Toronto.

Eastman, Julia, Glen Jones, Oliver Bégin-Caouette, Sharon X. Li, Christian Noumi, and Claude Trottier. 2018. "Provincial Oversight and University Autonomy." *Canadian Journal of Higher Education* 48(3): 65–81.

Eastman, Julia, Glen Jones, Oliver Bégin-Caouette, Christian Noumi, and Claude Trottier. 2019. "Federalism and University Governance." *Canadian Public Administration* 62(2): 1–23.

Eastman, Julia, and Daniel W. Lang. 2001. *Mergers in Higher Education: Lessons from Theory and Experience*. Toronto: University of Toronto Press.

*The Economist*. 2016. Briefing: "China invents the digital totalitarian state." 17 December 2016. https://www.economist.com/briefing/2016/12/17/china-invents-the-digital-totalitarian-state.

– 2018. Leader: "Does China's digital police state have echoes in the west?" *The Economist*. 31 May. https://www.economist.com/leaders/2018/05/31/does-chinas-digital-police-state-have-echoes-in-the-west.

Edmondson, Jill. 2020. "See you in court: Five instructive cases for universities." *University Affairs*, 10 August. https://www.universityaffairs.ca/opinion/in-my-opinion/see-you-in-court-five-instructive-cases-for-universities.

Ellis, Lindsay, and Nell Gluckman. 2019. "How University Labs Landed on the Front Lines of the Flight with China." *Chronicle of Higher Education*, 31 May. https://www.chronicle.com/article/how-university-research-landed-on-the-front-lines-of-the-fight-with-china.

Enders, Jürgen, Harry de Boer, and Elke Weyer. 2013. "Regulatory Autonomy and Performance: The Reform of Higher Education Re-visited." *Higher Education* 65(1): 5–23.

Environics Institute for Survey Research. 2021. "Canadian Youth Perspectives on Democracy, Global Issues and Civic Engagement." https://www.environicsinstitute.org/docs/default-source/project-documents/canadian-millennial-genz-social-values-study-2020/environics-institute-aisb-youth-perspectives-on-democracy-and-global-issues---final-report-eng-pdf.pdf?sfvrsn=a2b24487_2

Estermann, Thomas, Terhi Nokkala, and Monika Steinel. 2011. *University Autonomy in Europe II: The Scorecard*. Brussels: European University Association.

EUA (European University Association). 2019. "EUA Briefing: University Mergers in Europe." https://eua.eu/downloads/publications/eua%20merger%20brief%202904.pdf.

Fairtlough, Gerard. 2005. *The Three Ways of Getting Things Done: Hierarchy, Heterarchy, and Responsible Autonomy in Organizations*. Dorset: Triarchy Press.

FAECUM (Fédération des associations étudiantes du campus de l'Université de Montréal) and AGEEFEP (l'Association générale des étudiants et des étudiantes de la Faculté de l'éducation permanente de l'Université de Montréal). 2017. "Université de Montréal: il est temps que 'des chums cessent de juger des chums.'" *Le Devoir*, 29 November.

– 2018. "#OmertàUdeM." Campagne. http://www.faecum.qc.ca/campagne/omertaudem.

Fallis, George. 2007. *Multiversities, Ideas, and Democracy*. Toronto: University of Toronto Press.

Fife, Robert, and Stephen Chase. 2020. "China ramping up threats to activists in Canada: Report." *Globe and Mail*, 12 May. https://www.theglobeandmail.com/politics/article-china-ramps-up-bullying-and-intimidation-tactics-in-canada-report.

Finkelstein, Martin J. 2019. "United States: A story of Marketization, Professional Fragmentation, and Declining Opportunity." In *Professorial Pathways: Academic Careers in a Global Perspective*, edited by Martin

Finkelstein and Glen Jones, 220–42. Baltimore: Johns Hopkins University Press.

First Nations University of Canada. 2010. An Act respecting the First Nations University of Canada. https://www.fnuniv.ca/wp-content/uploads/2010_June_10_-_FN_University_of_Canada_Act_-_Amended.pdf.

Fisher, Donald, and Kjell Rubenson. 2014a. "Conclusion." In *The Development of Postsecondary Education Systems in Canada: A Comparison between British Columbia, Ontario. and Quebec 1980–2010*, edited by Donald Fisher, Kjell Rubenson, Teresa Shanahan, and Claude Trottier, 334–52. Montreal and Kingston: McGill-Queen's University Press.

– 2014b. "Introduction and Overview: PSE in Three Canadian Provinces." In *The Development of Postsecondary Education Systems in Canada: A Comparison between British Columbia, Ontario, and Quebec 1980–2010*, edited by Donald Fisher, Kjell Rubenson, Theresa Shanahan, and Claude Trottier, 3–34. Montreal and Kingston: McGill–Queen's University Press.

Ford, Reuben, Taylor Shek-wai Hui, and Cam Nguyen. 2019. *Postsecondary Participation and Household Income*. Toronto: Higher Education Quality Council of Ontario.

Fortier, Marco. 2016a. "L'Ecoles des sciences de la gestion prete a larguer l'UQAM." *Le Devoir*, 20 February. https://www.ledevoir.com/societe/education/463513/l-ecole-des-sciences-de-la-gestion-prete-a-larguer-l-uqam.

– 2016b. "L'integrite de l'UQAM est fondamentale." *Le Devoir*, 25 February. https://www.ledevoir.com/societe/education/463913/l-integrite-de-l-uqam-est-fondamentale.

– 2016c. "La 'loi du silence' choque les professeurs." *Le Devoir*, 27 February. https://www.ledevoir.com/societe/education/464155/uqam-la-loi-du-silence-choque-les-professeurs.

– 2017a. "Le Tribunal du travail blâme l'Université de Montréal." *Le Devoir*, 16 January. https://www.ledevoir.com/societe/education/489276/conflit-de-travail-le-tribunal-du-travail-blame-l-universite-de-montreal.

– 2017b. "Éducation – Levée de boucliers à l'Université de Montréal." *Le Devoir*, 20 January, A1. https://www.ledevoir.com/societe/education/489646/levee-de-boucliers-a-l-universite-de-montreal.

– 2017c. "Le recteur de l'UdeM propose un compromis aux professeurs inquiets." *Le Devoir*, 24 January. https://www.ledevoir.com/societe/education/489925/universite-de-montreal-le-recteur-propose-un-compromis-aux-professeurs-inquiets.

– 2017d. "Université de Montréal – Report de la réforme de la gouvernance." *Le Devoir*, 7 February, A4. https://www.ledevoir.com/societe/

education/491039/universite-de-montreal-report-de-la-reforme-de-la-gouvernance.

Fournier, Marcel, and D. Antonat. 2012. "Architecture et université nouvelle: l'UQAM." In *Les universités nouvelles: Enjeux et perspectives*, edited by Lyse Roy and Yves Gingras, 23–43. Québec: Presses de l'Université du Québec.

Foy, Cheryl. 2021. *An Introduction to University Governance*. Toronto: Irwin Law.

Frangou, Christina. 2019. "Alberta's universities tally up the budget cuts." *University Affairs*, 16 December. https://www.universityaffairs.ca/news/news-article/albertas-universities-tally-up-the-budget-cuts.

French, Janet. 2020. "Alberta universities, colleges face varied government funding cuts." *CBC News*, 8 March. https://www.cbc.ca/news/canada/edmonton/universities-colleges-technical-institutes-post-secondary-1.5489585.

Friedland, Martin L. 2002. *The University of Toronto: A History*. Toronto: University of Toronto Press.

Friesen, Joe. 2019. "Ontario government fighting to restore directive that made many fees optional for post-secondary students." *Globe and Mail*, 9 December. https://www.theglobeandmail.com/canada/article-ontario-government-fighting-to-restore-directive-that-made-many-fees.

– 2020a. "Coronavirus plunges universities into funding crisis amid threat of lost revenue from declining enrolment." *Globe and Mail*, 4 May, A1–A4.

– 2020b. "Ontario shelves plan for performance-based postsecondary funding, while Alberta pushes ahead." *Globe and Mail*, 6 May. https://www.theglobeandmail.com/canada/article-ontario-shelves-plan-for-performance-based-postsecondary-funding.

– 2020c. "Use of surveillance software to crack down on exam cheating has unintended consequences." *Globe and Mail*, 16 December. https://www.theglobeandmail.com/canada/article-use-of-surveillance-software-to-crack-down-on-exam-cheating-has.

Fung, Nathan. 2018. "U of A president defends honorary degree for David Suzuki." *The Gateway*, 24 April. https://thegatewayonline.ca/2018/04/ualberta-pres-defends-degree.

Galletta, A. 2013. *Mastering the Semi-Structured Interview and Beyond: From Research Design to Analysis and Publications*. New York: NYU Press.

Gazette [Montreal]. 2019. "Some Quebec universities and CEGEPs lag on sexual violence policies." 11 January. https://montrealgazette.com/news/some-quebec-universities-and-cegeps-lag-on-sexual-violence-policies.

Geiger, Roger L. 1991. "Private Higher Education." In *International Higher Education: An Encyclopedia*, edited by Philip Altbach. New York: Garland.

Gerbet, Thomas. 2018. "L'Université de Montréal se déchire au sujet des violences sexuelles." *Radio Canada*, 12 Novembre. https://ici.radio-canada.ca/nouvelle/1133595/udem-professeurs-etudiants-faecum-negociations-comite-discipline-diffamation.

Gill, Louis. 2017. "Quelques éléments d'histoire du syndicalisme professorale universitaire au Québec." UQAC: *Les classiques des sciences sociales*. http://classiques.uqac.ca/contemporains/gill_louis/quelques_elements_hist_syndicalisme_prof/hist_syndicalisme_prof_texte.html.

Giovannetti, Justin. 2019. "Kenney makes major changes to Alberta's universities, boards, and agencies." *Globe and Mail*, 16 August. https://www.theglobeandmail.com/canada/alberta/article-kenney-makes-major-changes-to-albertas-universities-boards-and.

Graney, Emma. 2018. "Minister slams University of Alberta budget cut, president pay." *Edmonton Journal*, 19 March. https://edmontonjournal.com/news/politics/minister-slams-university-of-alberta-budget-cut-president-pay.

– 2019. "UCP prepares to roll out Ford-flavoured post-secondary changes in Alberta." *Edmonton Journal*, 6 May. https://edmontonjournal.com/news/politics/ucp-prepares-to-roll-out-ford-flavoured-post-secondary-changes-in-alberta.

Graney, Juris. 2018. "NDP says new salary rules for Alberta university brass will save $5 million a year." *Edmonton Journal*, 10 April. https://edmontonjournal.com/news/politics/government-to-announce-pay-rules-for-alberta-university-top-brass.

Gregor, Alexander. 1997. "Higher education in Manitoba." In *Higher Education in Canada: Different Systems, Different Perspectives*, edited by Glen Jones, 115–35. New York: Garland.

Guillemet, Patrick. 2012. "D'une universite nouvelle a l'autre: La TELUQ et l'université bimodale." In *Les universités nouvelles: Enjeux et perspectives*, edited by Lyse Roy and Yves Gingras, 259–76. Quebec: Presses de l'Université du Québec.

Hache, Robert. 2021. Affadavit – sworn April 21, 2021. Section C-97 (p. 35). In the matter of the Companies' Creditors Arrangement Act, R.S.C. 1985, c. C-36, as amended; and in the matter of a plan of compromise or arrangement of Laurentian University of Sudbury. Ontario Superior Court of Justice.

Halliwell, Janet. 2013. *Centres of Excellence as a Tool for Capacity-Building: Case Study – Canada*. IMHE Higher Education Programme: OECD.

Halliwell, Janet, and Willie Smith. 2011. "Paradox and Potential: Trends in Science Policy and Practice in Canada and New Zealand." *Prometheus* 29(4): 373–91.

Hamilton, Graeme. 2015. "Quebec student activists dreaming of another Maple Spring." *National Post*, 6 March. https://nationalpost.com/news/politics/quebec-student-activists-dreaming-of-another-maple-spring-this-time-they-want-a-true-sharing-of-wealth.

Hanc, John. 2019. "For some colleges, the best move is to merge." *New York Times*, 10 October. https://www.nytimes.com/2019/10/10/education/learning/colleges-mergers.html.

Handy, Charles. 1989. *The Age of Unreason*. Boston: Harvard Business School Press.

Hannah, David and David Stack. 2015. "Students." In *Handbook of Canadian Higher Education Law*, edited by Teresa Shanahan, Michelle Nilson and Li-Jeen Broshko, 125–66. Montreal & Kingston: McGill-Queen's University Press.

Hannay, Chris. 2019. "Canada Research Chairs program taking new measures to close equity gaps among prestigious academic positions." *Globe and Mail*, 31July.https://www.theglobeandmail.com/politics/article-canada-research-chairs-program-taking-new-measures-to-close-equity.

Hardy, Cynthia. 1996. *The Politics of Collegiality*. Montreal and Kingston: McGill–Queen's University Press.

Harman, Grant. 1991. "Governance, Administration, and Finance". In *The Encyclopedia of Higher Education*, vol. 2, edited by Burton R. Clark and Guy R. Neave, 1279–93. Oxford: Pergamon Press.

Harmsen, Robert, and Allan Tupper. 2017. "A Post-Secondary Education Dialogue for Canada." In *How Ottawa Spends 2017–18*, edited by Katherine Graham and Allan Maslove, 20–30. Ottawa: Carleton University.

Harris, Robin S. 1976. *A History of Higher Education in Canada 1663–1960*. Toronto: University of Toronto Press.

Harris, Robin S. 1984. "The Universities of Canada." In *Commonwealth Universities Yearbook*. Association of Commonwealth Universities, London.

Harvey, Lee. 2004. "The Power of Accreditation: Views of Academics." *Journal of Higher Education Policy and Management* 26(2): 207–23.

Hatton, Michael J. 1990. *Corporations & Directors: Comparing the Profit and Not-for-Profit Sectors*. Toronto: Thompson Educational Publishing Inc.

Hayhoe, Ruth. 1996. *China's Universities, 1895–1995: A Century of Cultural Conflict*. New York: Garland.

Hébert, K. 2008. *Impatient d'être soi-même: Les étudiants montréalais, 1895–1960*. Sainte-Foy: PUQ.

Heydebrand, Wolf V. 2002. "New Organizational Forms." In *Central Currents in Organization Studies. II Contemporary Trends*, vol. 8, edited by Stewart Clegg. London: Sage.

Hilyer, Gail M. 1997. "Higher Education in the Northwest Territories." In *Higher Education in Canada: Different Systems, Different Perspectives*, edited by Glen Jones, 301–23. New York: Garland.

Hoffman, Andrew. 2021. *The Engaged Scholar*. Stanford, CA: Stanford University Press.

Horn, Michiel. 1999. *Academic Freedom in Canada: A History*. Toronto: University of Toronto Press.

Howard, Alison, and Jessica Edge. 2014. *Policies, Laws, and Regulations: Governing Post-Secondary Education and Skills in Canada*. Ottawa: Conference Board of Canada.

Huang, Futao. 2020a. "How to tackle academic misconduct among China's top scientists." *Times Higher Education*, 12 January. https://www.timeshighereducation.com/blog/how-tackle-academic-misconduct-among-chinas-top-scientists.

– 2020b. "Chinese plans for Green Card stir domestic criticism." *University World News*, 14 March. https://www.universityworldnews.com/post.php?story=20200310130 52338.

Huntelar, Adrian. 2017. "Breaking down the university-mandated leave of absence policy." *The Varsity*, 12 November. https://thevarsity.ca/2017/11/12/breaking-down-the-university-mandated-leave-of-absence-policy.

Hurtubise, Denis. 2019. "Thirty Years of Scholarly Literature on University Governance in Canada (1988–2016)." *Canadian Journal of Educational Administration and Policy* 191: 106–17.

Imai, Shin, and Ashley Stacey. 2014. "Municipalities and the Duty to Consult Aboriginal Peoples: A Case Comment on *Neskonlith Indian band v Salmon Arm*." *University of British Columbia Law Review* 47(1): 293–312.

Issawi, Hamdi. 2018. "Degree to disagree? Why the University of Alberta's decision to give David Suzuki an honorary degree is dividing Albertans." *StarMetro Edmonton*, 6 June. https://www.thestar.com/edmonton/2018/06/06/degree-to-disagree-why-the-university-of-albertas-decision-to-give-david-suzuki-an-honorary-doctorate-is-dividing-albertans.html.

Jamet, M. 2014. "Le gouvernement des universités au Québec et en France: Conceptions de l'autonomie et mouvements vers un pilotage stratégique." In *Réformes d'hier et réformes d'aujourd'hui: L'enseignement supérieur recomposé*, edited by T. Chevaillier and C. Musselin, 21–59. Rennes: Presses universitaires de Rennes.

Jeffords, Shawn. 2021. "Laurentian University's financial woes are long-standing, report suggests." *The Globe and Mail*. February 15, 2021.

Johnson, Lisa. 2020. "Alberta budget 2020: Advanced education funding cut 6.3 per cent, tuition to rise." *Edmonton Journal*, 28 February. https://

edmontonjournal.com/news/politics/alberta-budget-2020-advanced-education-funding-cut-6-3-per-cent-tuition-to-rise.

Jones, Glen A. 1996. "Governments, Governance and Canadian Universities." In *Higher Education: Handbook of Theory and Research*, vol. 11, edited by John C. Smart, 337–71. New York: Agathon Press.

– 1997. "Introduction." In *Higher Education in Canada: Different Systems, Different Perspectives*, edited by Jones, 1–8. New York: Garland.

– 2002. "The Structure of University Governance in Canada: A Policy Network Approach." In *Governing Higher Education: National Perspectives on Institutional Governance*, edited by Alberto Amaral, Glen Jones, and Berit Karseth, 213–34. Dordrecht: Kluwer Academic.

– 2013a. "The Horizontal and Vertical Fragmentation of Academic Work and the Challenge for Academic Governance and Leadership." *Asia Pacific Education Review* 14(1): 75–83.

– 2013b. "Trends in Academic Governance in Canada." In *Academic Governance 3.0: What Could It Be? How Can We Get There*, edited by Richard Kool, 6–12. Vancouver: Confederation of University Faculty Associations of British Columbia.

– 2018. "Decentralization, Provincial Systems, and the Challenge of Equity: High Participation Higher Education in Canada." In *High Participation Systems of Higher Education*, edited by Brendan Cantwell, Simon Marginson, and Anna Smolentseva, 203–26. Oxford: Oxford University Press.

– 2019. "Canada: Decentralization, Unionization and the Evolution of Academic Career Pathways." In *Professorial Pathways: Academic Careers in a Global Perspective*, edited by Martin J. Finkelstein and Glen A. Jones, 244–64. Baltimore: Johns Hopkins University Press.

Jones, Glen A., and Martin Finkelstein, 2019. "Looking across Systems: Implications for Comparative, International Studies of Academic Work." In *Professorial Pathways: Academic Careers in a Global Perspective*, edited by Martin Finkelstein and Glen Jones, 265–90. Baltimore: Johns Hopkins University Press.

Jones, Glen A., and Christian Noumi. 2018. "Canada: Provincial Responsibility, Federal Influence, and the Challenge of Coordination." In *Higher Education in Federal Countries*, edited by Martin Carnoy, Isak Froumin, Oleg Leshukov, and Simon Marginson, 96–125. New Delhi: Sage.

Jones, Glen A., Theresa Shanahan, and Paul Goyan. 2001. "University Governance in Canadian Higher Education." *Tertiary Education and Management* 7: 135–48.

Jones, Glen A., and Michael Skolnik. 1997. "Governing Boards in Canadian Universities." *Review of Higher Education* 20(3): 277–95.

Jones, Glen A., and Julian Weinrib. 2012. "The Organization of Academic Work and Faculty Remuneration at Canadian Universities." In *Paying the Professoriate: A Global Comparison of Compensation and Contracts*, edited by Philip Altbach, Liz Reisberg, Maria Yudkevich, Gregory Androushchak, and Iván F. Pacheco, 83–93. New York: Routledge.

Jones, Jeffrey M. 2018. "Confidence in higher education down since 2015." *Gallup* (blog), 9 October 2018. https://news.gallup.com/opinion/gallup/242441/confidence-higher-education-down-2015.aspx.

Kaiser, Ed. 2018. "NDP introduces bill to cap post-secondary tuition by 2020–21." *Edmonton Journal*, 29 October. https://edmontonjournal.com/news/local-news/ndp-introduces-bill-to-cap-post-secondary-tuition-by-2020-21.

Karram Stephenson, Grace, Glen A. Jones, Olivier Bégin-Caouette, and Amy Scott Metcalfe. 2020. "Teaching, Research, and the Canadian Professoriate: Findings from the 2018 APIKS Survey." *Higher Education Forum* 17: 25–41.

Karram Stephenson, Grace, Glen A. Jones, Olivier Begin-Caouette, Amy Metcalfe, and Arif Toor. 2017. *Responding to Change, Assessing Difference: A Review of the Literature on Professors at Canadian Universities*. Toronto: Centre for the Study of Canadian and International Higher Education, OISE–University of Toronto.

Kelchen, Robert. 2018. *Higher Education Accountability*. Baltimore: Johns Hopkins University Press.

Kempeneers, Marianne. 2019. "La réforme de la Charte de l'Université de Montréal: Chronique d'un projet imposé." In *De l'administration à la gouvernance: Progrès ou recul?*, edited by Louis Demers, Jean Bernatchez, and Michel Umbriaco, 135–46. Quebec: Presses de l'Université du Québec.

Kent, Gordon. 2018. "Controversial honorary degree for David Suzuki one of many University of Alberta handing out this month." *Edmonton Journal*, 5 June. https://edmontonjournal.com/news/local-news/controversial-honorary-degree-for-david-suzuki-one-of-many-university-of-alberta-handing-out-this-month.

Kerr, Clark. 2001. *The Uses of the University*, 5th ed. Cambridge, MA: Harvard University Press.

Kivinen, Osmo, and Petri Poikus. 2006. "Privileges of *Universitas Magistrorum et Scolarium* and Their Justification in Charters of Foundation from the 13th to the 21st centuries." *Higher Education* 52: 185–213.

Kniest, Paul. 2017. "Australian universities top world rankings ... for VC pay." (Advocate, 24 January). *National Tertiary Education Union*, 16 March. http://www.nteu.org.au/article/Australian-universities-top-world-rankings...-for-VC-pay-%28Advocate-24-01%29-19415.

Kool, Richard. 2013. "Introduction: Academic Governance: An End or a Means?" In *Academic Governance 3.0: A Conference Organized by the Confederation of University Faculty Associations of BC March 9–12, 2012*, edited by Richard Kool, 2–4. Vancouver: Confederation of University Faculty Associations of British Columbia.

KPMG. 2016. *Government of Nunavut University Feasibility Study – Final Draft: Phase II Analysis*. https://gov.nu.ca/sites/default/files/university_feasibility_study_phase_2_report_web_0.pdf.

Kuokkanen, Rauna. 2007. *Reshaping the University: Responsibility, Indigenous Epistemes, and the Logic of the Gift*. Vancouver: UBC Press.

Lacroix, Robert, and Louis Maheu. 2015. *Leading Research Universities in a Competitive World*. Montreal and Kingston: McGill-Queen's University Press.

Lafortune, Jean-Marie. 2019. "Préface." In *De l'administration à la gouvernance: Progrès ou recul?*, edited by Louis Demers, Jean Bernatchez, and Michel Umbriaco, vii–viii. Quebec: Presses de l'Université du Québec.

Lafortune, Jean-Marie, and Max Roy. 2019. "Quand décentralisation rime avec concentration des pouvoirs." In *De l'administration à la gouvernance: Progrès ou recul?*, edited by Louis Demers, Jean Bernatchez, and Michel Umbriaco, 121–34. Quebec: Presses de l'Université du Québec.

Lakehead University. 2019. Board Bylaws. Revised June 7 2019. https://www.lakeheadu.ca/sites/default/files/uploads/106/board/resource_documents/Board%20Bylaws%20-%20Approved%20June7-2019.pdf.

Lambert-Chan, Marie. 2013. "Proposed university framework causes a stir in Québec." *University Affairs*. September 18. https://www.universityaffairs.ca/news/news-article/proposed-university-framework-causes-a-stir-in-quebec/.

Lamont, Michèle. 2009. *How Professors Think*. Cambridge, MA: Harvard University Press.

Lang, Daniel W. 2003. "The Future of Merger: What Do We Want Mergers to Do: Efficiency or Diversity?" *Canadian Journal of Higher Education* 33(3): 19–46.

– 2016a. "Incentive Funding Meets Incentive-Based Budgeting: Can They Coexist?" *Canadian Journal of Higher Education* 46(4): 1–22.

– 2016b. "Five Case Studies of Governance in Tertiary Education." *Canadian Journal of Higher Education* 46(3): 42–58.

– 2019. "Financing Higher Education in a Federal System: The Case of Canada." Paper presented at the Annual Conference of the Society for the Study of Higher Education, Vancouver, BC, June.

– 2020. "Financing Higher Education in Canada: A Study in Fiscal Federalism System." *Researchgate*. DOI:10.13140/RG.2.2.19684.19846.

Laroche, Jean. 2015. "Nova Scotia universities face increased financial scrutiny with new bill." CBC News, 22 April. https://www.cbc.ca/news/canada/nova-scotia/nova-scotia-universities-face-increased-financial-scrutiny-with-new-bill-1.3044608.
Larouche, Catherine, and Denis Savard. 2019. "Les universités québécoises: une typologie." In *De l'administration à la gouvernance des universités: progress ou recul? L'experience du Québec*, edited by Louis Demers, Jean Bernatchez, and Michael Umbriaco, 83–104. Quebec: Presses de l'Université du Québec.
Lavallée, André. 1974. *Québec contre Montréal: La querelle universitaire 1876–1891*. Montreal: Les Presses de l'Université de Montréal.
Lavallee, Lynn. 2020. "Is Decolonization Possible in the Academy?" In *Decolonizing and Indigenizing Education in Canada*, edited by Sheila Cote-Meek and Taima Moeke-Pickering, 117–34. Toronto: Canadian Scholars.
Leclair, Jean, et al. 2017. "Projet de refonte de la charte de l'U de M: l'idée de l'université mise en péril." *La Presse*, 26 January. http://plus.lapresse.ca/screens/136cbb4f-de31-4d67-8d4a-e4dec9164352%7C_0.html.
Levasseur, Karine. 2009. "Universities and the Regulation of Research ethics." In *Research and Innovation Policy: Changing Federal Government–University Relations*, edited by G. Bruce Doern and Christopher Stoney, 242–64. Toronto: University of Toronto Press.
Levy, D.C. 1986. "'Public' and 'Private' Analysis and Ambiguity in Higher Education." In *Private Education: Studies in Choice and Public Policy*, edited by Daniel Levy. New York: Oxford University Press.
Lewis, Harriet, 2017. *Review of Governance Culture and Practices: Memorial University*. St John's: Memorial University of Newfoundland, 2017.
Li, Sharon X., and Glen A. Jones. 2015. "The 'Invisible' Sector: Private Higher Education in Canada." In *Private Higher Education: A Global Perspective*, edited by Kishore Joshi and Saeed Paiyandi, 1–33. Delhi: B.R.
Linteau, Paul-André, René Durocher, Jean-Claude Robert, and François Ricard. 1989. *Histoire du Québec contemporain*, vol. 2: *Le Québec depuis 1930*. Montréal: Les Editions du Boréal.
Logan, Harry T. 1958. *Tuum est: A History of the University of British Columbia*. Vancouver: University of British Columbia, Vancouver.
Longanecker, David A. 2006. "The 'New' New Challenge of Governance." In *Governance and the Public Good*, edited by William Tierney, 95–115. Albany: SUNY Press.
Lorinc, Jacob. 2019. "In Wake of Campus Suicides, U of T Students Push for Easier Access to Mental-Health Help." *Toronto Star*, 25 September. https://www.thestar.com/news/gta/2019/09/25/u-of-t-students-push-for-easier-access-to-mental-health-help.html.

Lougheed, Patrick, and Michelle Pidgeon. 2016. "Exploring Effective Academic Governance at a Canadian University." *Canadian Journal of Higher Education* 46(3): 90–104.

Lowe, Roy, and Yoshihito Yasuhara. 2017. *The Origins of Higher Learning: Knowledge Networks and the Early Development of Universities.* New York: Routledge.

MacDonald, Moira. 2018. "University Boards in the Spotlight." *University Affairs*, 3 January. https://www.universityaffairs.ca/features/feature-article/university-boards-spotlight.

MacKinnon, Peter. 2014. *University Leadership and Public Policy in the Twenty-First Century: A President's Perspective.* Toronto: University of Toronto Press.

– 2018. *University Commons Divided: Exploring Debate and Dissent on Campus.* Toronto: University of Toronto Press.

*Maclean's.* 2002. vol. 115. no 46. University Rankings: Finance. 18 November 2002.

– 2019a. "Canada's Best Medical Doctoral Universities: Rankings 2020." 3 October 2019. https://www.macleans.ca/education/university-rankings-2020-canadas-top-medical-doctoral-schools/.

– 2019b. "Canada's Best Comprehensive Universities: Rankings 2020." 3 October 2019. https://www.macleans.ca/education/university-rankings-2020-canadas-top-comprehensive-schools/.

Macleod, Rod. 2008. *All True Things: A History of the University of Alberta, 1908–2008.* Edmonton: University of Alberta Press.

Mandhane, Renu. 2018. "RE: University-Mandated Leave of Absence Policy Raises Human Rights Concerns." *Ontario Human Rights Commission* (Letters), 29 January. http://www.ohrc.on.ca/en/re-university-mandated-leave-absence-policy-%C2%ADraises-human-rights-concerns.

Marchand, Yannick, Jean Dubé, and Sébastien Breau. 2020. "Exploring the Causes and Consequences of Regional Income Inequality in Canada." *Economic Geography* 96(2): 83–107. DOI:10.1080/00130095.2020.1715793.

Marginson, Simon. 2008. "Global Field and Global Imagining: Bourdieu and Worldwide Higher Education." *British Journal of Sociology of Education* 29(3): 303–15.

– 2015. "Sustaining Resources." In *International Higher Education* 80: 11–12, edited by Anna Smolentseva, 3–38. Oxford: Oxford University Press.

– 2018a. "Australia: Benefits and Limits of the Centralized Approach." In *Higher Education in Federal Countries: A Comparative Study*, edited by Martin Carnoy, Isak Froumin, Oleg Leshukov, and Simon Marginson, 126–72. New Delhi: Sage.

– 2018b. "Equity." In *High Participation Systems of Higher Education*, edited by Brendan Cantwell, Simon Marginson, and Anna Smolentseva, 151–83. Oxford: Oxford University Press.

– 2018c. "High Participation Systems of Higher Education." In *High Participation Systems of Higher Education*, edited by Brendan Cantwell, Simon Marginson, and Anna Smolentseva, 3–38. Oxford: Oxford University Press.

– 2019. "How should universities respond to the new Cold War?" *University World News*, 16 November 2019. https://www.universityworldnews.com/post.php?story=20191112103413758.

Marginson, Simon, and Martin Carnoy. 2018. "Introduction: Higher Education in Federal Countries." In *Higher Education in Federal Countries*, edited by Martin Carnoy, Isak Froumin, Oleg Leshukov, and Simon Marginson, 1–36. New Delhi: Sage.

Marginson, Simon, and Mark Considine. 2000. *The Enterprise University: Power, Governance, and Reinvention in Australia.* Cambridge: Cambridge University Press.

Marginson, Simon, and Gary Rhoades. 2002. "Beyond National States, Markets, and Systems of Higher Education: A Glonacal Agency Heuristic." *Higher Education* 43: 281–309.

Marin, Michael. 2015. "Should the Charter Apply to Universities?" *National Journal of Constitutional Law* 35(1): 29–57.

Martin, Nick. 2017. "PC replaces NDP appointments on U of M board." *Winnipeg Free Press*, 25 January 2017. https://www.winnipegfreepress.com/local/pc-replaces-ndp-appointments-on-u-of-m-board-411777585.html.

Maslen, Geoff. 2021. "Vice-chancellors slash more than 17,000 university jobs." *University World News*, 3 February 2021. https://www.universityworldnews.com/post.php?story=20210203140358652.

Mastel, Jon. 2018. "Students protest potential increases to tuition, rent meal plan costs." *The Flame*, 15 March. https://theflame.su.ualberta.ca/en/blog/2018/03/15/students-protest-potential-increases-to-tuition-rent-meal-plan-costs.

Maton, Karl. 2005. "A Question of Autonomy: Bourdieu's Field Approach and Higher Education Policy." *Journal of Education Policy* 20(6): 687–704.

McEwan, Travis. 2018. "'U of A! Not OK!': Students, faculty and staff protest University of Alberta fee increases." *CBC News*, 6 April. https://www.cbc.ca/news/canada/edmonton/university-of-alberta-protest-against-fee-and-rent-hikes-1.4609530.

McGinn, Shauna. 2019. "Ontario's Student Unions Respond to Student Choice Initiative Fallout." *University Affairs* 12 November. https://www.

universityaffairs.ca/news/news-article/ontarios-student-unions-respond-to-student-choice-initiative-fallout.

McInnis, Craig. 2006. "Renewing the Place of Academic Expertise." In *Governance and the Public Good*, edited by William Tierney, 117–31. Albany: SUNY Press.

McLean, Tamara. 2018. "'Let us speak': Students boo University of Alberta president at forum on fee increases." *CBC News*, 28 March 2018. https://www.cbc.ca/news/canada/edmonton/let-us-speak-students-boo-university-of-alberta-president-at-forum-on-fee-increases-1.4598111.

McNutt, Ryan. 2019. "Five years of 'impact': Pres and Provost look back at Strategic Direction achievements in community town hall." *Dal News*, 27 June. https://www.dal.ca/news/2019/06/27/five-years-of--impact---pres-and-provost-look-back-at-strategic-.html.

Metcalfe, Amy Scott. 2010. "Revisiting Academic Capitalism in Canada: No Longer the Exception." *Journal of Higher Education* 81(4): 489–514.

Meunier, Hugo. 2009. "Grève des enseignants: perturbations à l'UQAM." *La Presse*, 20 March 2009. https://www.lapresse.ca/actualites/quebec-canada/education/200903/20/01-838421-greve-des-enseignants-perturbations-a-luqam.php.

Mintzberg, Henry. 1979. *The Structuring of Organizations*. Englewood Cliffs: Prentice-Hall.

Minzner, Carl. 2019. "Intelligentsia in the Crosshairs: Xi Jinping's Ideological Rectification of Higher Education in China." *China Leadership Monitor*, 1 December. https://www.prcleader.org/carl-minzner.

Moeke-Pickering, Tania. 2020. "The Future for Indigenous Education: How Social Media Is Changing Our Relationships in the Academy." In *Decolonizing and Indigenizing Education in Canada*, edited by Sheila Cote-Meek and Taima Moeke-Pickering, 267–78. Toronto: Canadian Scholars Press.

Morgan, Clara. 2009. "Higher Education Funding and Policy Trade-Offs: The AUCC and Federal Research in the Chrétien–Martin Era." In *Research and Innovation Policy: Changing Federal Government–University Relations*, edited by G. Bruce Doern and Christopher Stoney, 59–86. Toronto: University of Toronto Press.

Mortimer, Kenneth P., and Colleen O'Brien Sathre. 2006. "Be Mission Centered, Market Smart, and Politically Savvy." In *Governance and the Public Good*, edited by William Tierney, 73–94. Albany: SUNY Press.

MPHEC (Maritime Provinces Higher Education Commission). 2018. "Table 9: Total Enrolment by Province of Study, Immigration Status, Province of Residence, and Level of Study 2013–14 to 2017–18." 21 January 2019. http://www.mphec.ca/media/175160/Enr_Table9_2017-2018E.pdf.

Muir, William R. 1997. "Higher Education in Saskatchewan." In *Higher Education in Canada: Different Systems, Different Perspectives*, edited by Glen Jones, 93–113. New York: Garland.

Munn, Catharine. 2019. "Why are so many students struggling with their mental health?" *In my opinion [blog]*, University Affairs, 7 January. https://www.universityaffairs.ca/opinion/in-my-opinion/why-are-so-many-students-struggling-with-their-mental-health.

Musselin, Christine. 2004. *The Long March of the French Universities*. New York: Routledge Falmer.

– 2019a. "France: Marginal Formal Changes but Noticeable Evolutions." In *Professorial Pathways: Academic Careers in a Global Perspective*, edited by Martin Finkelstein and Glen Jones, 43–66. Baltimore: Johns Hopkins University Press.

– 2019b. *Propositions d'une chercheuse pour l'université*. Paris: Les Presses de Sciences Po.

Myers, Gordon. 2019. "Responsibility Centre Budgeting as a Mechanism to Deal with Academic Moral Hazard." *Canadian Journal of Higher Education* 49(3): 13–23.

Naidoo, R. 2003. "Repositioning Higher Education as a Global Commodity: Opportunities and Challenges for Future Sociology of Education Work." *British Journal of Sociology of Education* 24(2): 249–59.

Nanos. 2022. National Survey | Summary Conducted by Nanos Research, January 2022 Submission 2022-2066. https://nanos.co/wp-content/uploads/2022/02/2022-2066-Institutional-Tracking-Project-Populated-Report-with-tabs.pdf.

Neuman, Gerald L. 2020. "Populist Threats to the International Human Rights System." In *Human Rights in a Time of Populism: Challenges and Responses*, edited by Gerald Neuman, 1–19. Cambridge: Cambridge University Press.

Newman, Frank. 1987. *Choosing Quality: Reducing Conflict between the State and the University*. Denver: Education Commission of the States.

"Nothing about Us without Us: A Follow-Up Statement by University of Toronto Students Regarding the University-Wide Mental Health Crisis." 2019. https://drive.google.com/file/d/1sg-rwoRl2IziH9omU6ZdvSreXSN-lUTYJ/view?ths=true.

Nova Scotia. 2010. "Report on the University System: Prepared by Dr Tim O'Neill for Premier Darrell Dexter." *Documents – Higher Education*. https://novascotia.ca/lae/HigherEducation/documents.asp.

– 2014. "Chapter 29 of the Acts of 2014: St Francis Xavier University Act (amended)." https://nslegislature.ca/legc/bills/62nd_1st/3rd_read/b050.htm.

– 2015. "Legislation holds universities more accountable." *News – Labour and Advanced Education*, 22 April 2015. https://novascotia.ca/news/release/?id=20150422005.
– 2016. *Memorandum of Understanding between the Province of Nova Scotia and the Nova Scotia Universities, 2015–16 to 2018–19.* Halifax. https://novascotia.ca/lae/pubs/docs/MOU-2015-2019.pdf.
– 2021. "Ministerial Mandate Letter: Minister of Advanced Education." https://novascotia.ca/exec_council/letters-2021/ministerial-mandate-letter-2021-AE.pdf
OCUFA (Ontario Confederation of University Faculty Associations). 2019. "OCUFA's analysis of the 2019 Ontario Budget." OCUFA (blog), 1 May. https://ocufa.on.ca/blog-posts/ocufas-analysis-of-the-2019-ontario-budget.
– 2020. "OCUFA urges university administrations to respect collegial governance structures when addressing impacts of the COVID-19 pandemic." *News* (blog), 23 April. https://ocufa.on.ca/blog-posts/ocufa-urges-university-administrations-to-respect-collegial-governance-structures-when-addressing-impacts-of-the-covid-19-pandemic.
OECD (Organisation for Economic Co-operation and Development). 2017. *Educational Opportunity for All: Overcoming Inequality throughout the Life Course.* Paris. http://dx.doi.org/10.1787/9789264287457-en.
– 2018. *Education at a Glance 2018: OECD Indicators.* Paris. https://doi.org/10.1787/eag-2018-en.
– 2019. *Education at a Glance 2019: OECD Indicators.* Paris. https://doi.org/10.1787/f8d7880d-en.
– 2021. *Main Science and Technology Indicators* 20(2). https://doi.org/10.1787/0bd49050-en.
O'Malley, Brendan. 2020. "Universities Urge Trump to Drop Ban on Diversity Training." *University World News*, 17 October. https://www.universityworldnews.com/post.php?story=20201017110633690.
Ontario Superior Court of Justice. 2021. Court File No. CV-21-656040-00CL. Tab 2. Affidavit of Robert Haché sworn on April 21. 2021. pp. 30-108.
Orfali, Philippe. 2016a. "UQAM 'en peril' si l'ESG se sépare, selon les doyens." *Le Devoir*, 24 February. https://www.ledevoir.com/societe/education/463742/l-uqam-mise-en-peril-selon-un-doyen.
– 2016b. "Un projet de refonte de l'Universite de Montreal cree des remous." *Le Devoir*, 5 March, A3. https://www.ledevoir.com/societe/education/464719/un-projet-de-refonte-de-l-universite-de-montreal-cree-des-remous.
Ouellette-Vézina, Henri. 2021. "Legault veut 'protéger notre liberté d'expression.'" *La Presse*, 13 February. https://www.lapresse.ca/actualites/

education/2021-02-13/universites/legault-veut-proteger-notre-liberte-d-expression.php.

Papillon, Martin. 2020. "Canadian Federalism and Indigenous Multi-Level Governance." In *Nation to Nation: Canadian Federalism: Performance, Effectiveness, and Legitimacy*, edited by Herman Bakvis and Grace Skogstad, 395–426. Toronto: University of Toronto Press.

Parsons, Christopher. 2021. "The new security research rules threaten universities' ability to be open and inclusive." *The Globe and Mail*, 15 July 2021. https://www.theglobeandmail.com/opinion/article-the-new-security-research-rules-threaten-universities-ability-to-be/.

Patel, Vimal. 2019. "The New 'In Loco Parentis.'" *Chronicle of Higher Education*, 17 February. https://www.chronicle.com/interactives/Trend19-InLoco-Main.

Paul, Ross. 2015. *Leadership under Fire: The Challenging Role of the Canadian University President*. Montreal and Kingston: McGill-Queen's University Press.

Penner, Roland. 1994. "Unionization, Democracy, and the University." *Interchange* 25(1): 49–53.

Pennock, Lea, Glen A. Jones, Jeff M. Leclerc, and Sharon X. Li. 2015. "Assessing the Role and Structure of Academic Senates in Canadian Universities, 2000–2012." *Higher Education* 70(3): 503–18.

– 2016. "Challenges and Opportunities for Collegial Governance at Canadian Universities: Reflections on a Survey of Academic Senates." *Canadian Journal of Higher Education* 46(3): 73–89.

Pettigrew, Todd. 2012. "Dalhousie strike could get ugly." *MacLean's*, 7 March. https://www.macleans.ca/education/uniandcollege/dalhousie-strike-could-get-ugly.

Pocklington, Tom, and Allan Tupper. 2002. *No Place to Learn: Why Universities Aren't Working*. Vancouver: UBC Press.

Proulx, Robert. 2015. "L'heure juste à propos de l'UQAM." *Le Devoir*, 28 February. https://www.ledevoir.com/opinion/lettres/433164/l-heure-juste-a-propos-de-l-uqam.

Pruvot, Enora Bennetot, and Thomas Estermann. 2017. *University Autonomy in Europe III: The Scorecard 2017*. Brussels: European University Association. https://eua.eu/downloads/publications/university%20autonomy%20in%20europe%20iii%20the%20scorecard%202017.pdf.

PSAB (Public Sector Accounting Board). n.d. *20 Questions about the Government Reporting Entity*. Toronto: Canadian Institute of Chartered Accountants. http://www.frascanada.ca/standards-for-public-sector-entities/resources/referencematerials.item14956.pdf.

Quebec. 1963–1966. *Rapport de la Commission royale d'enquête sur l'enseignement dans la province de Québec* (Parent Report). 3 t. en 5 v. Quebec. http://www.bibliotheque.assnat.qc.ca/guides/fr/les-commissions-d-enquete-au-quebec-depuis-1867/7548-commission-parent-1963-66.
– 2013. *Cahier thématique: La gouvernance et le financement des universités.* Quebec: Ministere de l'enseignement superieur, recherché, science et technologie.
– 2021a. *L'université québécoise du future: tendances, enjeux, pistes d'action et recommandations.* Submitted by *Rémi* Quirion, chief scientist of Quebec, to Danielle McCann, minister of higher education.
– 2021b. *Commission scientifique et technique indépendante sur la reconnaissance de la liberté académique dans le milieu universitaire.* (webpage) https://www.quebec.ca/gouv/ ministere/enseignement-superieur/organismes-lies/commission-reconnaissance-liberte-academique.
Quebec National Assembly. 2018. "41st Legislature, 1st Session (20 May 2014 to 23 August 2018)." Journal des débats (Hansard) of the National Assembly. http://www.assnat.qc.ca/en/travaux-parlementaires/assemblee-nationale/41-1/journal-debats/20180327/216551.html#_Toc510020077.
Ramaley, Judith. 2006. "Governance in a Time of Transition." In *Governance and the Public Good*, edited by William Tierney, 157–77. Albany: SUNY Press.
Ramsay, Caley. 2018. "University of Alberta hikes international student tuition, rental, and meal costs." *Global News*, 16 March. https://globalnews.ca/news/4088039/university-of-alberta-hikes-international-student-tuition-rental-and-meal-costs.
Rancic, Michael. 2019. "A Fine Balance: Deciding Who Deserves an Honorary Degree." *University Affairs*, 1 May 2019. https://www.universityaffairs.ca/features/feature-article/a-fine-balance-deciding-who-deserves-an-honorary-degree.
RCAP (Royal Commission on Aboriginal Peoples). 1996. *Report of the Royal Commission on Aboriginal Peoples*, vol. 3. Ottawa.
RE$EARCH Infosource.com. 2014. "Canada's Top 50 Research Universities 2014." 7 November. https://researchinfosource.com/pdf/Canada_s%20 Top%2050%20research%20universities%202014.pdf.
– 2019. "Canada's Top 50 Research Universities 2019." https://researchinfosource.com/top-50-research-universities/2019/list.
Richardson, Geoffrey, and John Fielden. 1997. *Measuring the Grip of the State: The Relationship between Governments and Universities in Selected Commonwealth Countries.* London: Commonwealth Higher Education Management Service.

Riddle, Phyllis. 1989. *University and State: Political Competition and the Rise of the Universities 1200–1985*. Stanford: Stanford University Press.

Rizza, Alanna. 2018. "University of Toronto approves criticized student leave of absence policy." *Globe and Mail*, 27 June. https://www.theglobeandmail.com/canada/toronto/article-university-of-toronto-approves-criticized-student-leave-of-absence.

Rogers, Rory, and Jennifer Taylor. 2018. "Canada: An update on freedom of expression and Charter application to universities." *Mondaq*, 1 March. http://www.mondaq.com/canada/x/678606/Education/An+Update+On+Freedom+Of+Expression+Charter+Application+To+Universities.

Ross, Andrea. 2018. "U of A stands by Suzuki honorary degree as donors withdraw, Albertans protest." *CBC News*, 24 April. https://www.cbc.ca/news/canada/edmonton/david-suzuki-honorary-degree-backlash-1.4633770.

Ross, John. 2019a. "Australian task force to bolster campus cyber security." *Times Higher Education*, 27 August. https://www.timeshighereducation.com/news/australian-task-force-bolster-campus-cyber-security.

— 2019b. "Australian v-cs 'in a coma' over China collaboration risks." *Times Higher Education*, 14 October. https://www.timeshighereducation.com/news/australian-v-cs-coma-over-china-risks.

– 2019c. "New security guidelines for Australian universities." *Times Higher Education*, 14 November. https://www.timeshighereducation.com/news/contrasting-views-new-australian-security-guidelines.

Rowlands, Julie. 2015. "Turning Collegial Governance on Its Head: Symbolic Violence, Hegemony, and the Academic Board." *British Journal of Sociology of Education* 36(7): 1017–35.

– 2017. *Academic Governance in the Contemporary University*. Springer: Singapore.

– 2018. "Deepening Understanding of Bourdieu's Academic and Intellectual Capital through a Study of Academic Voice within Academic Governance." *Studies in Higher Education* 43(11): 1823–36.

Roy, Louise. 2017. "Idées – Pourquoi moderniser la charte de l'Université de Montréal." *Le Devoir*, 18 November, B9. https://www.ledevoir.com/opinion/idees/513340/pourquoi-moderniser-la-charte-de-l-universite-de-montreal.

Roy, Lyse, and Yves Gingras. 2012. "Introduction." In *Les universités nouvelles: Enjeux et perspectives*, edited by Lyse Roy and Yves Gingras, 1–8. Quebec: Presses de l'Université du Québec.

Royal Commission on the University of Toronto, Ontario. 1906. *Report*. Toronto: King's Printer.

Ruch, Richard S. 2001. *Higher Education Inc.: The Rise of the For-Profit University*. Baltimore: Johns Hopkins University Press.

Sa, Creso. 2019a. "The uncertain shelf life of the Fundamental Science Review." *University Affairs*, 8 July. https://www.universityaffairs.ca/opinion/policy-and-practice/the-uncertain-shelf-life-of-the-fundamental-science-review.

– 2019b. "The fault lines of the politics of science policy are firmly in place." *University Affairs*, 6 December. https://www.universityaffairs.ca/opinion/policy-and-practice/the-fault-lines-of-the-politics-of-science-policy-are-firmly-in-place.

Salmi, Jamil. 2011. "The Road to Academic Excellence: Lessons of Experience." In *The Road to Academic Excellence: The Making of World-Class Research Universities*, edited by Philip Altbach and Jamil Samil, 32–346. Washington, DC: World Bank.

Saskatchewan. 2005. Legislative Assembly. Debates and Proceedings (Hansard), N.S. Vol. XLVIII No. 14a Monday, 28 November 2005, 1:30 p.m.

Sauvé, Mathieu-Robert. 2006. "Solidarité chez les profs: Jaques Rouillard publie l'histoire du SGPUM." *Forum* 41(5), 25 September. http://www.iforum.umontreal.ca/Forum/2006-2007/20060925/AU_4.html.

Schoellhammer, Sarah. 2020. *Innovation Exposed: Case Studies of Strategy, Organization, and Culture in Heterarchies*. New York: Springer. https://doi.org/10.1007/978-3-658-29335-2.

Scholars at Risk. 2019. *Free to Think 2019: Report of the Scholars at Risk Academic Freedom Monitoring Project*. New York.

Schuetze, Hans G. 2012. "University Governance Reform: The Drivers and the Driven." In *University Governance and Reform: Policy, Fads, and Experience in International Perspective*, edited by Hans Schuetze, William Bruneau, and Garnet Grosjean, 3–10. New York: Palgrave Macmillan.

Scott, Peter. 2019. "United Kingdom: Institutional Autonomy and National Regulation, academic freedom and managerial authority." In *Professorial Pathways: Academic Careers in a Global Perspective*, edited by Martin Finkelstein and Glen Jones, 67–92. Baltimore: Johns Hopkins University Press.

Senkpiel, Aron. 1997. "Postsecondary Education in the Yukon: The Last Thirty Years." In *Higher Education in Canada: Different Systems, Different Perspectives*, edited by Glen Jones, 285–300. New York: Garland.

Shanahan, Theresa. 2015a. "The Role of the Federal Government in Postsecondary Education." In *Handbook of Canadian Higher Education Law*, edited by Theresa Shanahan, Michelle Nilson, and Li-Jeen Broshko, 17–36. Montreal: McGill-Queen's University Press.

– 2015b. "The role of the provincial government." In *Handbook of Canadian Higher Education Law*, edited by Teresa Shanahan, Michelle Nilson and Li-Jeen Broshko, 37–78. Montreal & Kingston: McGill-Queen's University Press.

– 2019. "Good governance and Canadian universities: Fiduciary duties of university governing boards and their implications for shared collegial governance." *International Journal of Education Policy & Leadership*. 14(8) https://doi.org/10.22230/ijepl.2019v14n8a861

Shanghai Rankings. n.d.a. "Shanghai Academic Ranking of World Universities 2018." http://www.shanghairanking.com/ARWU2018.html.

– n.d.b. "2019 Academic Ranking of World Universities 2019." https://www.shanghairanking.com/rankings/arwu/2019.

Sharma, Yojana. 2020. "Freedom curbs raise academic collaboration uncertainty." *University World News*, 10 January. https://www.universityworldnews.com/post.php?story=20200110071137628.

Shattock, Michael. 2014a. "The Context of 'Modernising' Reforms." In *International Trends in University Governance: Autonomy, Self-Government, and the Distribution of Authority*, edited by Michael Shattock, 1–14. Oxford: Routledge.

– 2014b. "University Governance in the UK: Bending the Traditional Model." In *International Trends in University Governance: Autonomy, Self-Government, and the Distribution of Authority*, edited by Michael Shattock, 127–43. Oxford: Routledge.

– 2014c. "Autonomy, Self-Government, and the Distribution of Authority: International Trends in University Governance." In *International Trends in University Governance: Autonomy, Self-government, and the Distribution of Authority*, edited by Michael Shattock, 184–97. Oxford: Routledge.

Shaw, Kenneth A. 1998. "Helping Public Institutions Act Like Private Ones." In *Seeking Excellence through Independence: Liberating Colleges and Universities from Excessive Regulation*, edited by Terence MacTaggart. San Francisco: Jossey-Bass.

Shen, Anqi. 2018. "Consultations are underway for a made-in-Canada Athena SWAN program." *University Affairs*, 2 October. https://www.universityaffairs.ca/news/news-article/consultations-are-underway-for-a-made-in-canada-athena-swan-program.

Shepherd, Christian. 2018. "In China, universities seek to plant 'Xi Thought' in minds of students." Reuters, 22 June. https://www.reuters.com/article/us-china-politics-education-idUSKBN1JI0I5.

Sherlock, Tracy. 2016. "UBC's next president needs to have it all." *Vancouver Sun*, 25 February. https://vancouversun.com/news/metro/ubcs-next-president-needs-to-have-it-all.

Shils, Edward. 1992. "Universities: Since 1900." In *The Encyclopedia of Higher Education*, vol. 1, edited by Burton R. Clark and Guy R. Neave, 1259–75. Oxford: Pergamon Press.

Simpson, Jeffrey. 2009. "Why Universities Shun Their Own for the Top Job." *Globe and Mail*, 11 February 2009. https://www.theglobeandmail.com/opinion/why-universities-shun-their-own-for-the-top-job/article1148759.

Skolnik, Michael L. 1997. "Putting It All Together: Viewing Canadian Higher Education from a Collection of Jurisdiction-Based Perspectives." In *Higher Education in Canada: Different Systems, Different Perspectives*, edited by Glen Jones, 32–41. New York: Garland.

– 2020. Email correspondance.

Slaughter, Sheila, and Larry Leslie. 1997. *Academic Capitalism: Politics, Policies, and the Entrepreneurial University*. Baltimore: Johns Hopkins University Press.

Smith, Lynn. 2015. "Summary of the fact-finding process and conclusions regarding alleged breaches of academic freedom and other university policies at the University of British Columbia." Office of the President. https://president.ubc.ca/files/2015/10/Summary-of-Process-and-Conclusions-Final.pdf.

Stake, R.E. 2006. *Multiple Case Study Analysis*. New York: Guilford Press.

Statistics Canada. 2003. "Full-time faculty by university, selected years" [unpublished data]. Special request. Received 5 June 2003.

– 2016. "Language Highlight Tables, 2016 Census." Updated 31 August 2017. https://www12.statcan.gc.ca/census-recensement/2016/dp-pd/hlt-fst/lang/index-eng.cfm.

– 2019. "Table 1: Enrolments in Canadian universities and colleges, by field of study, 2015/2016 and 2016/2017." Modified February 12, 2019. https://www150.statcan.gc.ca/n1/daily-quotidien/181128/t001c-eng.htm.

– 2020a. "Population estimates on July 1st, by age and sex. Table 17-10-0134-01." 29 September. https://doi.org/10.25318/1710000501-eng.

– 2020b. "Estimates of population (2016 Census and administrative data), by age group and sex for July 1st, Canada, provinces, territories, health regions (2018 boundaries) and peer groups." https://doi.org/10.25318/1710013401-eng.

– 2020c. "Postsecondary enrolments, by registration status, institution type, status of student in Canada and gender. Table 37-10-0018-01." 25 November. https://doi.org/10.25318/3710001801-eng.

– 2020d. "Number and Salaries of Full-Time Teaching Staff at Canadian Universities." Accessed 24 November 2020.

Stonechild, Blair. 2006. *The New Buffalo: The Struggle for Aboriginal Post-Secondary Education in Canada*. Winnipeg: University of Manitoba Press.

Swartz, David. 1997. *Culture and Power: The Sociology of Pierre Bourdieu*. Chicago: University of Chicago Press.

Syndicat des professeurs et professeures de l'UQAM (SPUQ). n.d.a. *Convention collective 2009-2013.*
– n.d.b. "Qui sommes-nous? Les faits marquants de l'historie du SPUQ: 1969 à 2007." Historique. https://spuq.uqam.ca/profil/historique/faits_marquants/.
Syndicat des professionnelles et professionnels de recherche de l'Université Laval (SPPRUL). 2016. *Mémoire sur l'examen du soutien fédéral aux sciences.* Quebec.
Takagi, Andy. 2019. "'How do you sleep at night?': Students confront admin on mental health." *The Varsity*, 6 October. https://thevarsity.ca/2019/10/06/how-do-you-sleep-at-night-students-confront-admin-on-mental-health.
Takagi, Andy, and Michael Teoh. 2019. "'We care deeply for their well-being': U of T admin addresses Bahen Centre death at Business Board meeting." *The Varsity*, 19 March. https://thevarsity.ca/2019/03/19/we-care-deeply-for-their-well-being-u-of-t-admin-addresses-bahen-centre-death-at-business-board-meeting.
Tamtik, Merli, Roopa Desai Trilokekar, and Glen A. Jones. 2020. "Conclusion: International Education as Public Policy – the Canadian Story." In *International Education as Public Policy in Canada*, edited by Merli Tamtik, Roopa Desai Trilokekar, and Glen Jones, 407–26. Montreal and Kingston: McGill-Queen's University Press.
Thériault, Joseph Yvon. 2016. "L'UQAM contre elle-même." *Le Devoir*, 6 May. https://www.ledevoir.com/opinion/idees/470119/l-uqam-contre-elle-meme.
Thompson, Walter P. 1970. *The University of Saskatchewan: A Personal History.* Toronto: University of Toronto Press.
Thorens, Justin. 2006. "Liberties, Freedom, and Autonomy: A Few Reflections on Academia's Estate." *Higher Education Policy* 19: 87–110.
Timmons, Vianne, and Peter Stoicheff. 2016. "Post-Secondary Education in Canada: A Response to the Truth and Reconciliation Commission of Canada." 12 December 2016. https://www.schoolofpublicpolicy.sk.ca/research/publications/policy-brief/Post-Secondary-Education-in-Canada-A-Response-to-the-Truth-and-Reconciliation-Commission-of-Canada.php.
Toth, Katie. 2020. "More academic freedom proposed for NWT's Aurora College in government's latest report." *CBC News*, 14 August. https://www.cbc.ca/news/canada/north/academic-freedom-aurora-college-1.5686406.
Toulouse, Jean-Marie. 2007. *Rapport de recherché sur la gouverance des institutions universitaires.* Montreal: Institut sur la gouvernance d'organisations privées et publiques.
TRC (Truth and Reconciliation Commission of Canada). 2015a. *Canada's Residential Schools: Reconciliation: The Final Report of the Truth and*

Reconciliation Commission of Canada, vols. 1–6. Montreal and Kingston: McGill-Queen's University Press. doi:10.2307/j.ctt19qghck.

– 2015b. *Honouring the Truth, Reconciling for the Future: Summary of the Final Report of the Truth and Reconciliation Commission of Canada.* https://publications.gc.ca/collections/collection_2015/trc/IR4-7-2015-eng.pdf.

Trotter, Lane D. 2009. "Building Boards: A Qualitative Analysis of the Perceptions of the Role of External Governors on University Governing Boards." PhD diss., Simon Fraser University.

Trottier, Claude, Jean Bernatchez, Donald Fisher, and Kjell Rubenson. 2014. "PSE Policy in Quebec: A Case Study." In *The Development of Postsecondary Education Systems in Canada: A Comparison between British Culombia, Ontario, and Québec 1980–2010*, edited by Donald Fisher, Kjell Rubenson, Theresa Shanahan, and Claude Trottier, 200–90. Montreal and Kingston: McGill-Queen's University Press.

Tupper, Allan. 2009. "Pushing Federalism to the Limit: Post-Secondary Education Policy in the Millennium." In *Research and Innovation Policy: Changing Federal Government–University Relations*, edited by G. Bruce Doern and Christopher Stoney, 35–58. Toronto: University of Toronto Press.

– 2013. "Higher Education: Leadership, Structure, and Power." *Canadian Public Administration* 56(2): 350–60.

Turpin, David H., Ludgard De Decker, and Brendan Boyd. 2014. "Historical Changes in the Canadian University Presidency: An Empirical Analysis of Changes in Length of Service and Experience since 1840." *Canadian Public Administration / Administration Publique du Canada* 57(4): 573–88.

UBC Faculty Association. 2010. "Ubyssey claims FA gave up right to strike earlier this year." *Bargaining* (blog), 12 October. https://www.facultyassociation.ubc.ca/bargaining/ubyssey-strike-earlier.

UK Department for Education. 2018. "New universities regulator comes into force". *GOV.UK*, 1 January 2018. https://www.gov.uk/government/news/new-universities-regulator-comes-into-force.

Université de Montréal. n.d. "Catalogue des archives. D35. Fonds du Secrétariat général." *Division de la gestion des documents et des archives.* http://www.archiv.umontreal.ca.

– n.d.a. "Vers une gouvernance réinventée." Gouvernance – Le projet. Accessed February 20, 2020. https://www.umontreal.ca/gouvernance/index.html.

– n.d.b. "Composition du Conseil de l'UdeM selon Ancienne ou la nouvelle Charte." https://www.umontreal.ca/gouvernance/documents/Composition du Conseil de l'UdeM.pdf.

– n.d.c. "Composition de l'Assemblée Universitaire." https://www.umontreal.ca/gouvernance/documents/tableau-compo-au.pdf.

- n.d.d. "In Figures." https://www.umontreal.ca/en/udem/in-figures/.
- 2014. Déclaration annuelle du recteur. 10 November. *Université de Montréal: Communications.* http://recteur.umontreal.ca/fileadmin/recteur/pdf/discours-allocutions/guy.breton/Allocution_declaration-annuelle-2014_20141110_protege.pdf.
- 2015. "Notre Histoire." http://www.umontreal.ca/udem-aujourdhui/Fr/histoire/1878-1919.html.
- 2016a. *Rapport synthèse de consultation: Version finale.* Montreal: Institut du Nouveau Monde. https://transformation.umontreal.ca/wp-content/uploads/2016/06/UdeM_Rapport_INM_Final.pdf.
- 2016b. "Declaration annuelle du recteur". https://recteur.umontreal.ca/fileadmin/recteur/pdf/discours-allocutions/guy.breton/Allocution_Declaration-annuelle-recteur-2016_20161214.pdf.
- 2017a. "Charte: l'Assemblée universitaire poursuit ses travaux." UdeMNouvelles, 1 February. https://nouvelles.umontreal.ca/article/2017/02/01/charte-l-assemblee-universitaire-poursuit-ses-travaux.
- 2017b. "Réforme de la Charte de l'UdeM: les motifs et les objectifs." *Gouvernance, Carnet du recteur*, 3 February. https://recteur.umontreal.ca/carnet-du-recteur/article/reforme-de-la-charte-de-ludem-les-motifs-et-les-objectifs.
- 2017c. "Charte de l'UdeM: cinq questions au président du CEPTI." *UdeMNouvelles*, 6 March. https://nouvelles.umontreal.ca/article/2017/03/06/charte-de-l-udem-cinq-questions-au-president-du-cepti.
- 2017d. "Charte: à un article d'un projet de loi." *UdeMNouvelles*, 18 April. https://nouvelles.umontreal.ca/article/2017/04/18/charte-a-un-article-d-un-projet-de-loi.
- 2017e. "L'Assemblee universitaire reaffirme son appui au projet de reforme de la Charte de l'Universite de Montreal." University Assembly. https://www.umontreal.ca/gouvernance/documents/2017-A0021-0593e-360_amende_Resolution_reaffirmer_appui_Charte.pdf.
- 2018. "L'Assemblée nationale adopte la loi modifiant la Charte de l'Université de Montréal." *UdeMNouvelles*, 27 March. https://nouvelles.umontreal.ca/article/2018/03/27/l-assemblee-nationale-adopte-la-loi-modifiant-la-charte-de-l-universite-de-montreal.
- 2019a. "L'Université de Montréal a de nouveaux statuts, qui s'harmonisent avec la charte entrée en vigueur le 28 septembre 2018." *UdeMNouvelles*, 28 February. https://nouvelles.umontreal.ca/article/2019/02/28/les-nouveaux-statuts-de-l-udem.
- 2019b. "Rapport du recteur 2019." http://www.rr.umontreal.ca/rapport2019/.

Université de Montréal and Institut du Nouveau Monde. 2016. *Construire notre avenir ensemble: Consultation: Guide de réflexion.* Montreal: University of Montreal. http://transformation.umontreal.ca/wp-content/uploads/2016/02/VR-TRANSFO_REV_07B_HR.pdf.

Universities Canada. n.d. "Three categories of membership: institutional members." *Universities Canada: Membership Criteria.* https://www.univcan.ca/about-us/membership-and-governance/membership-criteria.

– 2017. "Indigenous student education." https://www.univcan.ca/priorities/indigenous-education.

– 2019a. "2019 full-time and part-time fall enrolment at Canadian universities." Facts and Statistics. https://www.univcan.ca/universities/facts-and-stats/enrolment-by-university.

– 2019b. "Enrolment by university 2018." Facts and Statistics. https://www.univcan.ca/universities/facts-and-stats/enrolment-by-university.

– 2019c. *Equity, Diversity and Inclusion at Canadian Universities: Report on the 2019 National Survey.* Ottawa. https://www.univcan.ca/wp-content/uploads/2019/11/Equity-diversity-and-inclusion-at-Canadian-universities-report-on-the-2019-national-survey-Nov-2019-1.pdf.

– 2020a. "2019 full-time and part-time fall enrolment at Canadian universities." Facts and Statistics. https://www.univcan.ca/universities/facts-and-stats/enrolment-by-university.

– 2020b. "COVID-19 and Canadian universities: Information and resources." https://www.univcan.ca/coronavirus-covid-19-and-canadian-universities-information-and-resources.

University of Alberta. n.d. "Colleges and Faculties." Accessed 18 November 2020. https://www.ualberta.ca/faculties/index.html.

– 2007. "Dare to Deliver: Academic Plan 2007–2011." https://www.su.ualberta.ca/about/news/entry/330/donors-redirecting-gifts-to-university-of-alberta-students.

– 2018a. "Board of Governors Open Session Minutes." 6 March. https://www.ualberta.ca/governance/media-library/documents/member-zone/board-of-governors/board-minutes/2018-03-16-approved-open-session-minutes.pdf.

– 2018b. "Message from Fraser Forbes." Office of the Dean of Engineering. https://www.ualberta.ca/engineering/news/2018/april/message-from-fraser-forbes.

– 2018c. "Message from Dean Doucet regarding UAlberta honorary degrees." Office of the Dean of Business. https://www.ualberta.ca/business/about/news/articles-and-press-releases/2018/april/message-from-dean-doucet-regarding-ualberta-honorary-degrees.

– 2018d. "Board of Governors Open Session Minutes." 11 May. https://www.ualberta.ca/governance/media-library/documents/member-zone/board-of-governors/board-minutes/2018-05-11-approved-open-session-minutes.pdf.

- 2019a. *Ad hoc Committee on Honorary Degrees: Report to Senate.* Edmonton. https://drive.google.com/file/d/1D1el68GaCAGDi34B-rN-Bo30BhVRqrwOm/view.
- 2019b. "Facts." University of Alberta website. Prepared on 19 March 2019. https://www.ualberta.ca/about/facts.html.

University of Alberta Student Union. 2018. "Donors Redirecting Gifts to University of Alberta Students." *University of Alberta Student Union News*, 26April.https://www.su.ualberta.ca/about/news/entry/330/donors-redirecting-gifts-to-university-of-alberta-students.

University of British Columbia. n.d. *Trek 2000: A vision for the 21$^{st}$ century.*
- 2019. "University of British Columbia 2018/19 Annual Enrolment Report." Prepared by Ananya Mukherjee-Reed and Andrew Szeri. https://senate.ubc.ca/sites/senate.ubc.ca/files/downloads/Item%208a%202018-19%20Enrolment%20Report.pdf.

University of Saskatchewan. n.d. "Senate Responsibilities." Governance Office. https://secretariat.usask.ca/senate/#Responsibilities.

University of Toronto. n.d.a. "A brief history and description of the governing council of the university of Toronto." Office of the Governing Council. https://governingcouncil.utoronto.ca/brief-history-governing-council.
- n.d.b. "A letter to students, faculty and staff from President Gertler on student mental health at U of T." Office of the President. https://www.president.utoronto.ca/a-letter-from-president-gertler-on-student-mental-health-at-u-of-t.
- 2015. *Report of the University Ombudsperson: 1 July 2014 to June 30 2015.* https://governingcouncil.utoronto.ca/sites/default/files/import-files/OmbudsAnnualReport2014-15.pdf.
- 2017a. *Report no. 202 of the University Affairs Board.* https://governingcouncil.utoronto.ca/sites/default/files/ogc/reports/r1002-2017-2018uab.pdf.
- 2017b. *Report no. 203 of the University Affairs Board.* https://governingcouncil.utoronto.ca/sites/default/files/ogc/reports/r1120-2017-2018uab.pdf.
- 2017c. *Report no. 212 of the Academic Board.* https://governingcouncil.utoronto.ca/sites/default/files/ogc/reports/r1123-2017-2018ab.pdf.
- 2018a. "Financial Report, April 30, 2018." Financial services. https://finance.utoronto.ca/wp-content/uploads/2018f.pdf.
- 2018b. *Minutes of the Meeting of the Governing Council of June 27, 2018.* https://governingcouncil.utoronto.ca/sites/default/files/ogc/reports/r0627-2017-2018gc.pdf.
- 2018c. *Report No. 204 of University Affairs Board.* https://governingcouncil.utoronto.ca/sites/default/files/ogc/reports/r0130-2017-2018uab.pdf.
- 2018d. *Report Number 216 of the Academic Board.* https://governingcouncil.utoronto.ca/sites/default/files/ogc/reports/r0531-2017-2018ab.pdf.

– 2019a. *Presidential and Provostial Task Force on Student Mental Health: Final Report and Recommendations – December 2019*. https://www.provost.utoronto.ca/wp-content/uploads/sites/155/2020/01/Presidential-and-Provostial-Task-Force-Final-Report-and-Recommendations-Dec-2019.pdf.
– 2019b. "Enrolment Report 2018–19." 5 February 2019. https://planningandbudget.utoronto.ca/wp-content/uploads/2021/03/Enrolment-Report-2018-19.pdf.
– 2019c. "Facts and Figures 2019." Prepared by the Office of Planning and Budget. March 2019. https://data.utoronto.ca/wp-content/uploads/2020/06/Finalized-Factbook-2019.pdf.
UQAM (Université du Québec à Montréal). n.d. " Faits saillants des 40 ans de l'UQAM." http://www.40ans.uqam.ca/page/faits_saillants.php.
– n.d.b. "UQAM in Numbers." https://uqam.ca/en/information/numbers/.
– 2014. "Il était une fois l'UQAM." *Magazine INTER*- 7(1). http://www.40ans.uqam.ca/page/histoire.php.
– 2016. "L'Ecole des sciences de la gestion questionne son appartenance à l'UQAM." *AMEQ en ligne*, 25 February 2016. http://www.ameqenligne.com/detail_news.php?ID=566180&cat=;21.
UQAM (Université du Québec à Montréal) et Syndicat des professeurs et professeures de l'Université du Québec à Montréal. 2009. Convention collective 2009–2013. https://spuq.uqam.ca/documents/x_documents/1_convention_collective_professeurs.pdf.
Usher, Alex. 2016a. "A marginally less mediocre set of provincial budgets." *One Thought Blog*, 13 June. http://higheredstrategy.com/a-marginally-less-mediocre-set-of-provincial-budgets.
– 2016b. "Boards of governors." *One Thought Blog*, 2 February.
– 2017a. "Presidential compensation." *One Thought Blog*, 18 September. https://higheredstrategy.com/presidential-compensation.
– 2017b. "The financial landscape of Canadian universities." *One Thought Blog*, 31 May. http://higheredstrategy.com/the-financial-landscape-of-canadian-universities.
– 2018a. "Canada's Growing Reliance on International Students." *Policy Options*, 29 August. https://policyoptions.irpp.org/magazines/august-2018/canadas-growing-reliance-on-international-students.
– 2018b. "Canadian University Finances 2016–17 (Expenditures)." *One Thought Blog*, 5 September. http://higheredstrategy.com/canadian-university-finances-2016-17-expenditures.
– 2018c. "Management (or lack thereof)." *One Thought Blog*, 21 June. https://higheredstrategy.com/management-or-lack-thereof.
– 2018d. *The State of Post-Secondary Education in Canada, 2018*. Toronto: Higher Education Strategy Associates.

– 2019a. "'Cape Breton, You have to be kidding me.'" *One Thought Blog*, 17 October 17. http://higheredstrategy.com/cape-breton-you-have-to-be-kidding-me.
– 2019b. "Antipodean student organization struggles." *One Thought Blog*, 23 January. http://higheredstrategy.com/antipodean-student-organization-struggles.
– 2019c. "Big news on free speech." *One Thought Blog*, 6 November. http://higheredstrategy.com/big-news-on-free-speech.
– 2019d. "Canadian PSE funding is weirder than you think." *One Thought Blog*, 3 September. https://higheredstrategy.com/canadian-pse-funding-is-weirder-than-you-think.
– 2019e. "Canadian university expenses, 2017–18." *One Thought Blog*, 13 September. http://higheredstrategy.com/canadian-university-expenses-2017-18.
– 2019f. "Education at a glance, 2019: The key data." *One Thought Blog*, 11 September. http://higheredstrategy.com/education-at-a-glance-2019-the-key-data.
– 2019g. "If Canada were serious about higher education (Part 1)." *One Thought Blog*, 8 April. http://higheredstrategy.com/if-canada-were-serious-about-higher-education-part-1.
– 2019h. "Know your incoming students (2019 edition)." *One Thought Blog*, 28 August. http://higheredstrategy.com/know-your-incoming-students-2019-edition.
– 2019i. "Student affairs." *One Thought Blog*, 29 June. http://higheredstrategy.com/student-affairs.
– 2019j. "The bombshell in the Ontario budget." *One Thought Blog*, 12 April. http://higheredstrategy.com/the-bombshell-in-the-ontario-budget.
– 2019k. *The State of Postsecondary Education in Canada, 2019*. Toronto: Higher Education Strategy Associates.
– 2020a. "Coronavirus (3)." *One Thought Blog*, 16 March. http://higheredstrategy.com/coronavirus-3.
– 2020b. "Counter-intuitive faculty salary data." *One Thought Blog*, 4 February. https://higheredstrategy.com/counter-intuitive-faculty-salary-data.
– 2020c. "Postcard from Alberta (2)." *One Thought Blog*, 28 January. http://higheredstrategy.com/postcard-from-alberta-2.
Usher, Alex, Collin McLeod, and Linda Green. 2010. *Courting Success in Senior Hiring at Canadian Universities*. Toronto: Higher Education Strategy Associates.
Vancouver Senate. 2015. "Vancouver Senate: Minutes of 21 October 2015." University of British Columbia. https://senate.ubc.ca/sites/senate.ubc.ca/files/downloads/20151021-va-minutesapproved.pdf.

Venne, Jean-François, 2017a. "The dubious legacy of Quebec's Maple Spring." *University Affairs*, 1 March. https://www.universityaffairs.ca/features/feature-article/dubious-legacy-quebecs-maple-spring.
– 2017b. "The tough job of university rector in Quebec." *University Affairs*, 5 July. https://www.universityaffairs.ca/news/news-article/tough-job-university-rector-quebec.
– 2018. "Major changes to the funding formula for Quebec universities." *University Affairs*, 19 June. https://www.universityaffairs.ca/news/news-article/major-changes-to-the-funding-formula-for-quebec-universities.
Verge, Pierre G. 2017. "Il faut moderniser la charte de l'Universite de Montreal." *Le Devoir*, 5 December, A6. https://www.ledevoir.com/opinion/libre-opinion/514658/il-faut-moderniser-la-charte-de-l-universite-de-montreal.
Vérificateur Général du Québec. 2008. "Rapport à l'Assemblée nationale concernant la vérification particulaire menée auprès de l'Université du Québec a Montréal, Partie 2." Library of the National Assembly of Québec.
Waite, Peter B. 1987. *Lord of Point Grey: Larry MacKenzie of UBC*. Vancouver: UBC Press.
– 1994. *The Lives of Dalhousie University*, vol. 1: *1818–1925*. Montreal and Kingston: McGill-Queen's University Press.
– 1998. *The Lives of Dalhousie University*, vol. 2: *1925–1980*. Montreal and Kingston: McGill-Queen's University Press.
Wang, Li. 2010. "Higher Education Governance and University Autonomy in China." *Globalisation, Societies, and Education* 8(4): 477–95.
Wang, Rong, and Po Yang. 2018. "China: The 'Commanding Heights' Strategy Revisited." In *Higher Education in Federal Countries: A Comparative Study*, edited by Martin Carnoy, Isak Froumin, Oleg Leshukov, and Simon Marginson, 408–54. New Delhi: Sage.
Wang, Siyi, and Glen A. Jones. 2020. "Competing Institutional Logics of Academic Personnel System Reforms in Leading Chinese Universities." *Journal of Higher Education Policy and Management* 43(1): 49–66.
Warren, May. 2019. "Students criticize U of T after third death at same building in under two years." *Toronto Star*, 30 September. https://www.thestar.com/news/gta/2019/09/30/safety-barriers-installed-at-bahen-centre-after-student-death-u-of-t-says.html.
Watts, Ronald. 1992. "The Federal Context for Higher Education." In *Higher Education in Federal Systems: Proceedings of an International Colloquium, Queen's University, Kingston*, edited by Douglas Brown, Pierre Cazalis, and Gilles Jasmin, 3–22. Renouf: Ottawa.

Webber, Jeremy. 2020. "Constitutionalism in the Age of Populism." Paper presented at the annual conference Constitutionalism in the Age of Populism, Victoria, BC, March.

Webber, Michelle, and Jonah Butovsky. 2018. "Faculty Associations Confront Accountability Governance." *Canadian Journal of Higher Education* 48(3): 165–81.

Weber, Bob. 2018. "Environmentalist David Suzuki receives honorary degree from University of Alberta." *Globe and Mail*, 7 June. https://www.theglobeandmail.com/canada/alberta/article-environmentalist-david-suzuki-receives-honorary-degree-from-university.

Weinrib, Julian, and Glen A. Jones. 2014. "Largely a Matter of Degrees: Quality Assurance and Canadian Universities." *Policy and Society* 33(3): 225–36.

Welch, Anthony. 2012. "Academic Salaries, Massification, and the Rise of an Underclass in Australia." In *Paying the Professoriate: A Global Comparison of Compensation and Contracts*, edited by Philip Altbach, Liz Reisberg, Maria Yudkevich, Gregory Androushchak, and Iván F. Pacheco, 61–71. New York: Routledge.

Weyland, Kurt. 2001. "Clarifying a Contested Concept: Populism in the Study of Latin American Politics." *Comparative Politics* 34(1): 1–22.

WHED (World Higher Education Database). n.d. "IAU WHED." https://www.whed.net/home.php.

WID (Workplace Information Division). 2020. "Report on university strikes since 1970" [unpublished data], received via email, 14 July. Labour Program. Employment and Social Development Canada.

Williams, Garett. 2017. "Progressive Conservatives stock U of M board of governors." *The Manitoban*, 1 February 2017. http://www.themanitoban.com/2017/02/progressive-conservatives-stock-u-m-board-governors/30634.

Wolfe, David A. 2009. "Universities and Knowledge Transfer: Powering Local Economic and Cluster Development." In *Research and Innovation Policy: Changing Federal Government–University Relations*, edited by G. Bruce Doern and Christopher Stoney, 265–87. Toronto: University of Toronto Press.

Woolf, Daniel. 2019. "An overview of challenges – both local and global – facing Canadian universities." *Principal's Blog*, 8 March. https://www.queensu.ca/connect/principal/2019/03/08.

Xu, Chenggang. 2011. "The Fundamental Institutions of China's Reforms and Development." *Journal of Economics Literature* 49(4): 1076–51.

Yakabuski, Konrad. 2020. "The University of Ottawa throws academic freedom under the bus." *Globe and Mail*, 21 October. https://www.

theglobeandmail.com/opinion/article-the-university-of-ottawa-throws-academic-freedom-under-the-bus.

Yan, Fengqiao, and Dan Mao. 2019. "China: The Changing Relationship among Academics, Institutions, and the State." In *Professorial Pathways: Academic Careers in a Global Perspective*, edited by Martin Finkelstein and Glen Jones, 172–99. Baltimore: Johns Hopkins University Press.

Yang, Rui, Lesley Vidovich, and Jan Currie. 2007. "'Dancing in a cage': Changing Autonomy in Chinese Higher Education." *Higher Education* 54(4): 575–92.

Yeung, Linda. 2015. "Campus crackdown on 'Western values.'" *University World News*, 7 February. https://www.universityworldnews.com/post.php?story=20150207101411455.

Young, David C. and Wendy L. Kraglund-Gauthier. "Canadian post-secondary education associations." In *Handbook of Canadian Higher Education Law*, edited by Teresa Shanahan, Michelle Nilson and Li-Jeen Broshko, 113–21. Montreal & Kingston: McGill-Queen's University Press.

Yukon Legislative Council Office. 2019. "Yukon University Act, SY 2019, c. 15, s. 3(2))." Acts and Regulations. http://www.gov.yk.ca/legislation/acts/yuun_c.pdf.

Zhuang, T., and B. Liu. 2020. "Power Landscapes within Chinese Universities: A Three-Dimensional Discourse Analysis of University Statues." *Cambridge Journal of Education* 50(5): 639–56.

Ziegler, Dominic. 2020. "China wants to put itself back at the centre of the world." *The Economist*. https://www.economist.com/special-report/2020/02/06/china-wants-to-put-itself-back-at-the-centre-of-the-world.

# Index

academic capitalism, 68, 325–6
academic departments, 78, 189–90, 301, 322–3
academic freedom, 6–7, 56–8, 221–3, 233–4, 275–8, 327–8, 343–4, 352–3
academic guilds, 11, 330
academic judgment, 7, 221, 227
academic oligarchy, 165, 332–3
Acadia University, 16, 95
access, 22, 25, 30, 33–4, 57, 60–1, 112–13, 147, 153, 240, 306, 312, 316, 349
accessibility, 317, 324, 333; low-income families in Ontario, 59; post-secondary institutions in Alberta, 46. *See also* access; massification
accountability, 145–53, 231, 240, 290–1, 297–9
accreditation, 63–4, 166–7, 297, 298, 339
administration, 14, 24, 42, 69, 79–80, 87–9, 162, 181, 191, 195–7, 243, 291, 308
advisory body, 26, 225. *See also* buffer body
Algoma University, 63
Alliance of Canadian Comprehensive Universities, 51
alumni, 73, 101, 175–7, 259–60, 273–7, 282–4, 300, 338, 365
appointment processes, board, 48, 63, 139–40, 150, 334–5; administrative, 199, 200, 221; presidential, 82–5, 115, 232, 255, 259
Association of Accrediting Agencies of Canada (AAAC), 64
Association of Universities and Colleges of Canada (AUCC), 21, 109, 111, 130, 159. *See also* Universities Canada
Athabasca University, 45
Australia, 289–90, 296–8, 319–21, 321–2, 325–6, 328, 333–5, 339, 343, 349

bicameral model, 19, 24, 31, 40–4, 49, 79–80, 87, 107, 119, 122, 126, 138, 152–4, 174, 180, 218, 229, 292, 327, 334
Bishop's University, 16, 31, 36
board (general), 17–19, 23–6, 36, 40, 47–8, 63, 71–7, 79–81, 85–6, 101, 138–41, 174–82, 218, 220, 282–5, 320, 334–8, 344, 353–6
board chair, 48, 74, 82, 85–6, 106, 124, 139–40, 150–5, 173, 179–84, 190–1, 197, 216, 272, 275–7, 359–60
board member, 24, 73–5, 334–6, 353–6
Bologna Process, 305
Brandon University, 45
British North America Act (BNA), 16–17, 32, 39, 118
budget, 79, 111, 126, 129, 149, 151–3, 172, 181, 184–6, 188, 198,

202, 216–17, 235–40, 264, 271–2, 308, 327, 353
buffer body, 26, 40, 46, 296
business: board (University of Toronto), 173, 180, 220, 269, 299; as a discipline or faculty, 89, 94, 14, 265, 276, 303; as external stakeholders, 65, 82, 120, 168; as occupation, 73

Canada Council, 20
Canadian Alliance of Student Associations (CASA), 94
Canadian Association of University Business Officers, 89
Canadian Association of University Teachers (CAUT), 24, 42, 77, 81, 114, 258, 278, 337, 340, 347, 352
Canadian Federation of Students, 94, 235
chair (of academic department), 88, 167, 190, 201–5, 241, 262, 359–60
chair of board. See board chair
chancellor, 44, 117, 120, 122, 175–7, 256, 258, 273, 277, 282, 297, 371
Charter (Canadian Charter of Rights and Freedoms), 64–5
China, 50, 242, 289, 310–18, 324, 327–9
church, 11–13, 17, 23, 30, 33, 37–40, 43, 63, 107, 110–11, 117–18
Coalition Avenir Québec (CAQ), 36, 233
collective bargaining, 35, 42, 219, 235, 295, 336–8
College Act, 50
College de Quebec, 16, 30, 32
Colleges d'enseignement general et professionnel (CEGEPs), 33–4
collegiality, 218–19, 263–4
commercialization, 68, 159–60, 166, 326, 347
commission des études, 79, 114, 162, 183–5, 209, 212–13, 259, 264. See also general faculties council; senate (general)
Concordia University, 36, 75, 95, 234
conflict of interest, 195, 336, 355–6
conseil d'administration, 19, 178, 262, 308. See also board (general)
conservative government, 58, 159, 212, 231, 234, 237
corporatization, 68–71, 320, 332, 345
Council of Ministers of Education, Canada (CMEC), 20
cultural capital, 5–8

Dalhousie Act, 107–8
dean, selection of, 87–8
delegation, 119, 354
denominational, 19, 39, 43–4, 117–18
disciplines, 78, 101, 187–90, 221, 223–4, 229–30, 315, 322, 333, 338–9, 364, 367
donors, 65, 168, 177, 226, 273–4, 300
Duff–Berdahl Report, 24, 56, 336, 340

École Polytechnique de Montréal, 32, 36, 110–11
economic capital, 5–6
election, 25, 33, 36, 48, 83, 87–8, 138, 140, 184–5, 193, 199, 225, 237–9, 240, 254, 362
enrolment, institution (students), 25, 34, 41, 105, 111, 121, 214, 130, 152, 203, 260–1, 296, 306, 313, 363; funding, 22, 25, 127, 148, 216, 261, 291, 297, 312, 317, 326
equity (or equity and diversity), 241, 243, 250, 325, 338, 347, 349–50
European University Association, 57, 305

faculties, 187–9, 196–7
faculty associations, 91, 116, 207–8, 219, 235, 278, 352; Ontario Confederation of University Faculty Associations (OCUFA), 331

# Index

faculty councils, 18, 78, 92–3, 189, 205–6
faculty members. *See* professors (general, duties, powers)
faculty unions, 35, 80–1, 91, 207–10, 219, 221, 323, 331, 336–7
federal government, 163–4, 166, 169, 171, 241–2, 303, 326, 334, 345–6
federalism, 60–2, 170–1, 318–19
federation, 16, 39–40, 171, 296, 298; of students, 94, 111, 213–14, 235
Federation of Saskatchewan Indian Nations, 45, 63, 69
fiduciary responsibility, 27, 335
fields, 15; of global higher education, 5; of large-scale production, 5, 52, 166; of restricted production, 5
First Nations governments, 63
First Nations University of Canada Act, 63
First Nations University of Canada, 45, 63
Flavelle Commission, 18–19, 24, 40, 44, 100, 119, 220, 340–1, 343
for-profit institutions, 15, 26, 290, 299–303, 345, 348
France, 13, 50, 113, 289, 304–10, 319, 323, 327, 332
freedom of speech, 221
funding, government, 14, 18–20, 22, 25, 28, 32, 40–1, 60, 69, 108–10, 112, 117, 121, 123–4, 127, 130, 141, 148, 154, 158–9, 170, 234–5, 239, 245, 261, 290, 315, 317, 326, 333–5, 347; research, 65, 124, 161, 293, 308, 312–13, 326, 346. *See also* tuition
fundraising, 40, 42, 69, 124, 142, 189, 226, 293

general faculties council, 46, 79, 123, 162, 185, 211, 273
governance, defined, 3–8
governance models, 232, 327, 344

governing council, 117, 120, 139, 174, 177, 179, 185, 191, 212, 266–8, 270
government reporting entity (GRE), 47–8, 138–9, 146, 149, 153, 156, 170
graduate education, 51
granting council, 158, 160, 241

hierarchy, 7; within institutions, 203, 225; within system, 51–2, 68, 161
higher education in Canada, history of, 16–54
Higher Education Quality Council of Ontario, 137
Humboldtian model, 13
Hungary, 305

Indian Act, 17
Indigenization, 338
Indigenous knowledge, 16, 245, 338
Indigenous peoples, 16–17, 26–7, 49, 54, 63, 84–5, 90, 93, 98, 125, 145, 240–1, 245, 334, 338, 349–50, 367
institutional autonomy. *See* university autonomy
intermediary body, 2, 100. *See also* buffer body
international students, 52, 93, 130, 142, 152, 234, 296–7, 313, 318
isomorphism, 15, 218, 334

Johns Hopkins University, 18

King's Colleges, 16, 37–9, 95, 107–8, 117–18

Lakehead University, 63
Land Act, 125
Laurentian University, 236
Liberal Arts, 30, 301
Liberal government, 33, 35–6, 152–4, 231–4, 240–1

*Maclean's*, 111
managerialism, 68–9, 196, 321
Maple Spring, 143, 232
Maritime Provinces Higher Education Commission (MPHEC), 40, 53, 137
marketization, 26, 329, 331; in China, 316; in Quebec, 37
massification, 13–14, 40, 45, 291, 363
McGill University, 16, 18–19, 21, 31–3, 36, 45, 51, 67, 95, 125–6, 234
media, 60, 82, 99, 145–6, 234, 277, 302, 352; social media, 97–8, 233, 246, 250, 275–6
Medical Research Council (MRC), 20
Memorial University of Newfoundland (MUN), 41, 95
mission groups, 295, 321
missions, 14, 54, 57–9, 243, 331–2, 342–3, 345–7, 350–1, 365–7
Mount Allison University, 39, 95
multiversity, 14, 98–9, 350
municipal government, 62, 168

National Conference of Canadian Universities (NCCU), 20–1, 340
National Survey of Student Engagement (NSSE), 94–6
Natural Sciences and Engineering Research Council (NSERC), 21–2, 242
neoliberal, 29, 58
New Democratic Party, 48, 237
Norway, 50
Nunavut Artic College, 49

OECD, 3, 52, 317–18, 349–50
Ontario Labour Act, 208
Ottawa, 20, 106, 157, 328, 345
Oxford University, 16, 38, 72, 117, 292

Parent Commission, 32–5, 64, 112, 340
Parti Québécois, 33, 36, 143, 153, 232, 260

performance indicators, 29, 147, 244, 313
postmodernism, 99
Post-Secondary Learning Act (PSLA), 47, 138, 149–50, 179, 208, 211, 237, 273
president (university), 17, 19, 27, 72–3, 76, 80, 82–8, 106, 140, 175, 191–201, 208, 225, 280, 282, 300, 304, 314, 322, 340, 354–9; Dalhousie University, 107–9, 177, 183, 246, 250; student union (University of Toronto), 266–70; Université de Montréal, 110, 183, 254, 258–9; Université du Québec à Montréal, 114, 116, 140, 264; University of Alberta, 122–4, 150, 181, 185–6, 272, 274–5; University of British Columbia, 45, 75, 126–30, 182, 186, 275–7, 280; University of Ottawa, 233; University of Saskatchewan, 43–4; University of Toronto, 117–21, 180
private universities, 29, 299, 320, 324, 348
privatization, 345
professional bodies, 37, 53, 64, 136, 167
professional bureaucracy, 67, 87, 172, 193, 333, 361
professional programs, 37, 51, 105, 215; accreditation, 64, 166
professors (general, duties, powers), 6, 11, 13, 27, 89–92, 205–7, 291, 360–2
provincial government, 136–7, 139, 153–7, 318, 342, 344–5, 354; Alberta, 44, 123, 140, 156, 237, 239, 271; British Columbia, 48, 126–8, 153; Newfoundland and Labrador, 41; Nova Scotia, 38, 109, 111, 116, 142, 231, 232; Ontario, 18, 154, 234–5; Quebec, 20, 32, 36, 74, 83, 145, 150; Saskatchewan, 44

provost, 83, 87–8, 193, 198–9, 201, 250, 357
Public Administration Act, 35–6
public sector, 156, 164, 302–3, 332

quality assurance, 37, 62, 319
Queen's University, 40, 87, 95
Quest University, 96
Quiet Revolution, 33

rankings, 7, 15, 51, 53–4, 59–60, 89, 117, 121, 124, 170, 250, 260, 296, 305, 307, 316
rector, 27, 83, 85, 115, 140, 147, 178–9, 191–5, 199, 259, 264–5. *See also* president (university)
regulation, 25–6, 64, 68, 71, 75, 77, 116, 136, 139, 145–6, 148, 158–9, 165, 168, 179, 183, 196, 220, 227, 229, 234, 237, 240, 243–4, 290, 294–8, 305, 315, 317, 319, 329, 342–3, 353
research councils, 46, 53, 158, 294
research ethics, 159, 161
Research Excellence Framework (REF) UK, 294
Respecting Educational Institutions at the University Level Act, 35, 145
revenue. *See* funding, government
Royal Commission of Inquiry on Education in the Province of Quebec, 33, 112. *See also* Parent Commission
Royal Commission on Aboriginal Peoples, 26, 334
Royal Commission on the University of Toronto. *See* Flavelle Commission

self-governance, 78, 333, 337
senate (general), 18–19, 24, 79–81, 154, 162, 175–6, 182–8, 282–4, 297, 301, 357–9
senate chair, 79, 109, 183–6, 191
senate member, 79, 357–8

sessionals, 92
Simon Fraser University, 45, 96
Social Sciences and Humanities Research Council of Canada (SSHRC), 9, 21
staff (non-academic), 88–9, 92–3, 100–1, 162, 362
stakeholders, 15, 36, 54, 65–7, 70, 73, 75, 77, 82, 87, 107, 136, 143–4, 153, 177, 193, 209, 222, 224–9, 233, 238–9, 243, 245, 269, 275, 290, 306, 340–2, 352–4, 366–7
state (role of), 6, 11, 14, 18, 33, 37–8, 55–62, 119, 144, 146, 156, 243, 290, 292–3, 304–6, 310–12, 319, 332–3, 343, 365–6
St Boniface College, 42
St Francis Xavier University, 63, 95
strategic planning, 72, 215–16
student associations, 53, 94, 210, 212–14, 235, 237; unions, 93, 212, 230, 268, 298, 331, 363
Student Choice Initiative, 235
student mental health, 269–71
student participation in governance, 24, 210–15, 219, 230
Supreme Court of Canada, 64, 237
system structure, 52, 57; stratification, 347–9

Teaching Excellence Framework (TEF) UK, 294
tenure, 24, 78, 89–92, 99–100, 128–9, 163, 198, 200–2, 262, 291, 295, 302, 309, 315, 321, 323, 354, 362
tricameral, 138, 174, 218
trust, 86, 182, 189, 208, 263, 303, 327, 256, 358–9, 361; political, 6, 69; public, 326, 333–4, 340, 342, 350, 361, 365
Truth and Reconciliation Commission, 17, 54, 240–1, 245
tuition: control of, 129, 130, 141, 143, 146, 148, 152, 170, 216, 226, 233,

234–40, 271–2, 292, 295–6, 303, 307, 313–15, 325–7, 331, 349, 363; as source of revenue, 26, 29, 35–6, 39, 60, 75, 93, 110, 112, 117, 121, 124, 129, 303, 363

U15, 51, 105, 109, 121, 161, 321
unicameral, 31, 120, 138, 174, 179–80, 218
United Empire Loyalists, 37, 39
United Kingdom, 292, 321–2, 325–6, 328, 33, 343; as UK, 13, 16, 33, 50–2, 58, 289–90, 292–5, 318–28, 333, 343
United States (US), 13, 16, 33, 50–2, 58, 68, 94, 96, 117, 244, 289, 298–9, 302, 300–4, 316–21, 323–28, 333–5, 339, 343
Université de Moncton, 40, 95
Université de Montréal (UdeM), 32, 34, 36, 105, 110–12, 137–9, 162, 170, 174, 177–9, 183–4, 191–4, 195, 198–200, 203, 208–10, 219, 251–60, 279, 371
Université du Québec (UQ), 33, 36–7, 105, 112–17, 146, 162, 170
Université du Québec à Montréal (UQAM), 14, 35, 105, 114, 115, 138, 140, 162, 168, 170, 174, 178–9, 184–5, 187, 190, 193–5, 197, 199–204, 213–15, 218–19, 225, 227, 260–5
Université Laval, 17, 31–2, 34–6, 83, 92, 95, 110, 192
Universities Act, 45, 47, 80
Universities Canada, 21–3, 49–50, 84, 159, 164, 245, 278, 340, 350, 352
university associations, 53, 91, 94, 101, 210–15, 235–7, 352
university autonomy, 6–8, 12–13, 19, 22, 41, 44, 48, 56–8, 61–7, 138, 144–5, 156, 168, 234–5, 243, 275, 279, 290, 294–9, 305–7, 310–14, 318–19, 327, 342–3, 352, 354, 366

University of Alberta (U of A), 46–7, 96, 105, 121–5, 137, 169–70, 180–2, 208, 227, 238–9, 271–5
University of Berlin, 13
University of Bologna, 11
University of British Columbia (UBC), 45, 75, 81, 96, 105, 125–30, 137, 162, 173, 182, 186, 195, 220, 226, 275–8, 280–1
University of Calgary, 45, 95, 238–9
University of Edinburgh, 16, 107
University of London, 39, 41, 118
University of Manitoba, 43, 47–8, 96
University of New Brunswick, 17, 39–40, 42, 95
University of Northern British Columbia (UNBC), 45
University of Ottawa, 96, 233, 240–3
University of Paris, 11
University of Prince Edward Island (UPEI), 41–2, 95
University of Regina, 45, 48
University of Saskatchewan, 43–6, 48, 95
University of Sherbrooke, 32, 34, 36, 95
University of Toronto, 17–19, 21, 39, 40, 51, 95, 105, 117–19, 121, 131, 137, 180, 185, 265–71, 336
University of Victoria, 16, 45, 95, 125, 128
University of Western Ontario, 40, 75–6, 95–6
University of Winnipeg, 45, 95
university secretary, 9, 195
U of T Act, 180

Yukon University, 50, 63
Yukon University Act, 63